AF473974

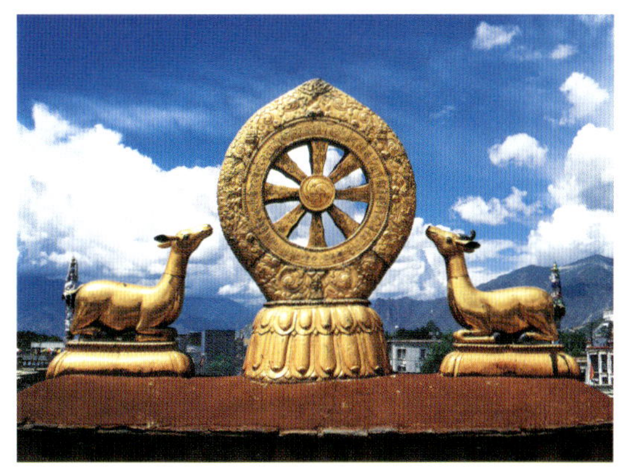

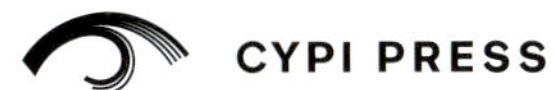

CYPI PRESS

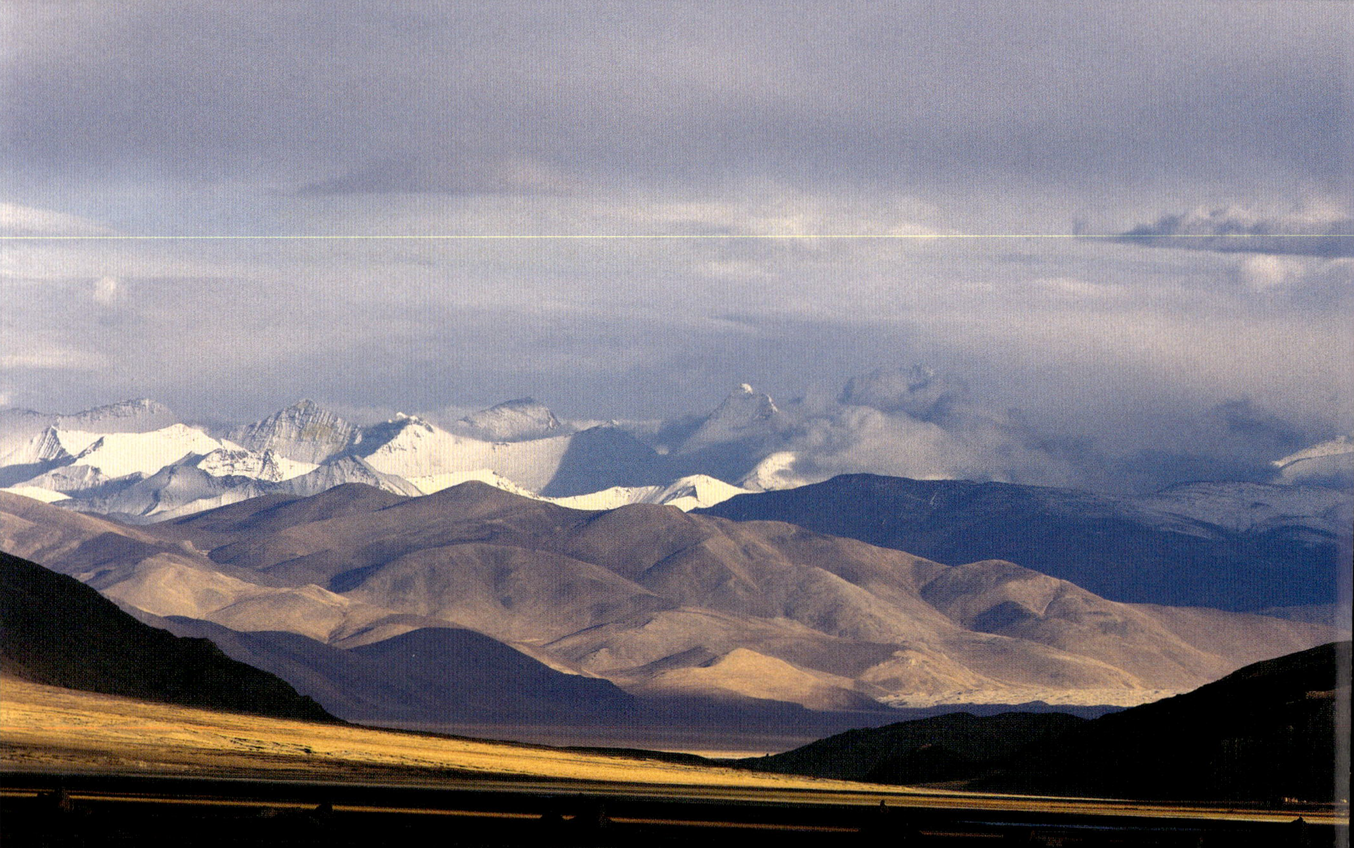

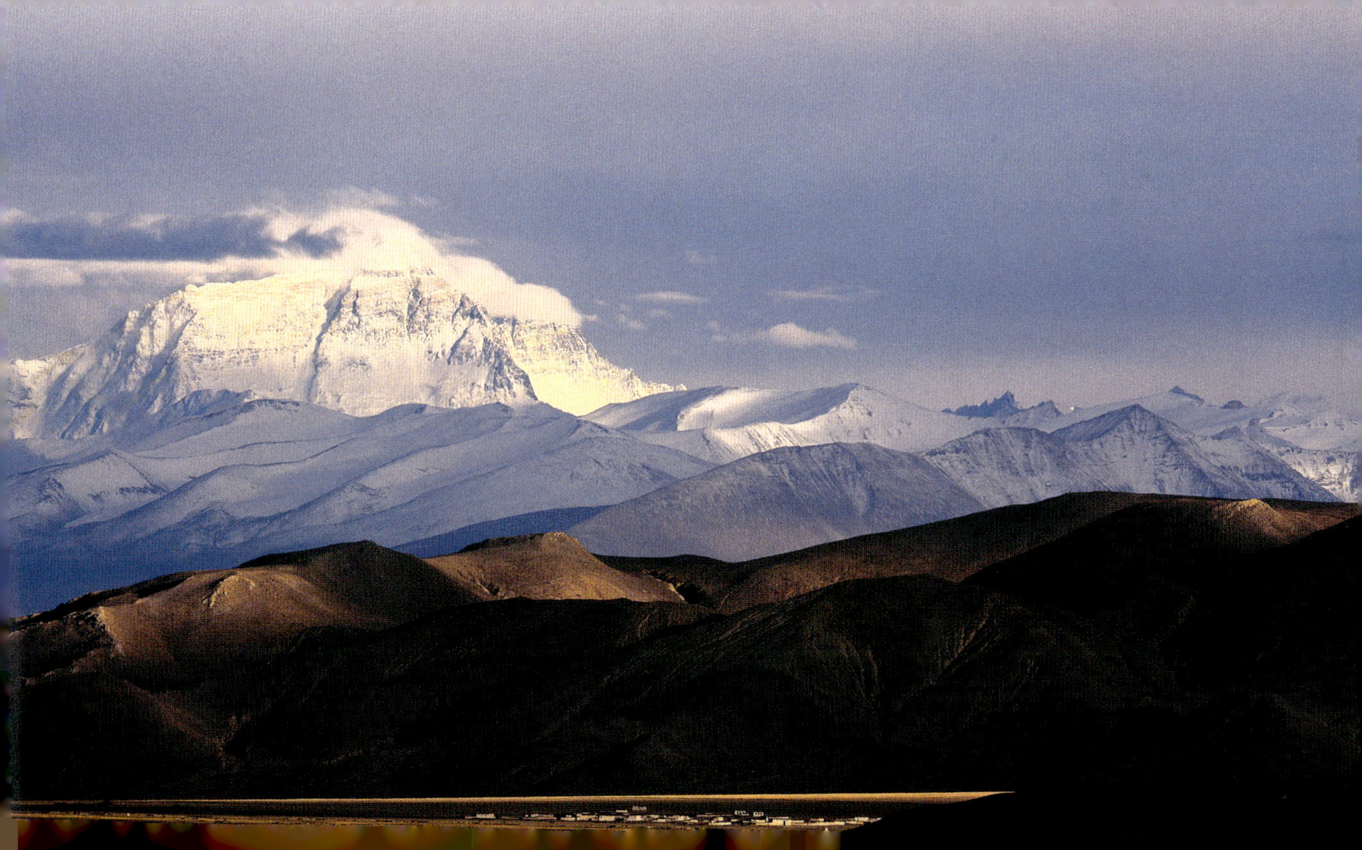

西藏

TI

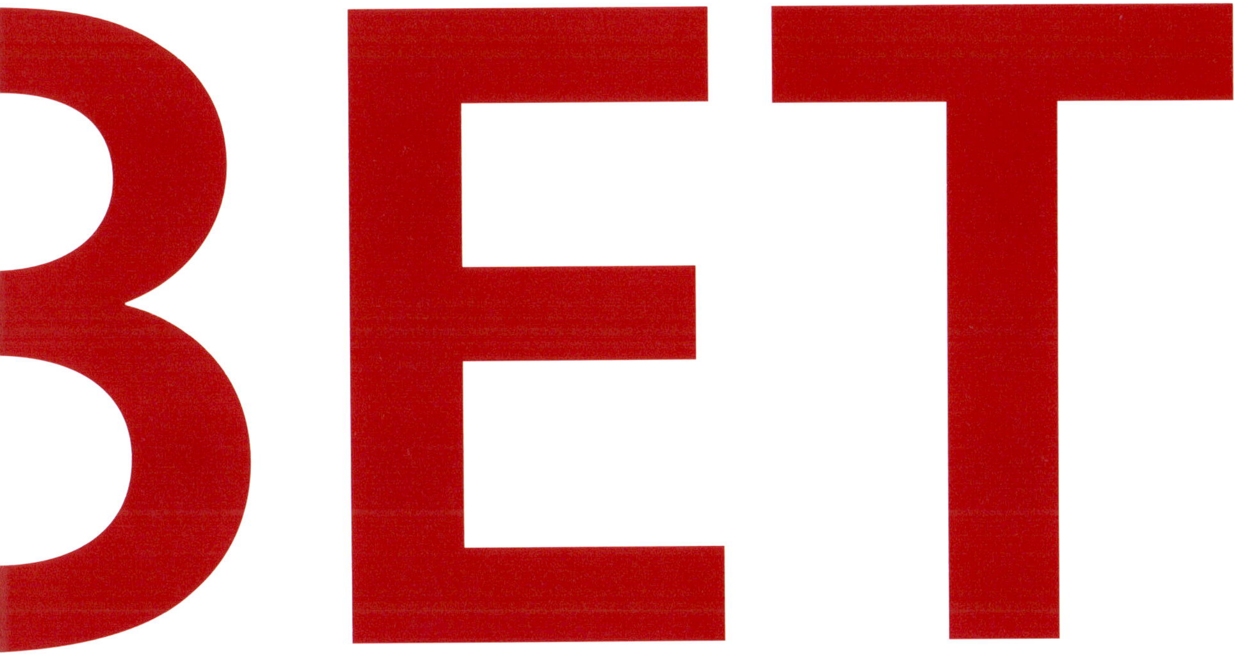
BET

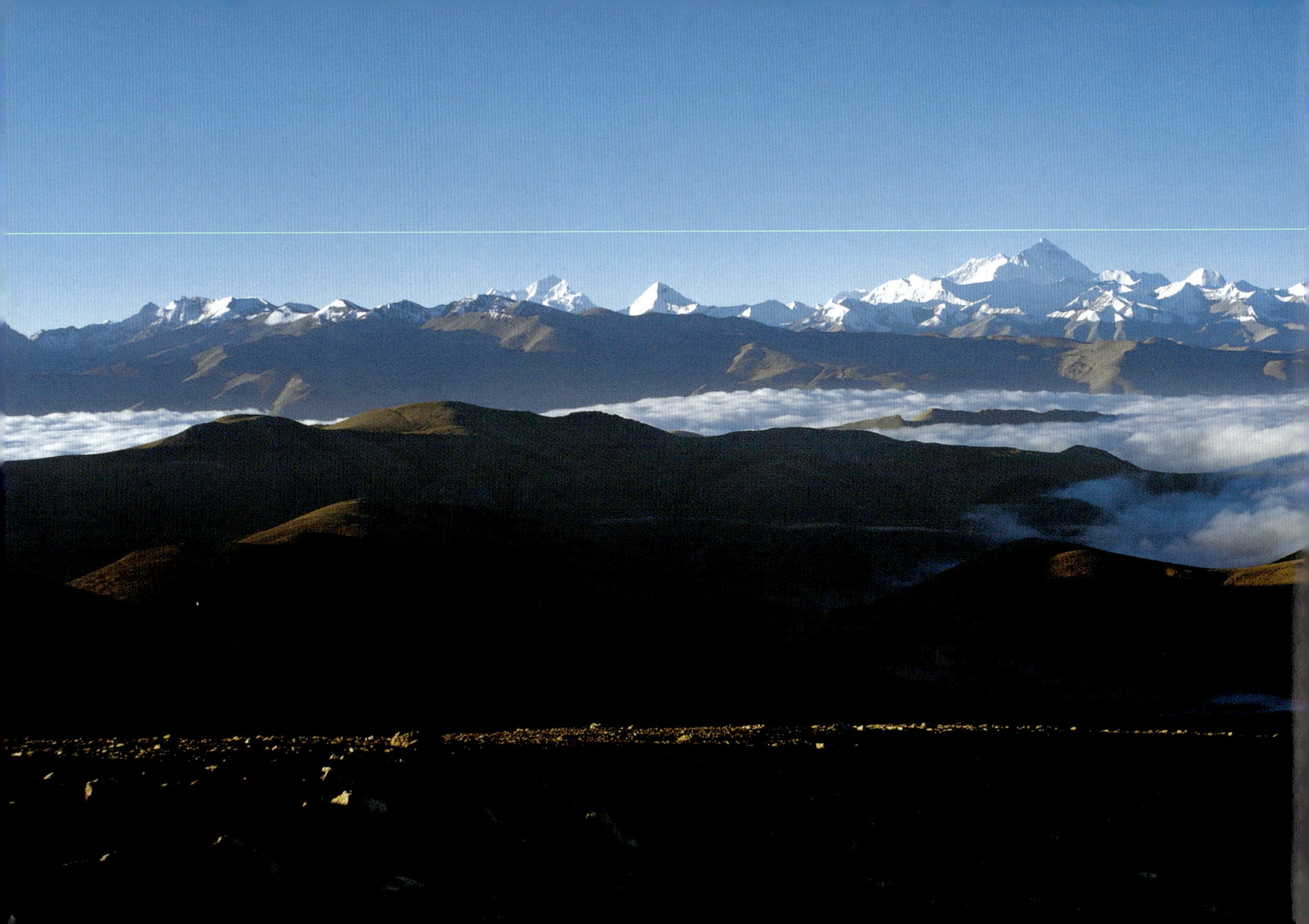

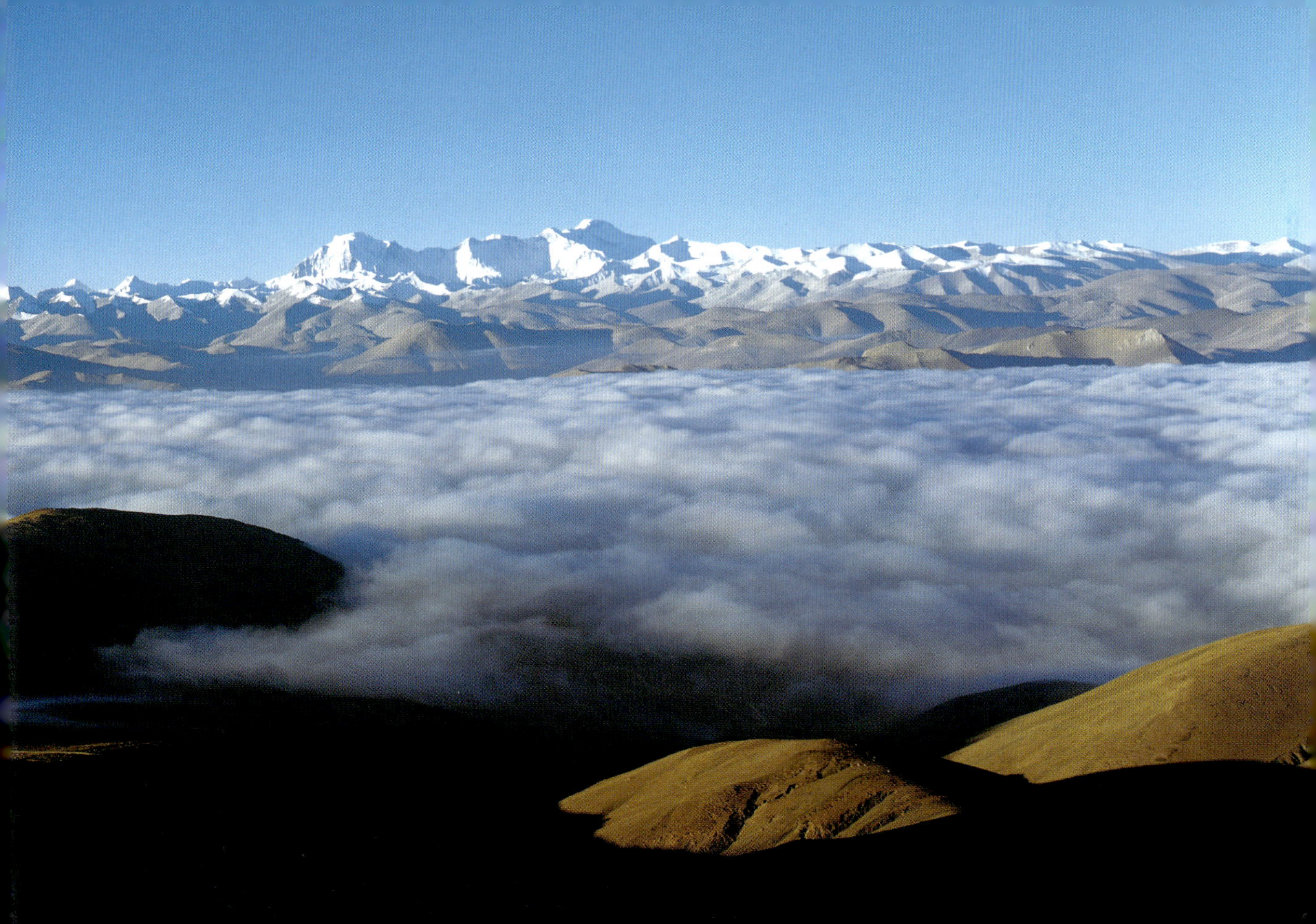

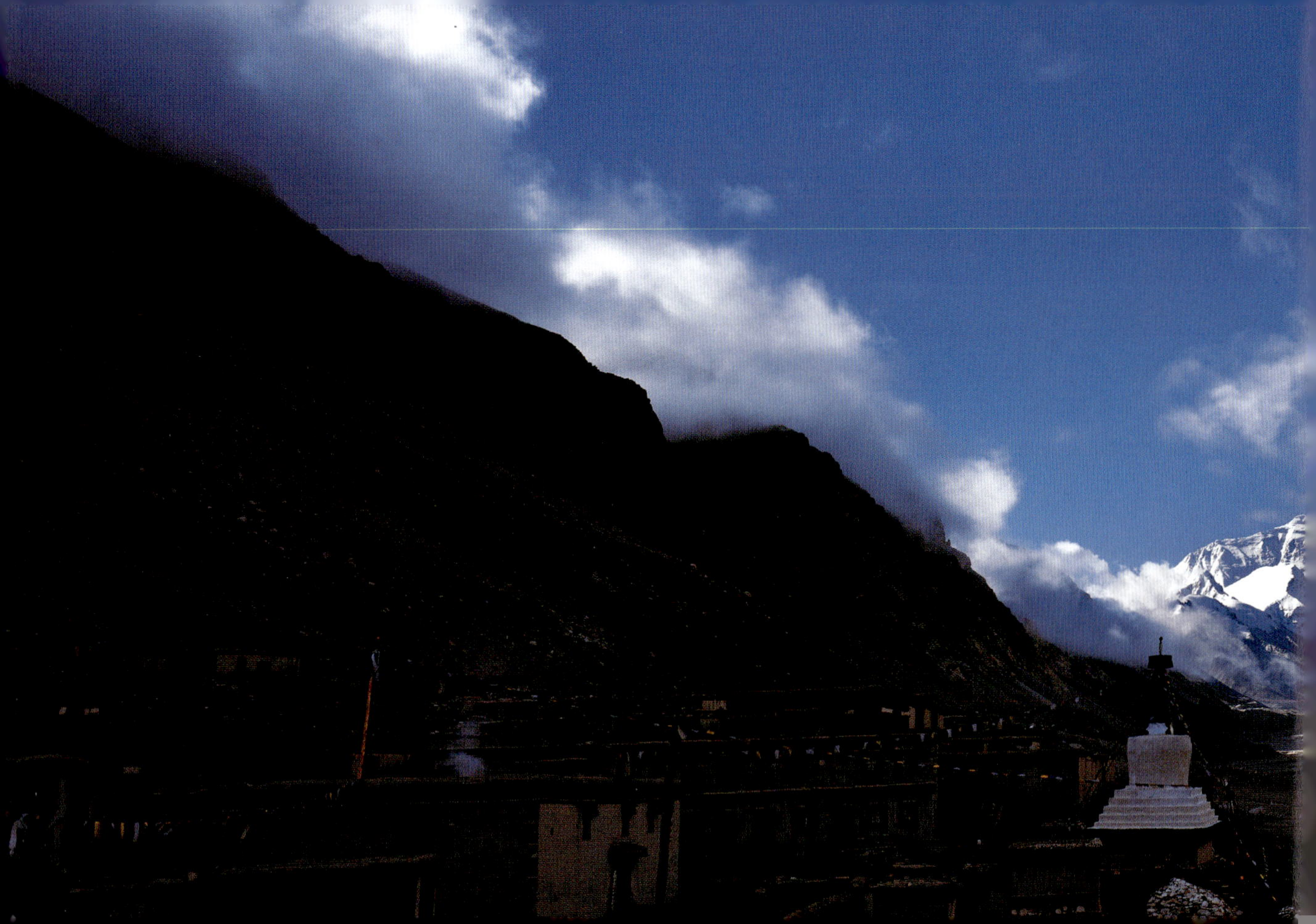

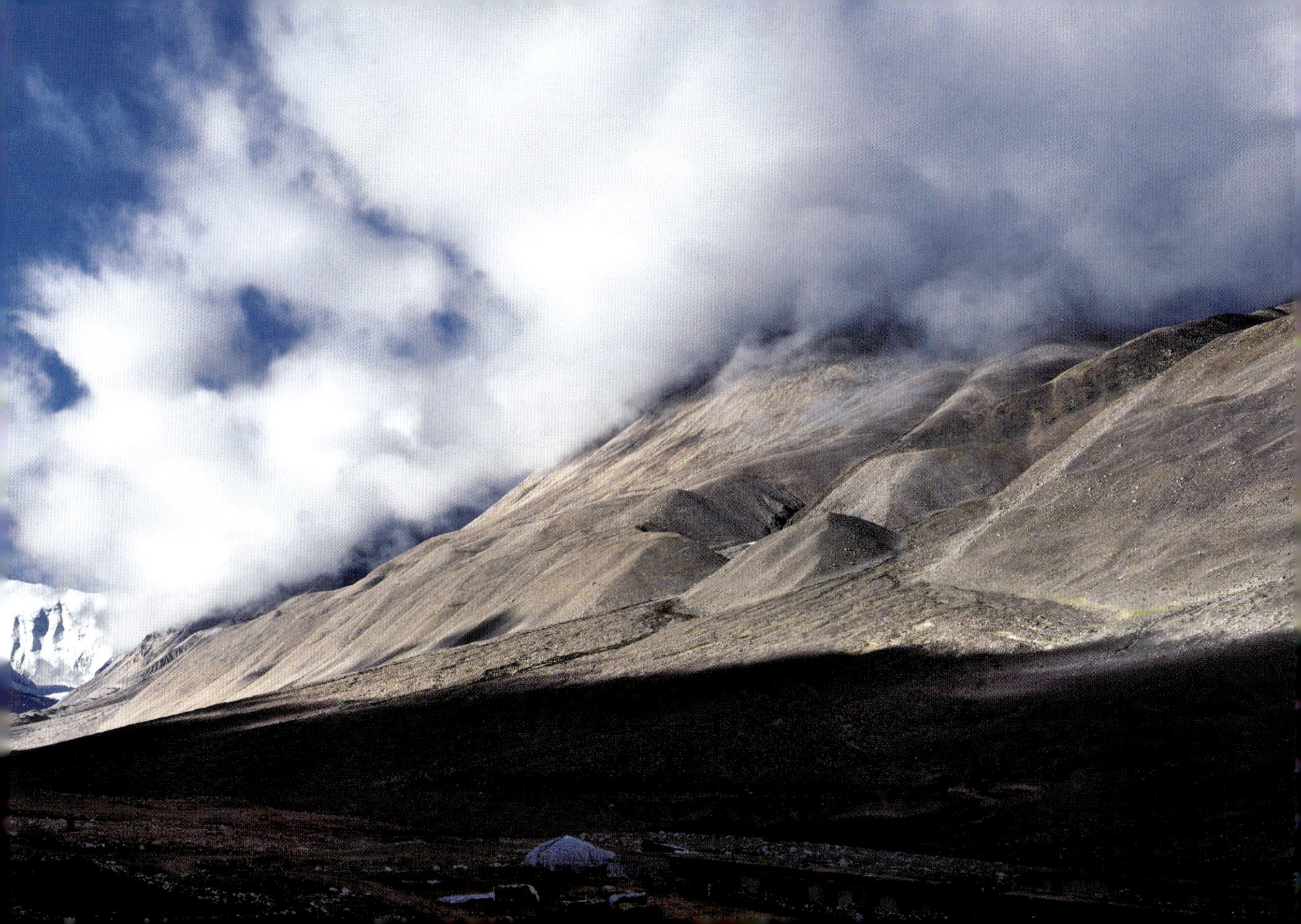

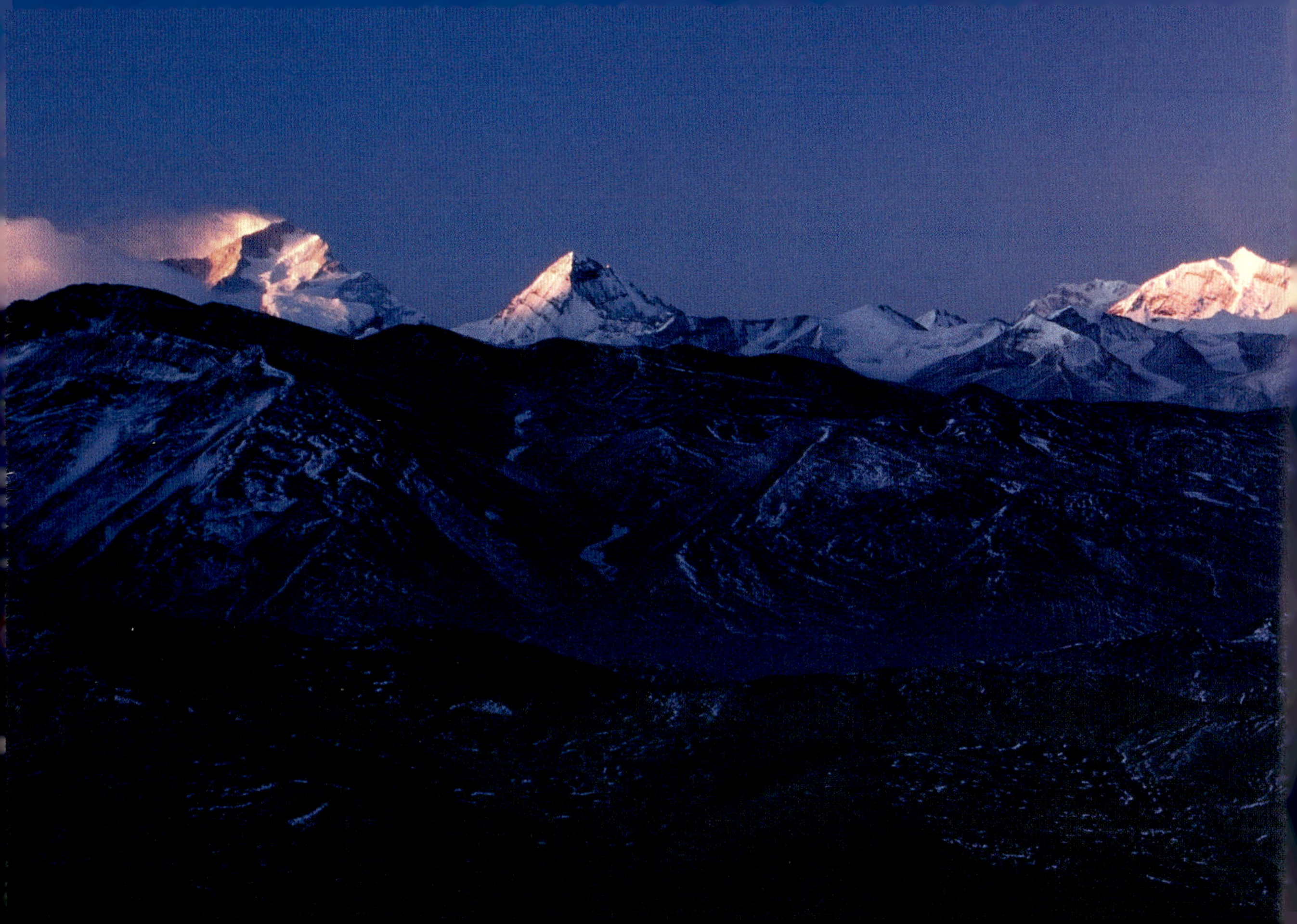

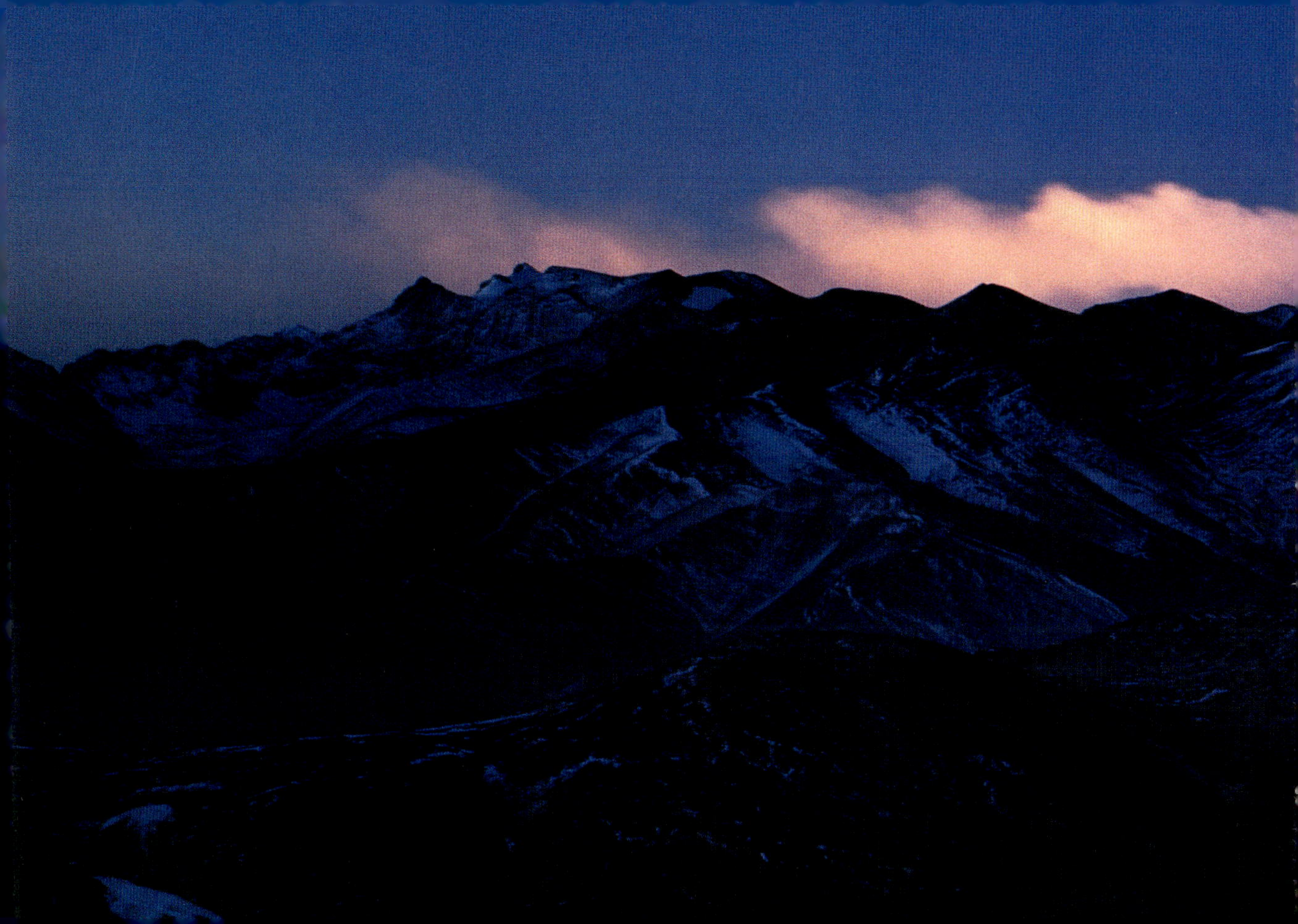

FOREWORD

The beauty and holiness of Mount Everest have helped seal the mesmerizing grip it has long held on those who live in its shadow, as well as a touch of the thrill felt by all who have known the irresistible compulsion to scale its peaks. Through the power of the photographic images and the elegant phrasing of the accompanying text in this volume, you are about to have an intense experience of Tibet, To fully appreciate the incredible forces of nature on the land that is now the Qinghai-Tibetan plateau and the Himalayas, you must first understand that this great land was long ago completely under the sea.

When the Indian plate and the Eurasian plate slammed against each other, the ancient sea retreated, giving birth to what would become today's Eurasian continent. Starting between 3.4 million and 150,000 years ago, this young landmass experienced three major uplifts before it finally entered into an entirely new era some 10,000 years ago.

Today, with an average elevation of 4,700 meters (15,400 ft), the Qinghai-Tibetan plateau is dominated by high mountain ranges over 6,000 meters (19,700 ft) well above the perpetual snow line. The spectacle of these snow-clad peaks has earned Tibet its reputation as the "Land of Snows." The Himalayas, the great mountain range south of the plateau, is home to numerous towering peaks, including Mount Everest, the world's highest at 8,844.43 meters (29,035 ft) above sea level.

As the sea bed was elevated into high peaks, the ancient sea left behind an array of lakes and pools nestled in the valleys of these snowy mountains. Crashing waves and tides quieted into gentle ripples, their colors simple and as elemental as the crayons and paints of the young.

Constant upheavals of shifting tectonic plates are still producing a mosaic of soaring mountains and deep valleys, leaving immensely diversified ecosystems as spectacularly charming as those in fairy tales.

The plateau itself is also birthplace to some of the greatest rivers of Asia. Both the Yangtze and the Yellow Rivers, cradles of ancient Chinese civilization, start here and flow eastward to the sea. Presumably, the valleys carved by the Yarlung Tsangpo River were home to the earliest known Tibetan settlers, since the valleys today are filled with the most fertile fields of all Tibet. The farmers here still live the agricultural and herding life of their ancestors.

Where the imposing mountains level off into a sea of rolling grasslands, generation after generation of Tibetan nomads share a peaceful existence with their herds of yaks, sheep, goats, and horses, although the climate out there is harsh and very cold for most of the year.

According to archeologists, the ancestors of the Tibetan people were living on the plateau as far back as the Neolithic Age. To survive in this unforgiving environment of vast spaces, but few people, the Tibetans have learned to devote more attention to their lasting relationship with nature. That explains why they respectfully refer to snowy mountains as "Divine Stones", and lakes as "Holy Waters". Legends endure that tell the story of the mutual love between divine mountains and holy lakes, as well as their battles against evil forces. Tibetan worship of nature and its elements—mountains, rocks, and trees—continues among the locals. The ritual-oriented primitive religion, with totem worship as one of its main tenets, began to give way to Buddhism in the early 7th century, when Buddhism was first introduced to Tibet. Centuries of conflicts and cultural encounters finally led to the establishment of Tibetan Buddhism, a unique religion characteristic of the plateau.

Rich and profound, Tibetan Buddhist culture has been a lifelong pursuit for numerous eminent monks and scholars. Tibetan Buddhism is, in essence, very heavy on ritual. Grand religious ceremonies, small prayer beads in the hands of an old Tibetan, flapping prayer flags printed with scriptures at mountain passes and river crossings, rocks inscribed with prayers, even piles of small stones along the roadsides—all serve as reminders of the religious atmosphere that surrounds Tibetan life. Meanwhile, they are believed to contribute, in one way or another, to strengthening the positive values inherent in the Buddhist tradition.

Historically, temples and monasteries are the most splendid structures on the plateau, the most visible embodiments of the ritual-oriented Tibetan Buddhism. To better express the intricacy of their inner world, the Tibetans used their wealth to create a huge variety of religious architecture, most of it at the pinnacle of Buddhist art. Lhasa, the most ancient city in Tibet, was developed partly out of the need for pilgrims to pay homage to the Buddhist shrines at the Jokhang and Ramoche Monasteries. To refine their virtues and gain merit in this life, pilgrims trek a long distance to these holy sites to perform energetic prostrations as they make kora—holy circuits—around the temples. Brightly lit with butter lamps and enshrined with the most venerated Buddhist images, the temples are where Buddhist monks, a unique hermit community on the plateau, spend all their lives meditating and cultivating wisdom.

The daily life of the Tibetan people is, however, as secular as it is religious. Farm tools and articles of daily use, for example, are often exquisitely fashioned to harmonize with the hues of sky and earth, richly and vibrantly colored like the tanned skin of the Tibetan people glowing in the sun. During festivities, they dress up with traditional costumes, trying to out bloom each other in beauty and color. Here on the plateau, the Tibetans, with their loud, sonorous voices, sing their way onto the summits of the snowy mountains, and across the depths of the green grasslands. Here on the plateau, the Tibetans, radiant and fit from their healthy way of life, dance so vigorously that even the mighty rivers seem to roar in unison with them and the laughter of the fruitful fields, all in affirmation of the rich abundance of life on this bountiful land. Their love flows freely in this sea of song and dance. With love flowing from their hearts, life goes on as it seems it always has in this most wonderful place on our planet.

The Tibetan sky is as bright and clear as the eyes of the Tibetan people are fathomless and deep. Although the plateau is geologically young, it is nevertheless wide enough, real and exciting, to embrace the enduring, enterprising, and optimistic Tibetan pilgrims with grateful and humble hearts.

So, with the heart of a pilgrim, let's continue through the pages of this Tibetan album, to experience the passions of the plateau, to explore this timeless land of exotic mystery, and to feel the Tibetans' elevated love of life.

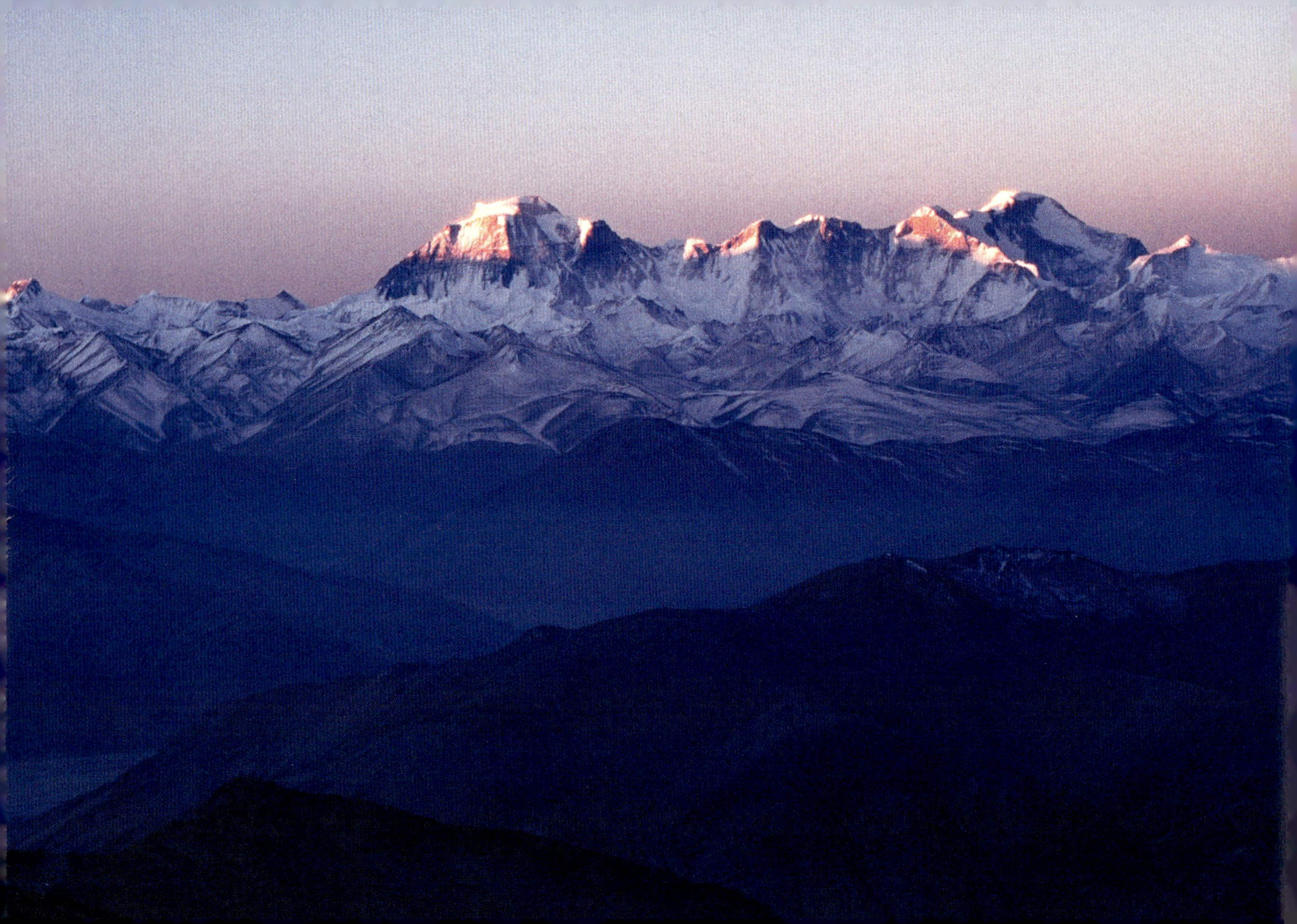

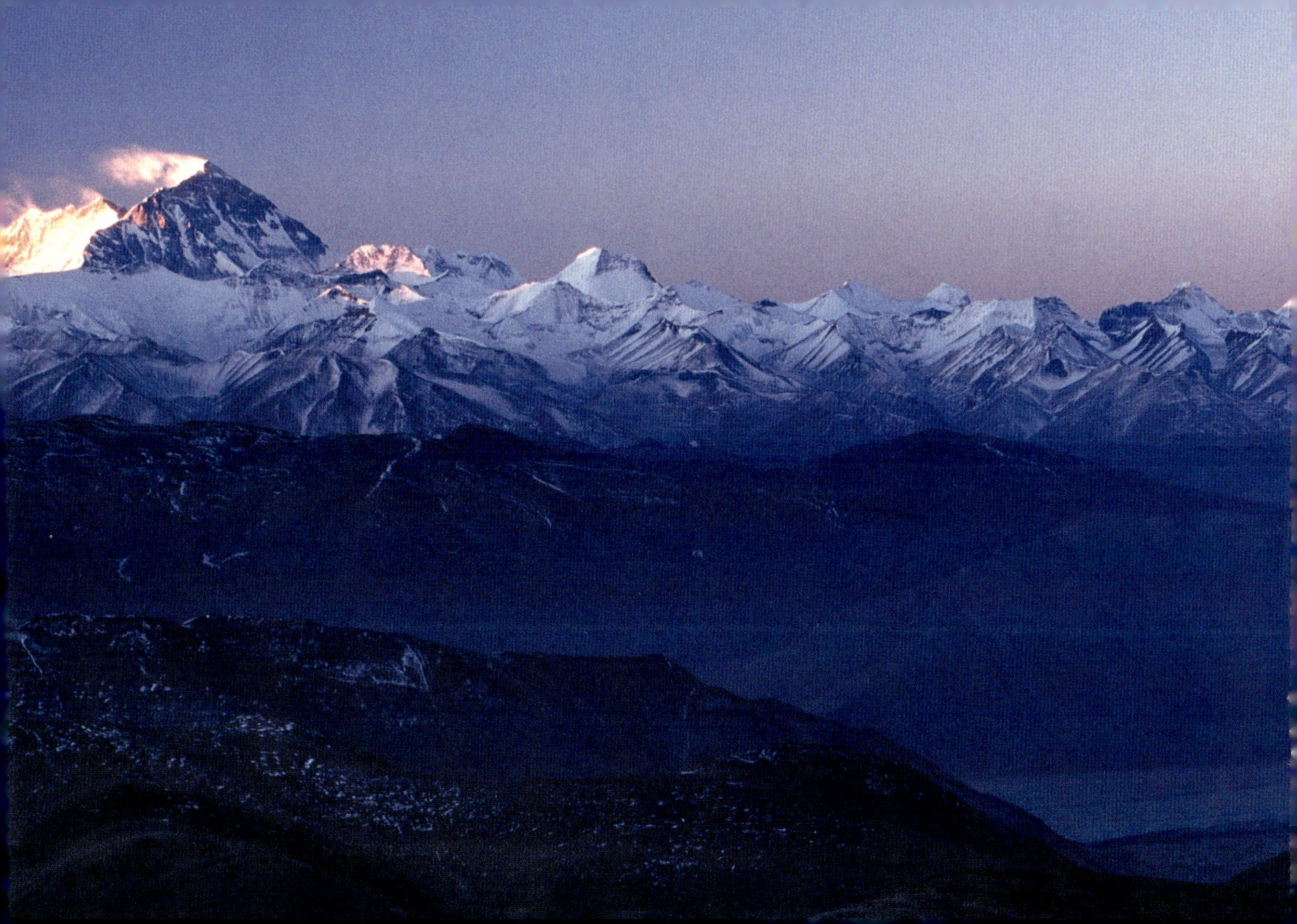

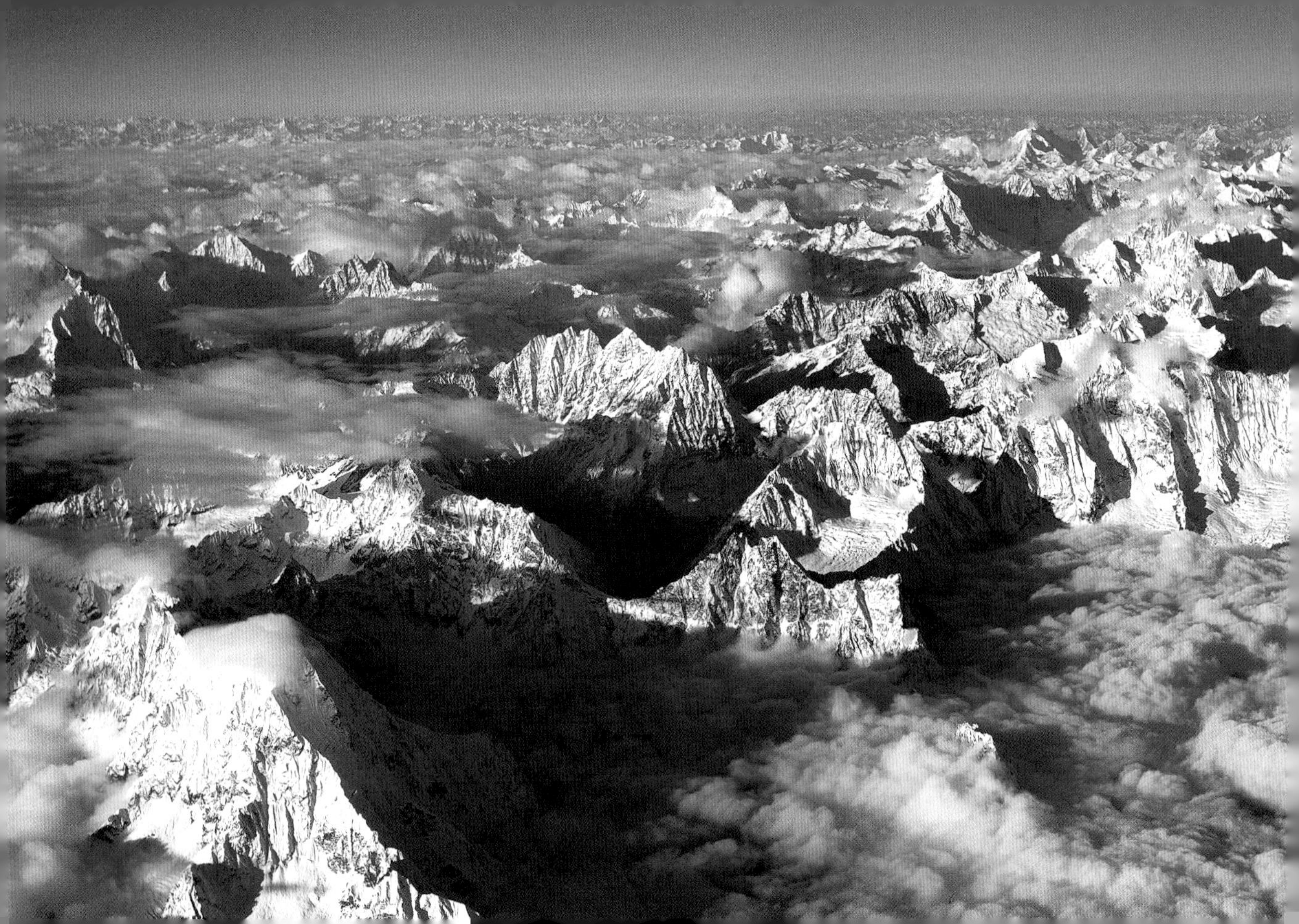

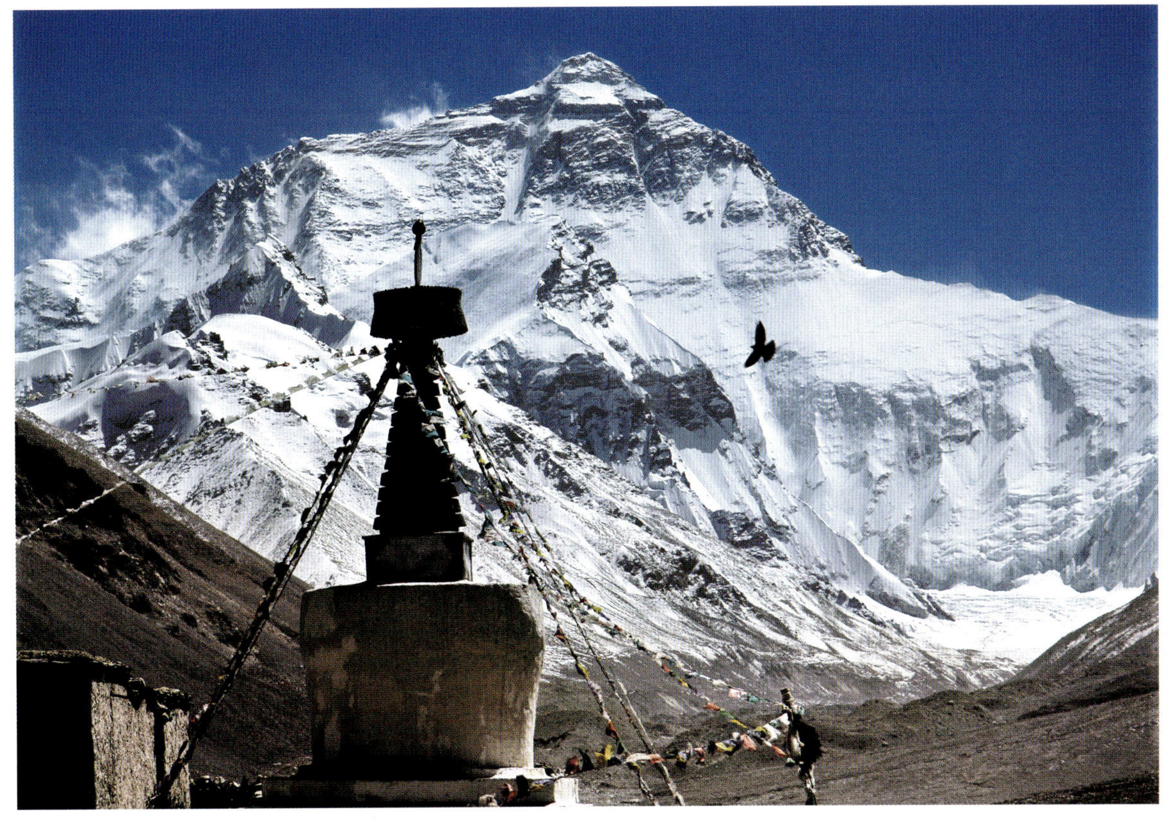

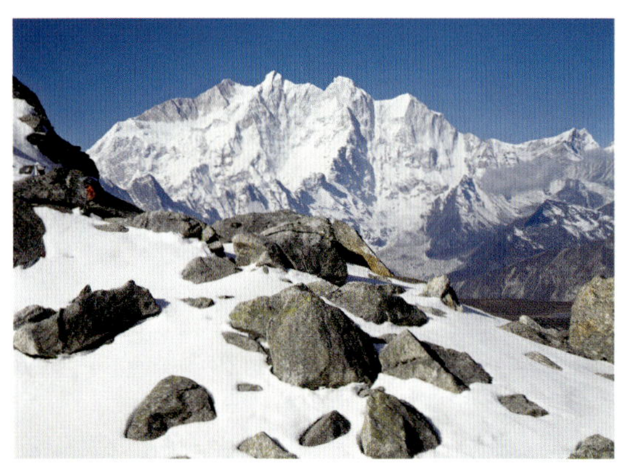

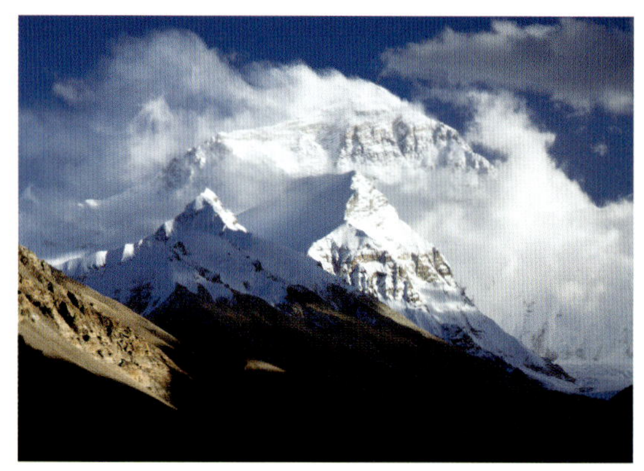

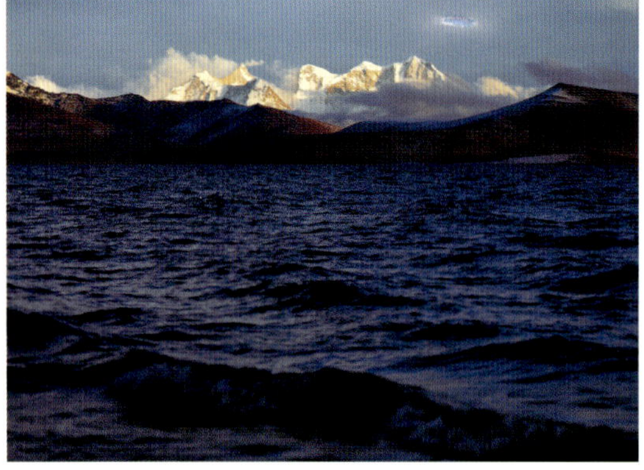

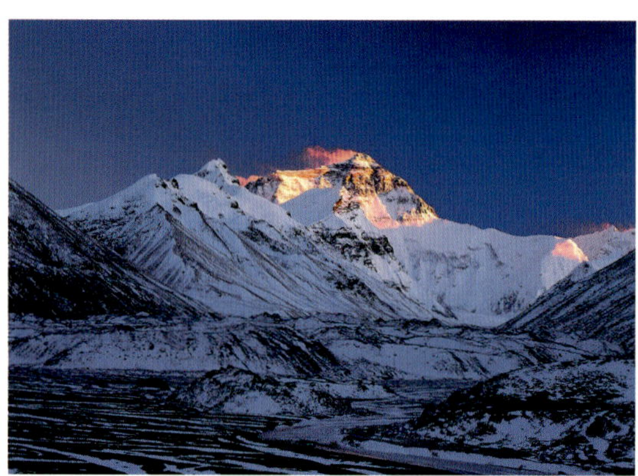

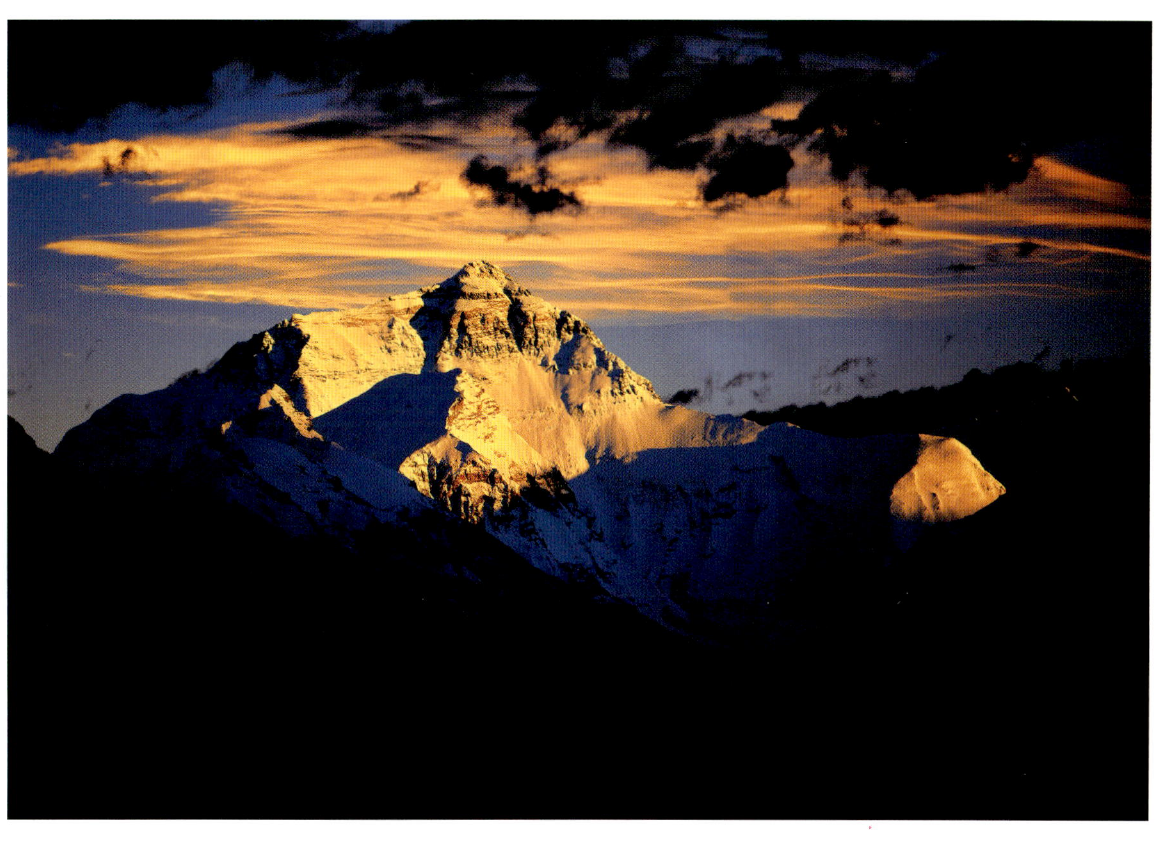

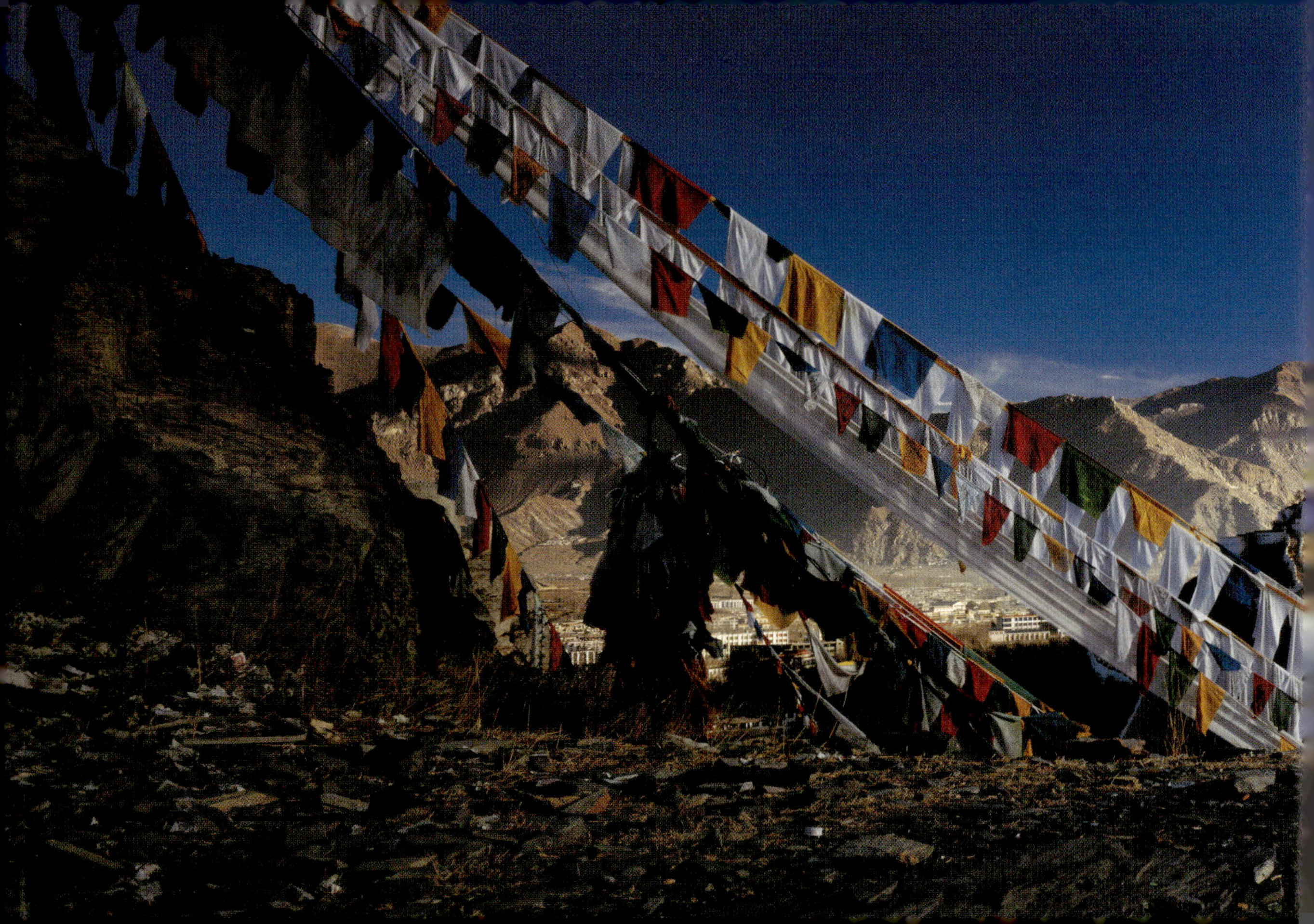

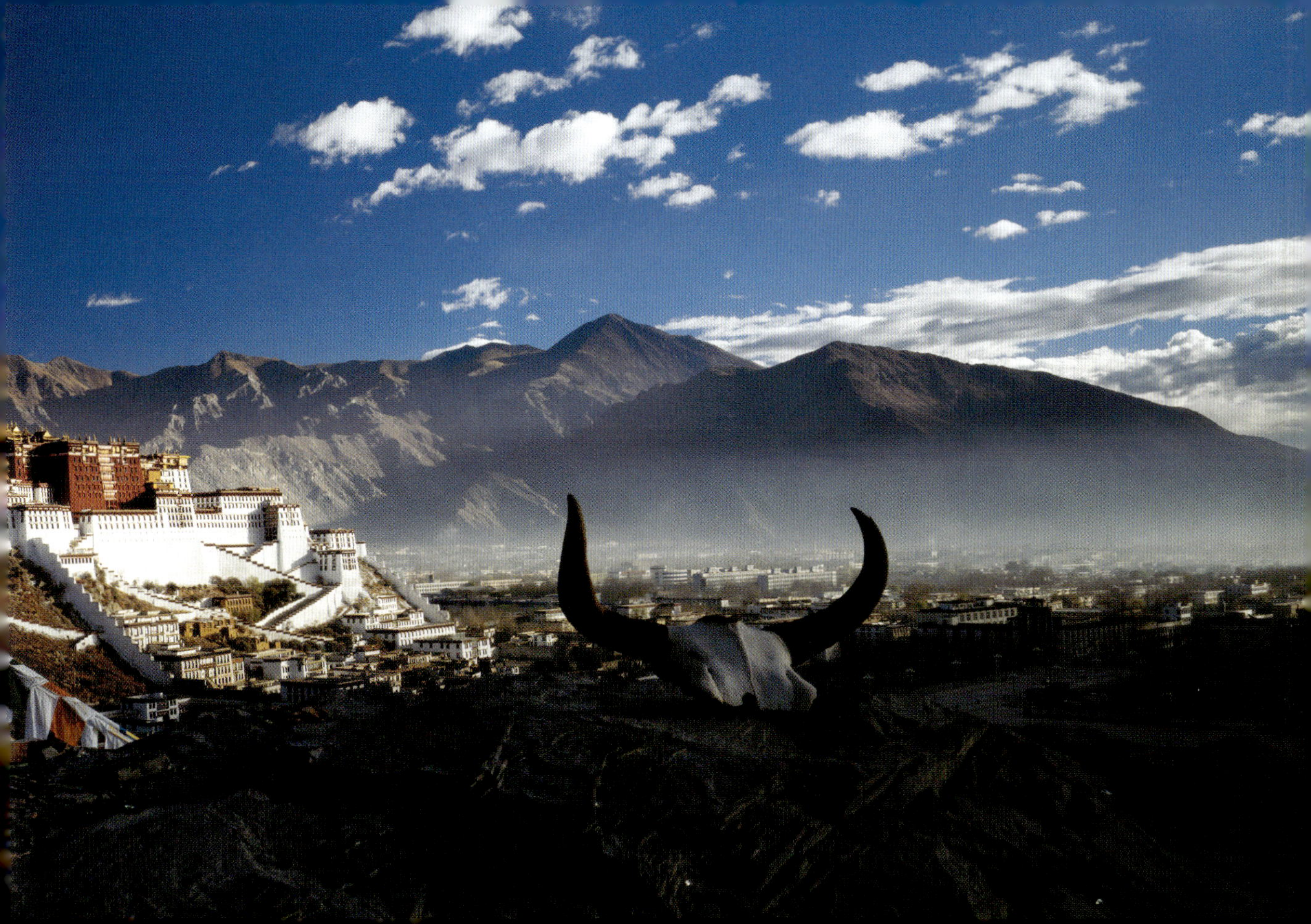

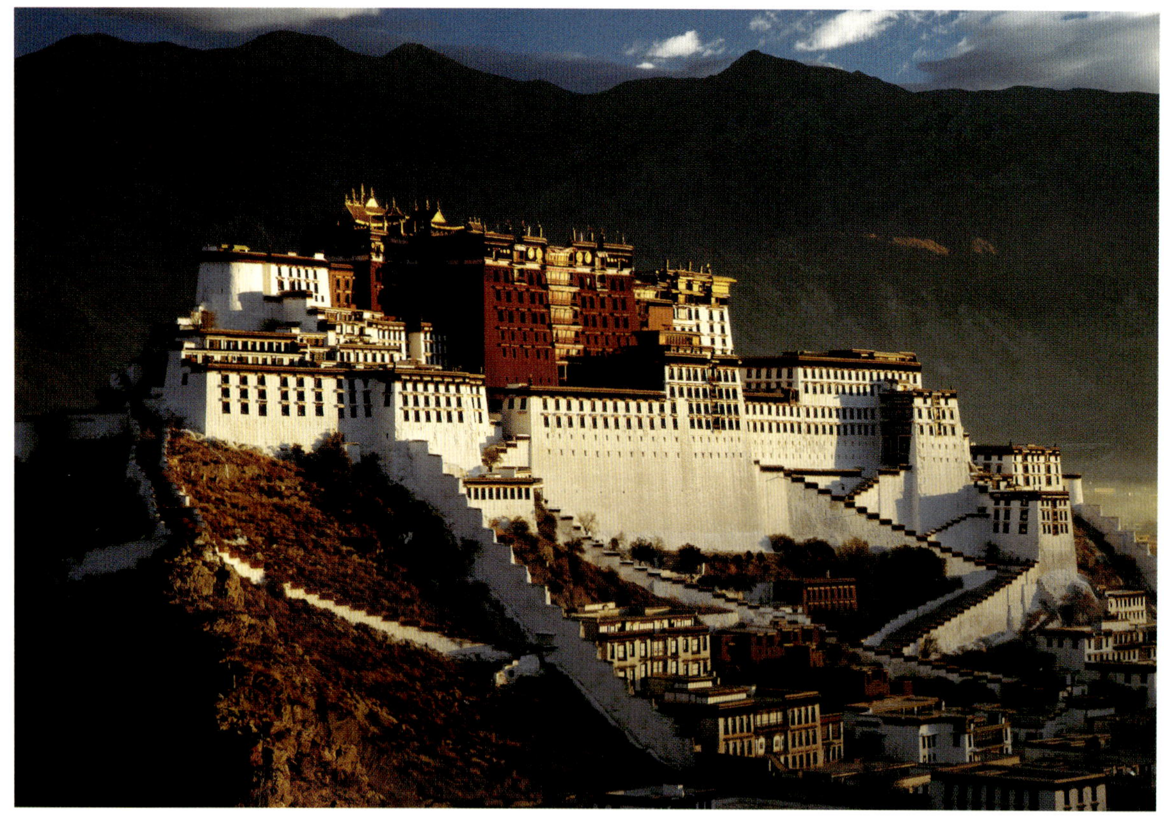

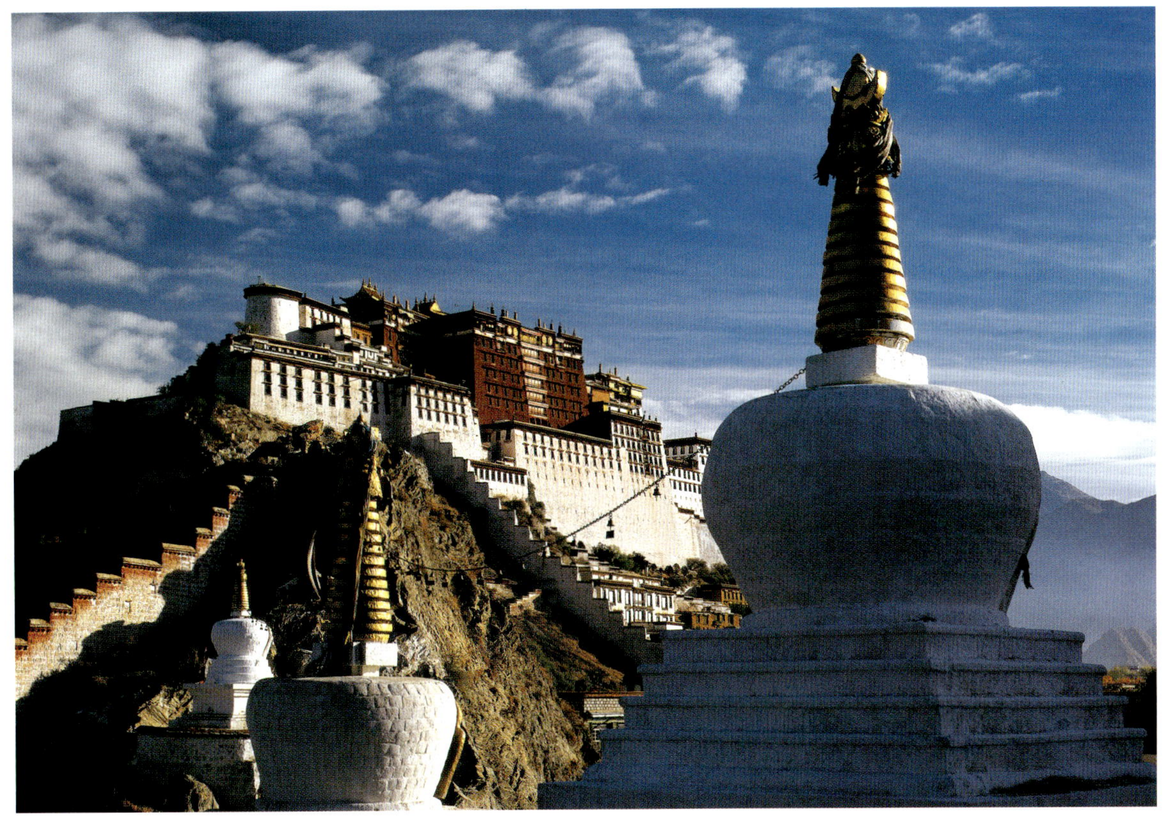

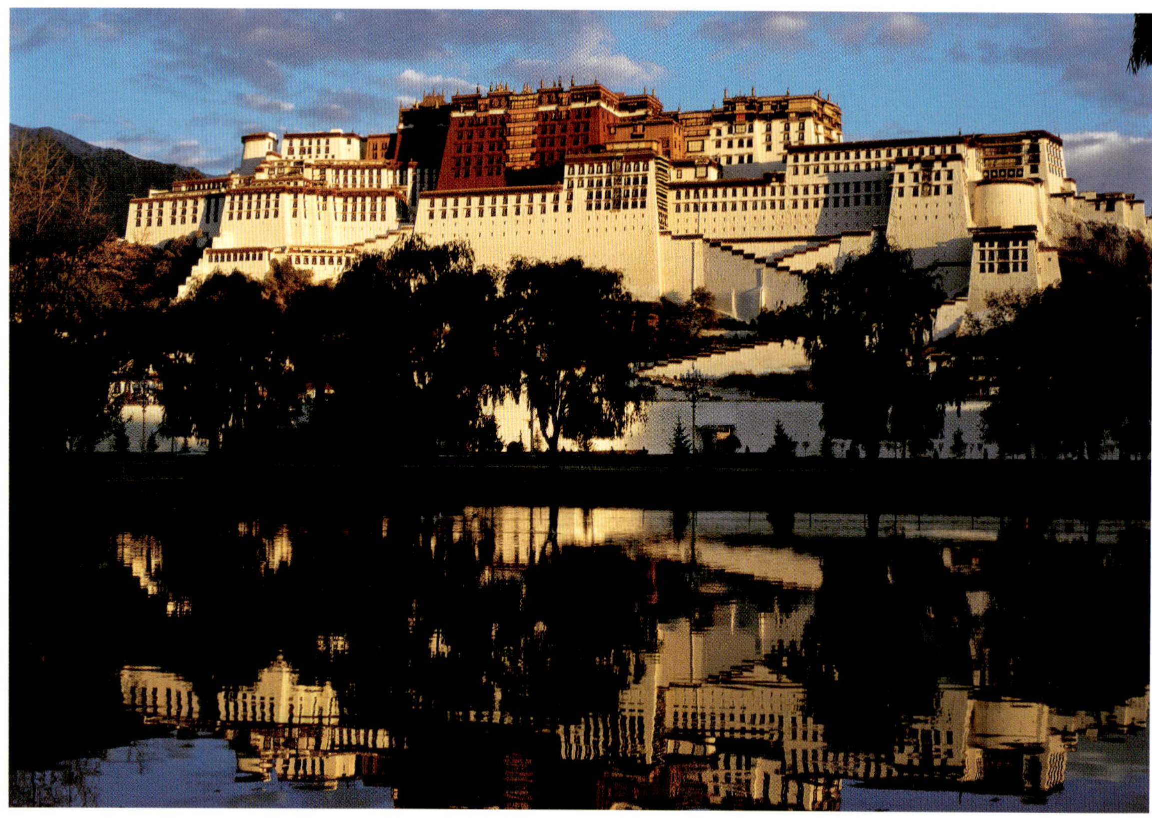

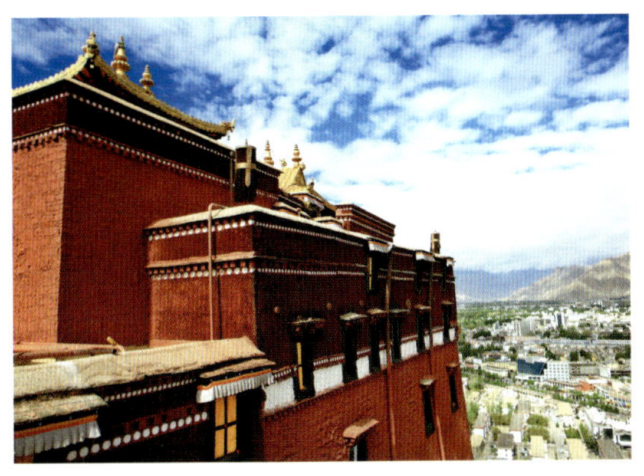
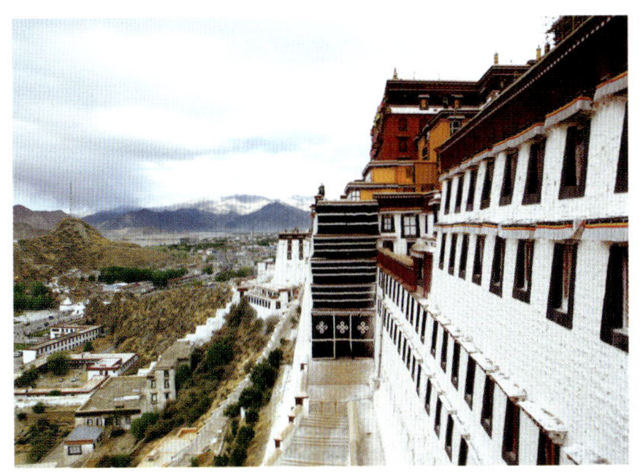
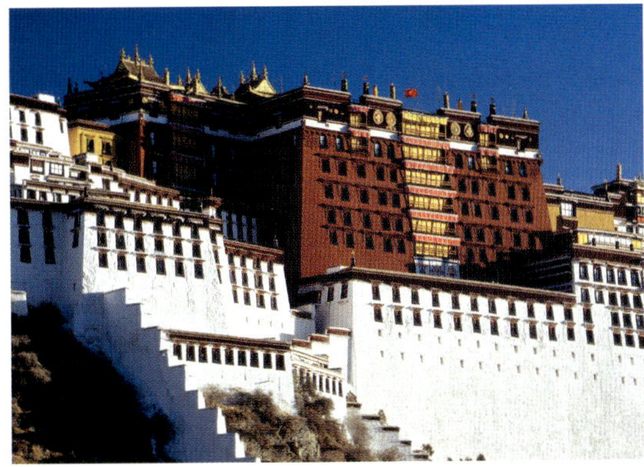
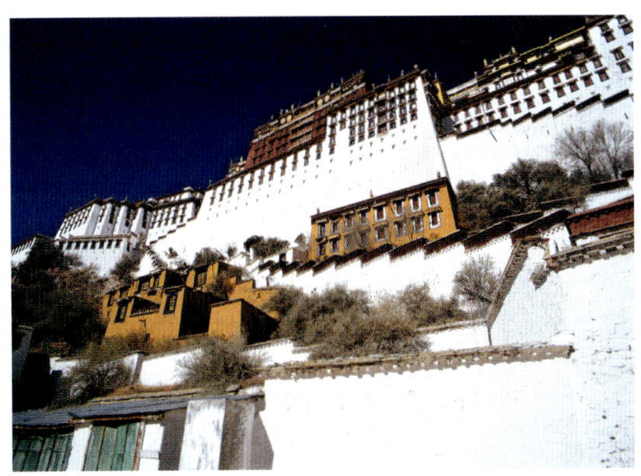

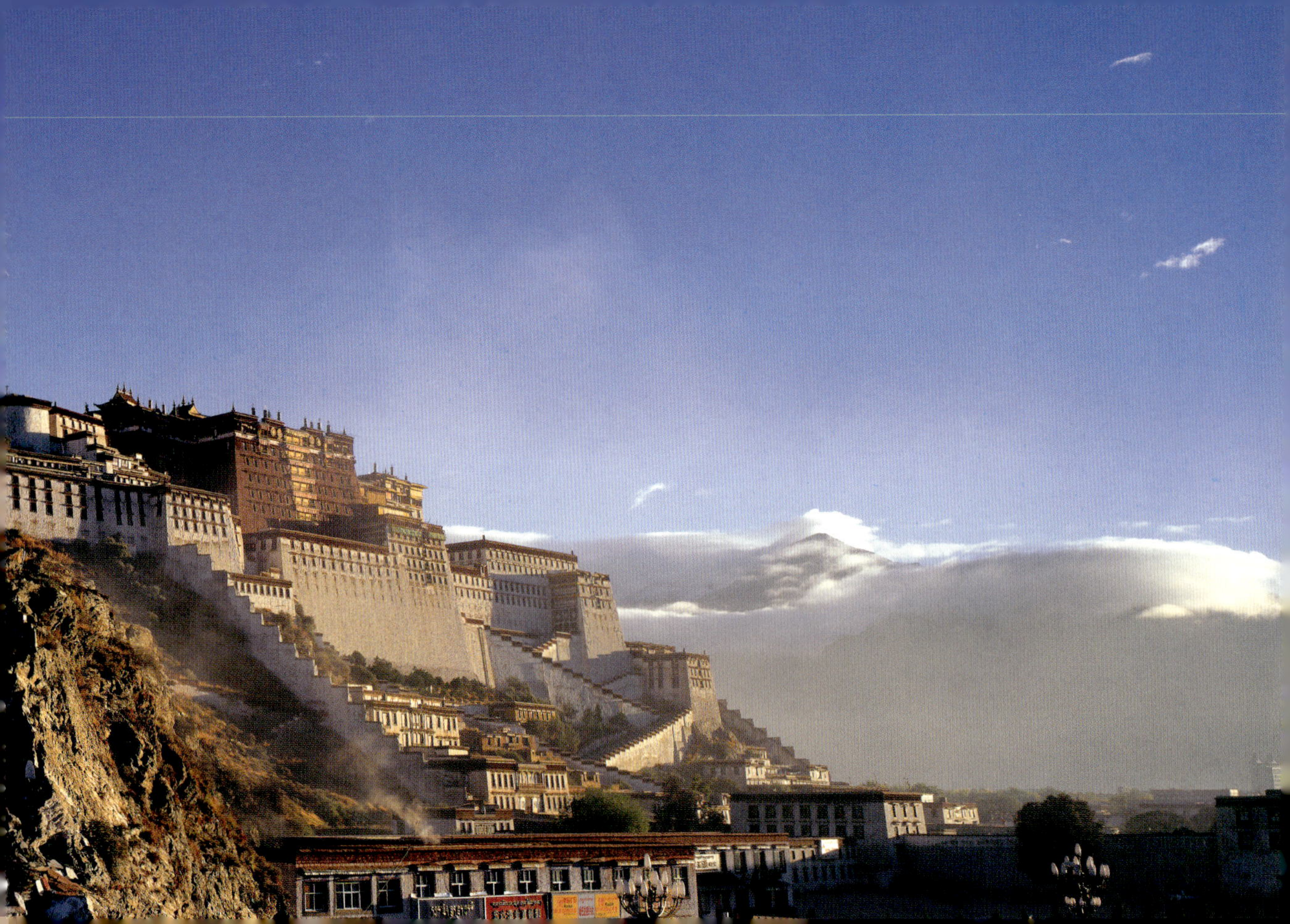

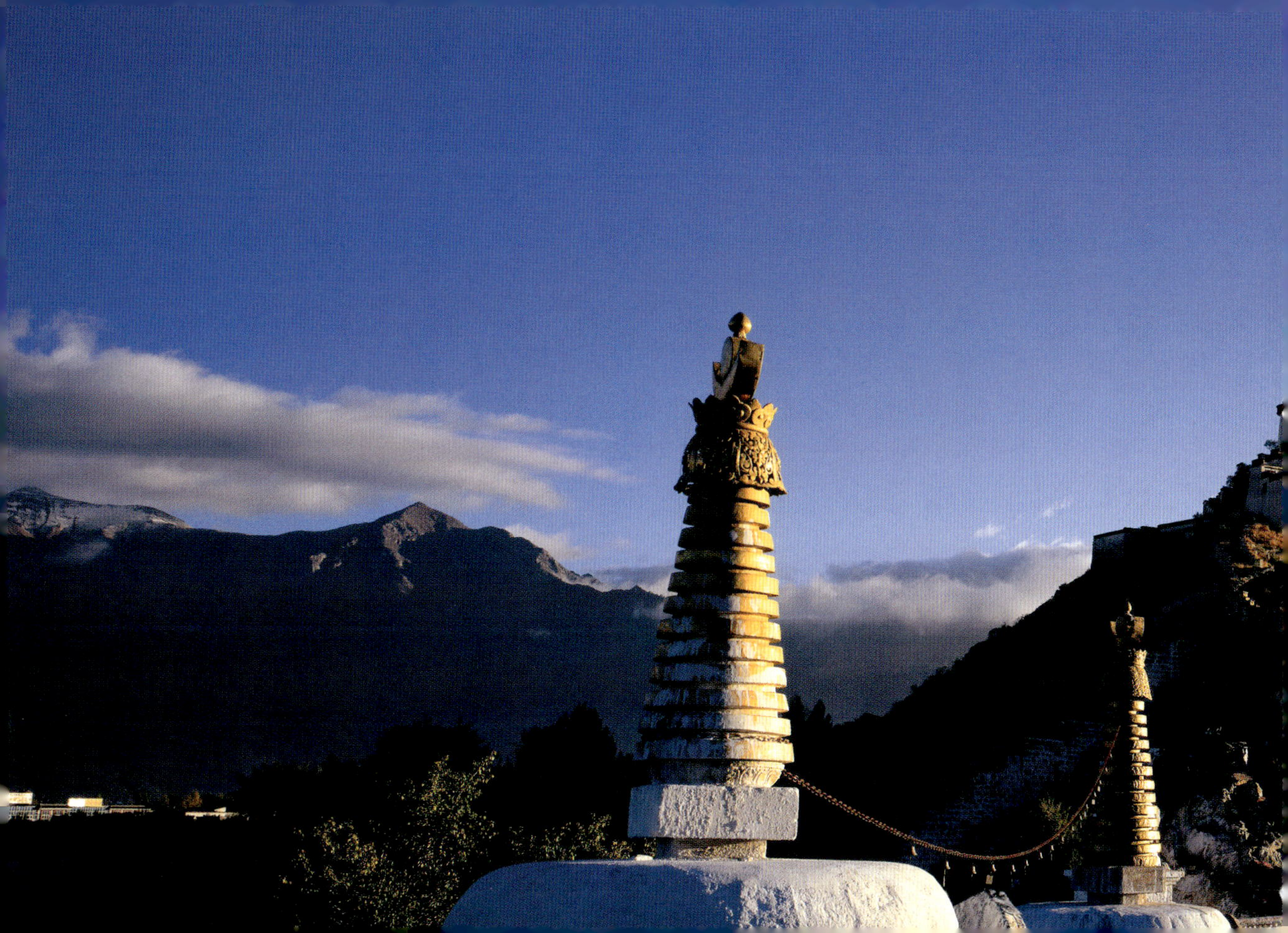

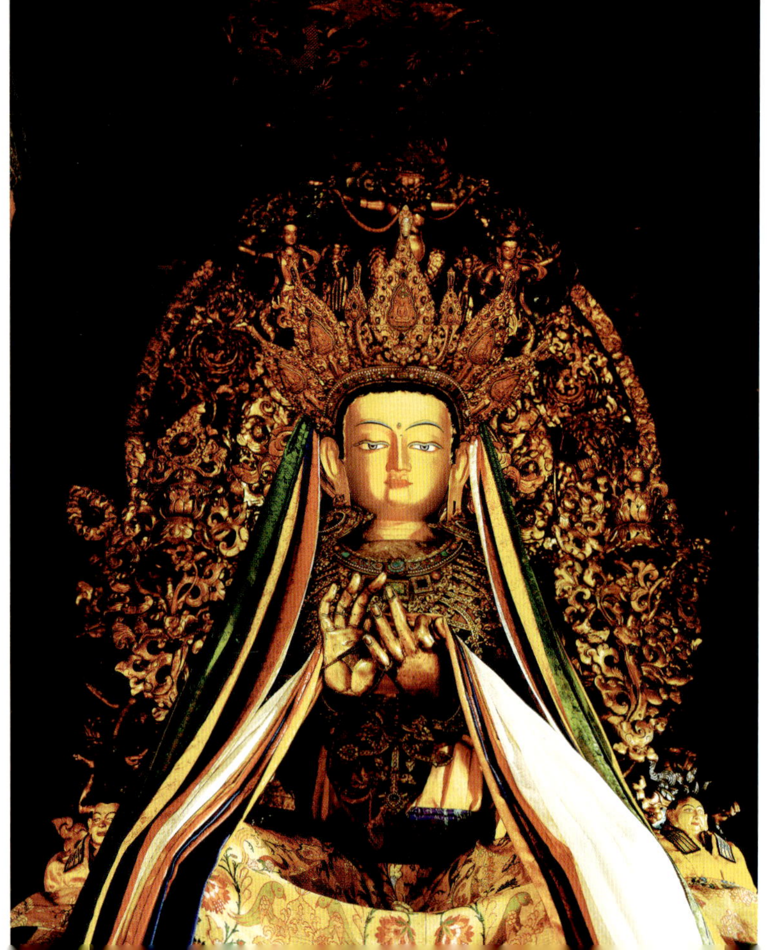

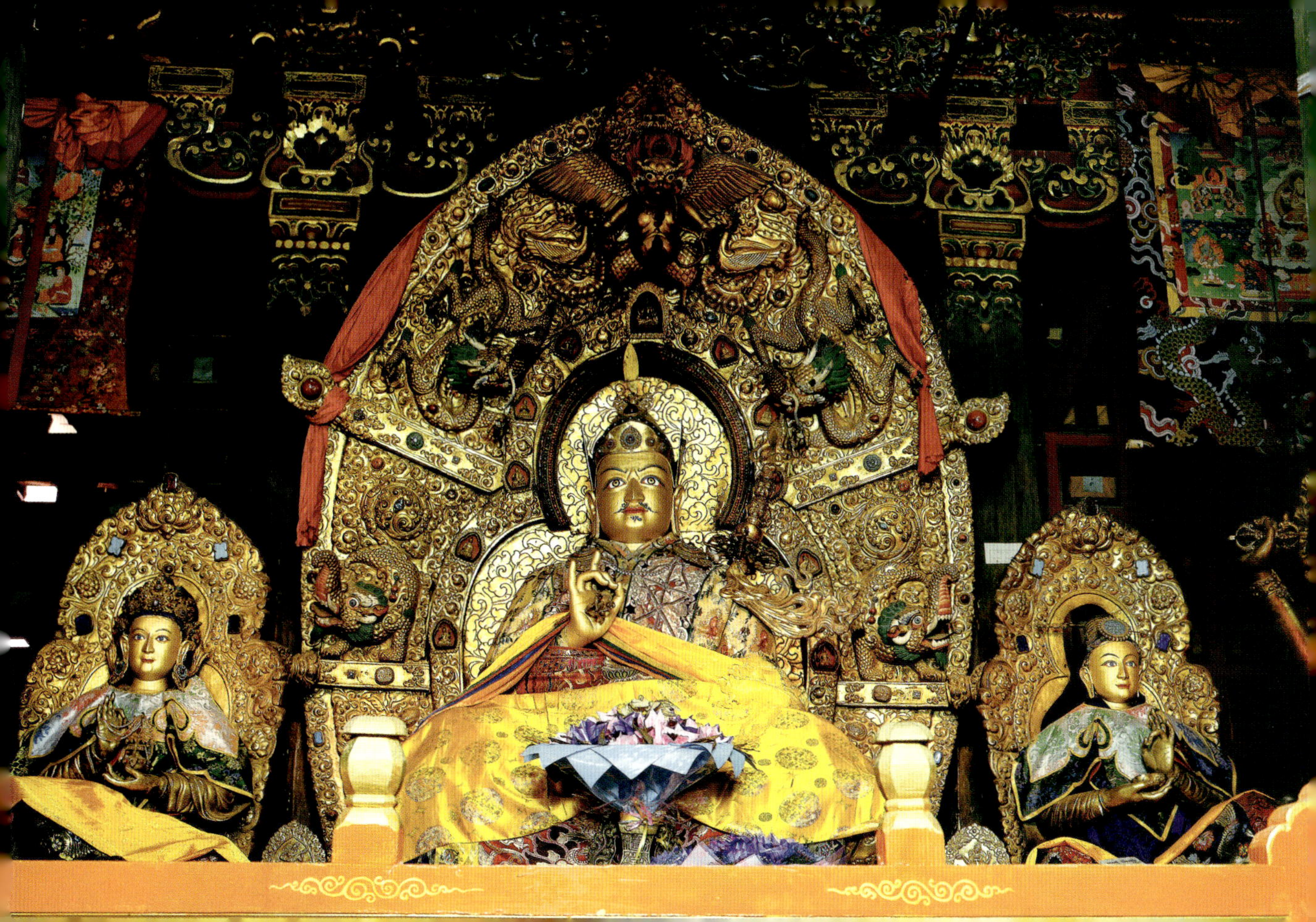

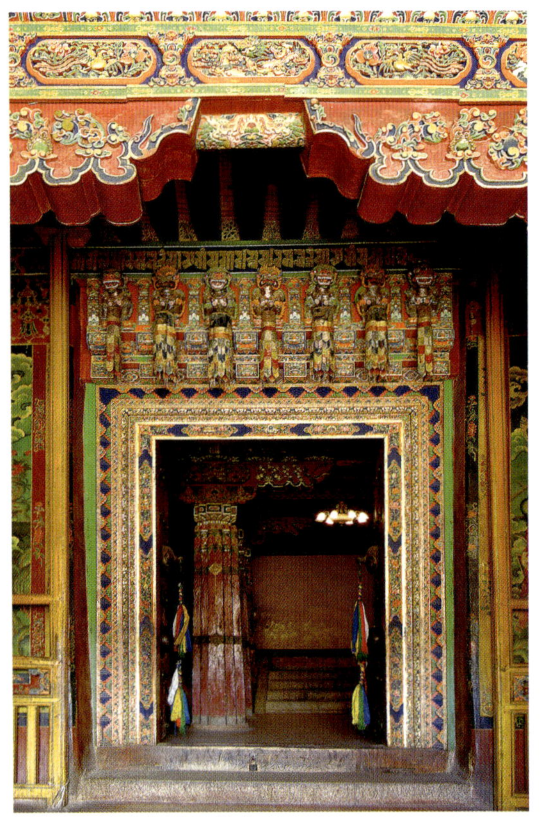

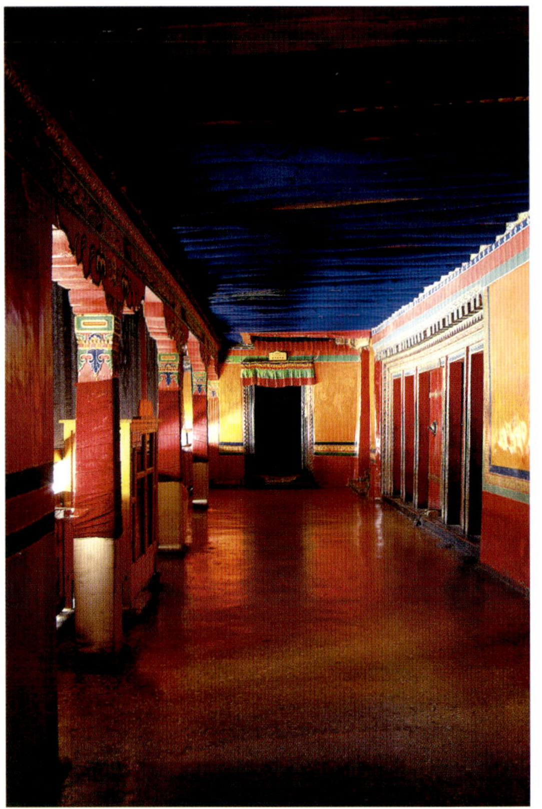

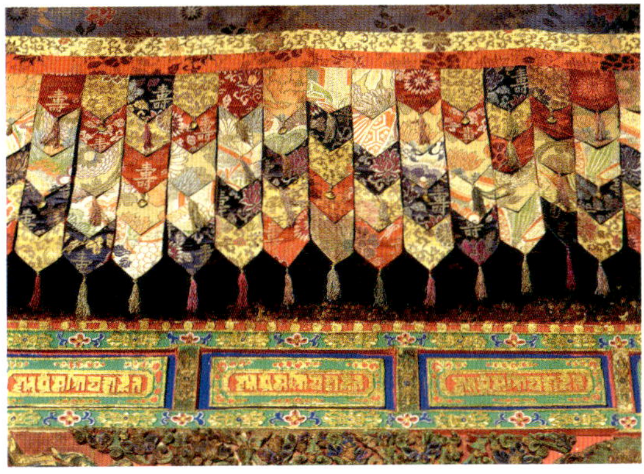

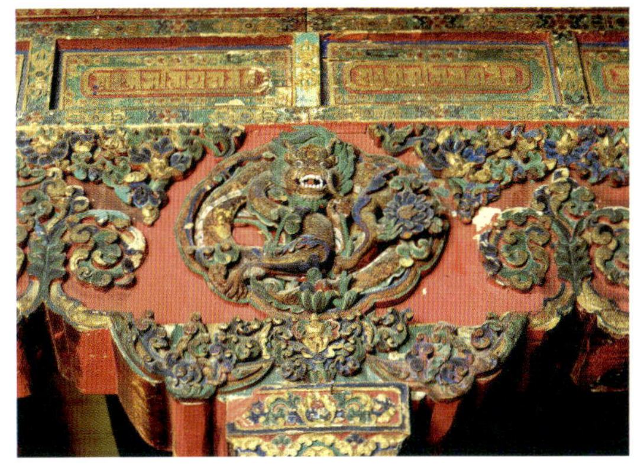

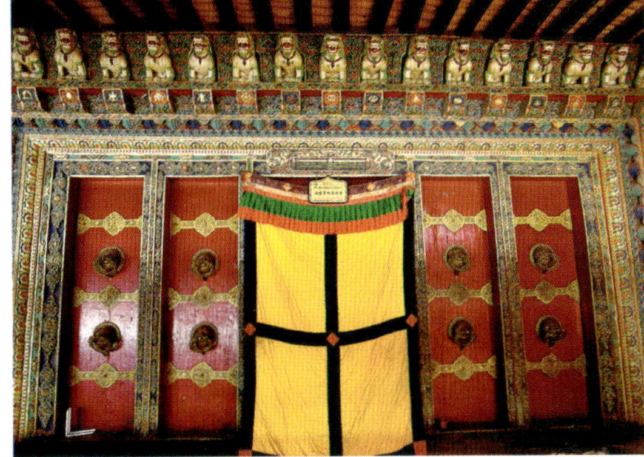

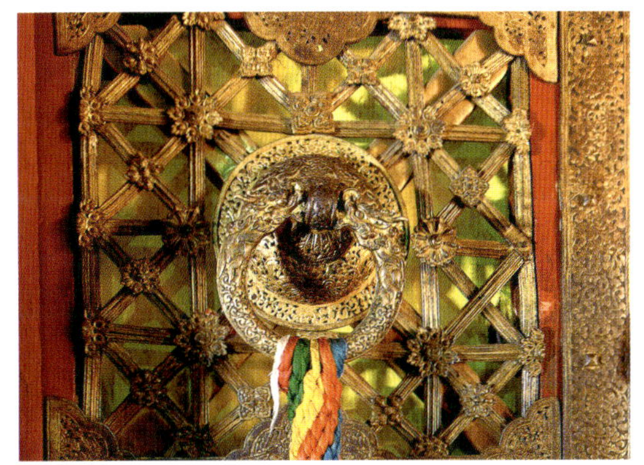

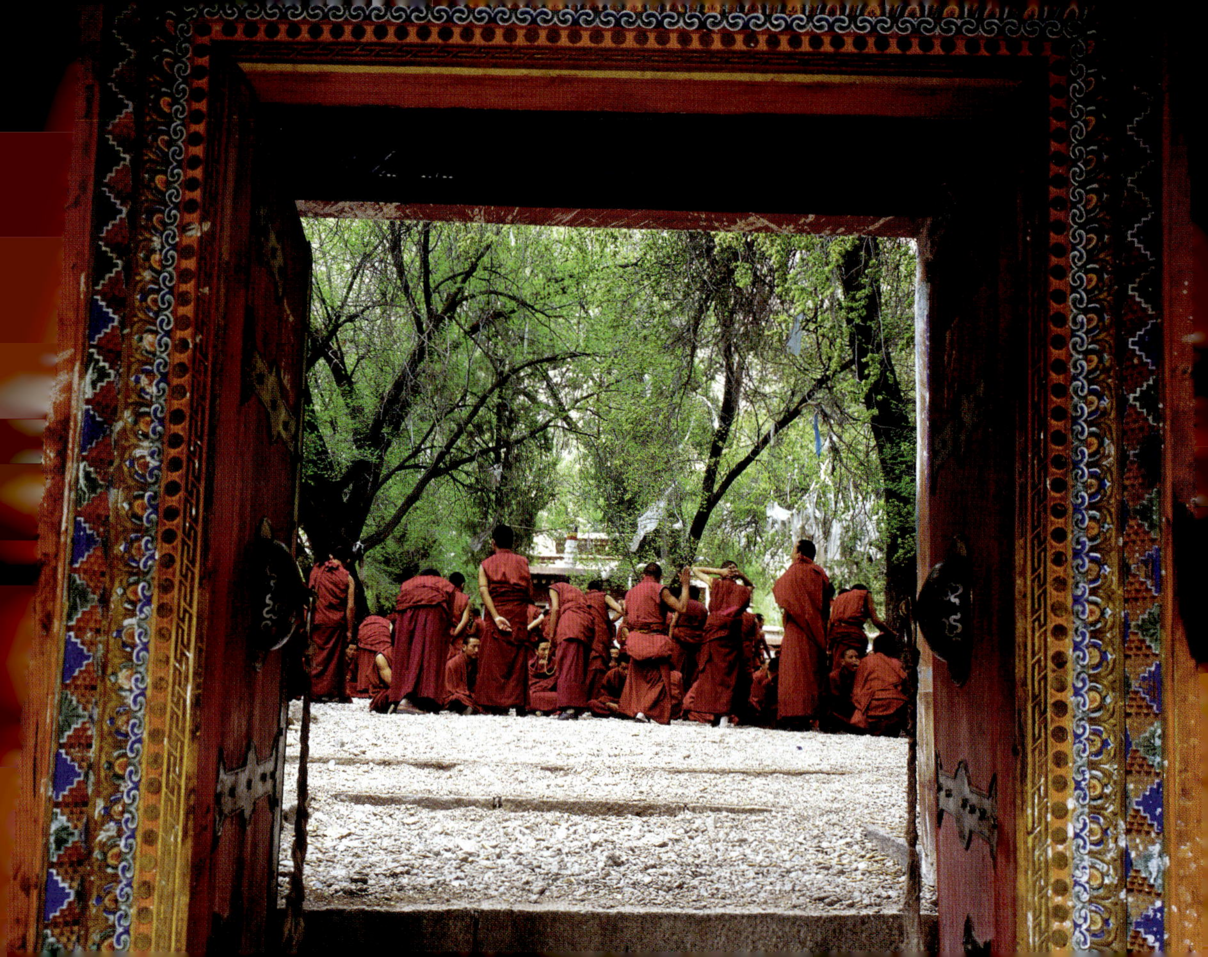

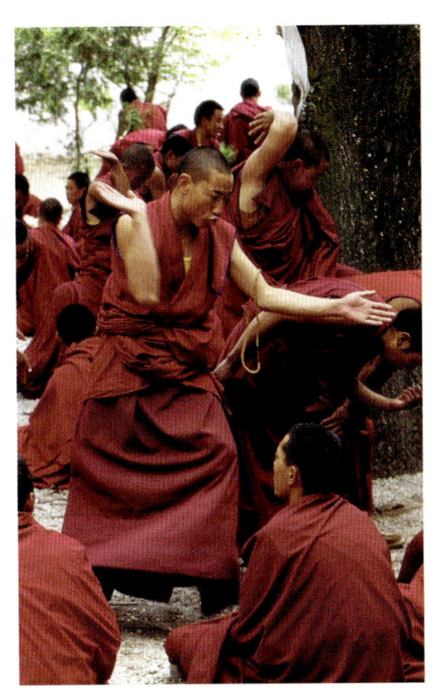

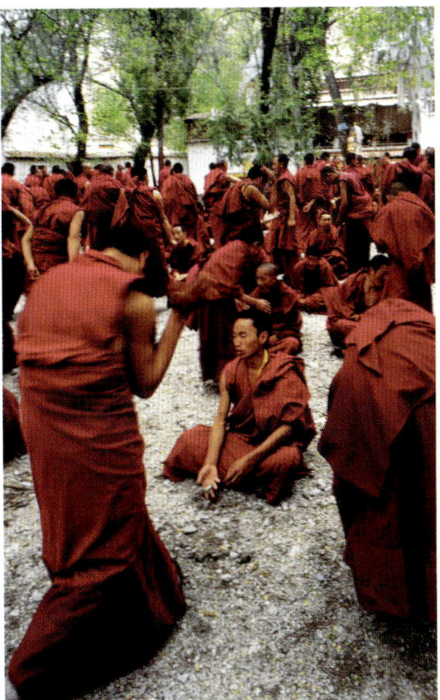

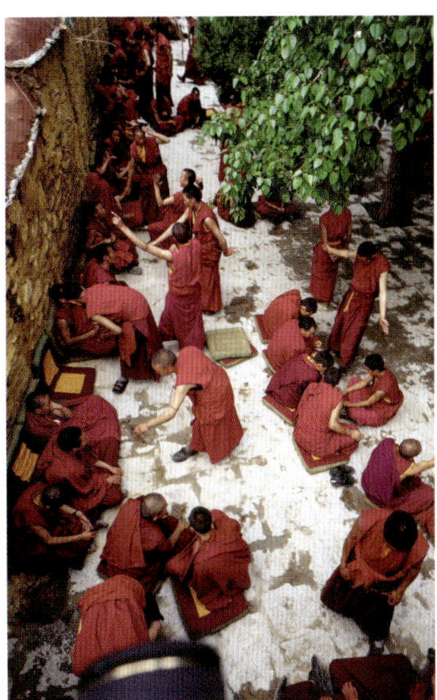

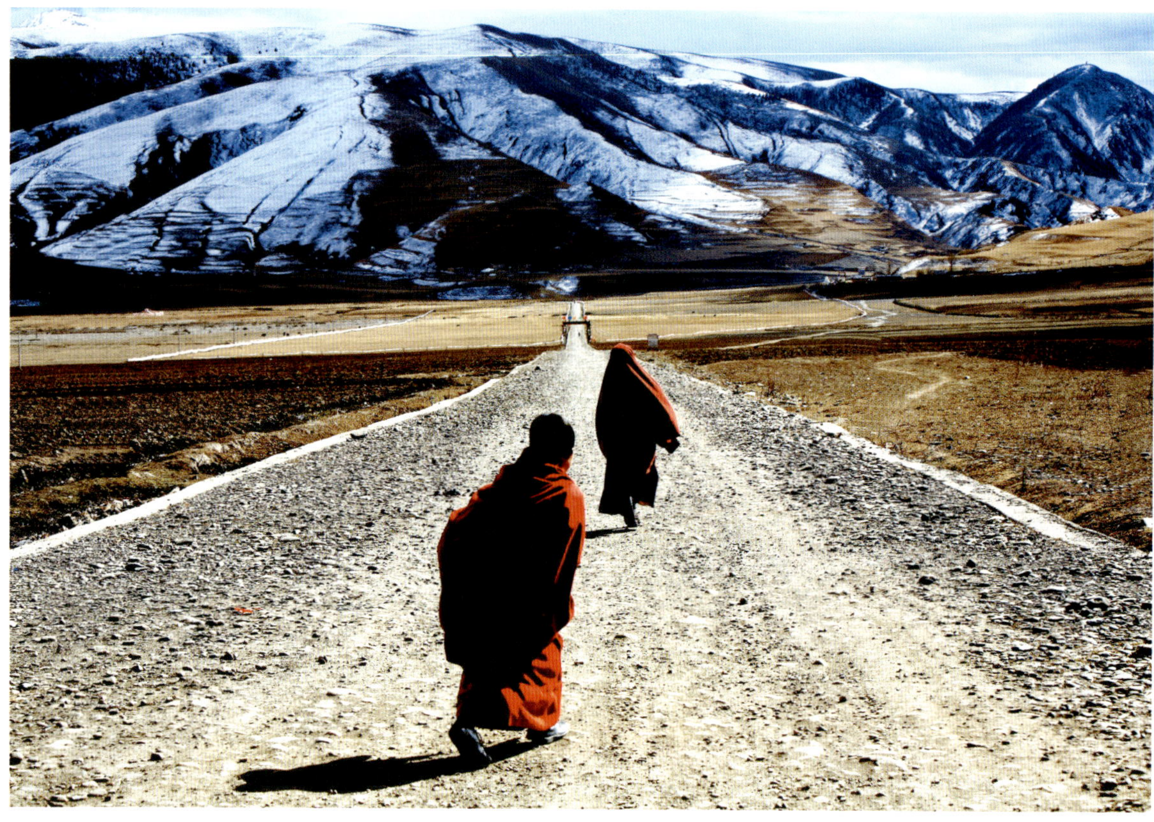

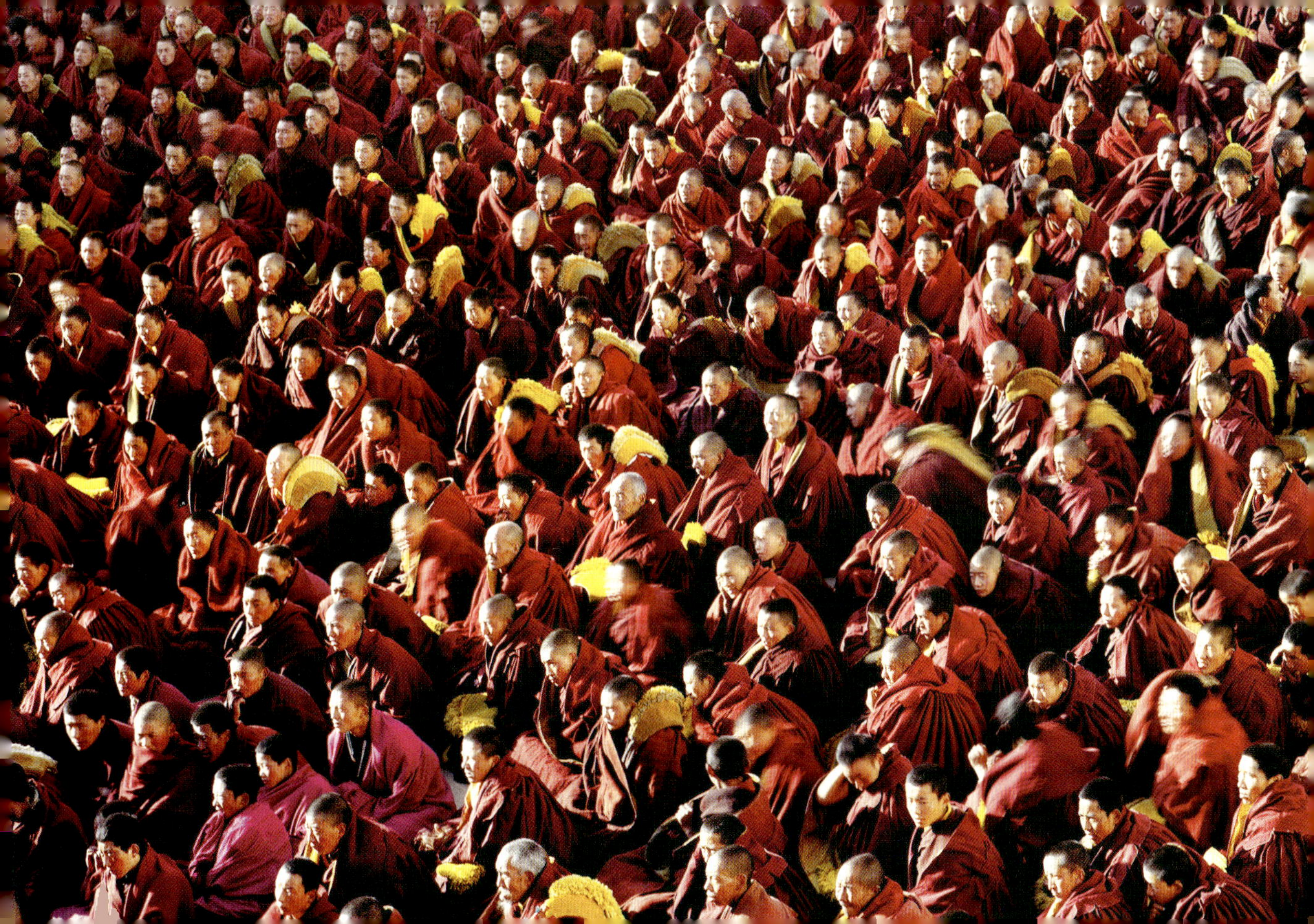

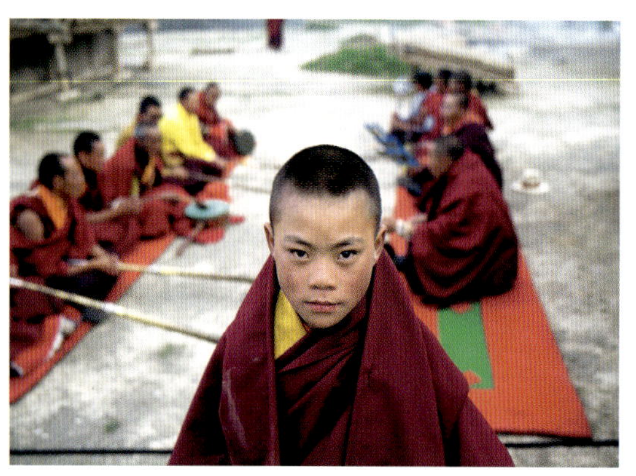

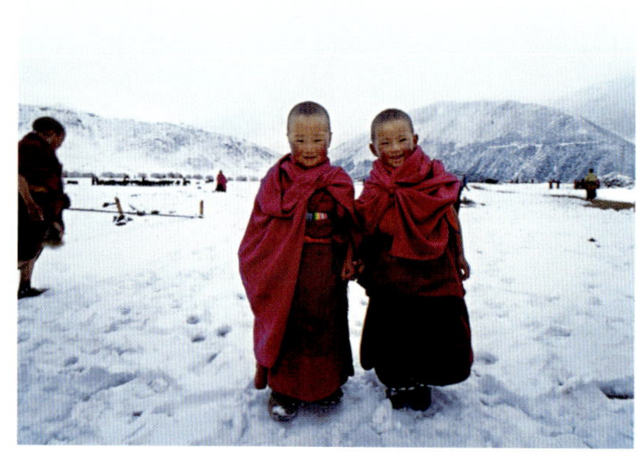

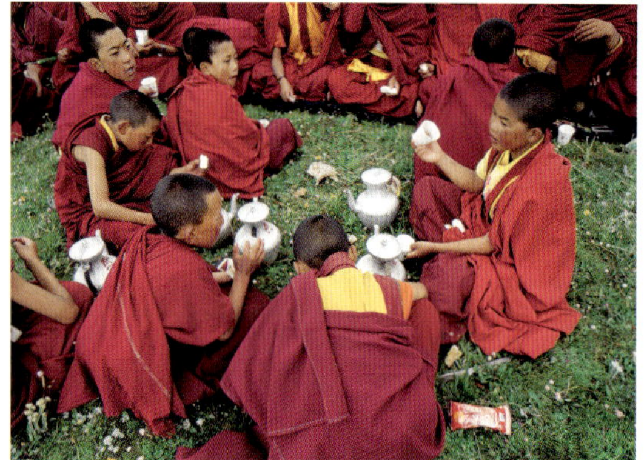

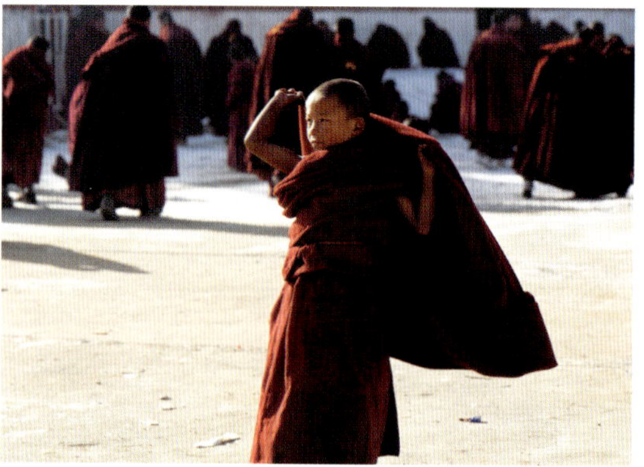

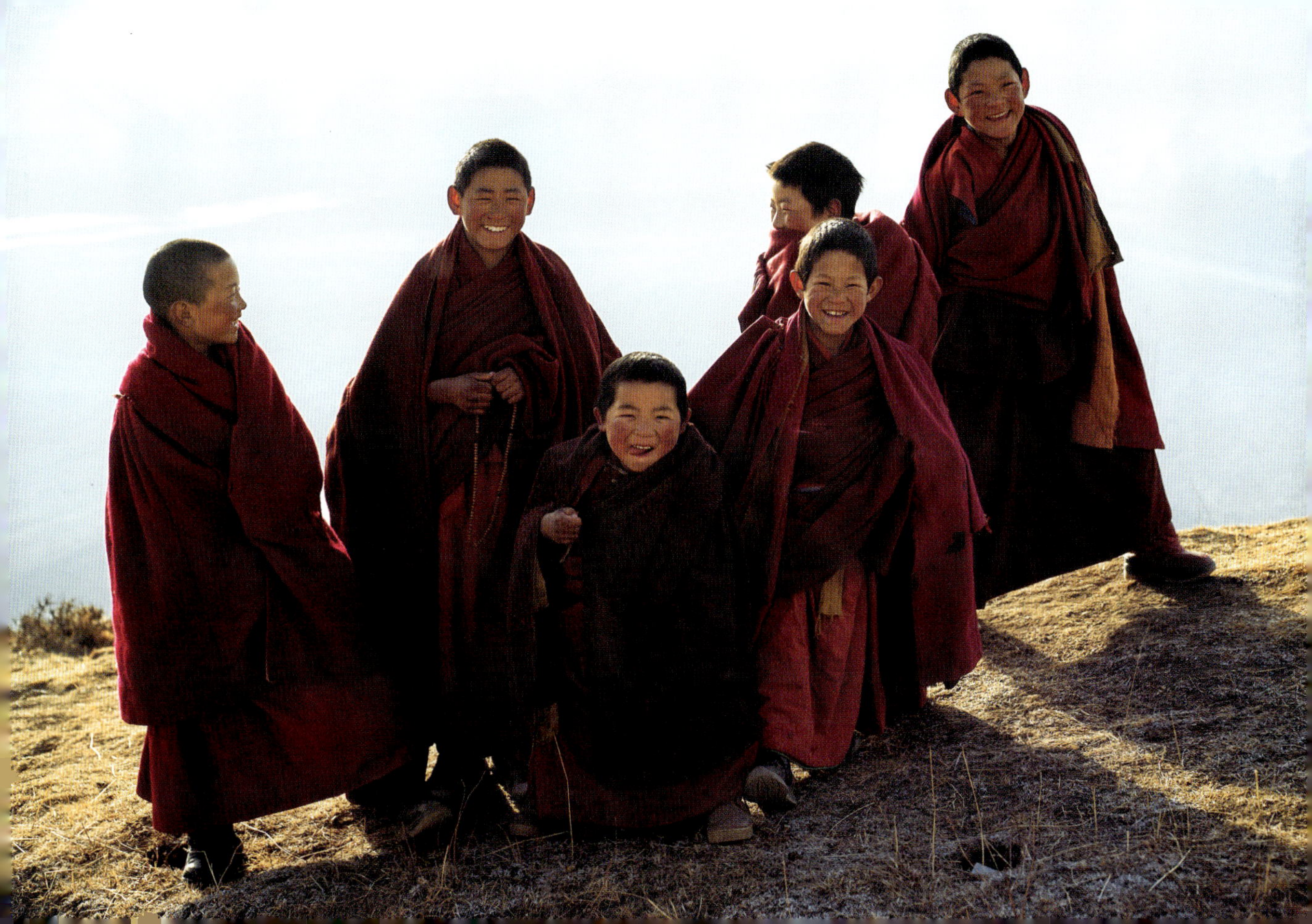

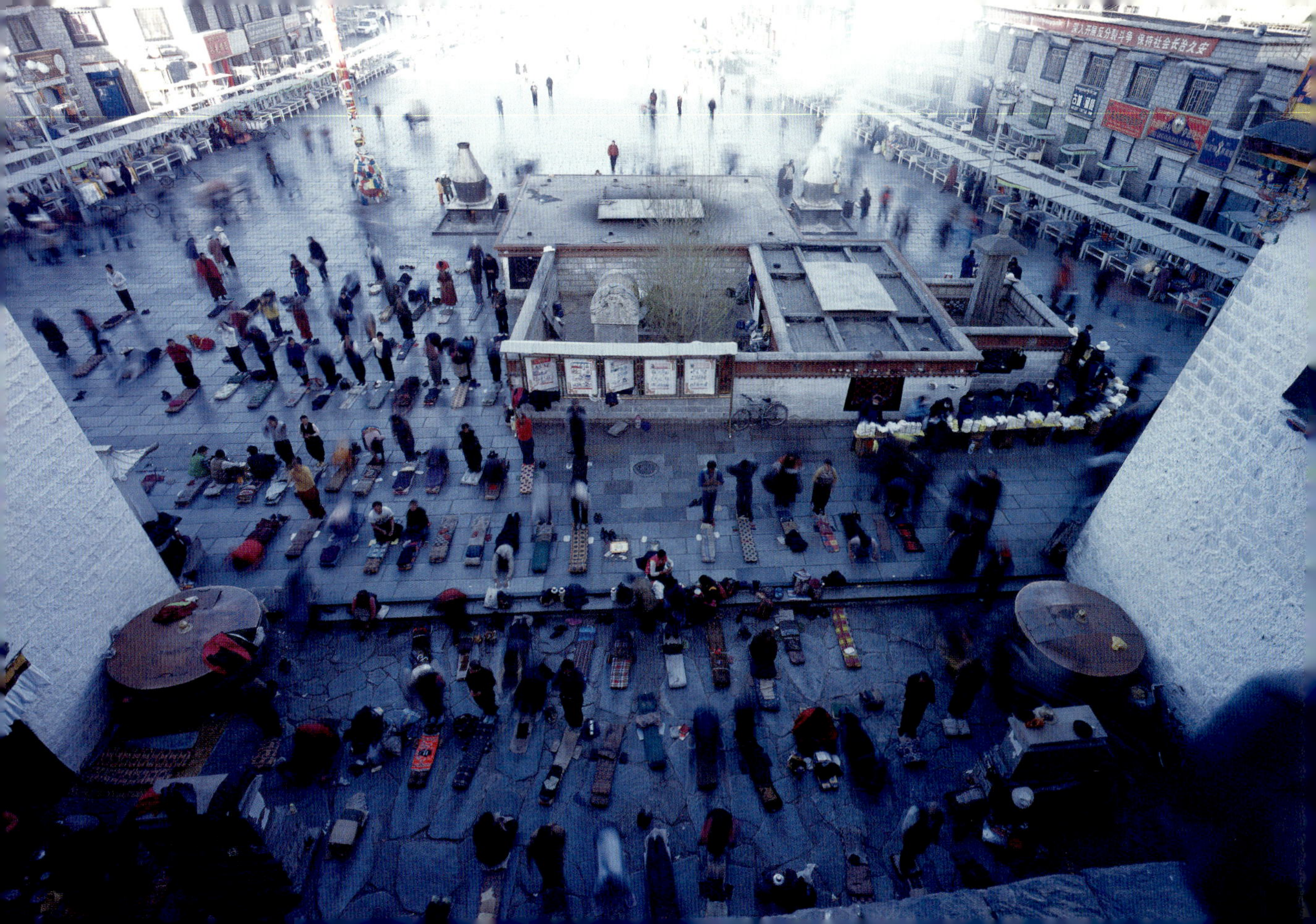
深入开展反分裂斗争 保持社会长治久安

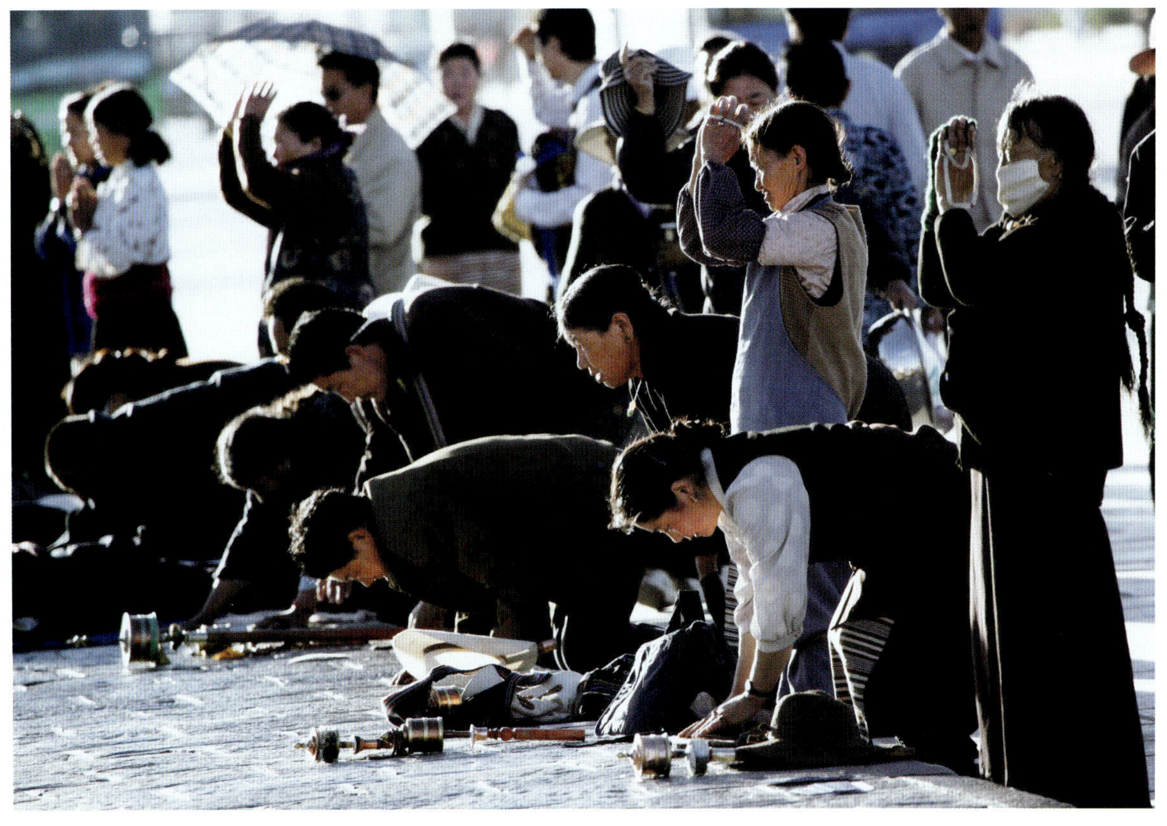

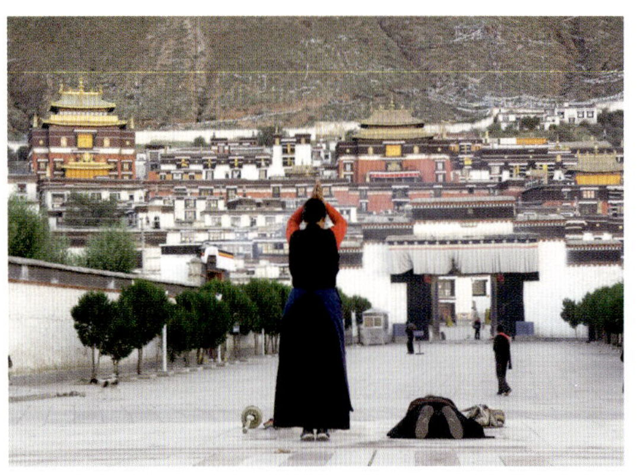

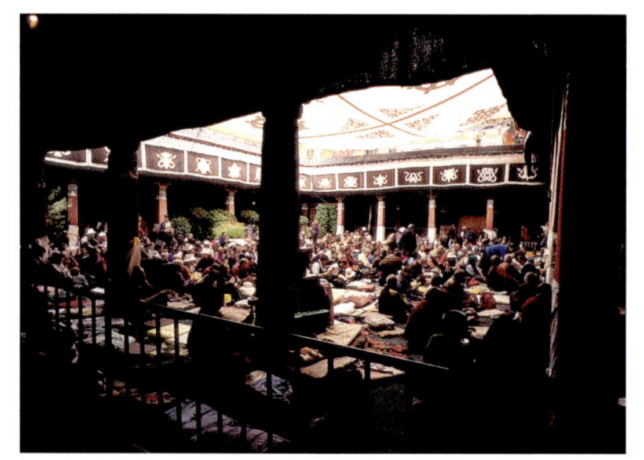

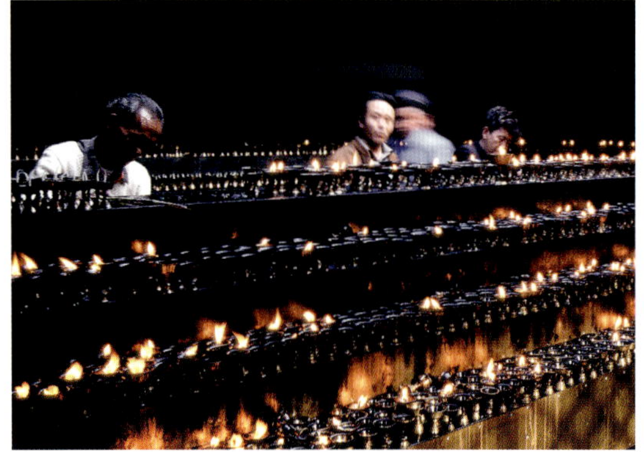

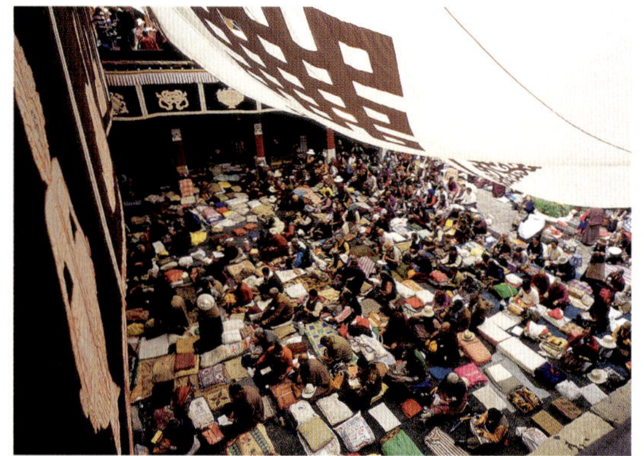

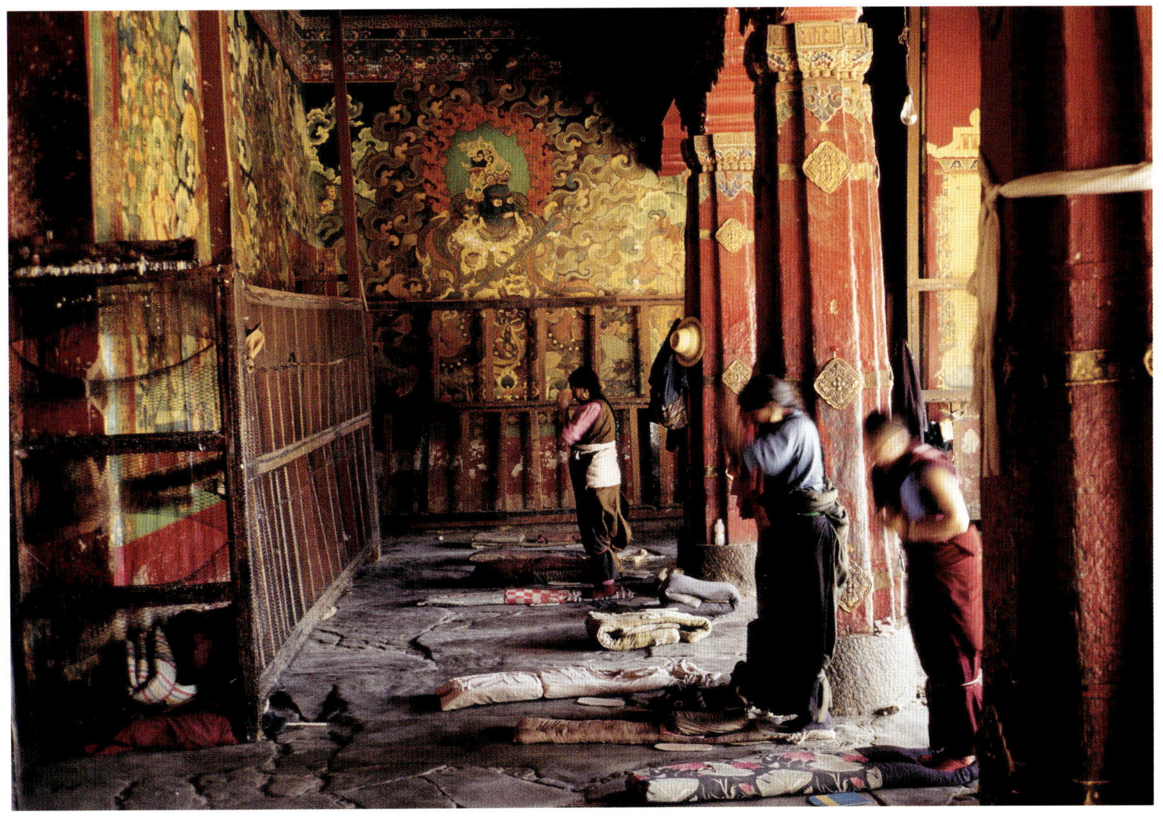

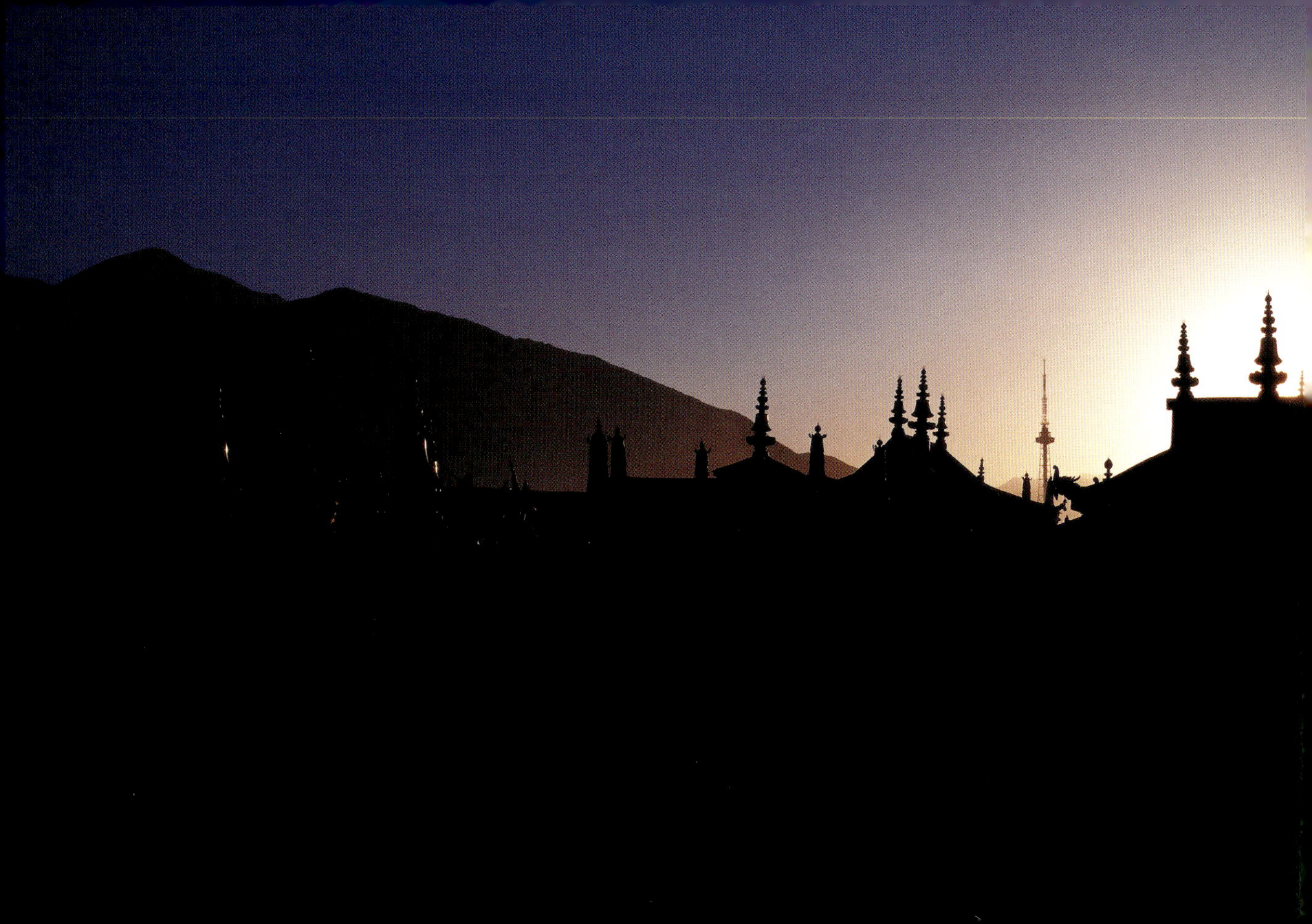

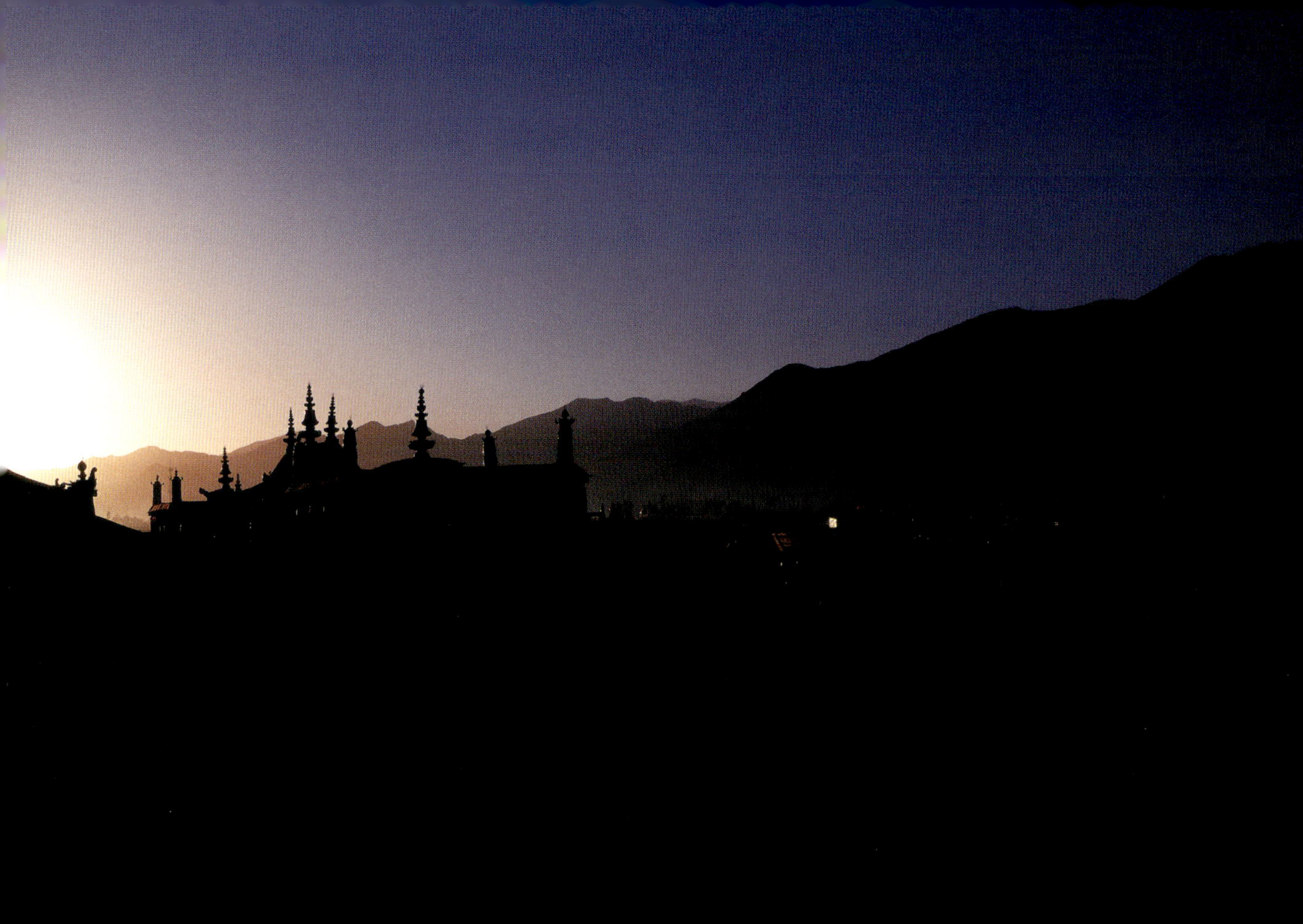

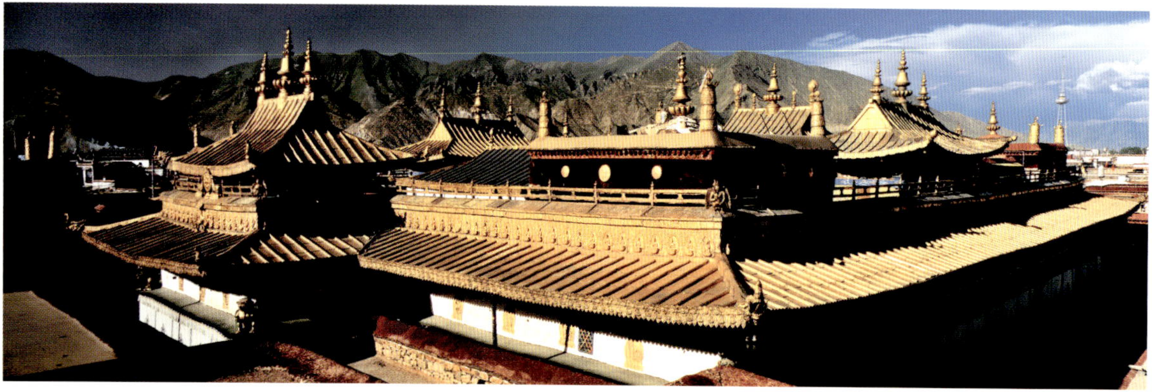

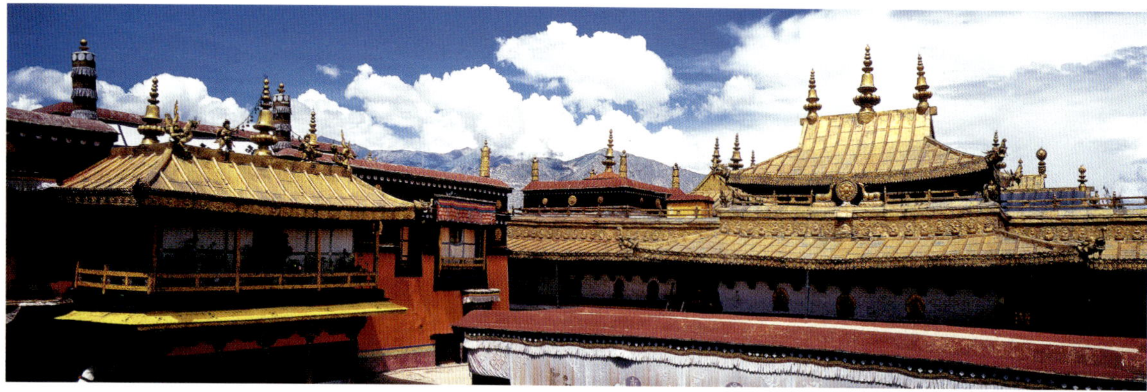

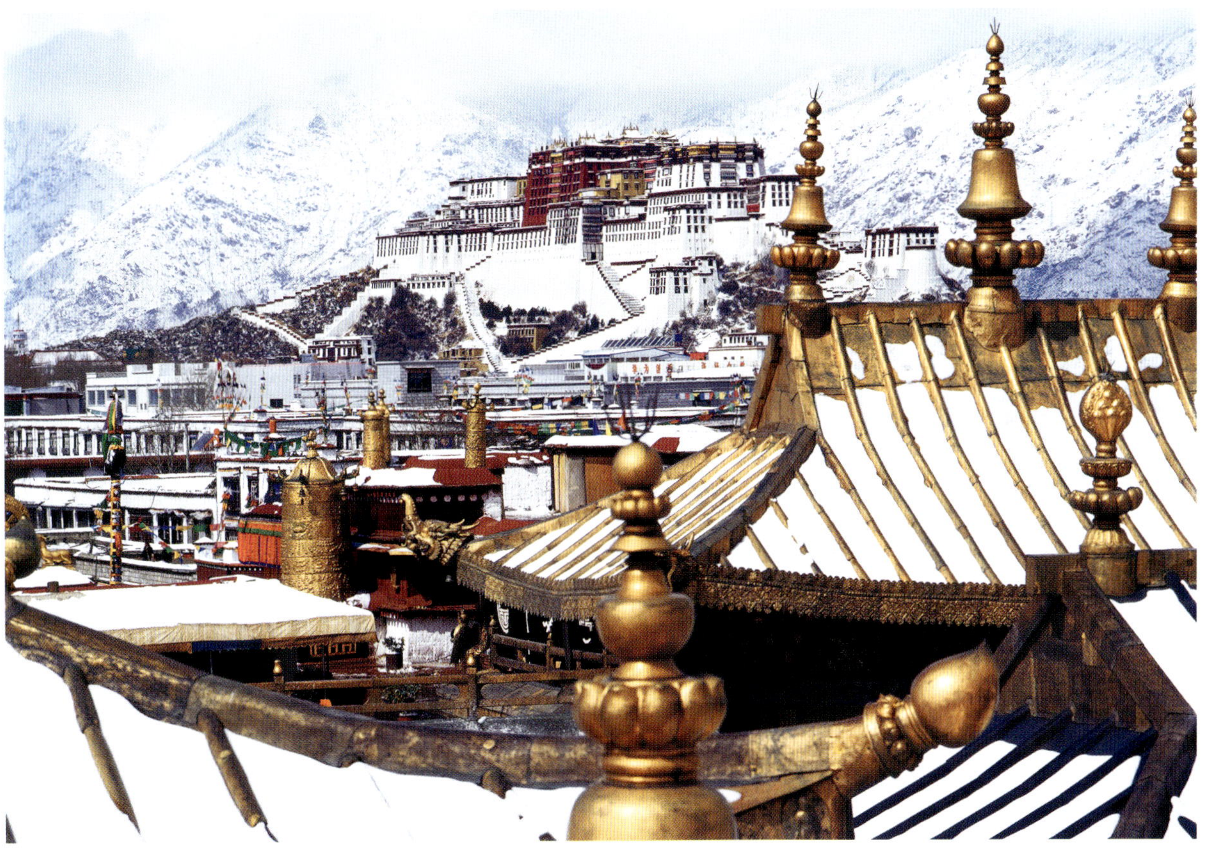

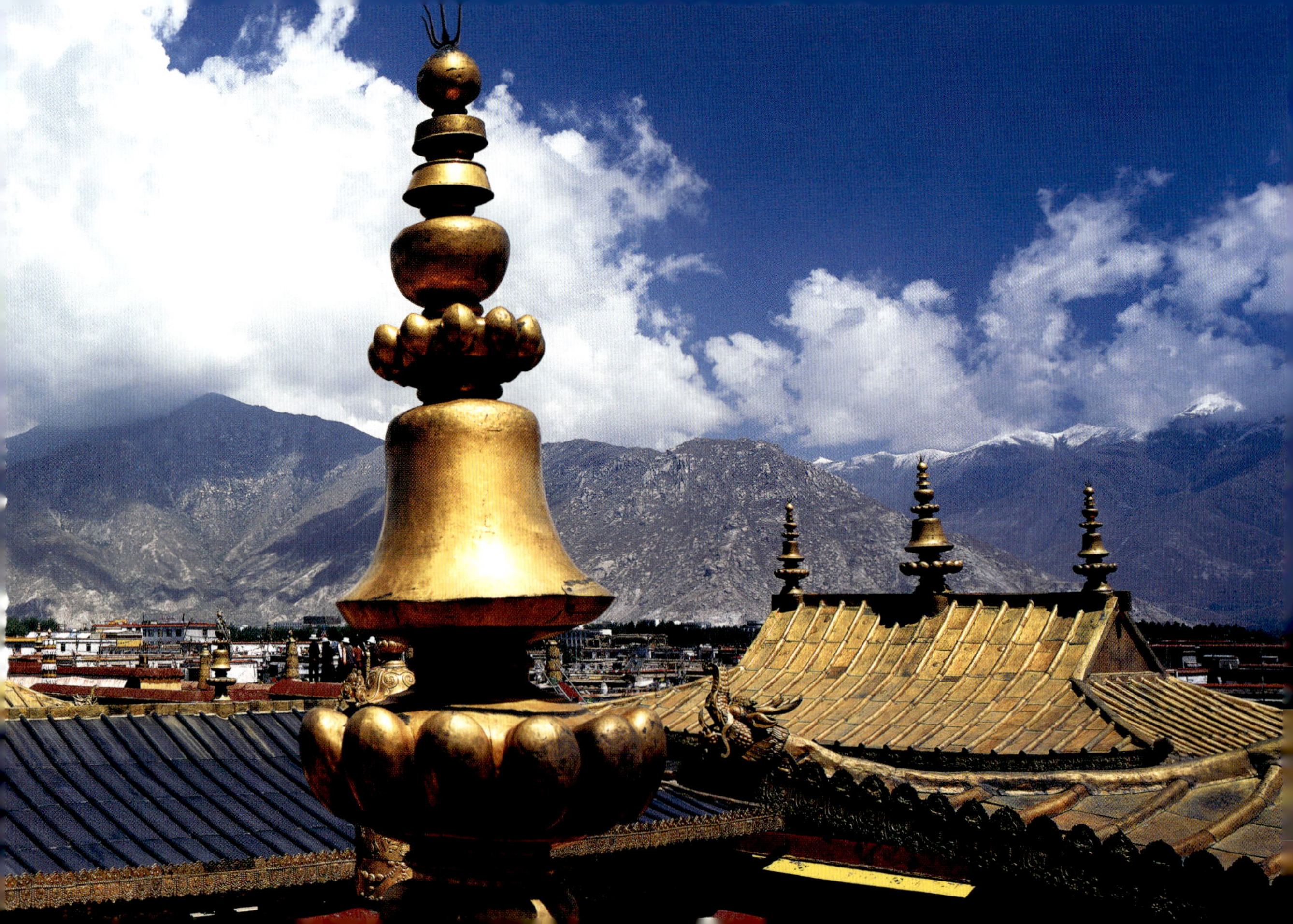

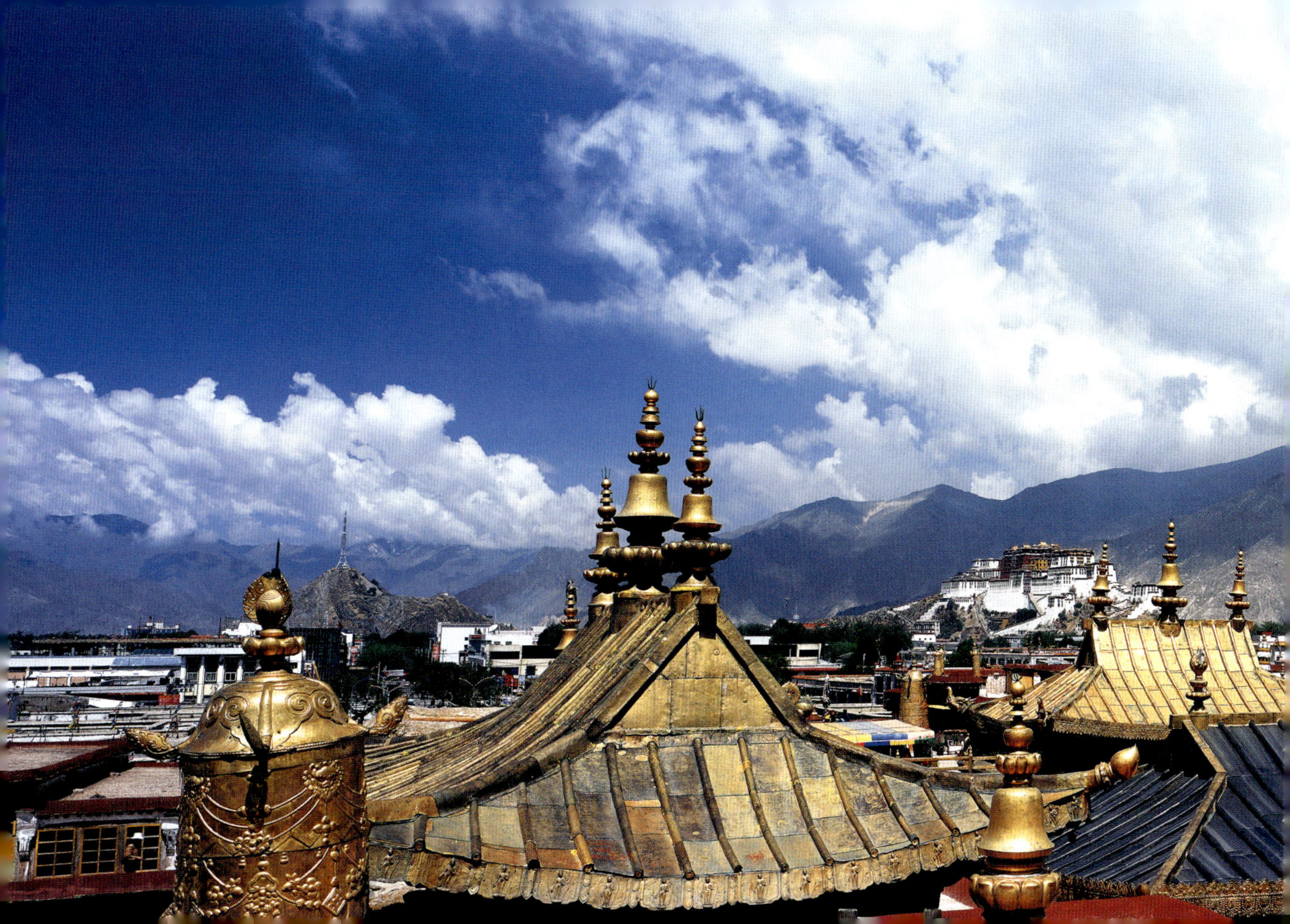

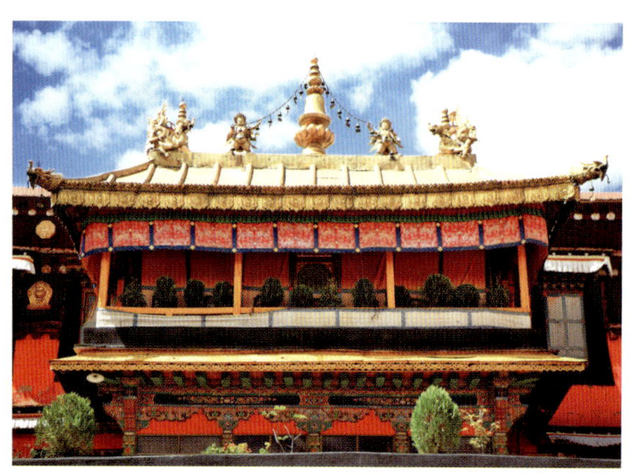

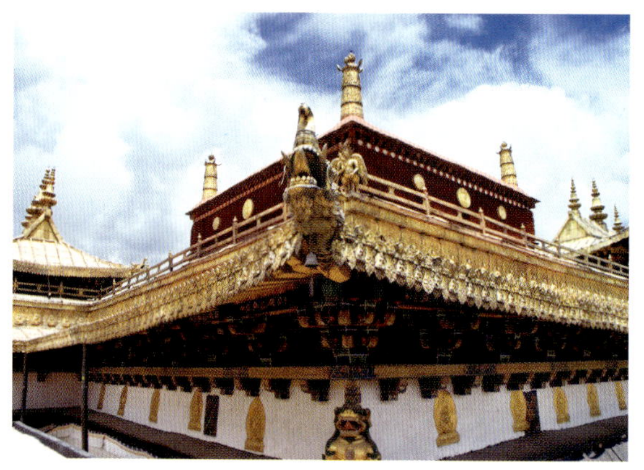

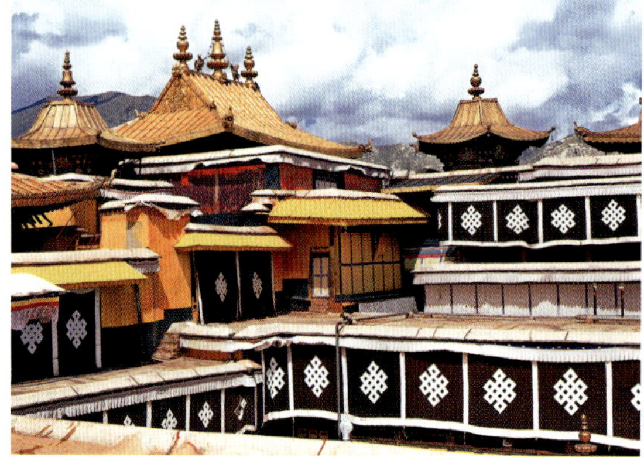

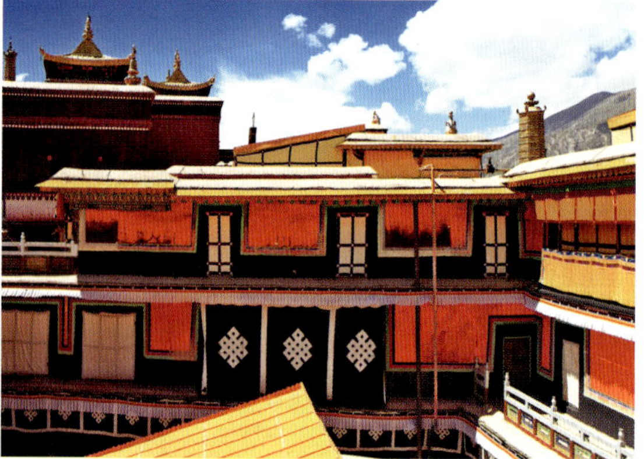

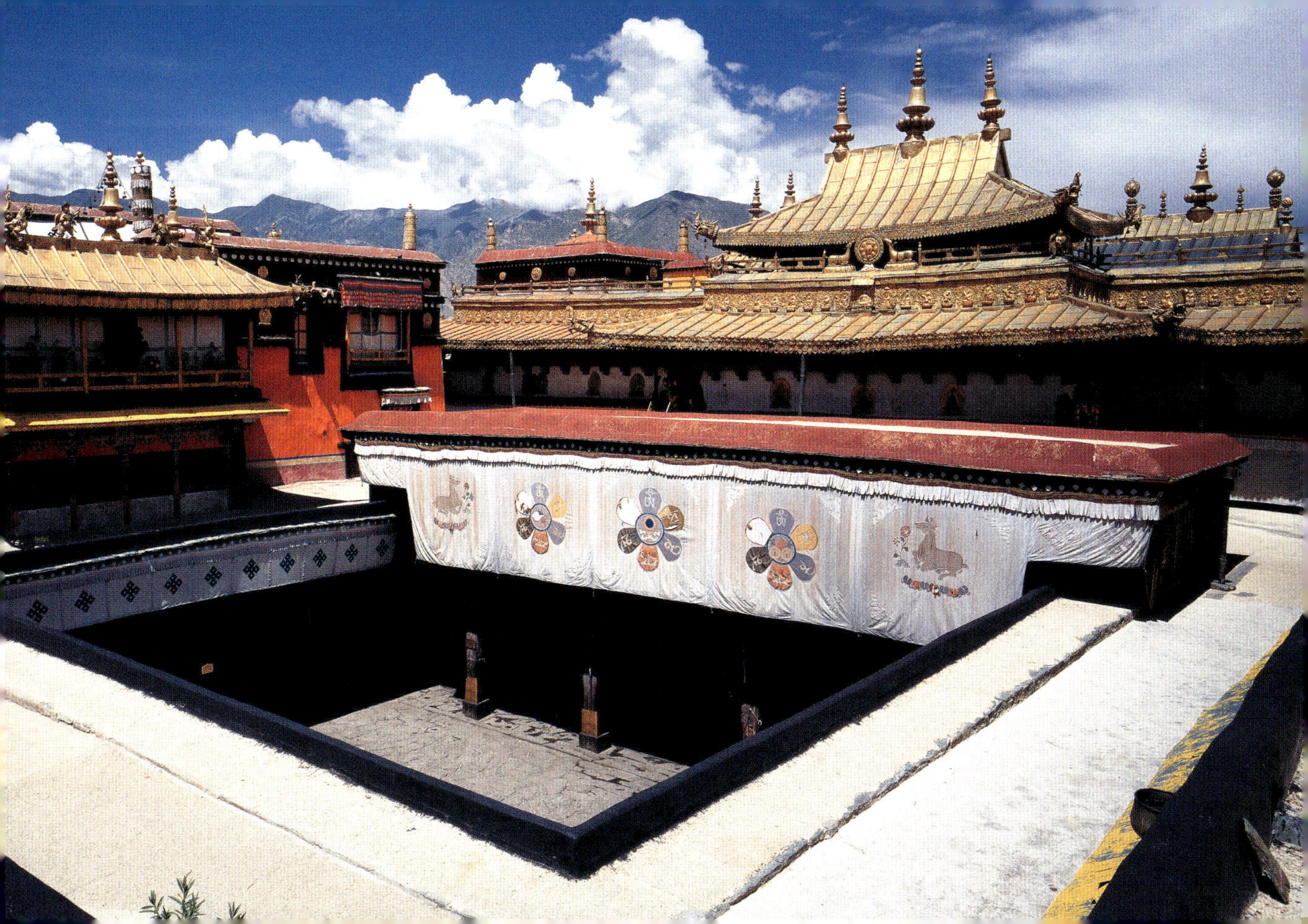

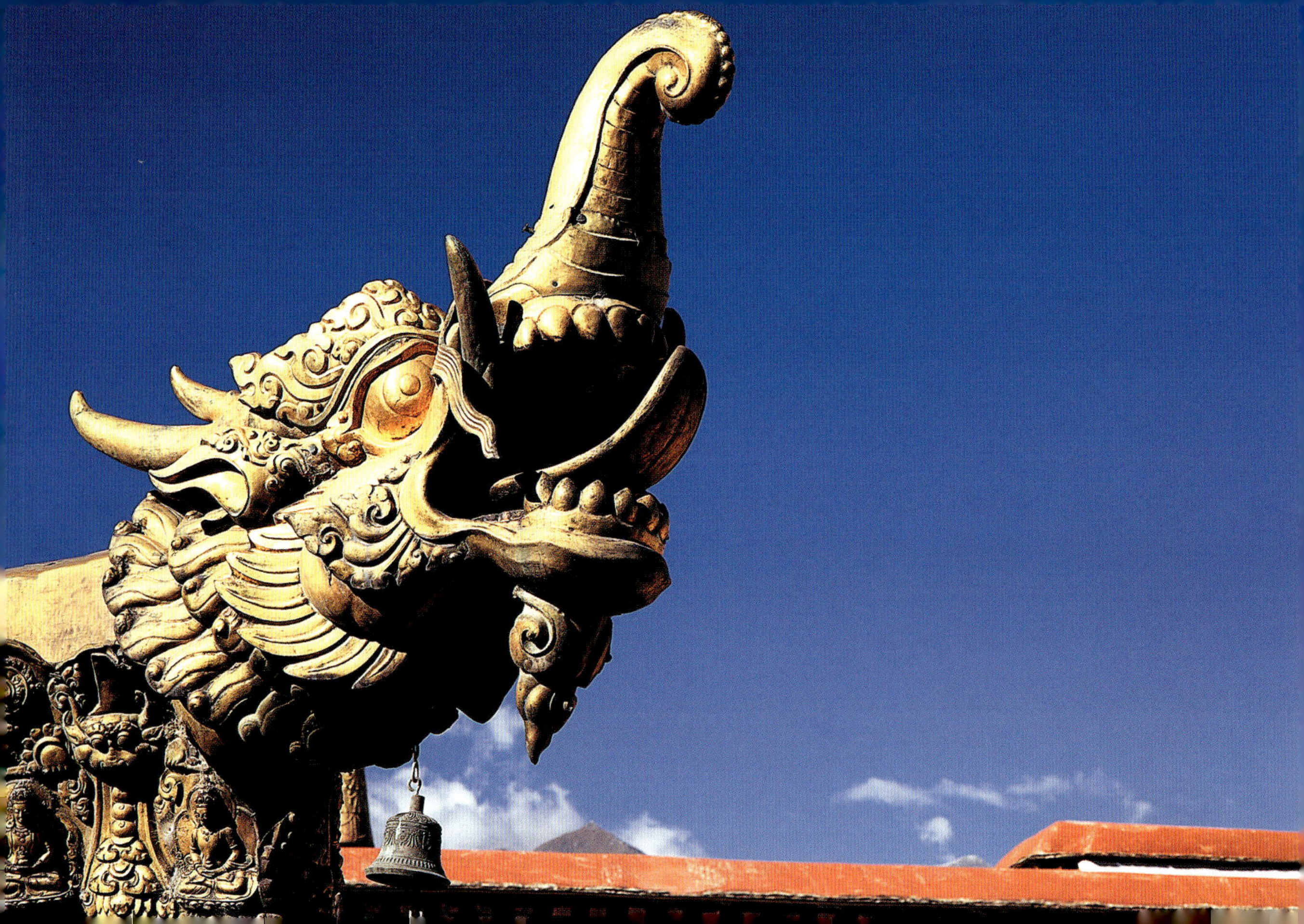

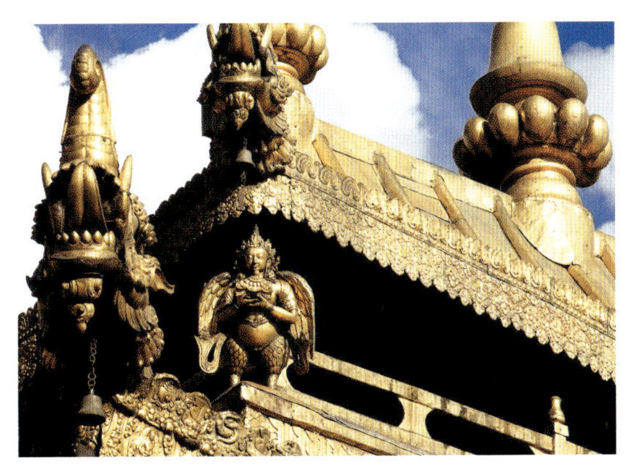

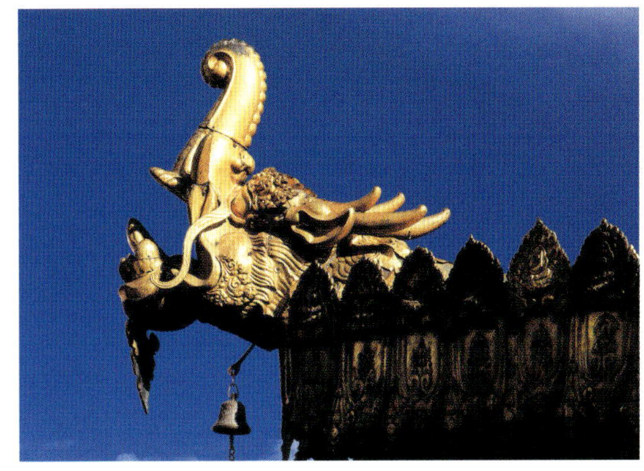

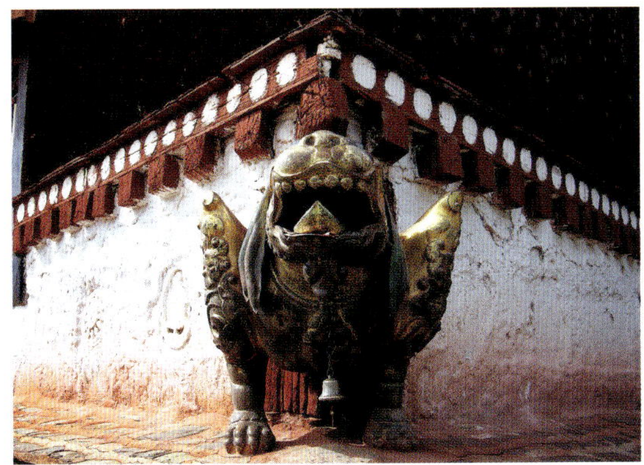

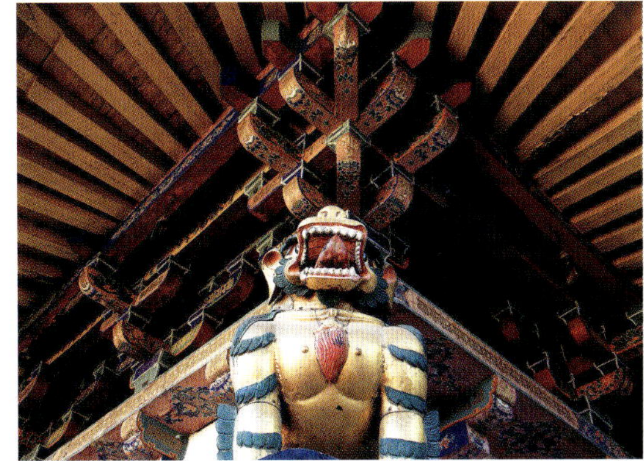

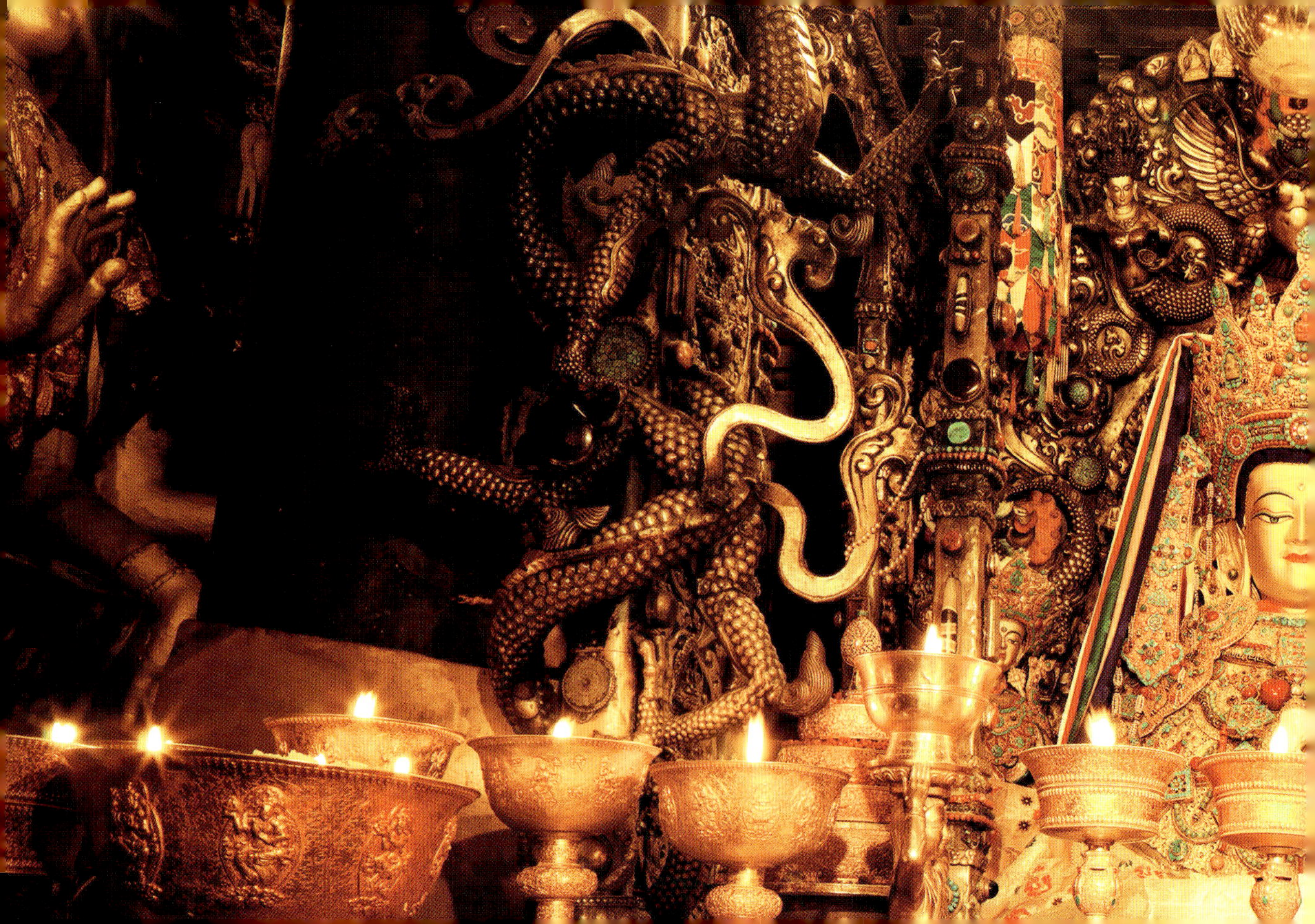

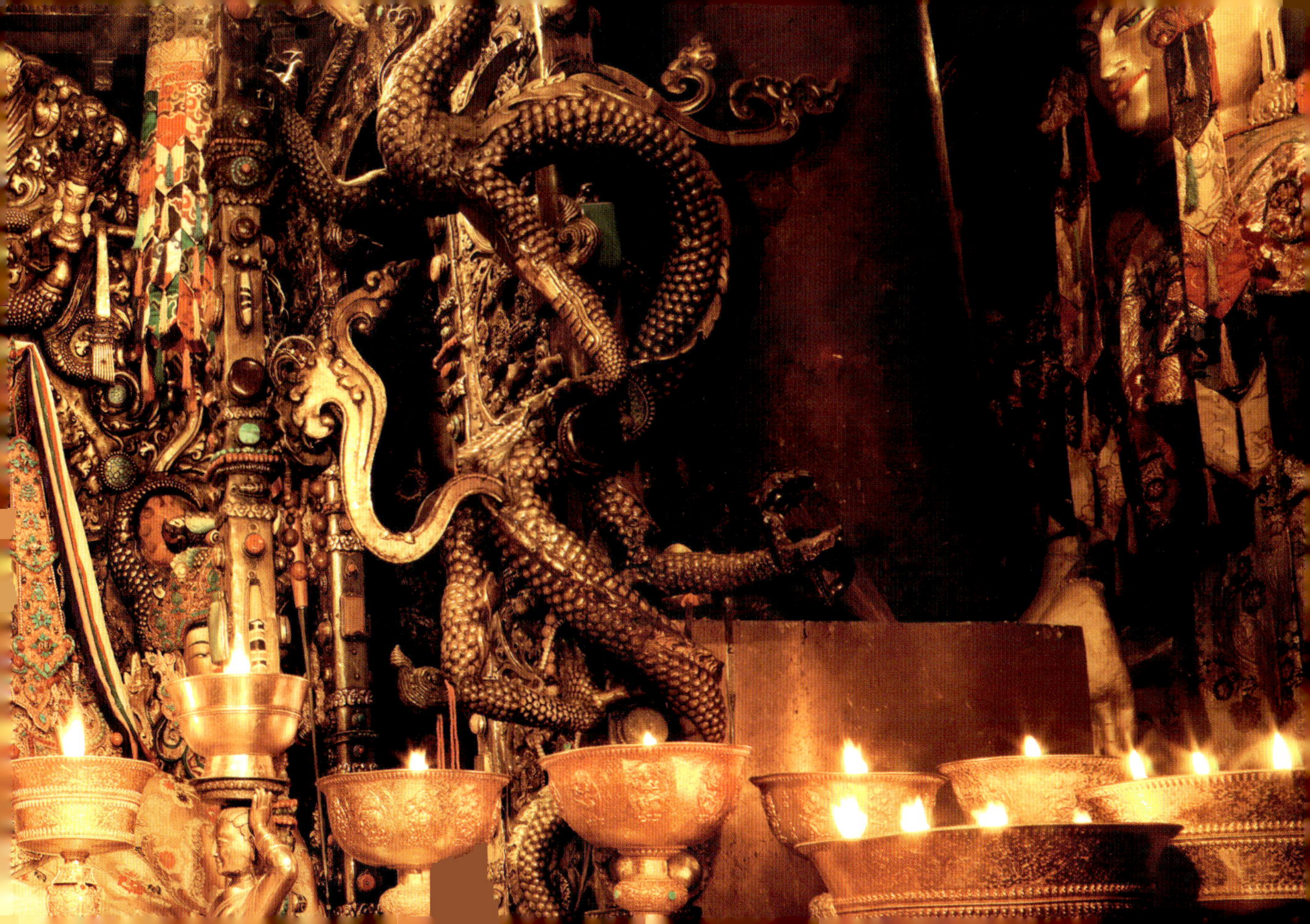

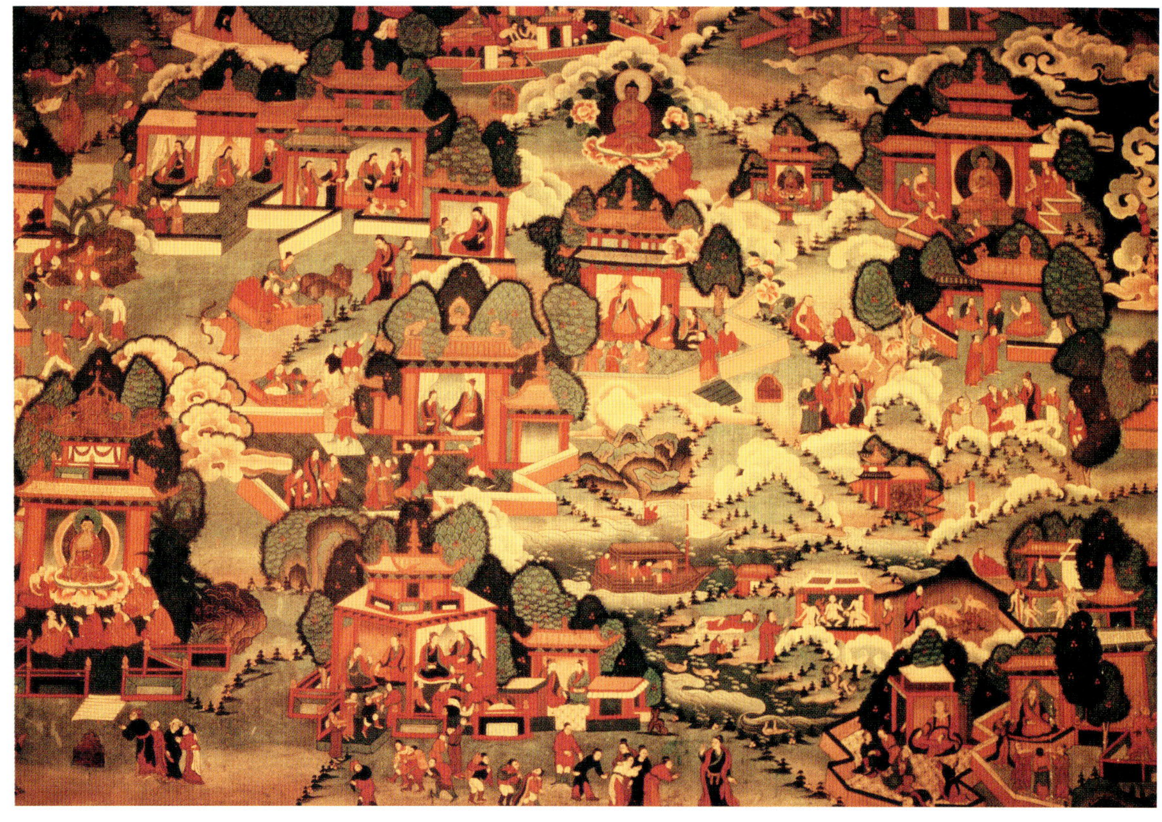

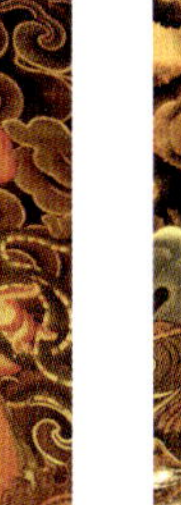

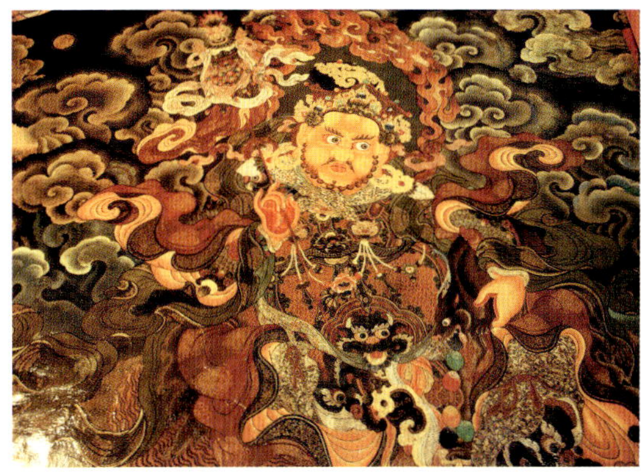

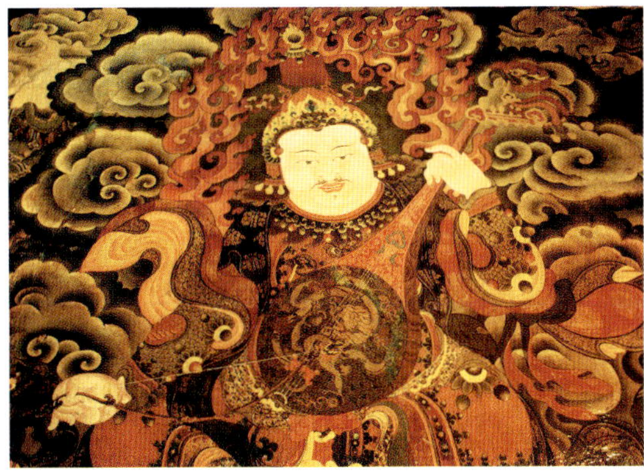

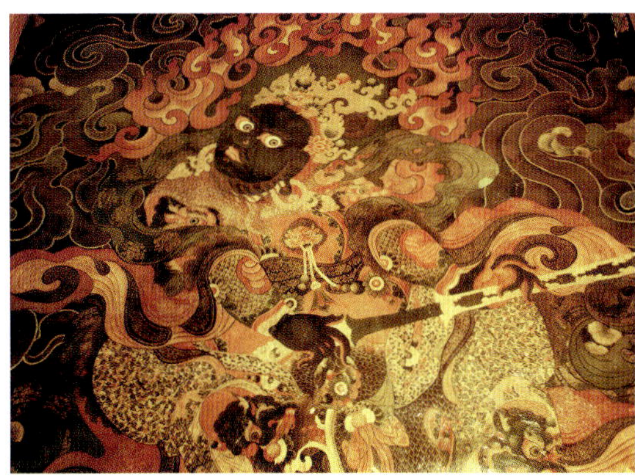

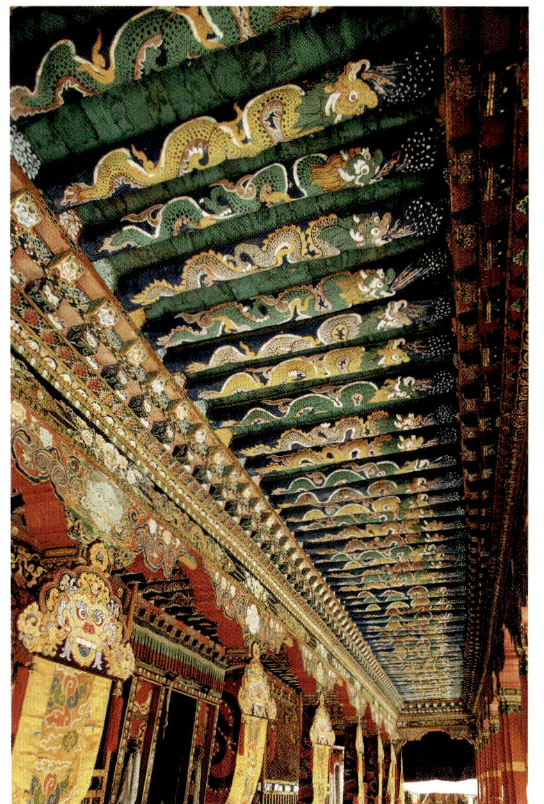

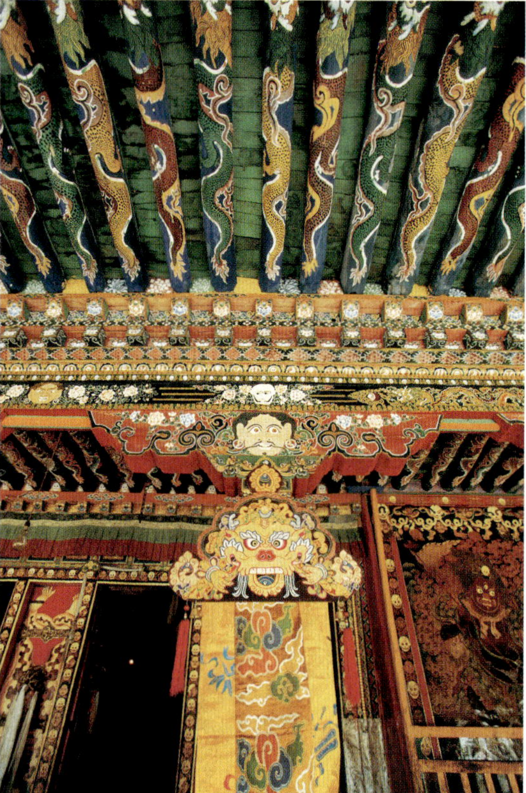

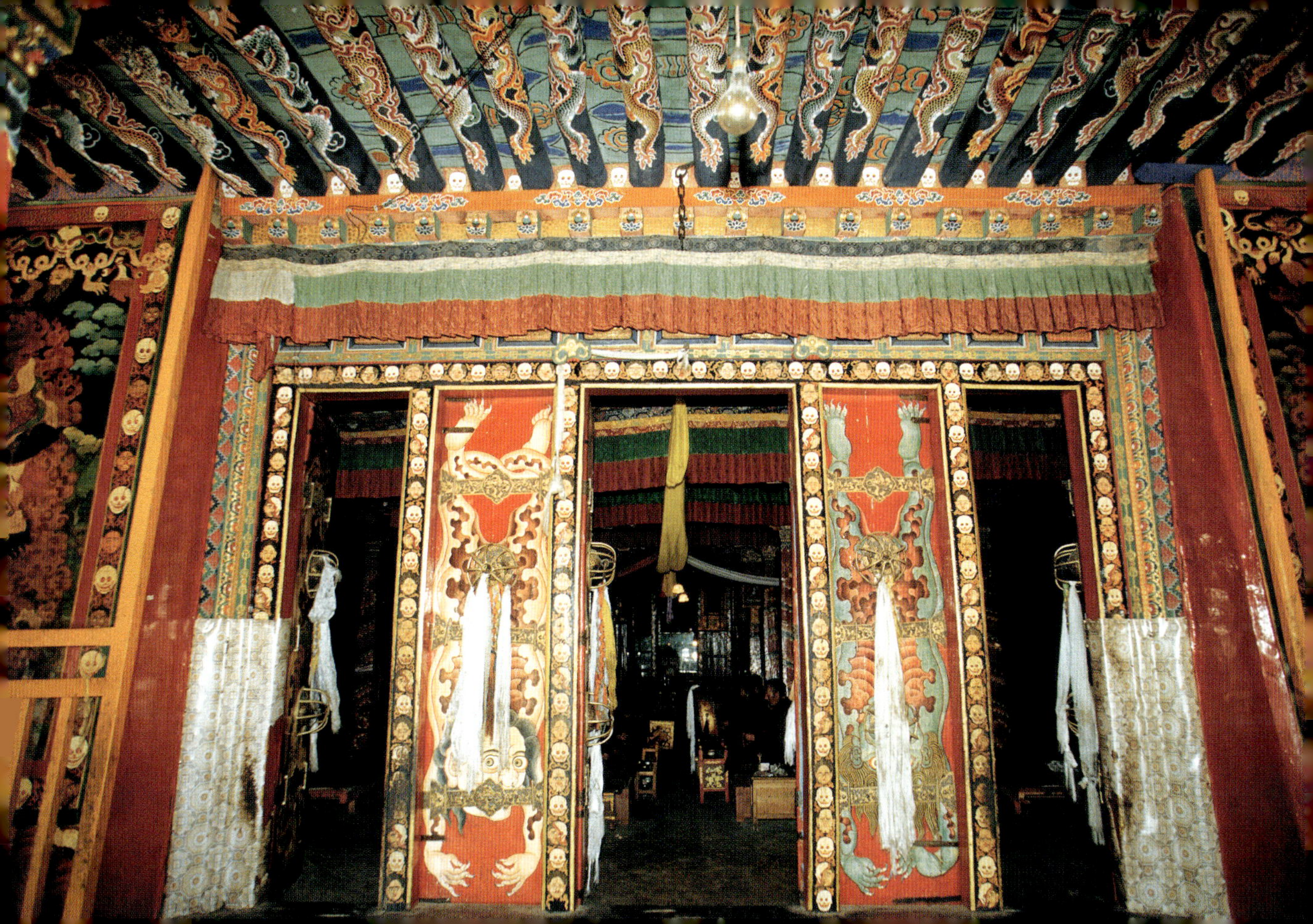

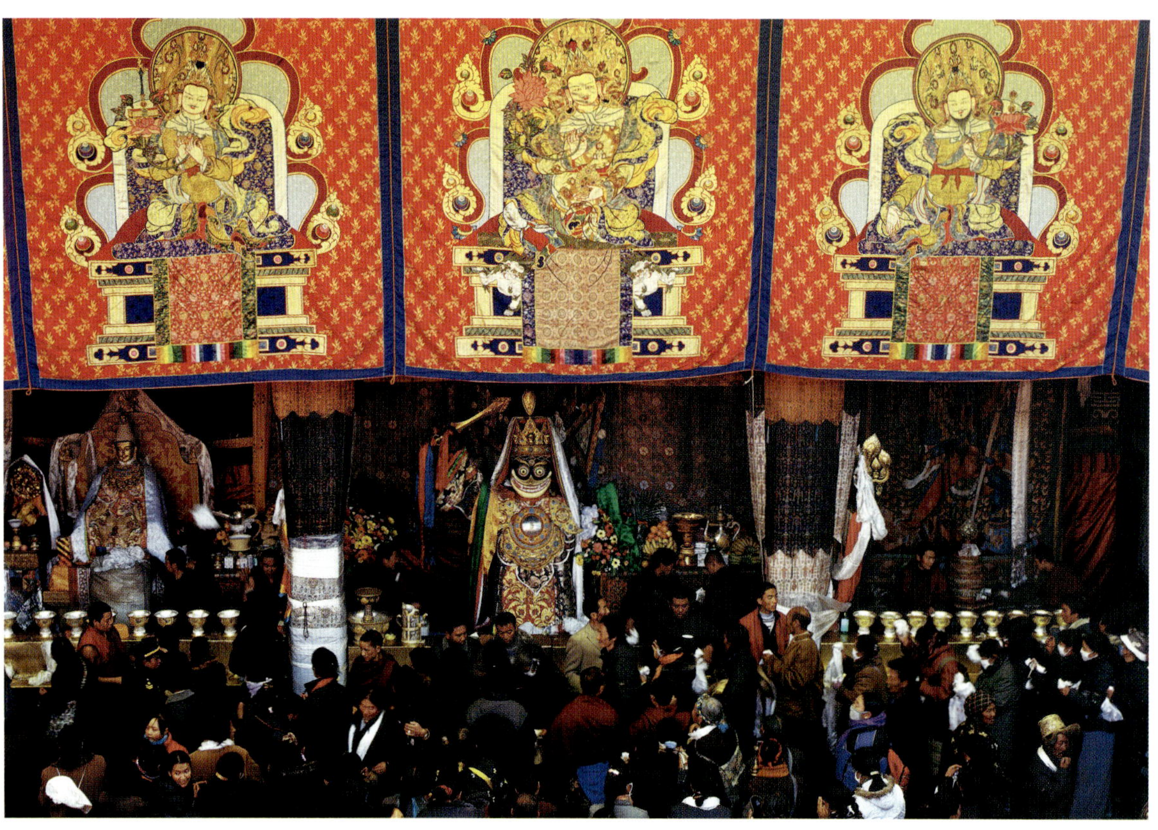

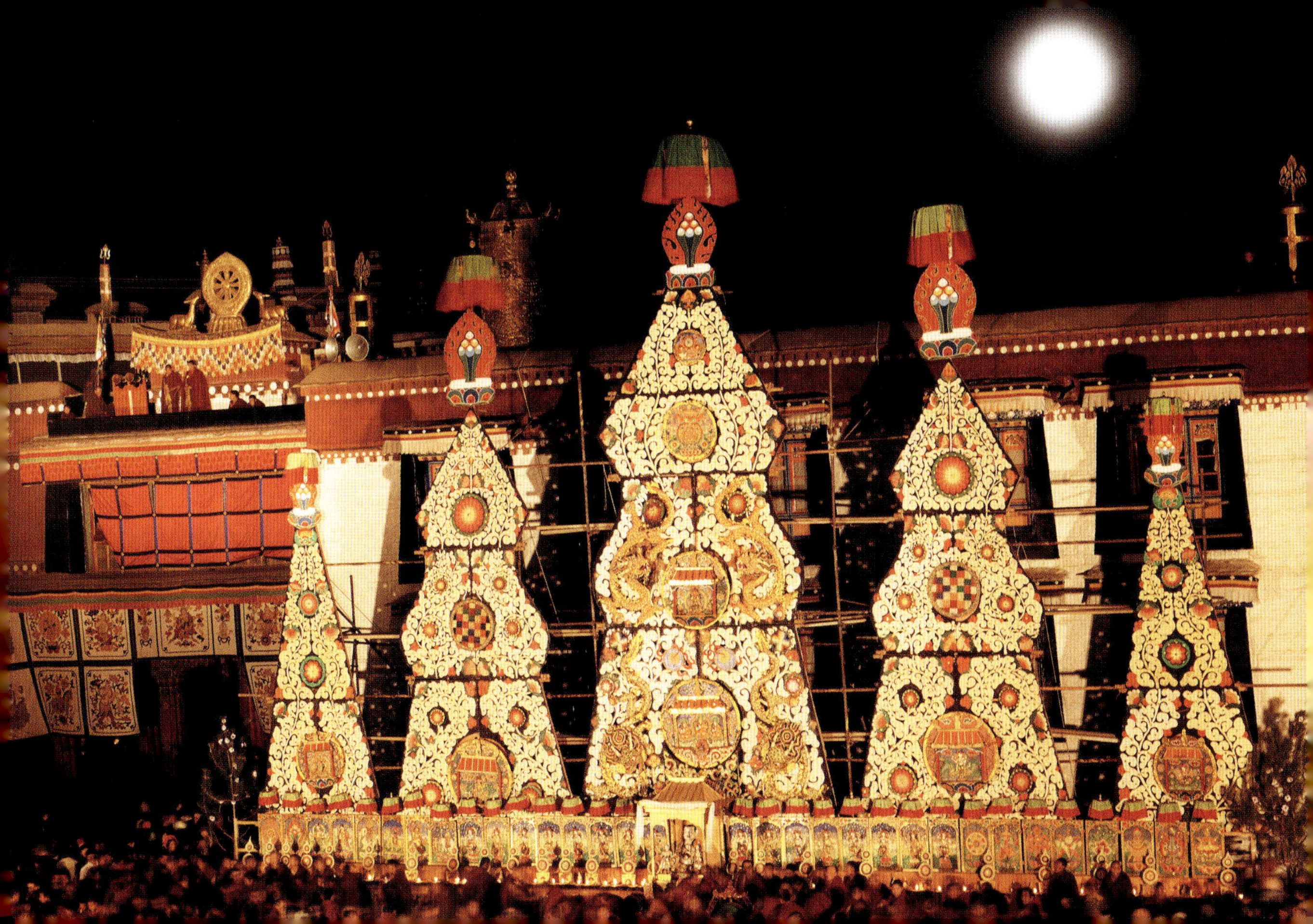

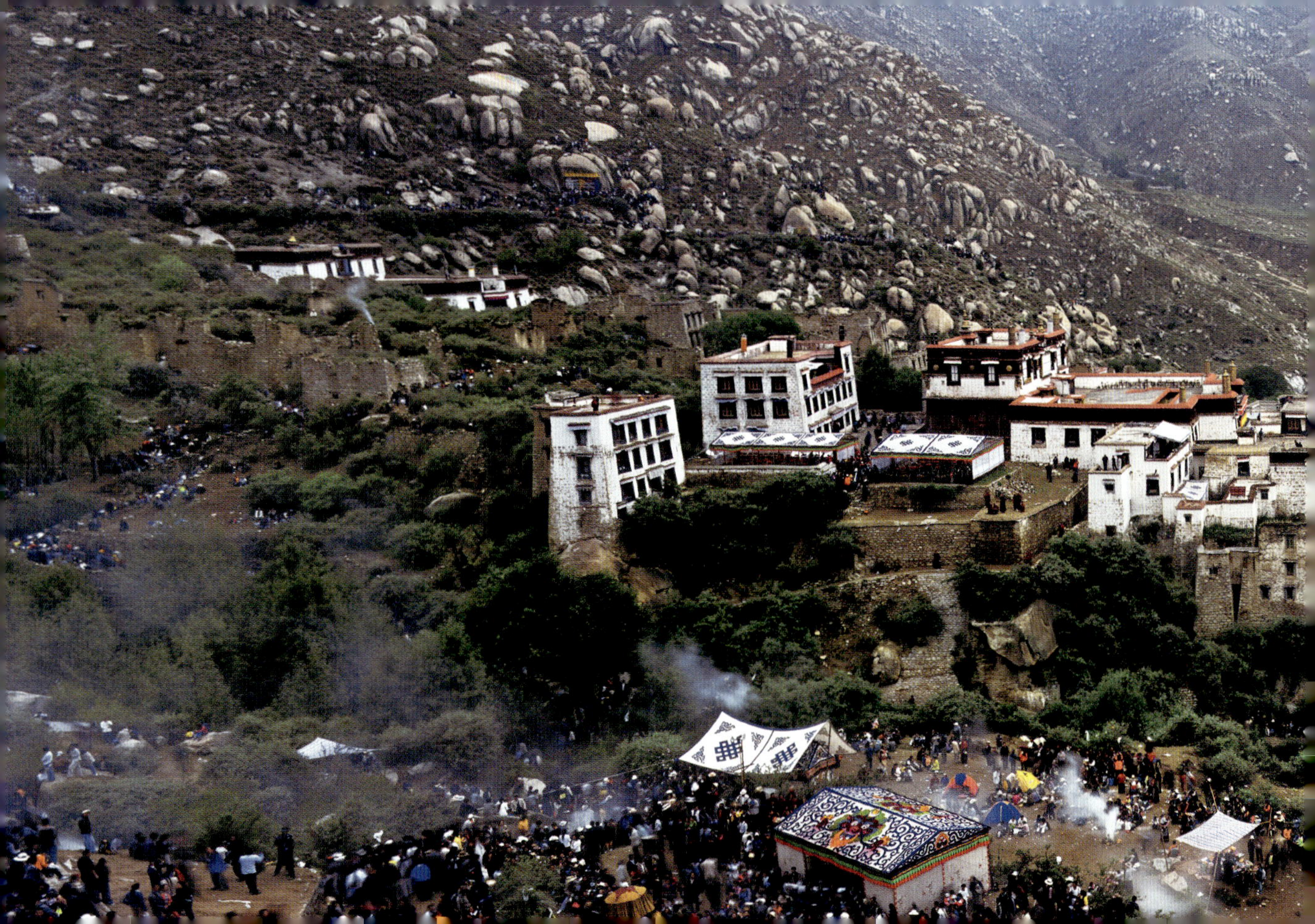

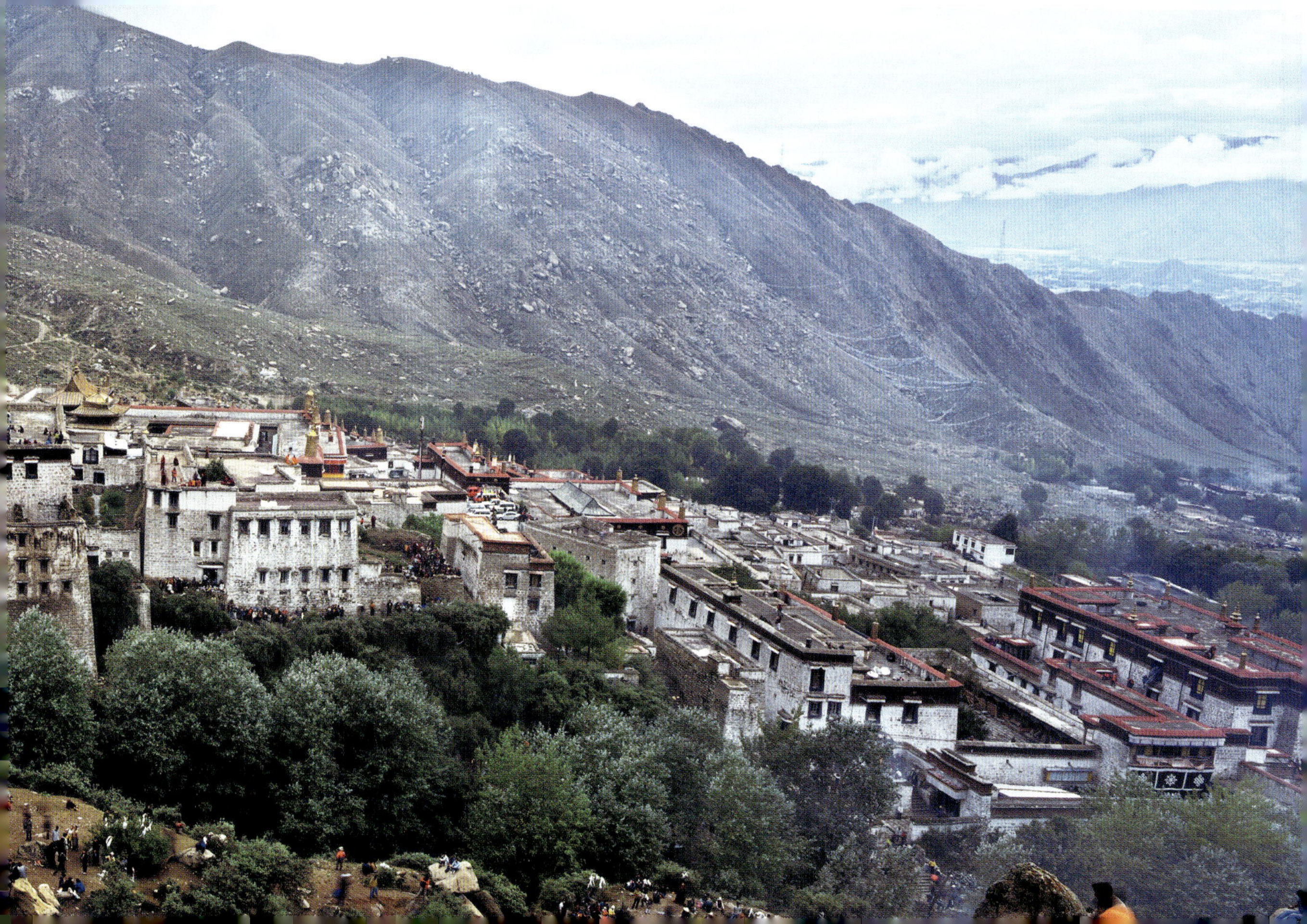

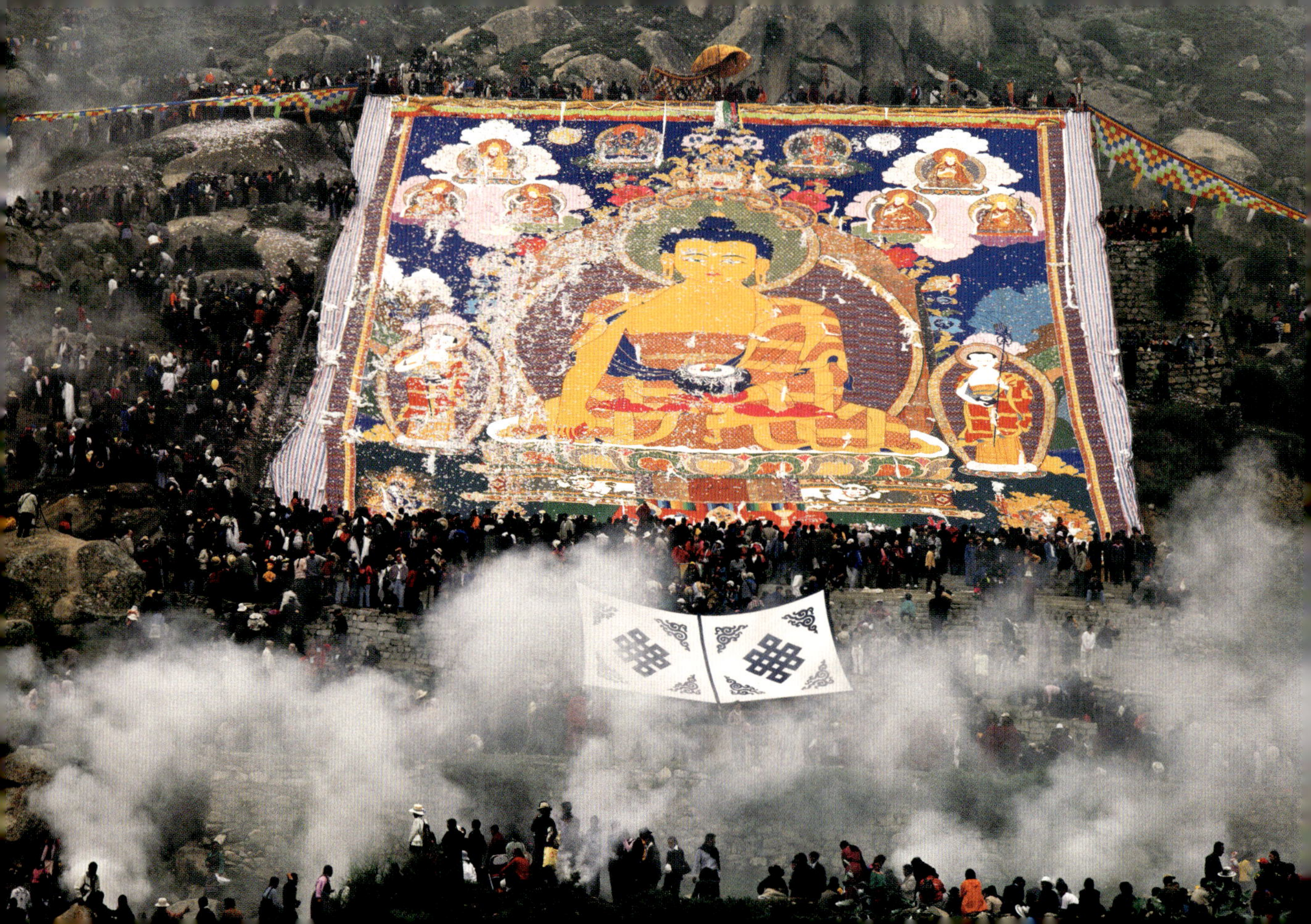

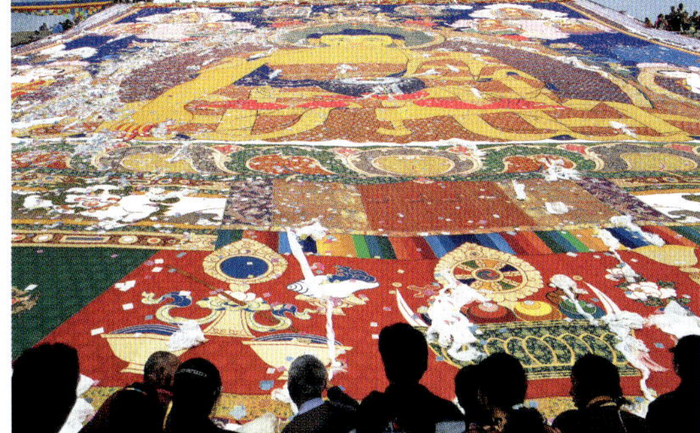

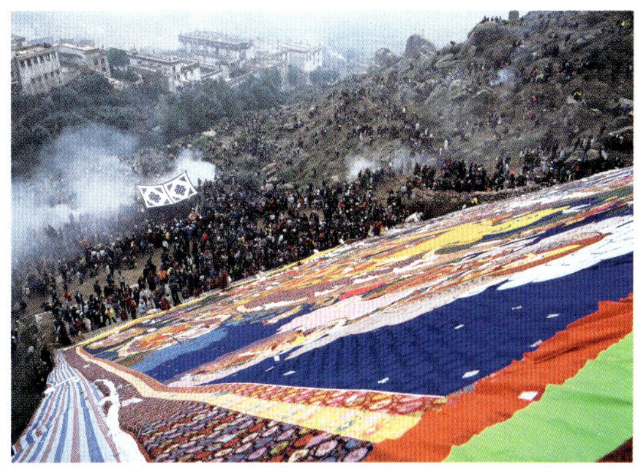

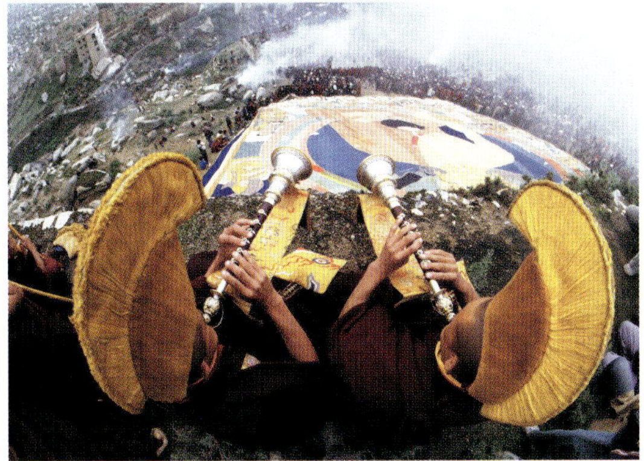

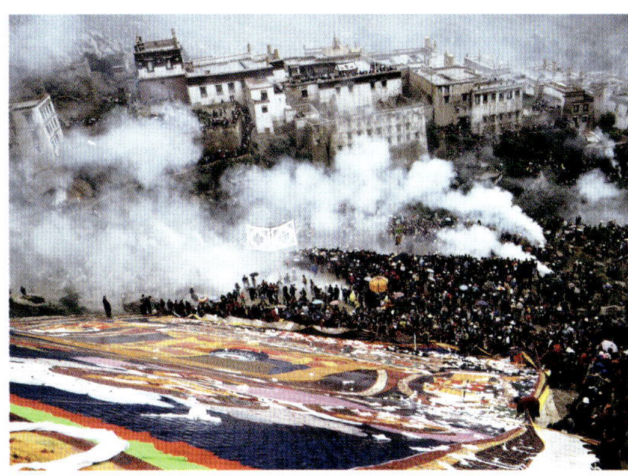

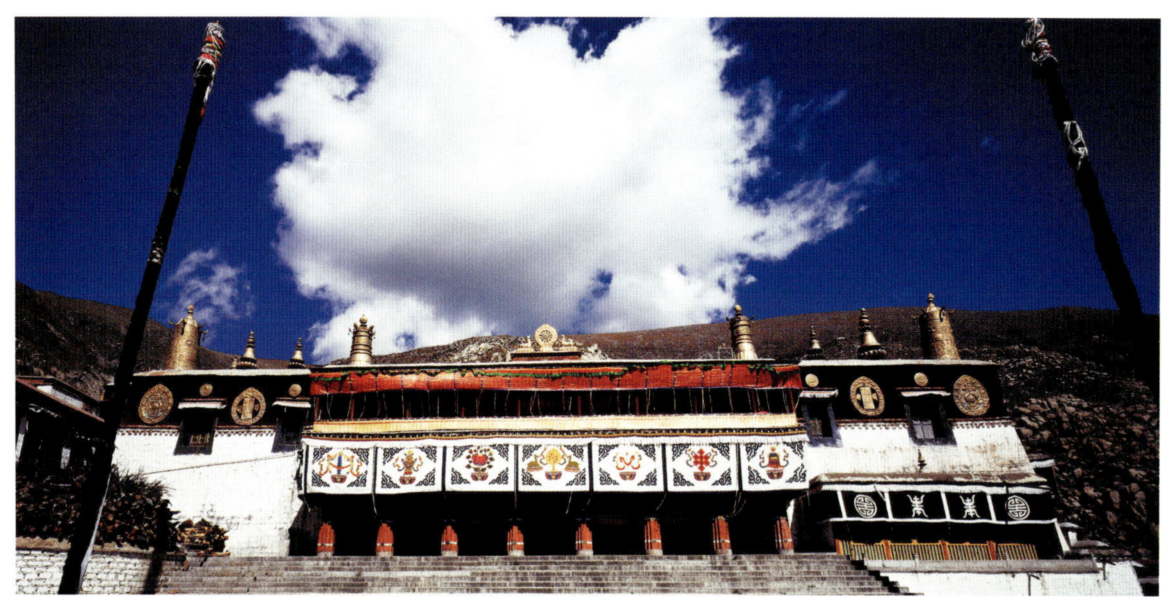

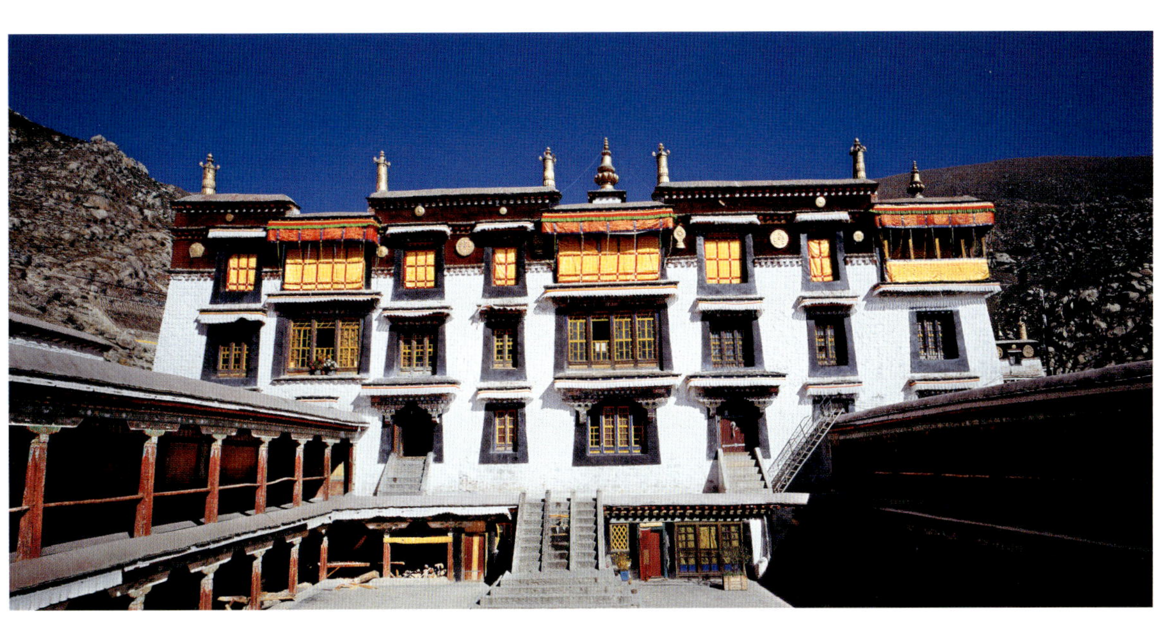

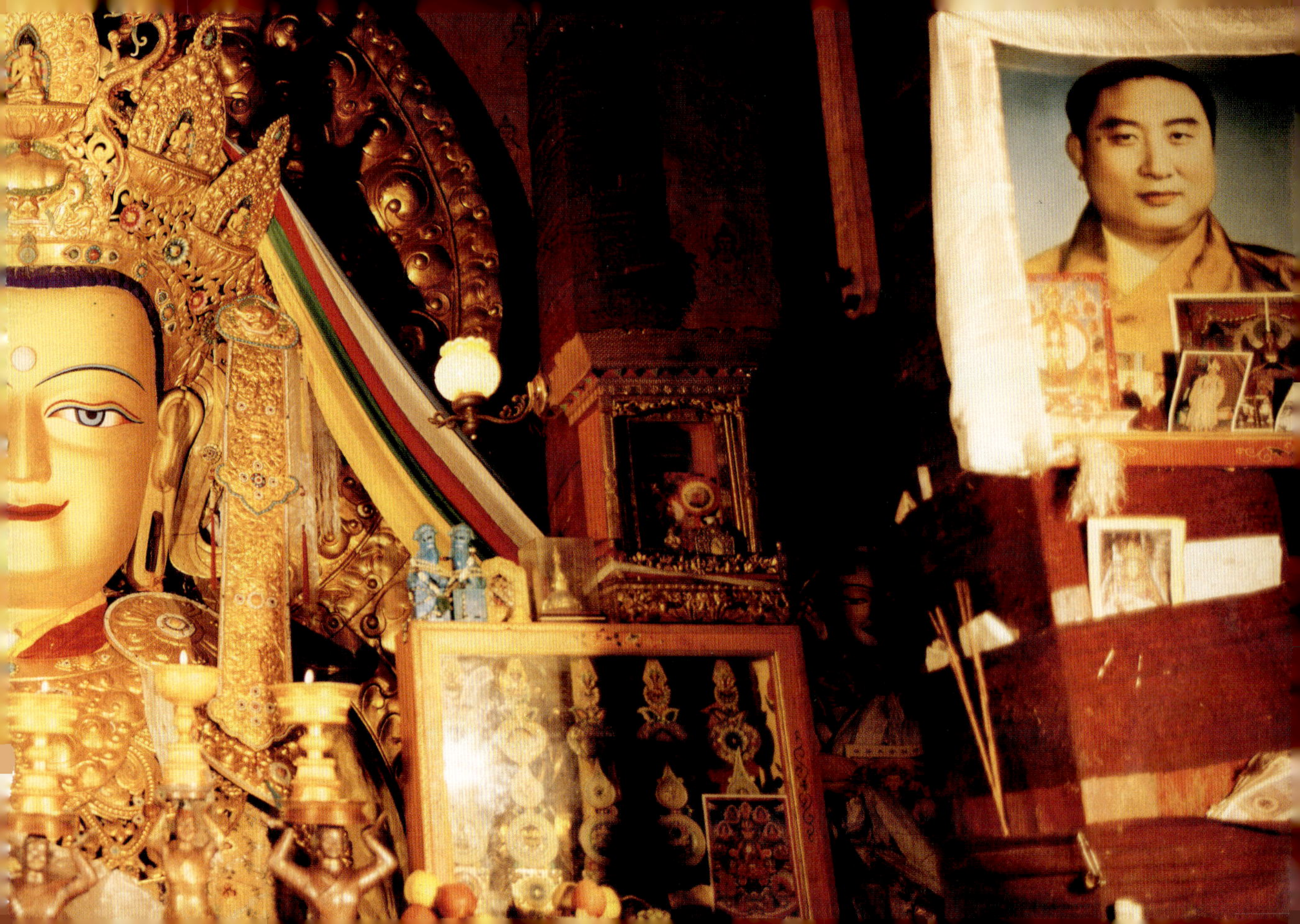

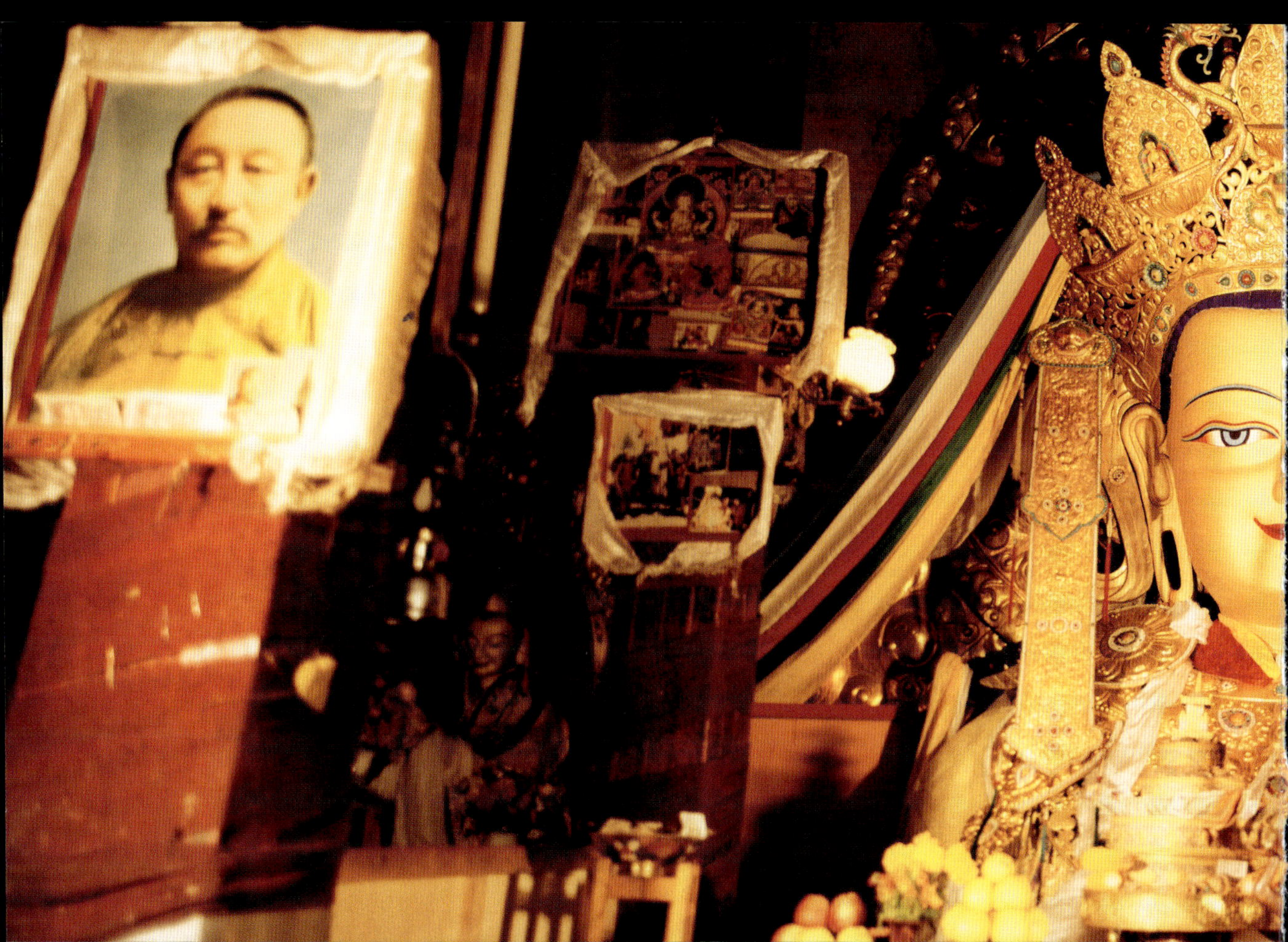

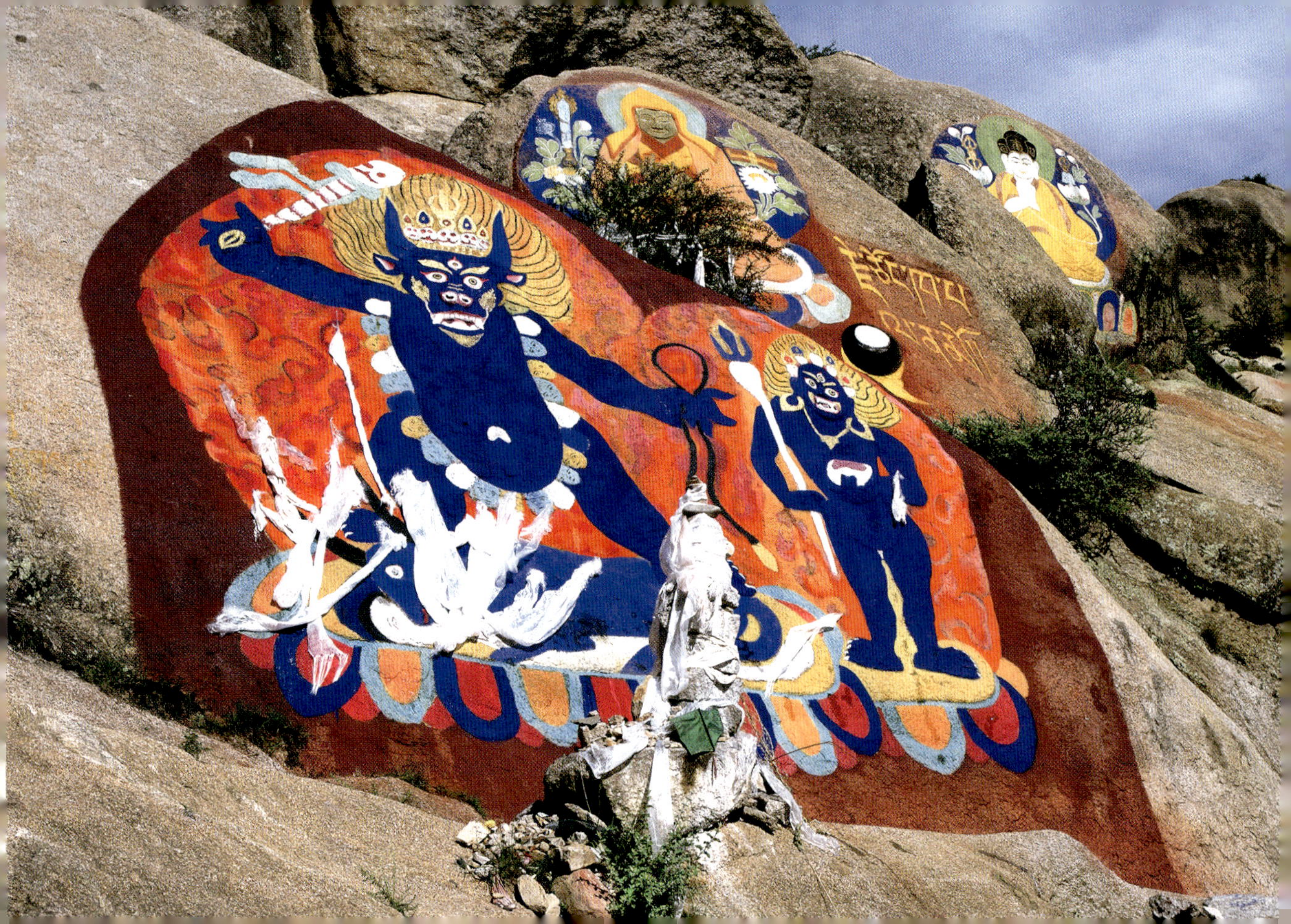

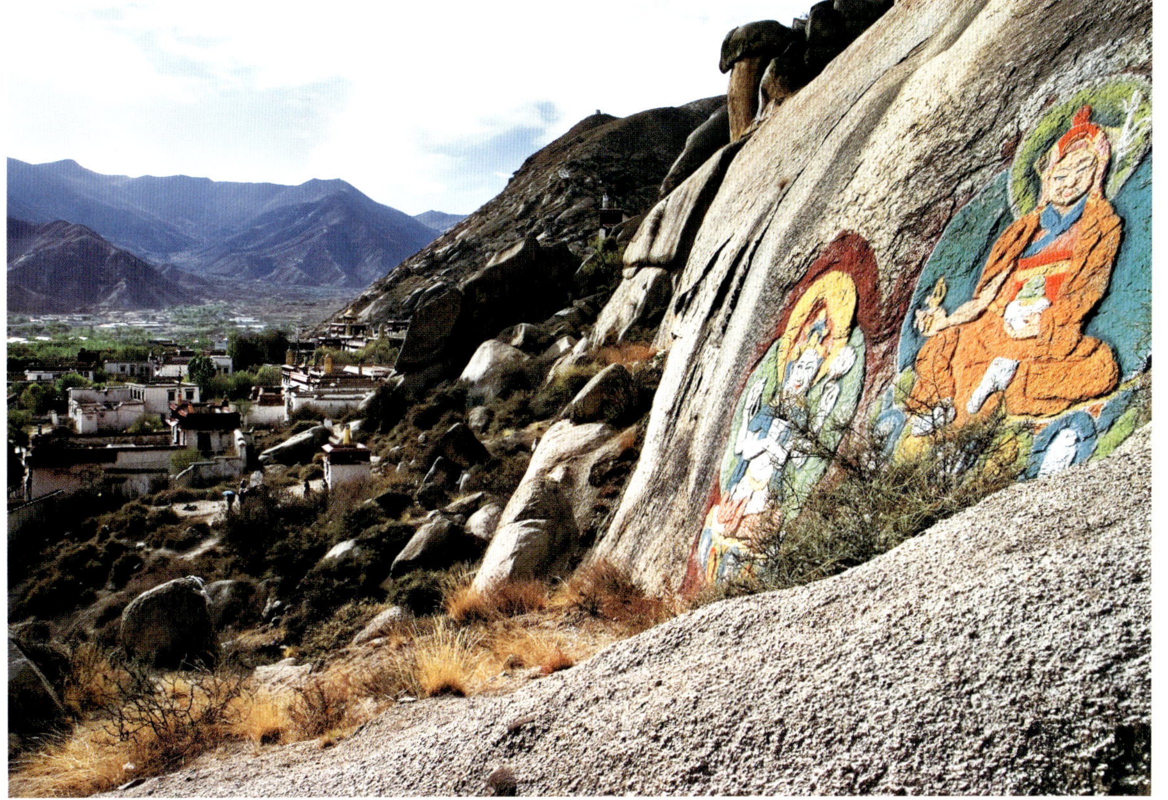

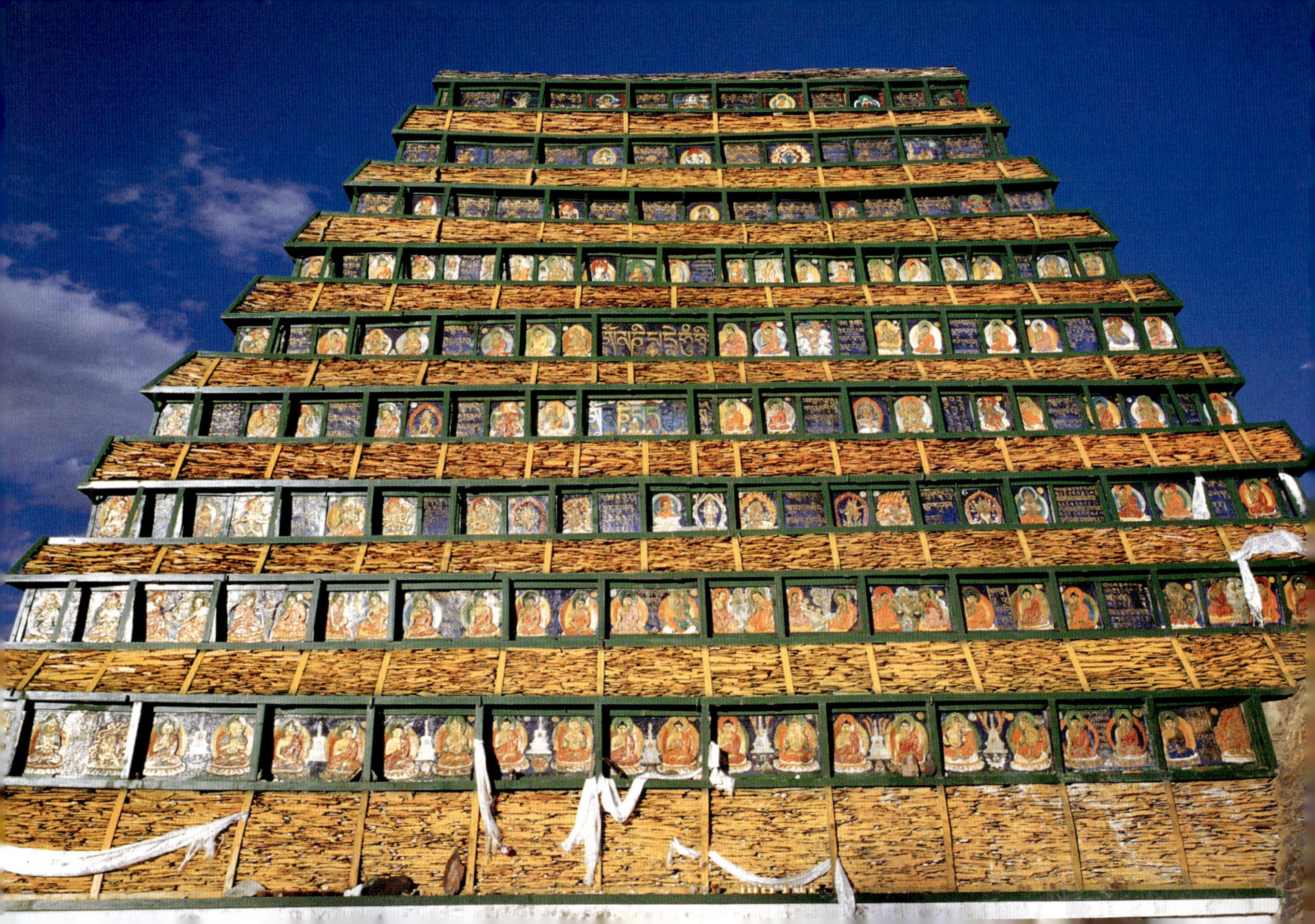

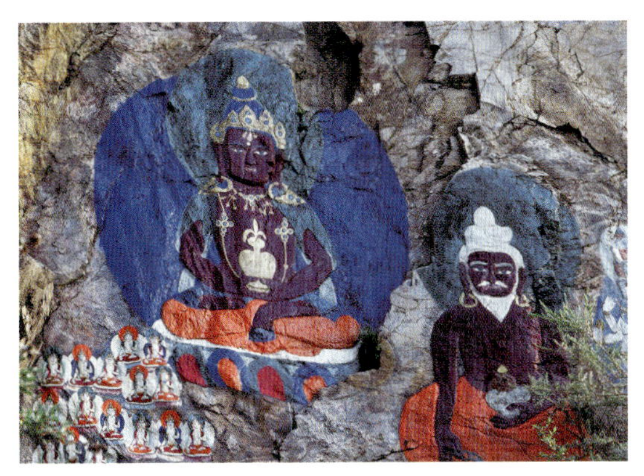

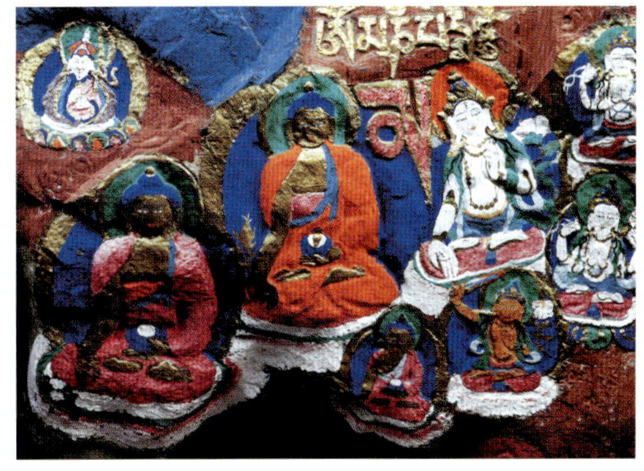

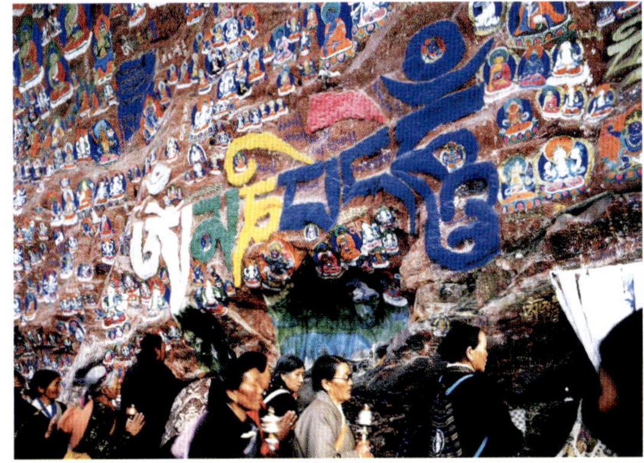

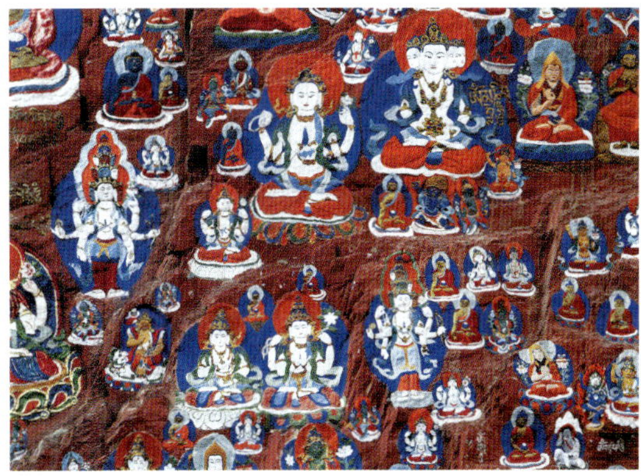

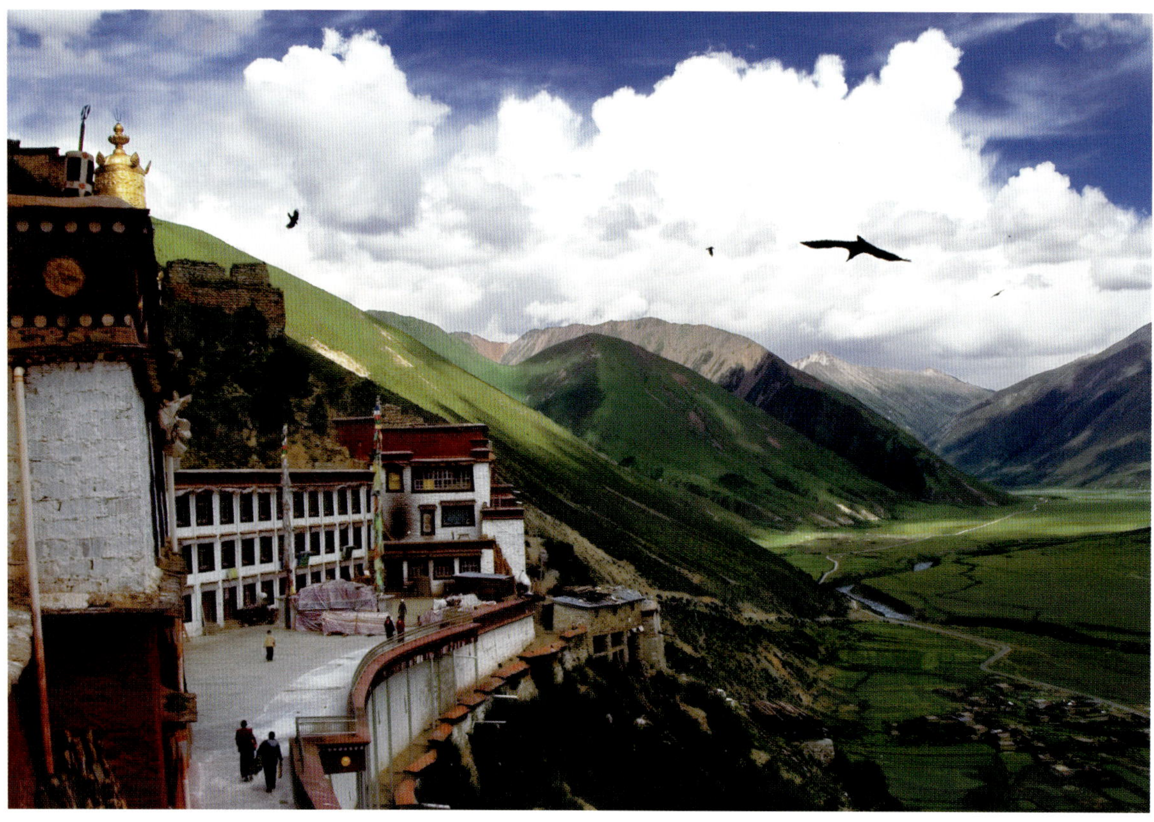

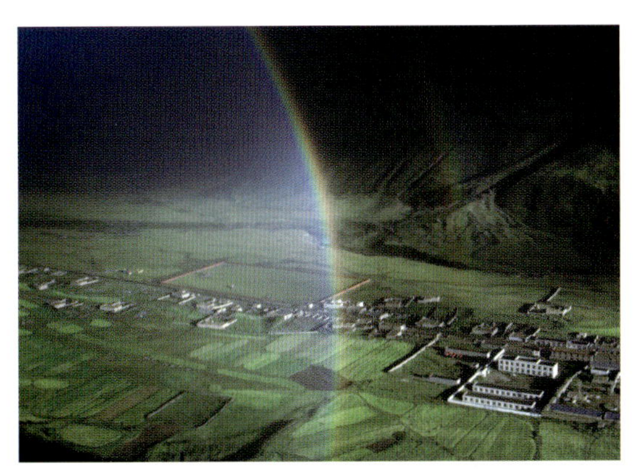

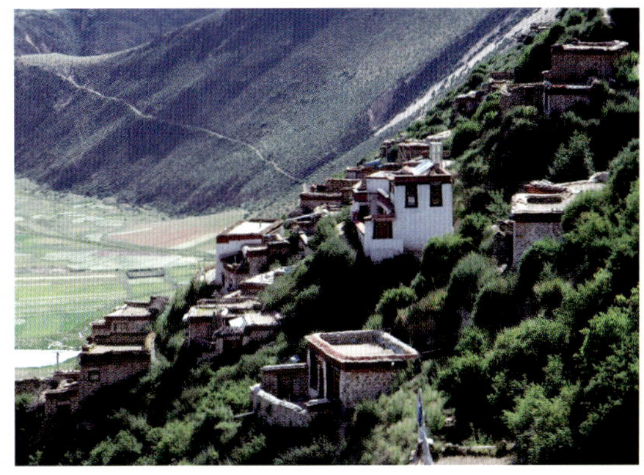

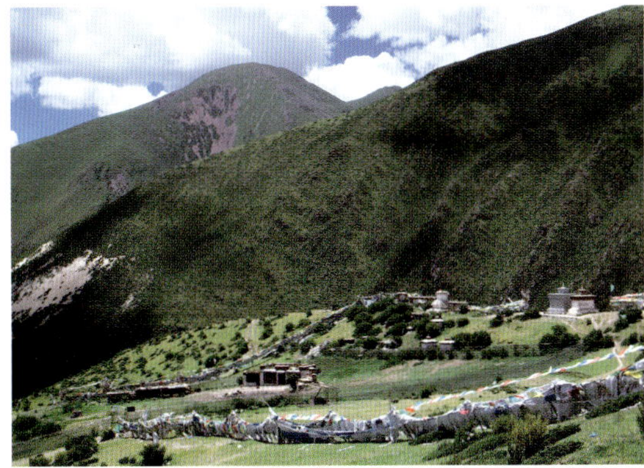

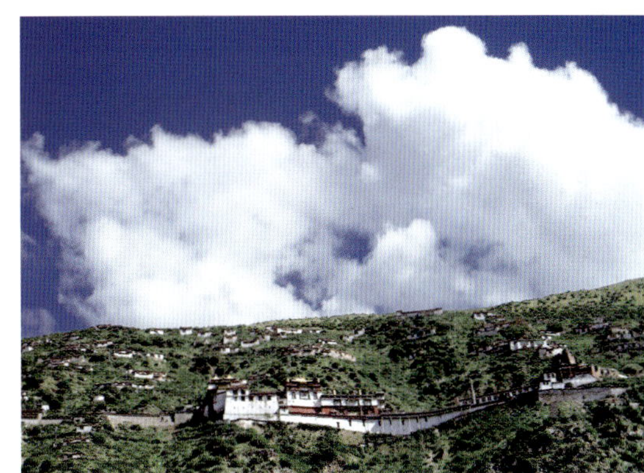

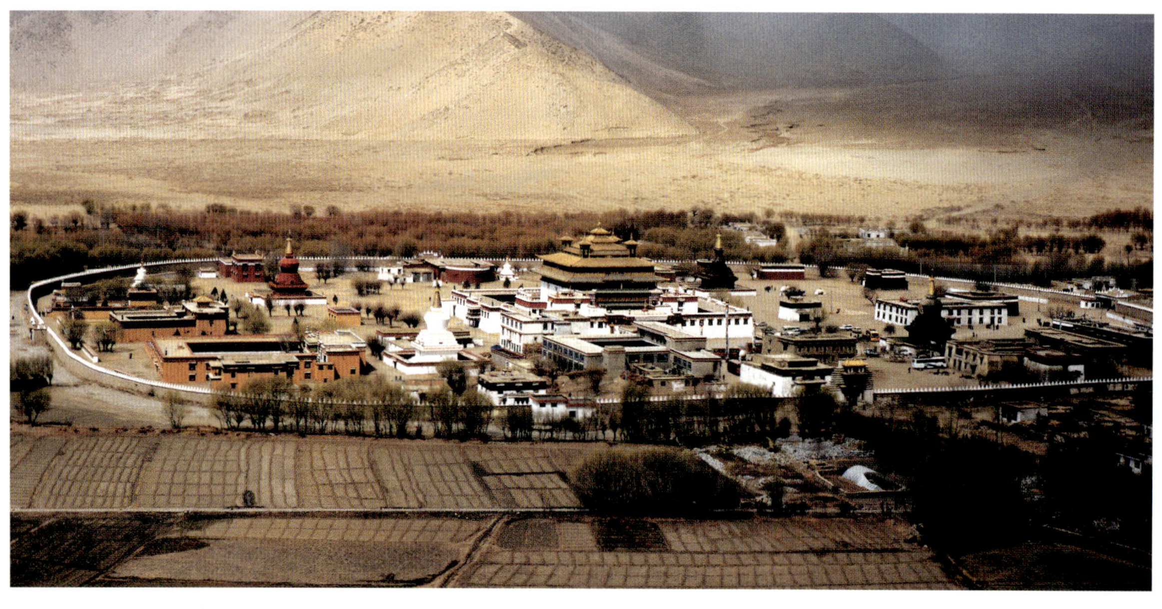

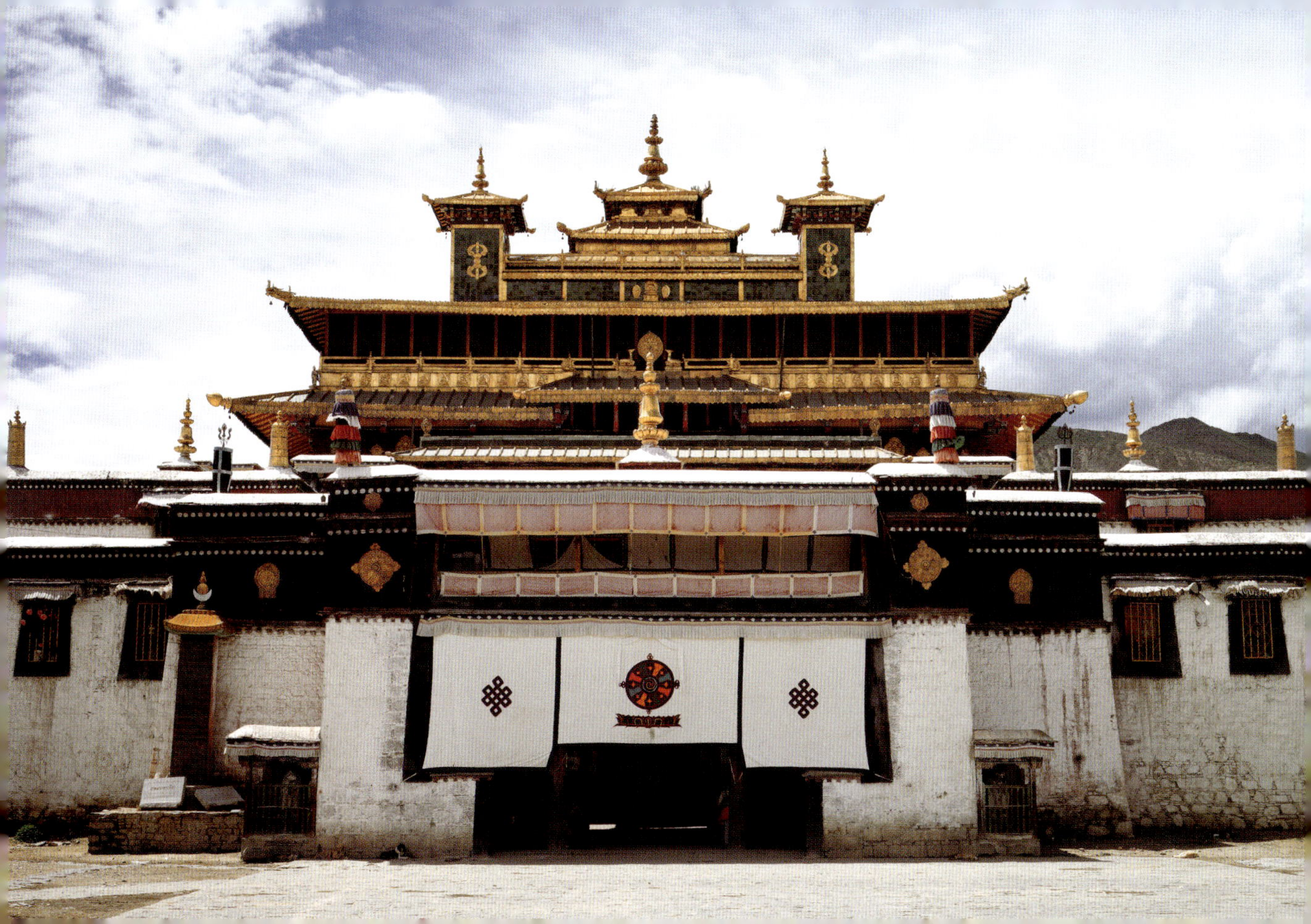

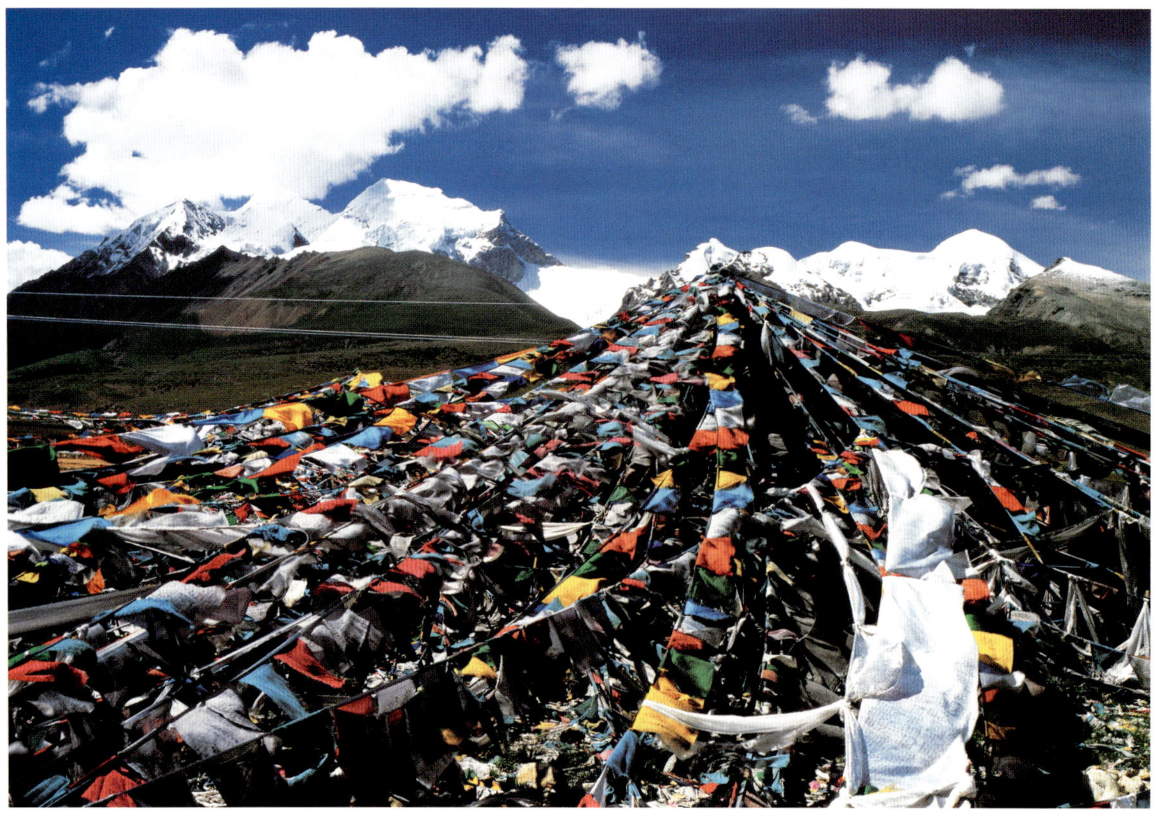

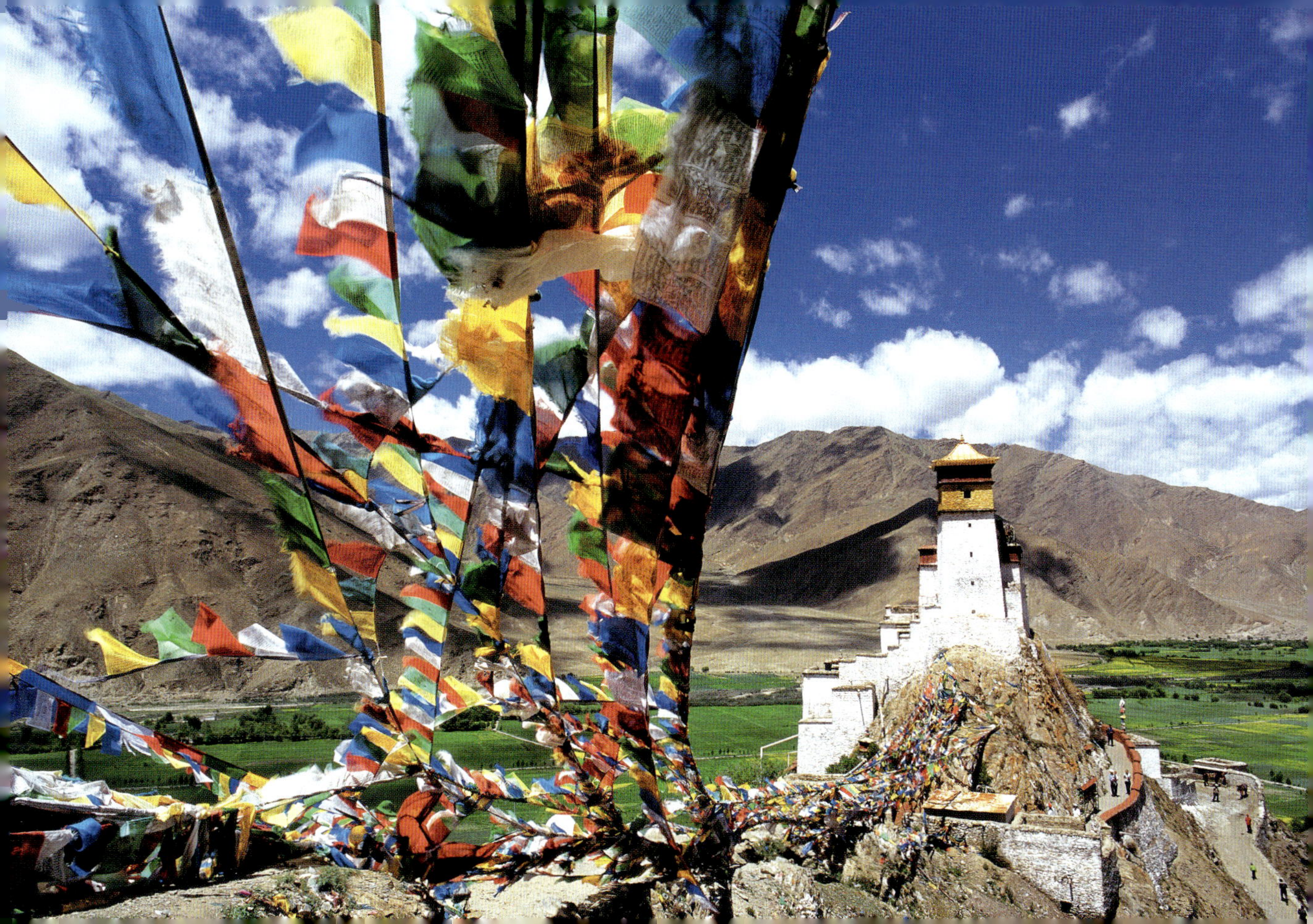

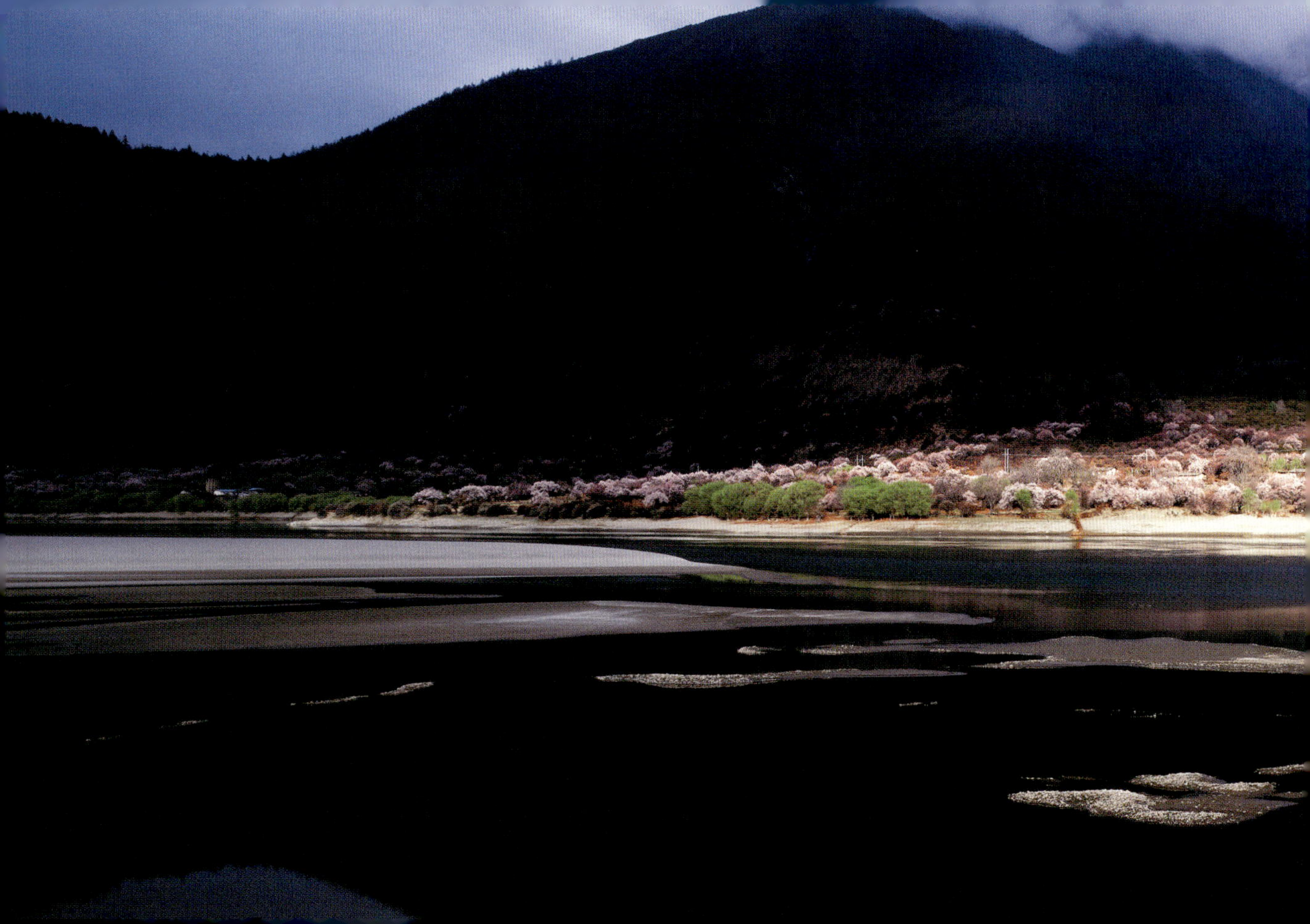

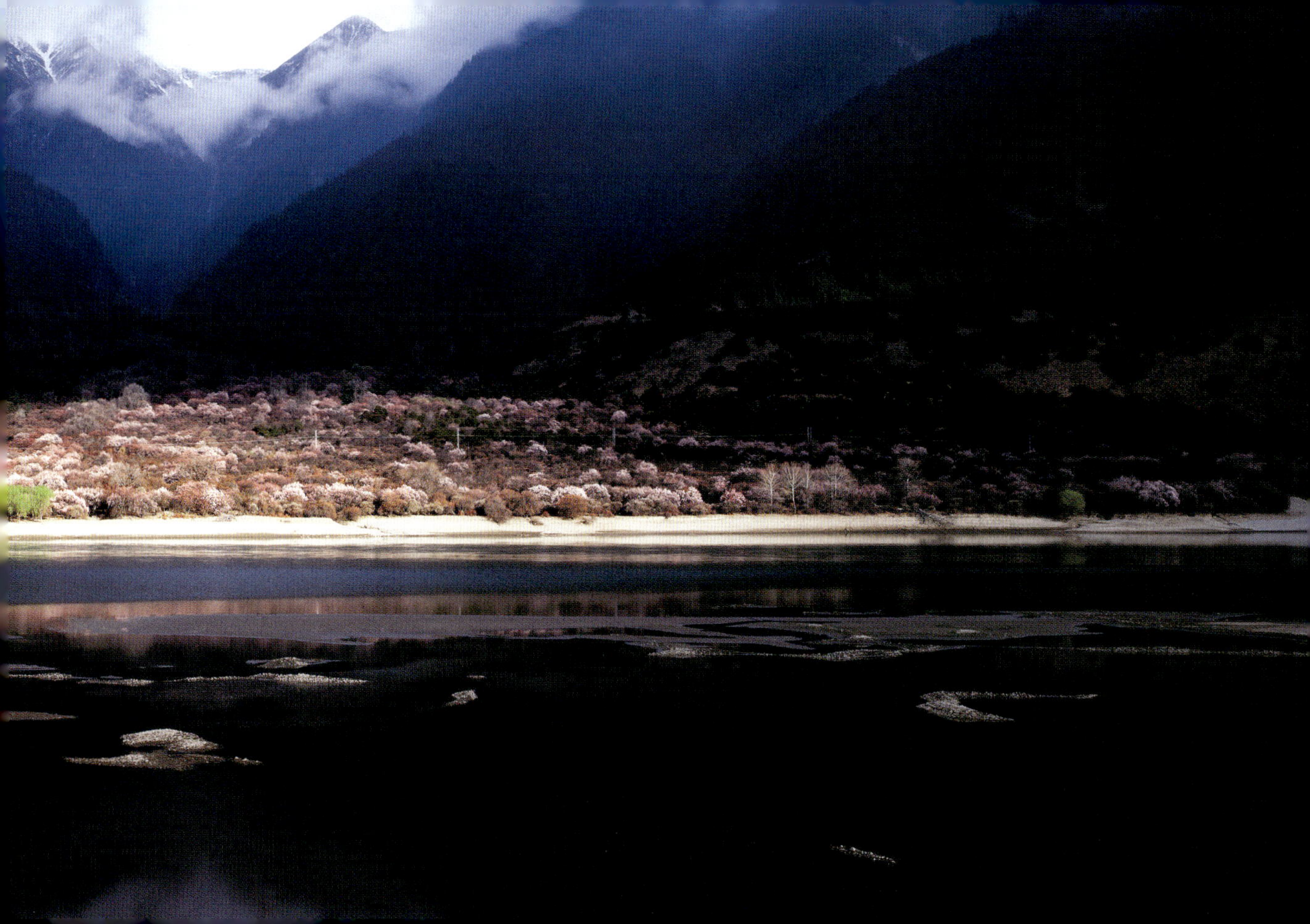

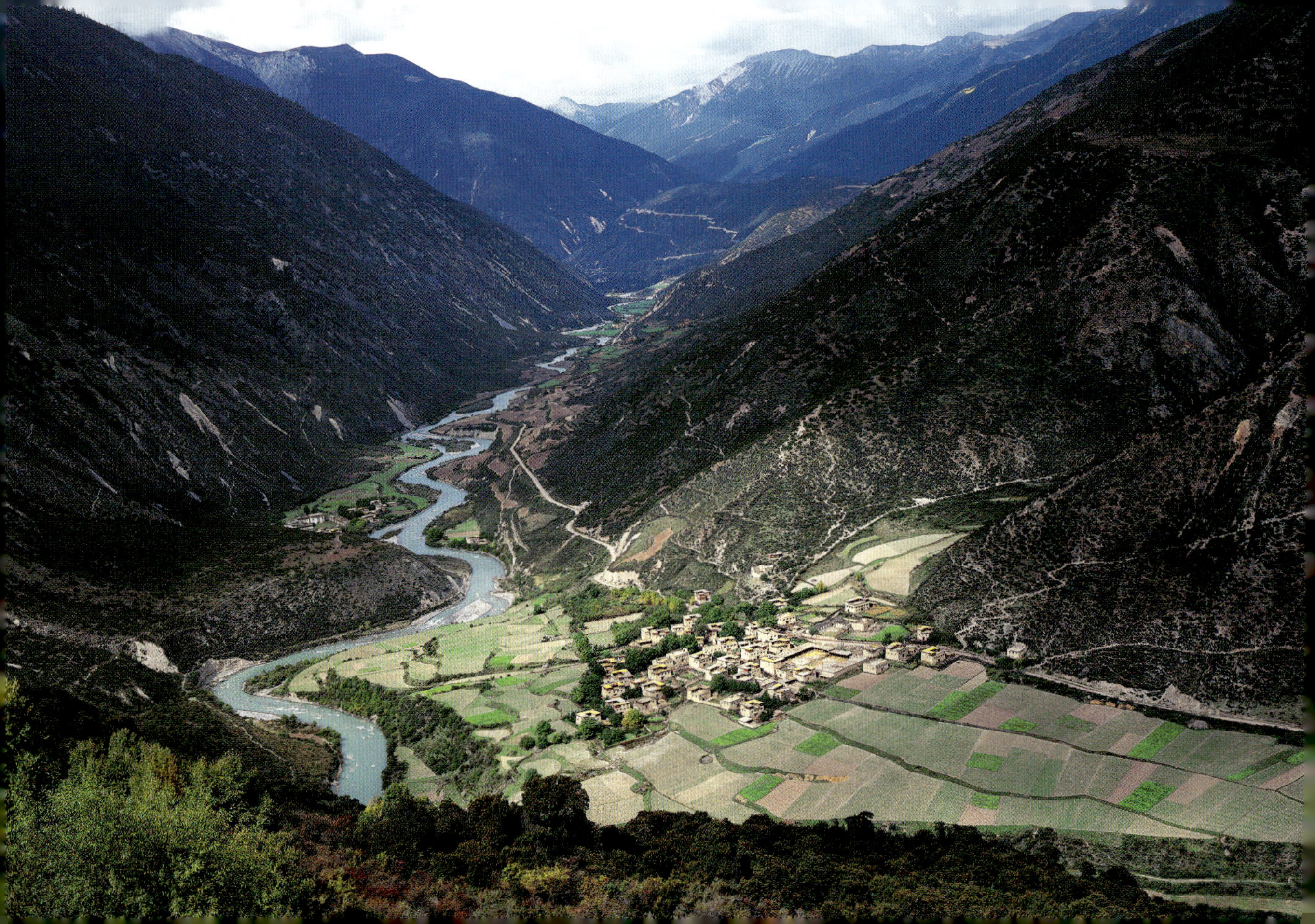

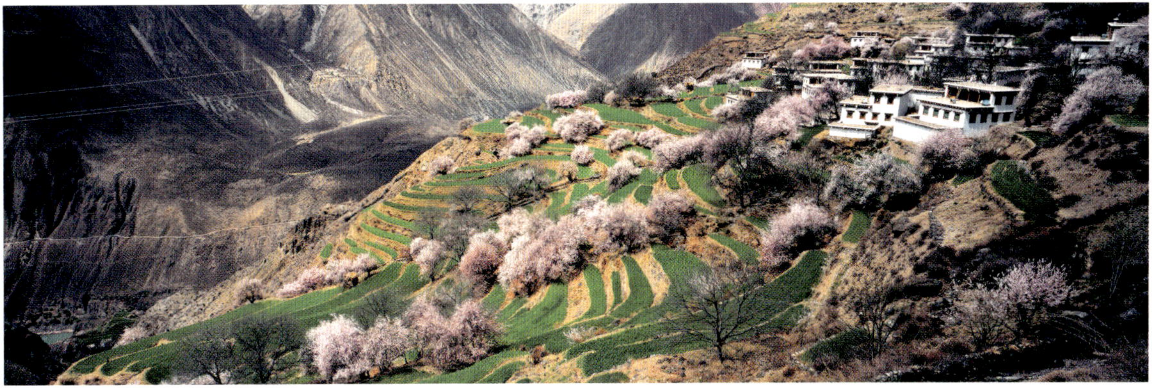

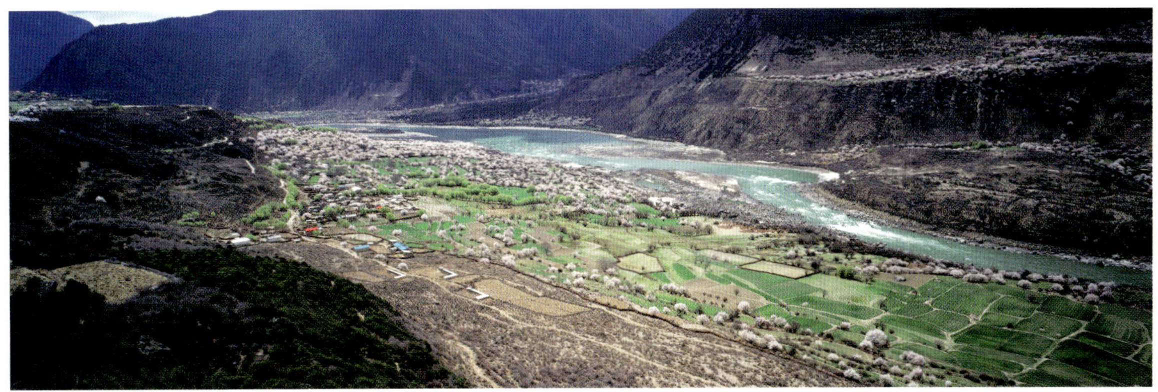

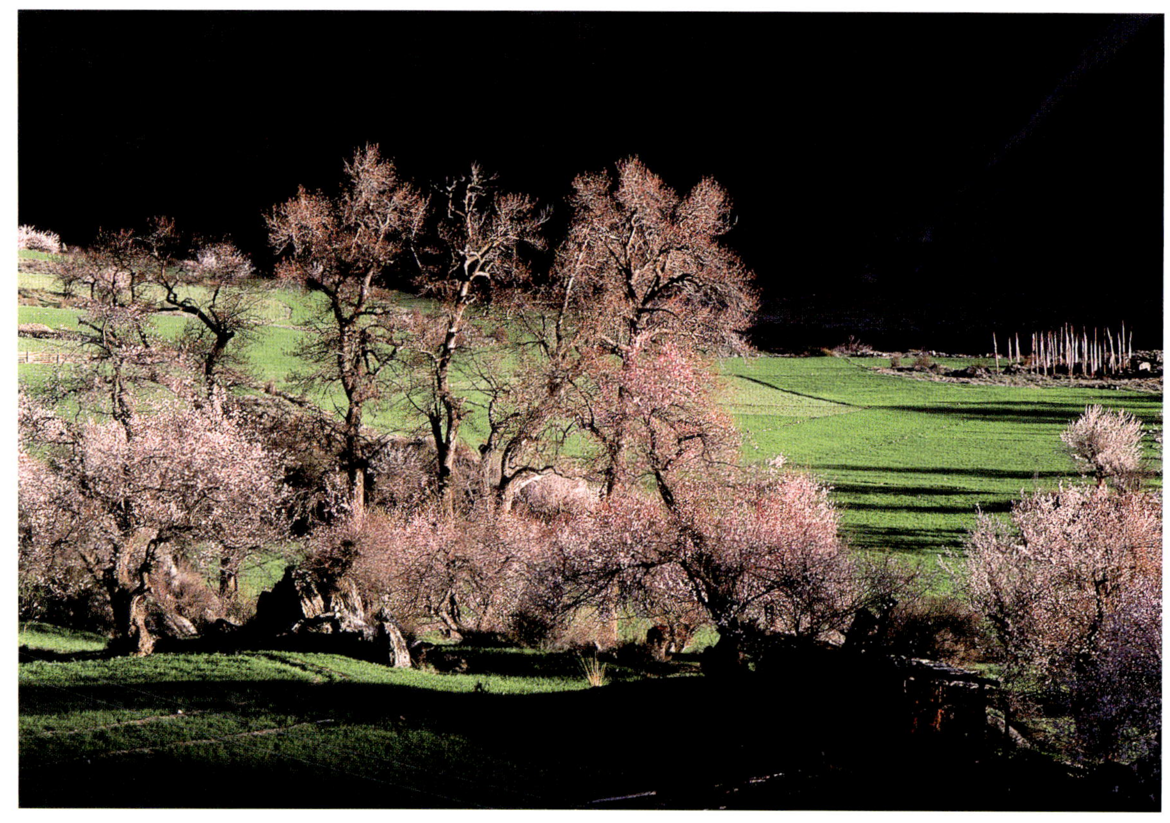

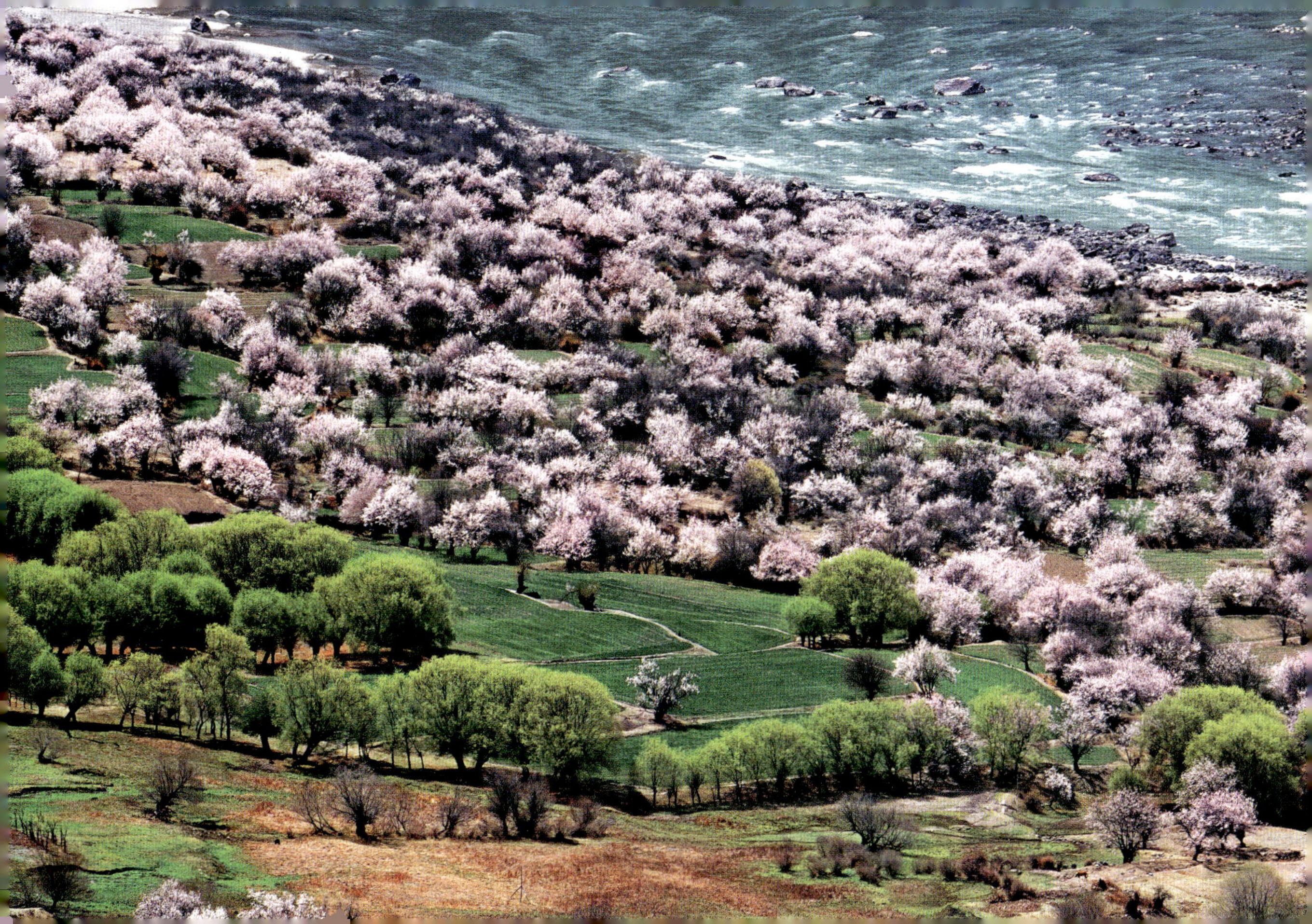

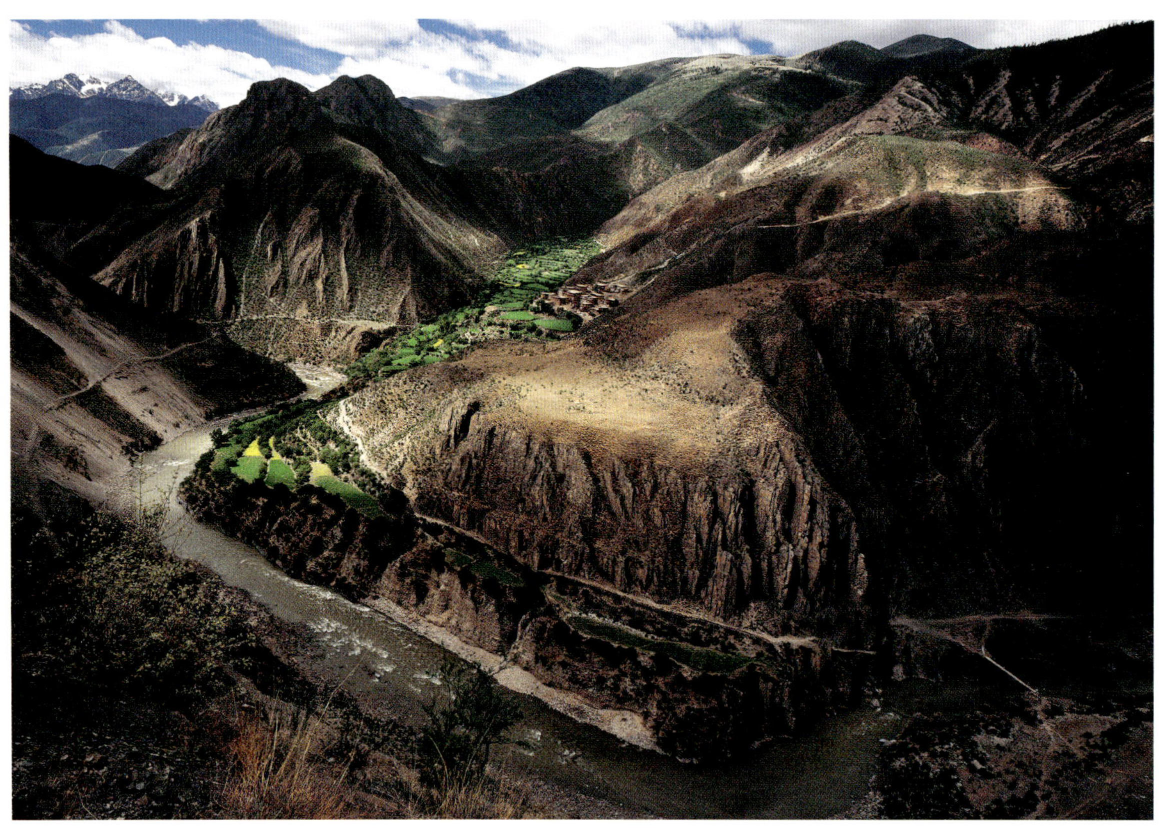

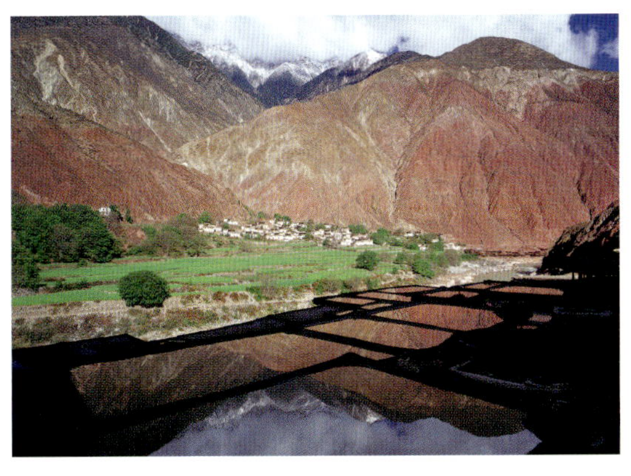
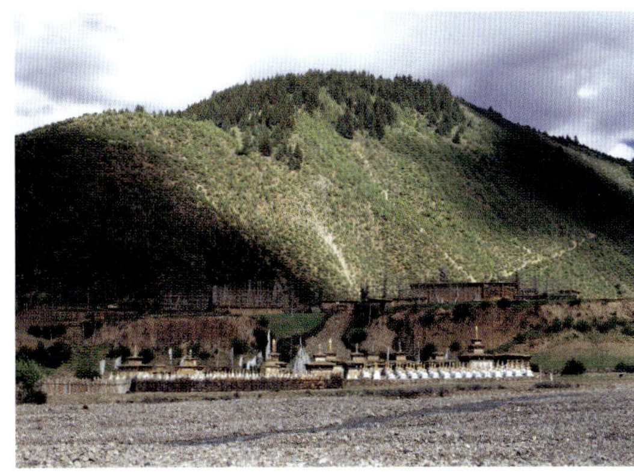
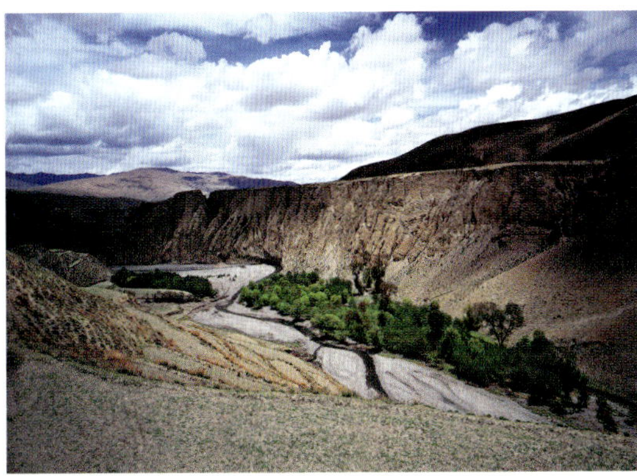
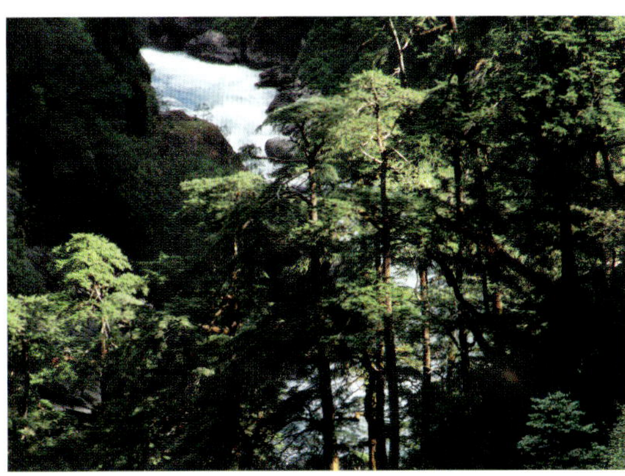

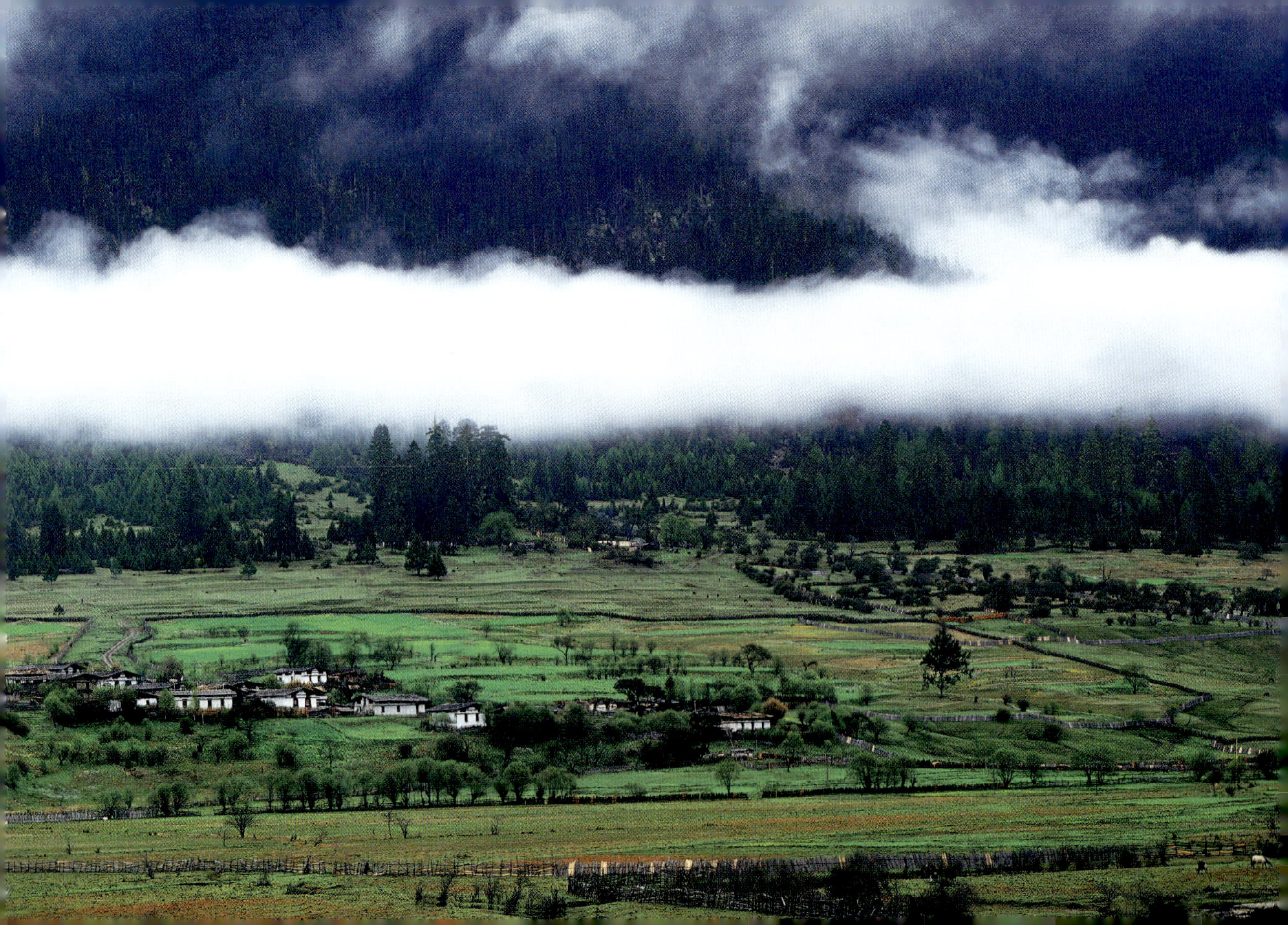

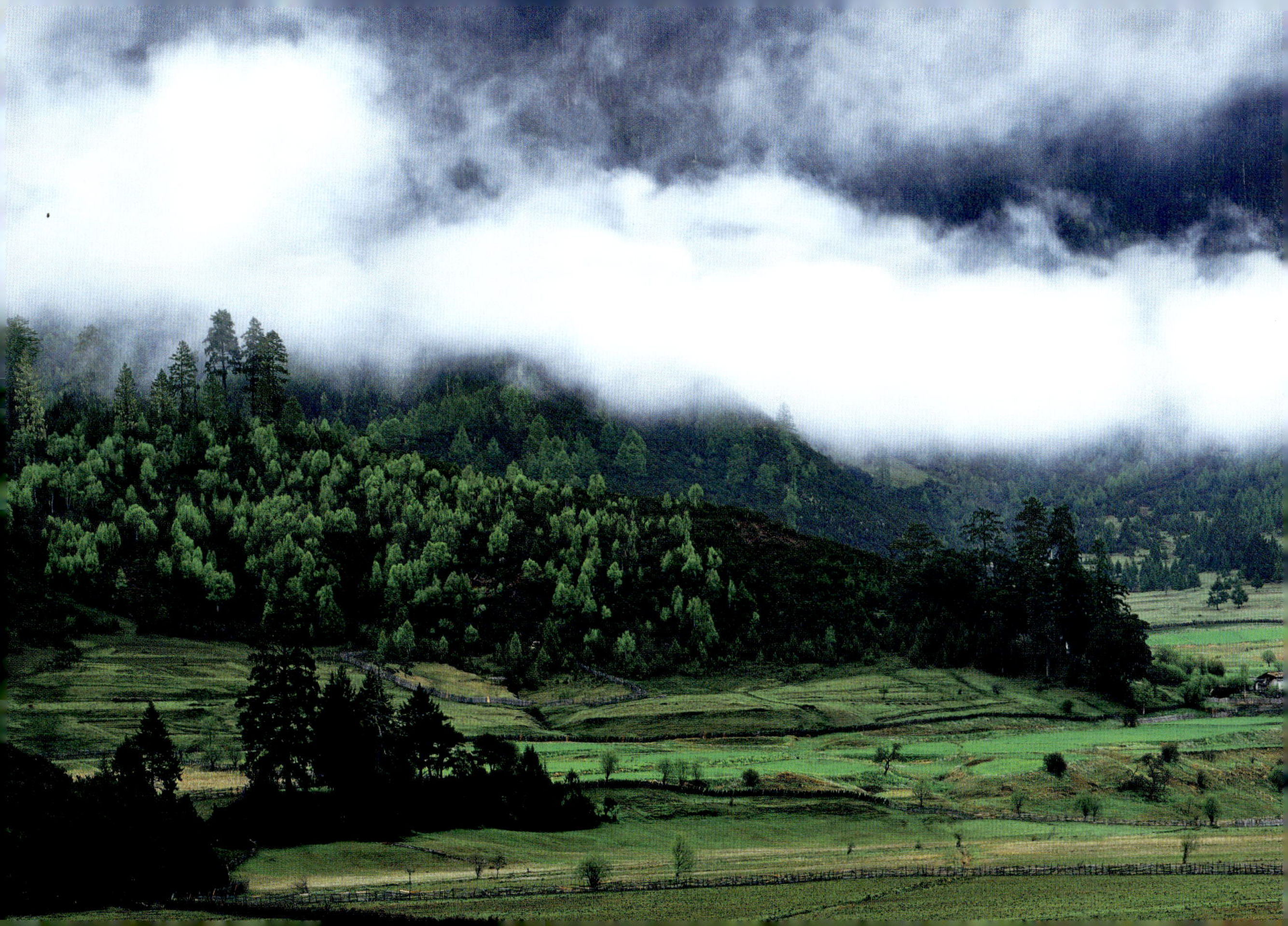

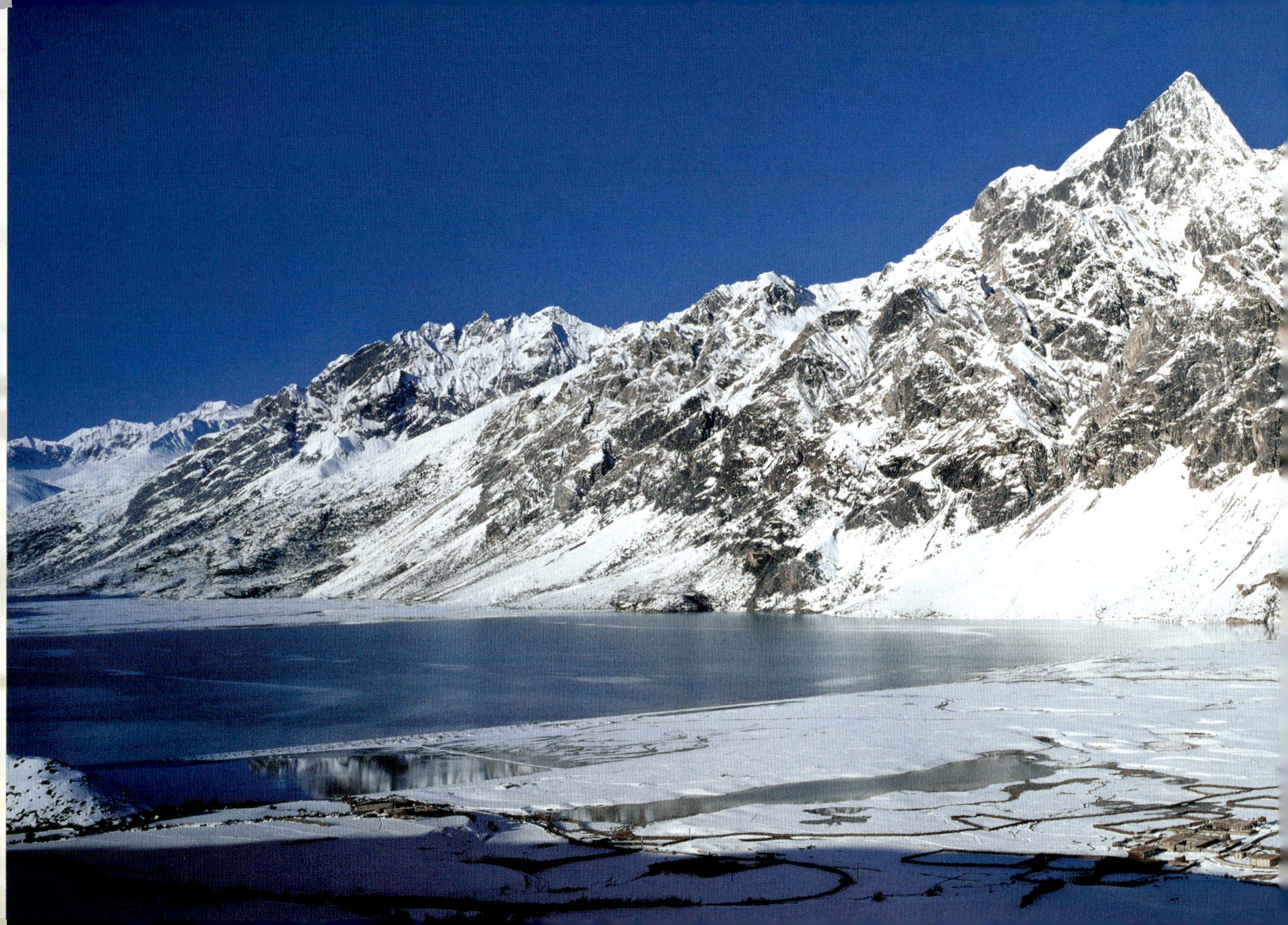

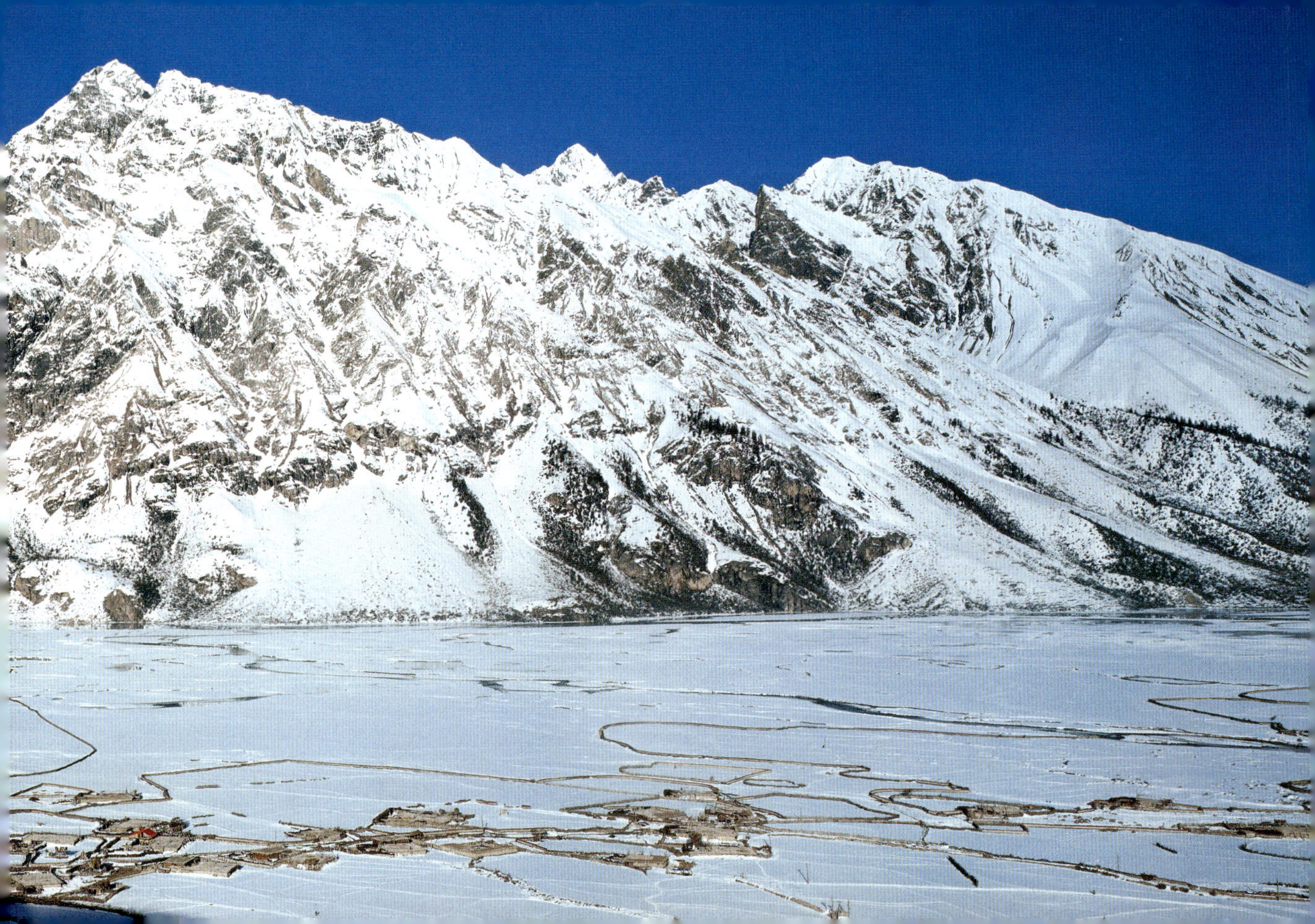

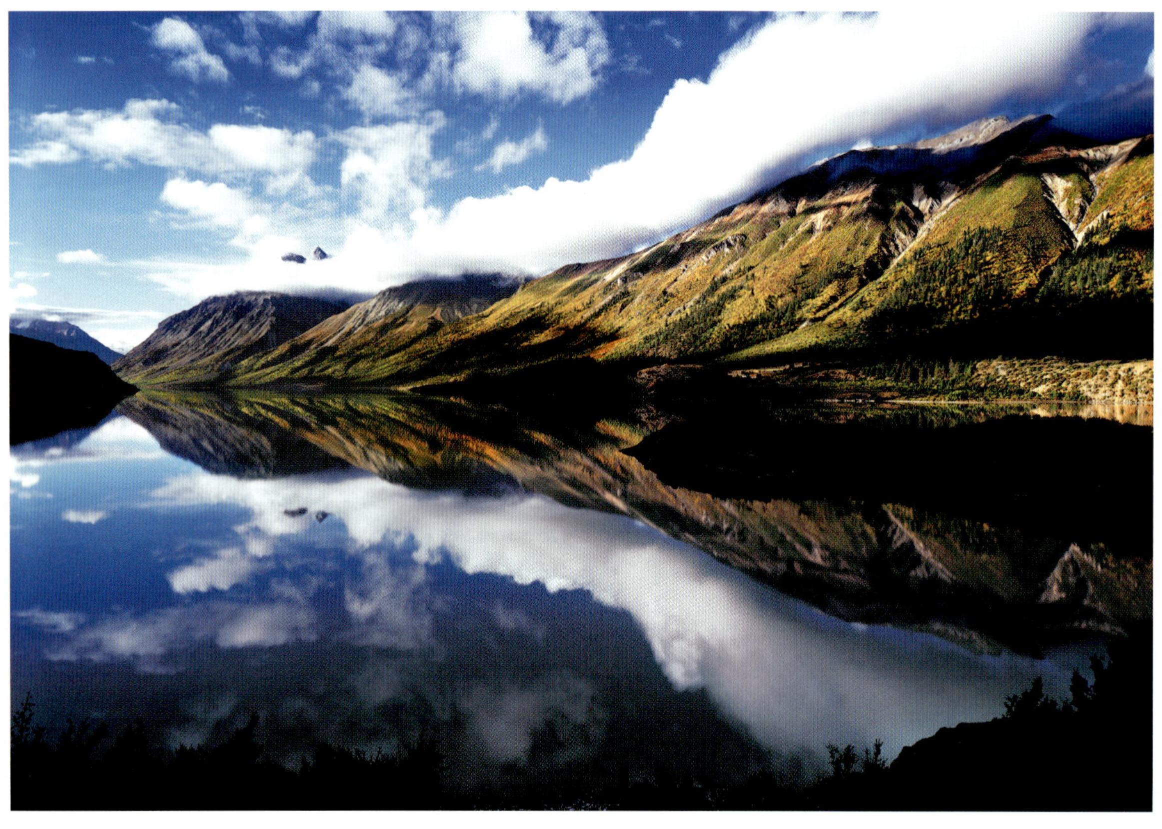

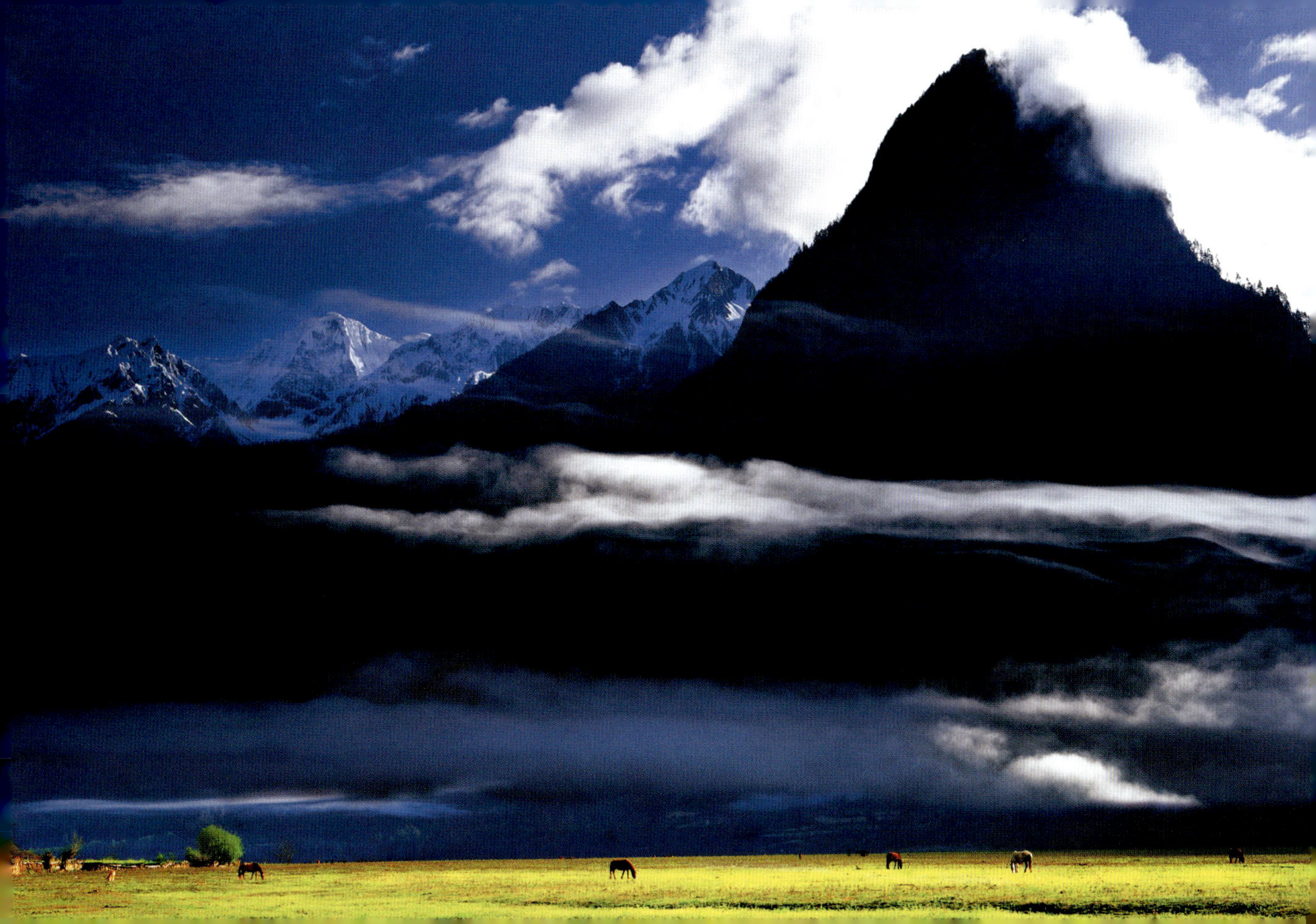

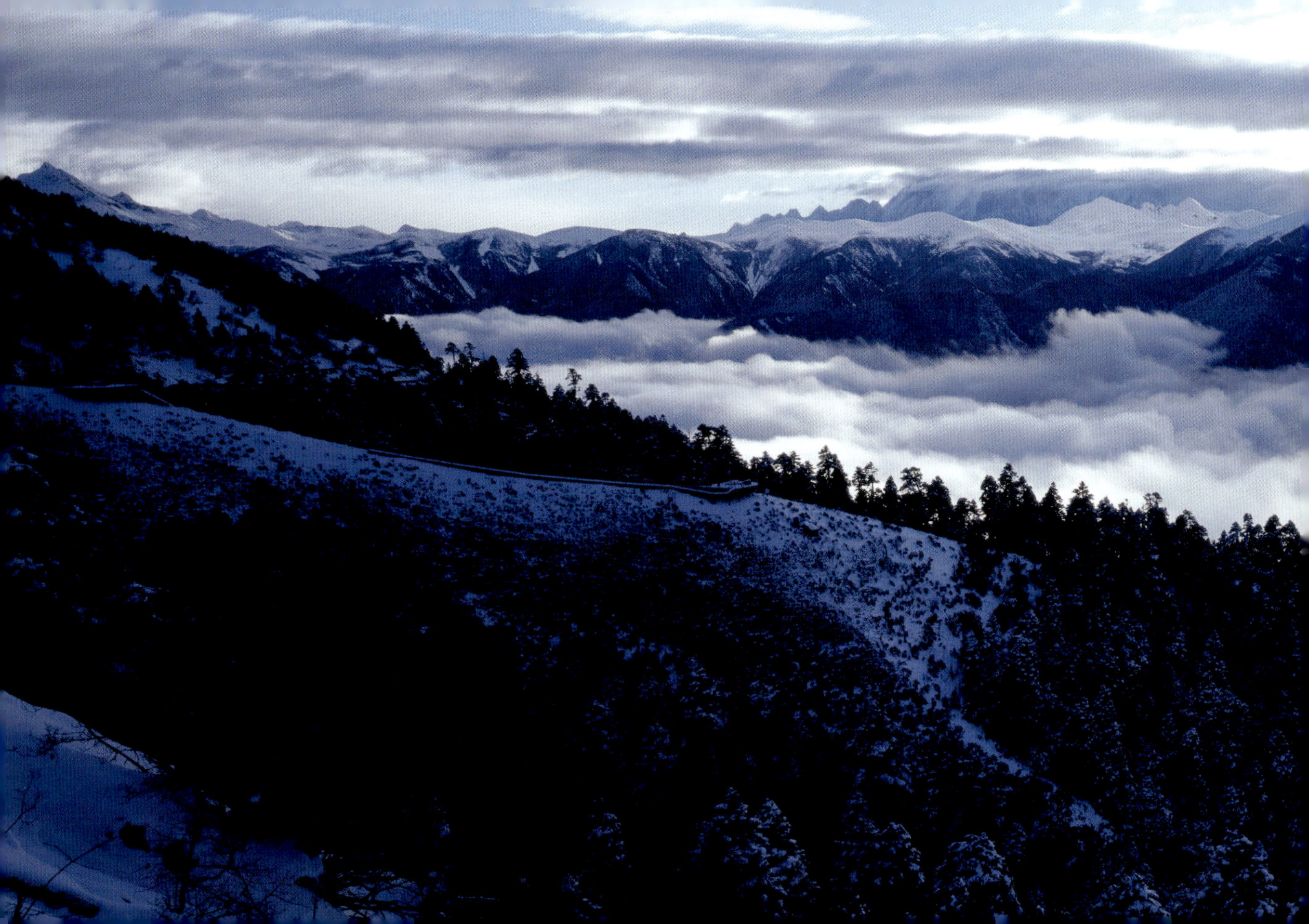

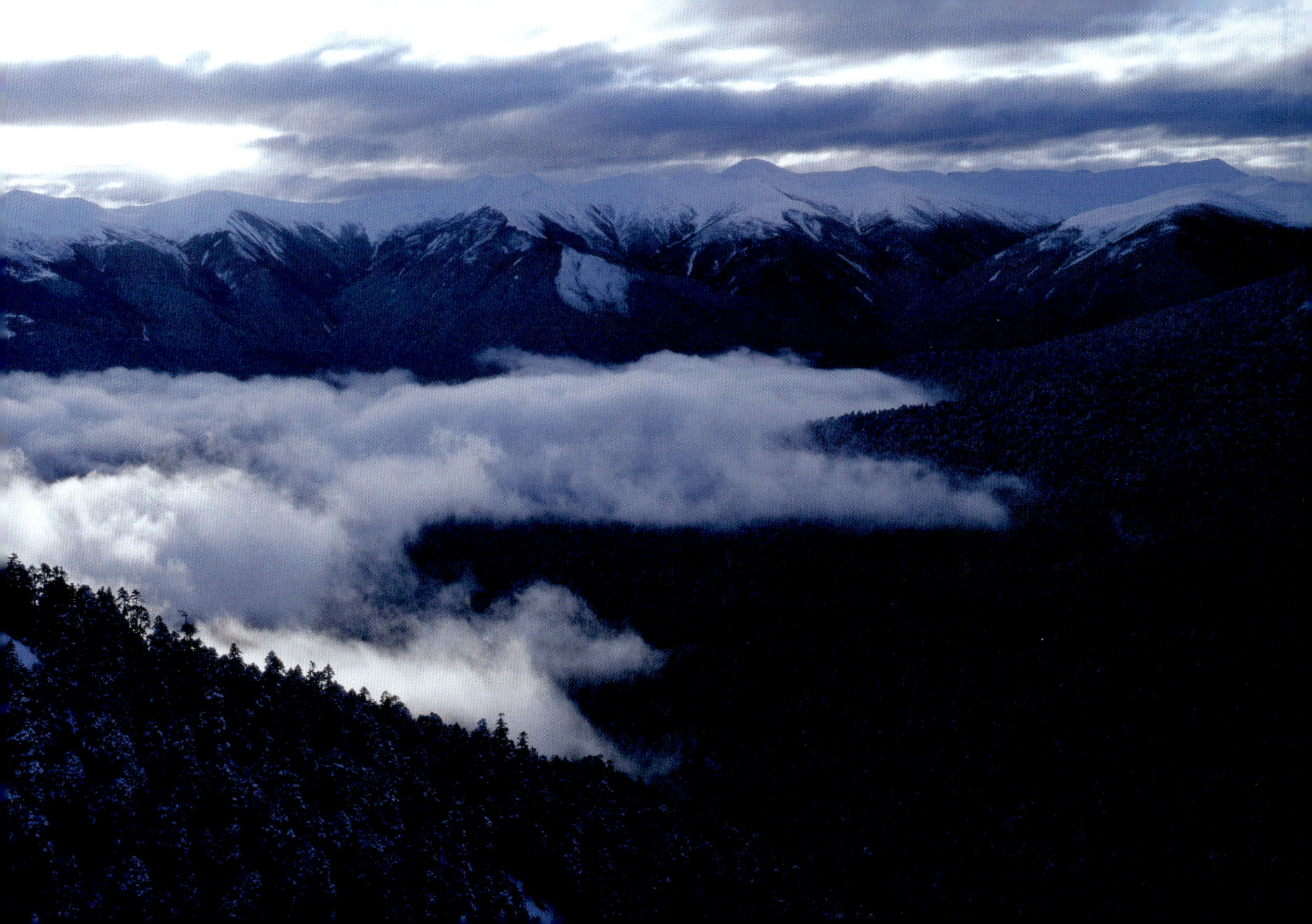

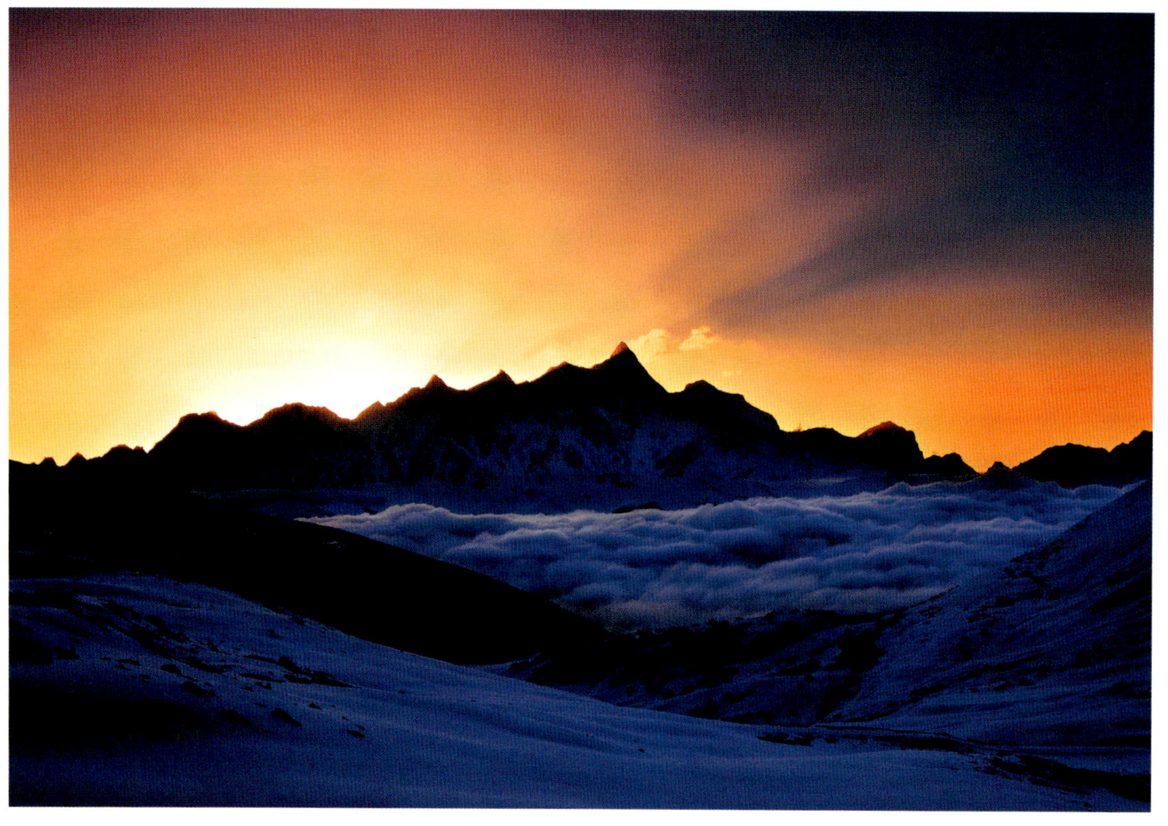

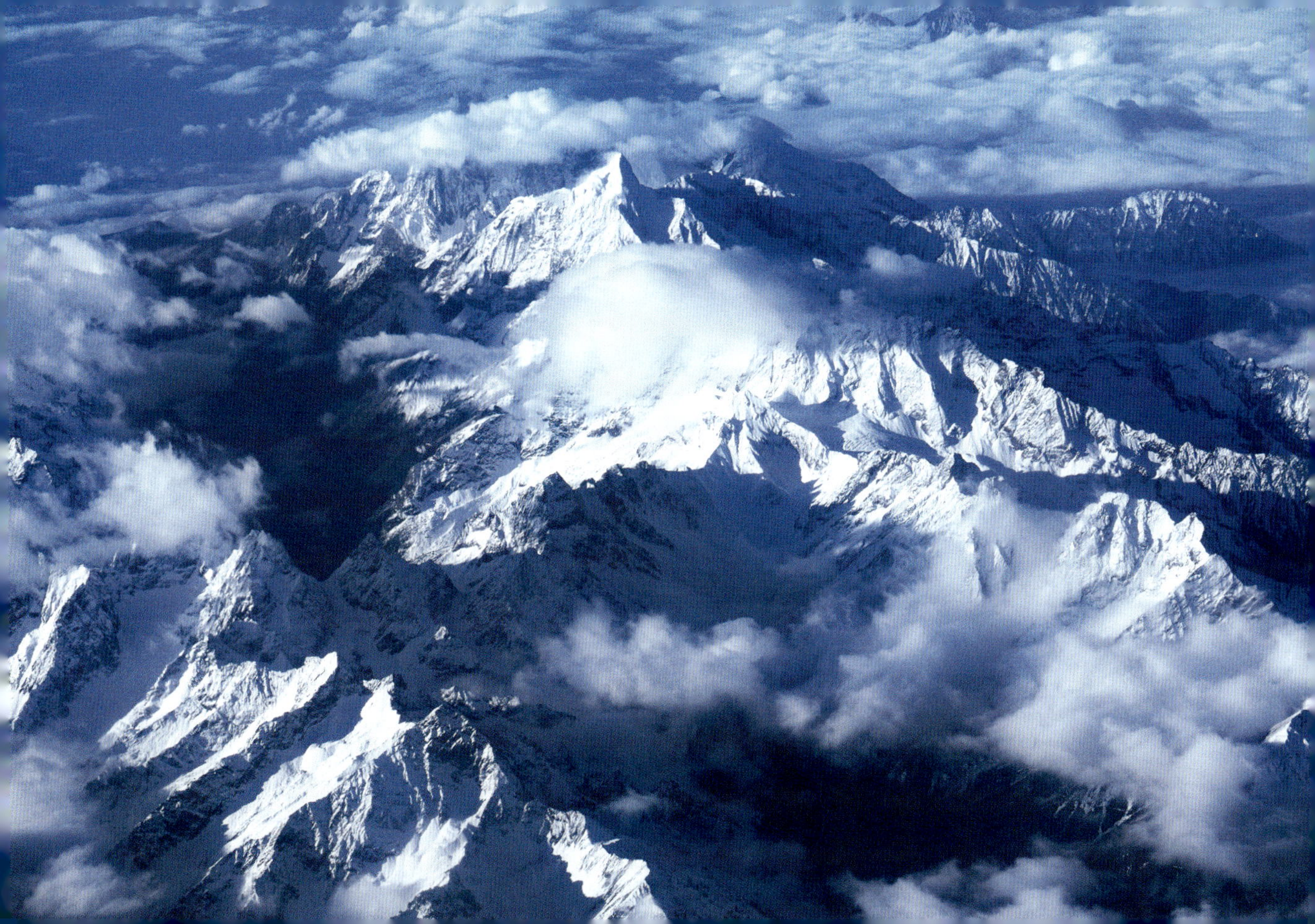

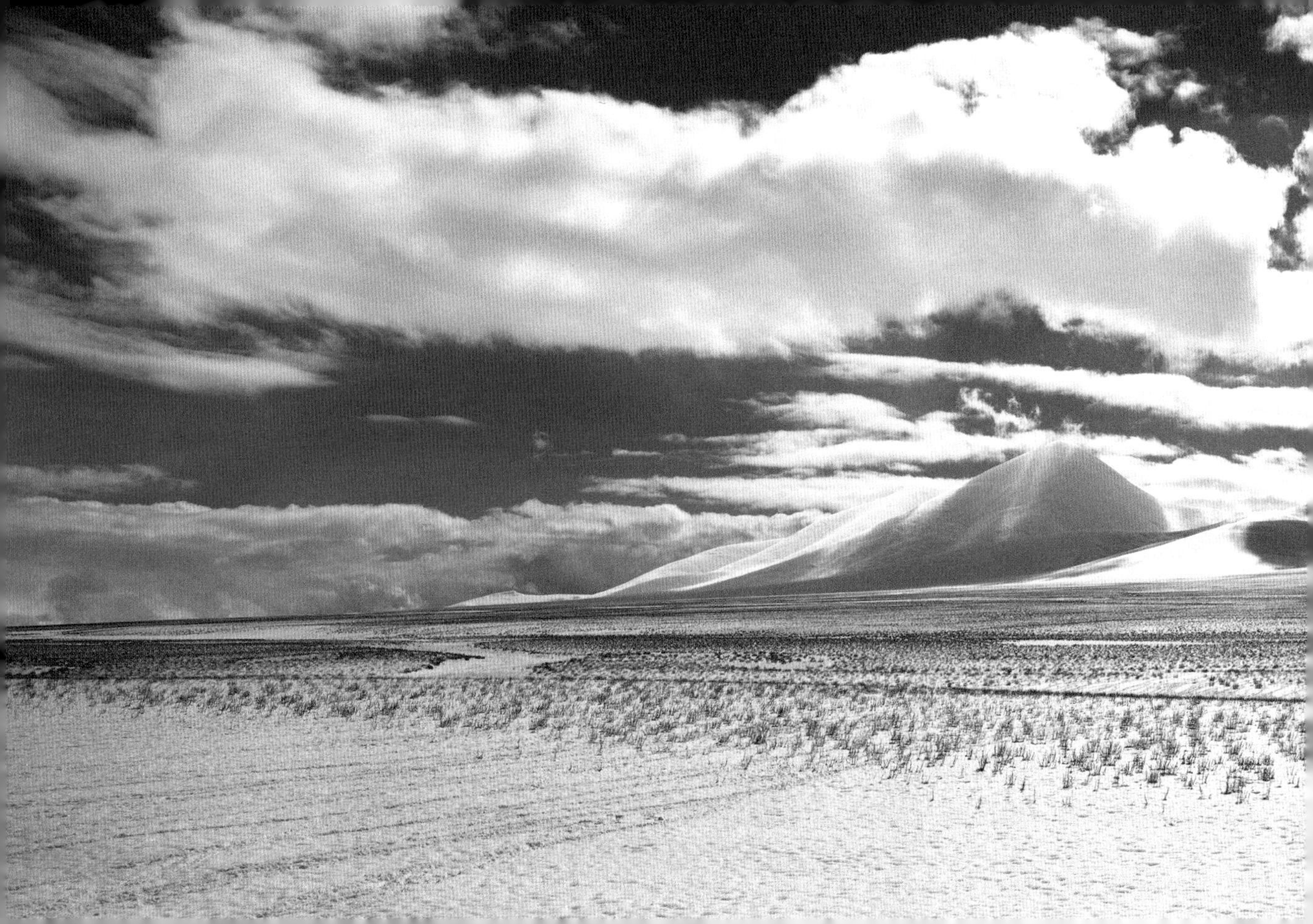

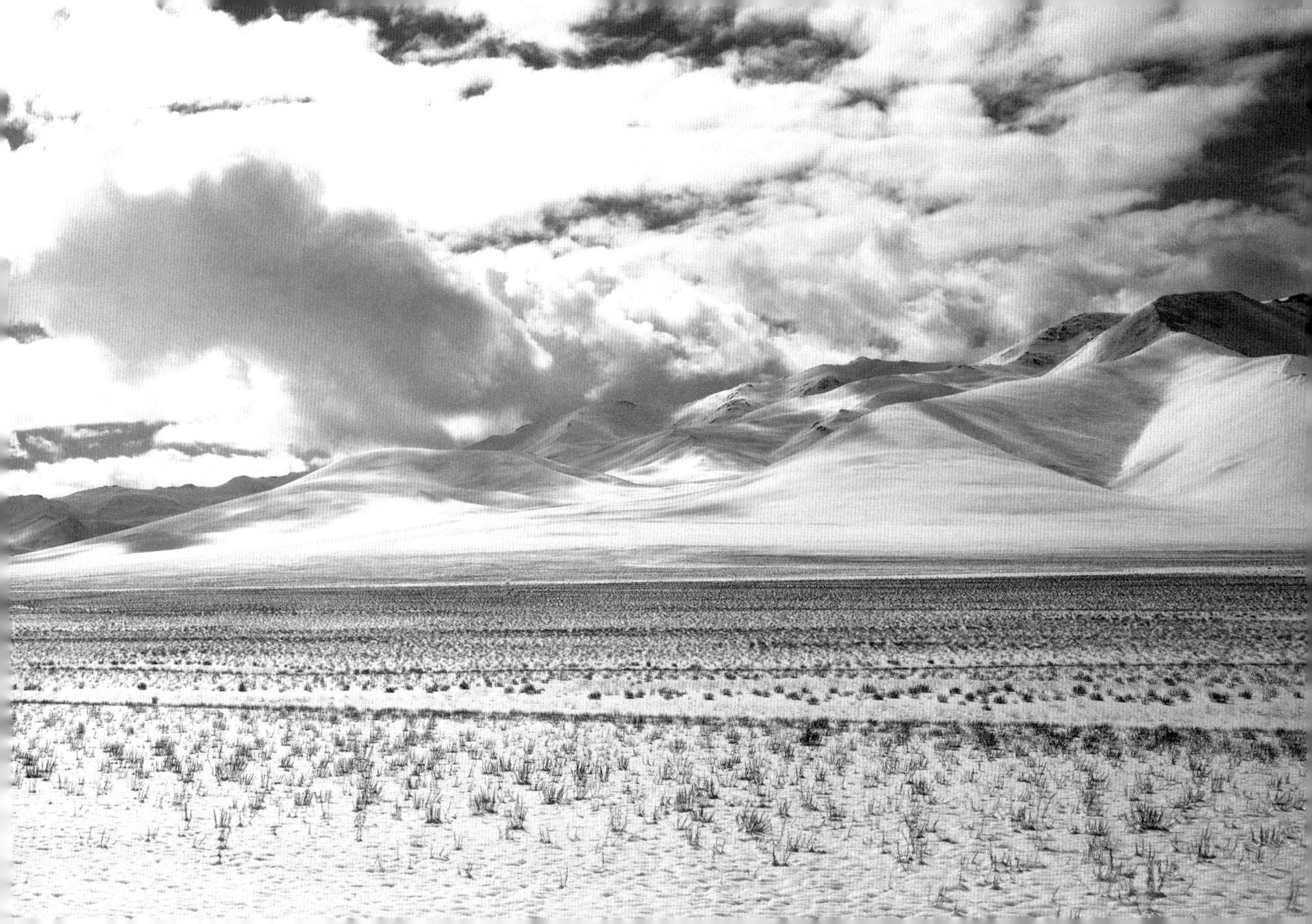

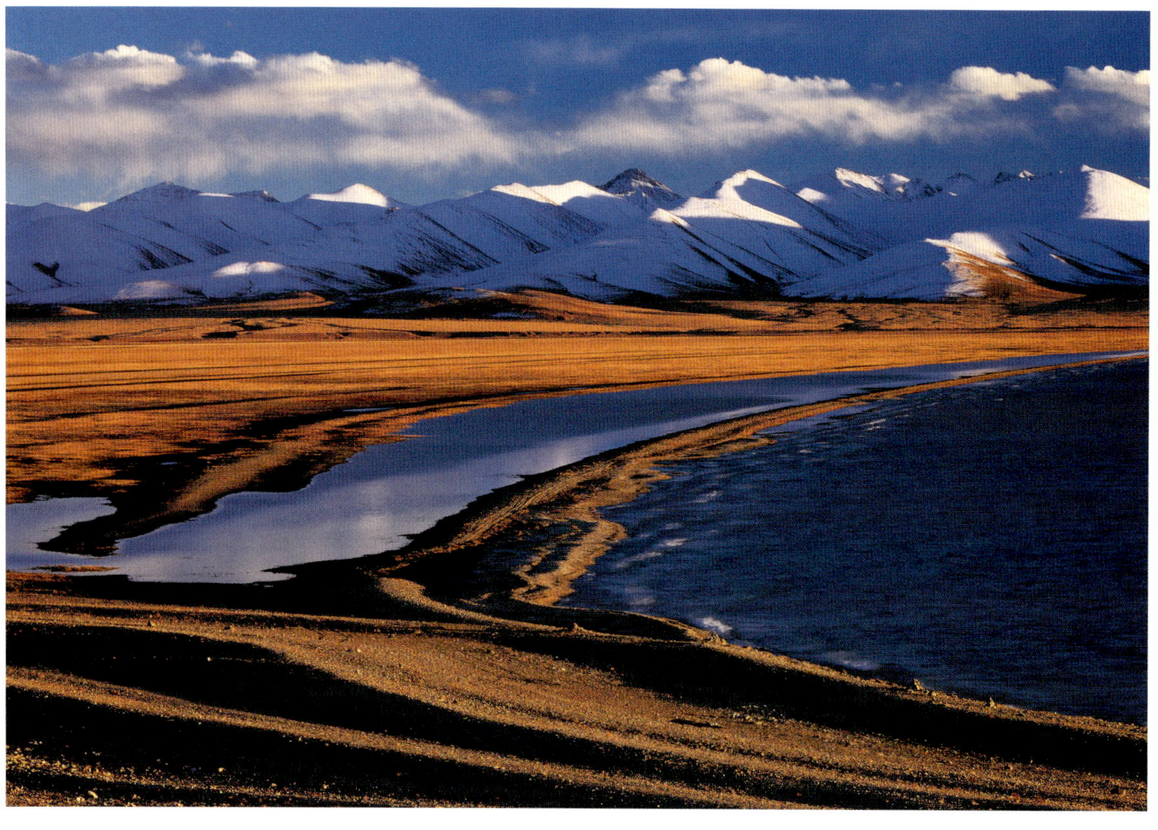

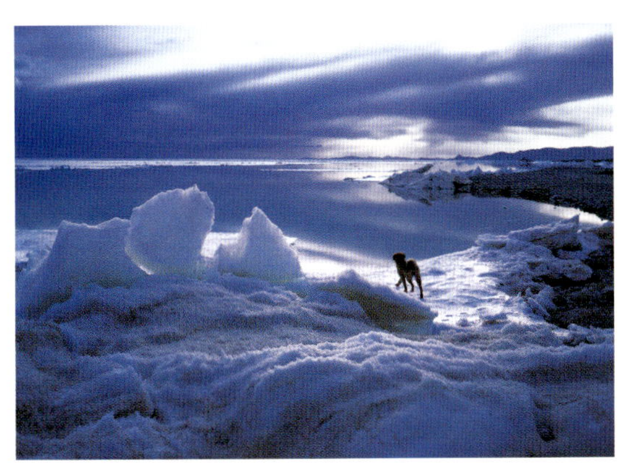

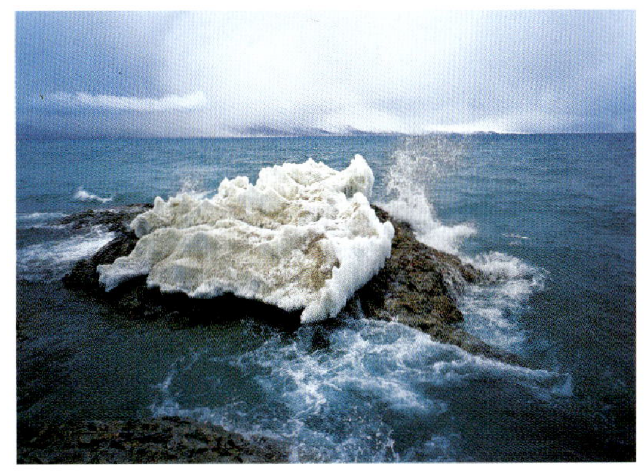

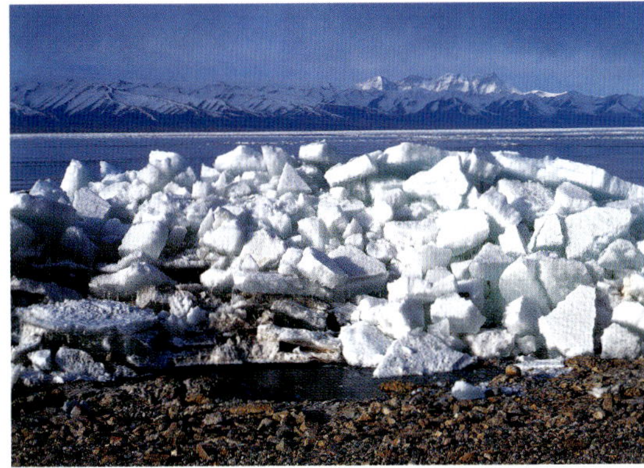

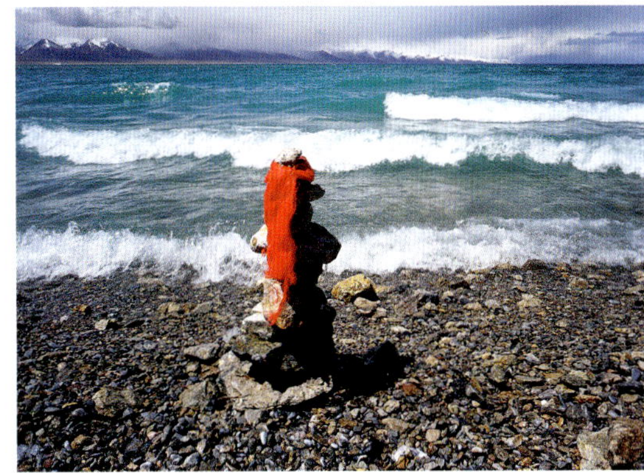

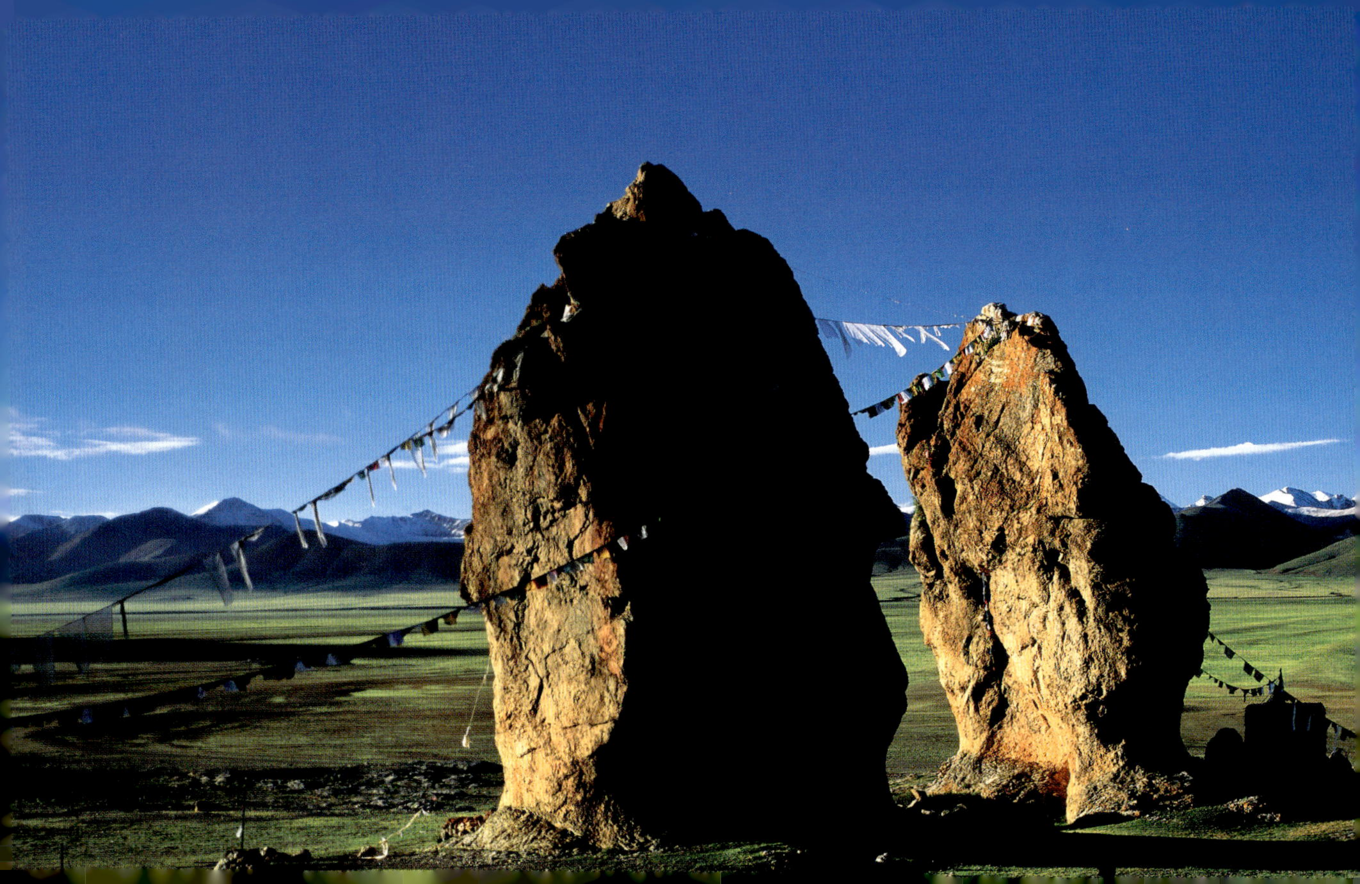

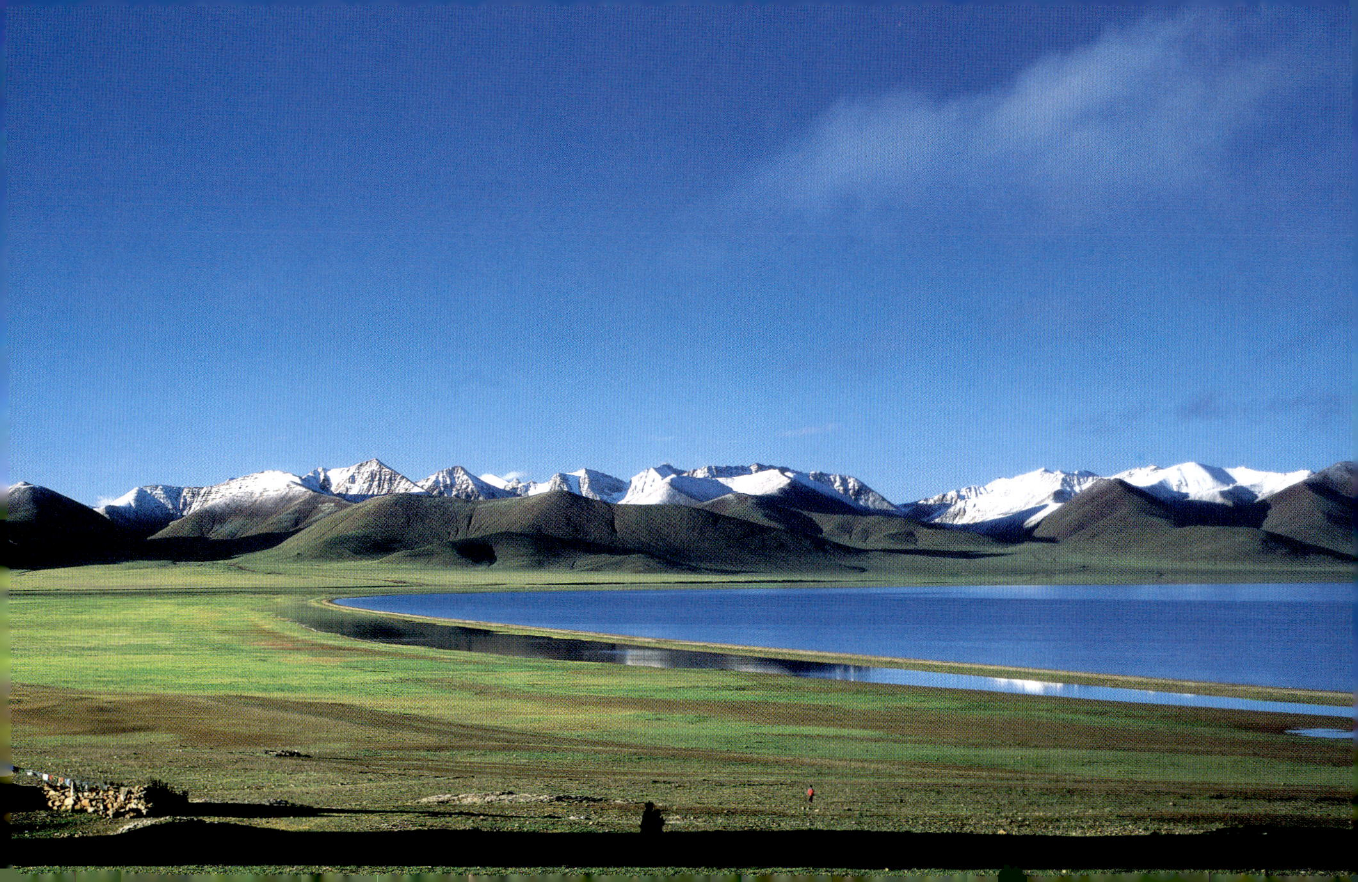

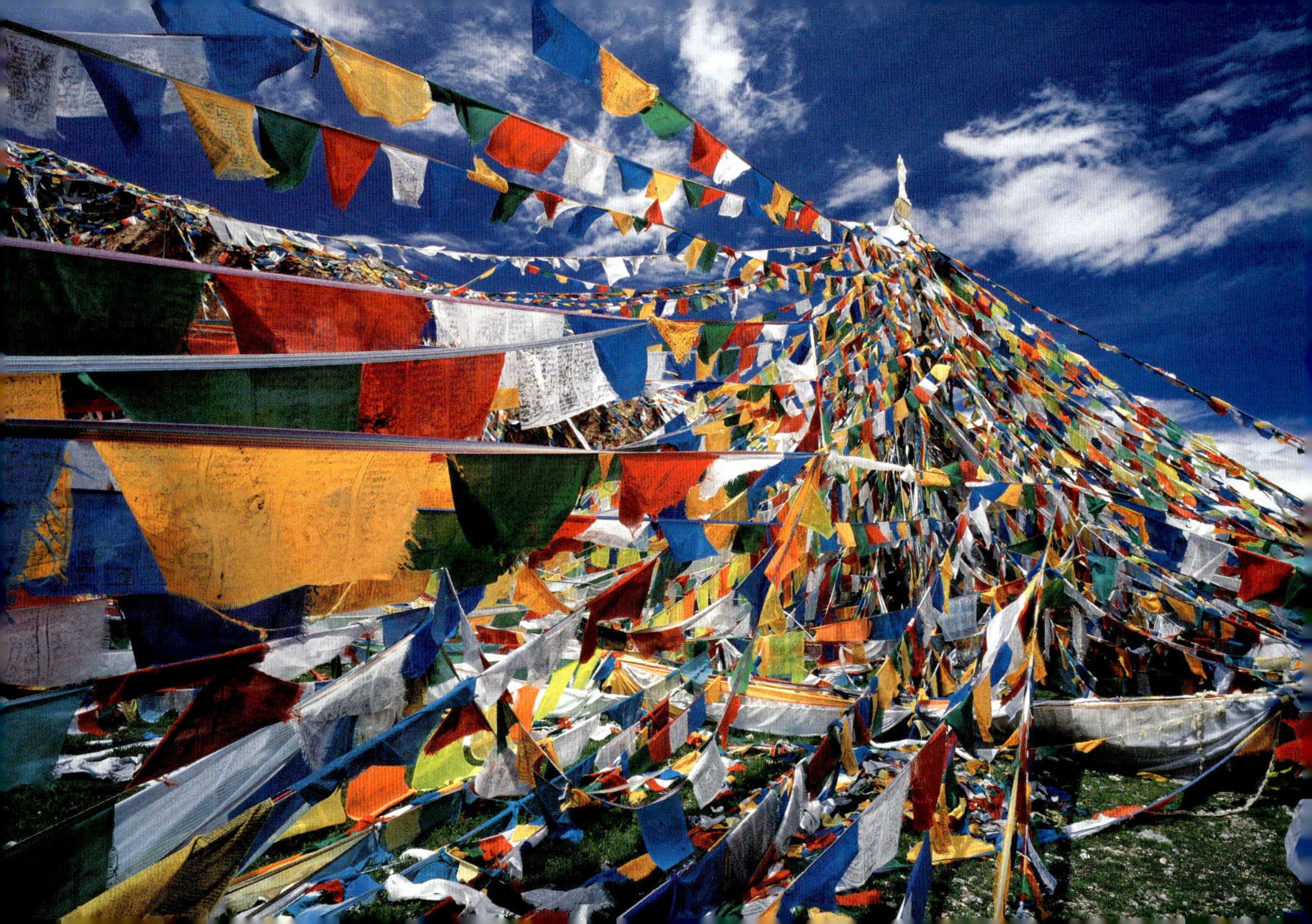

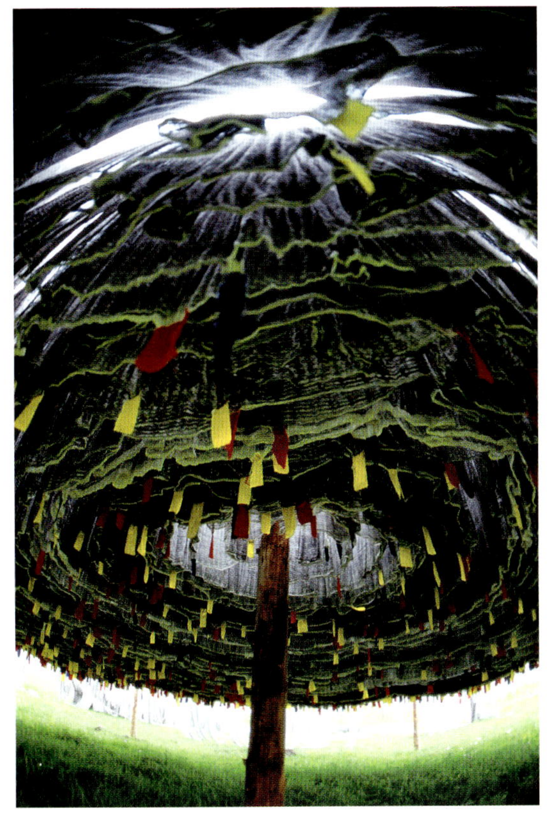

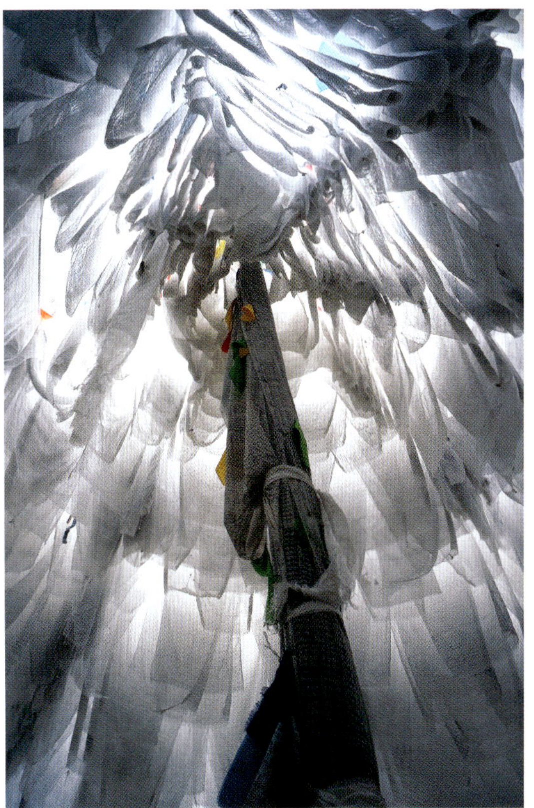

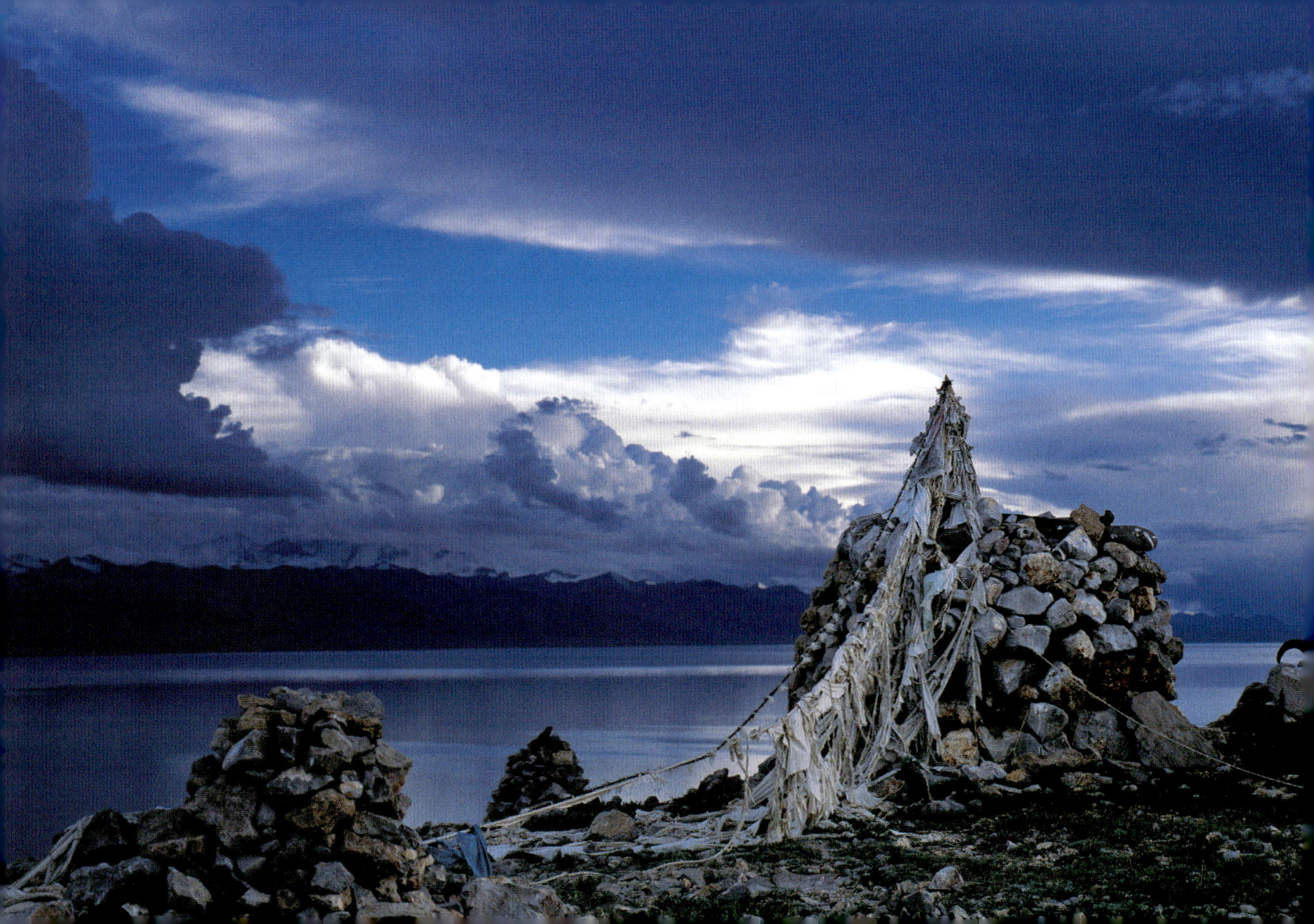

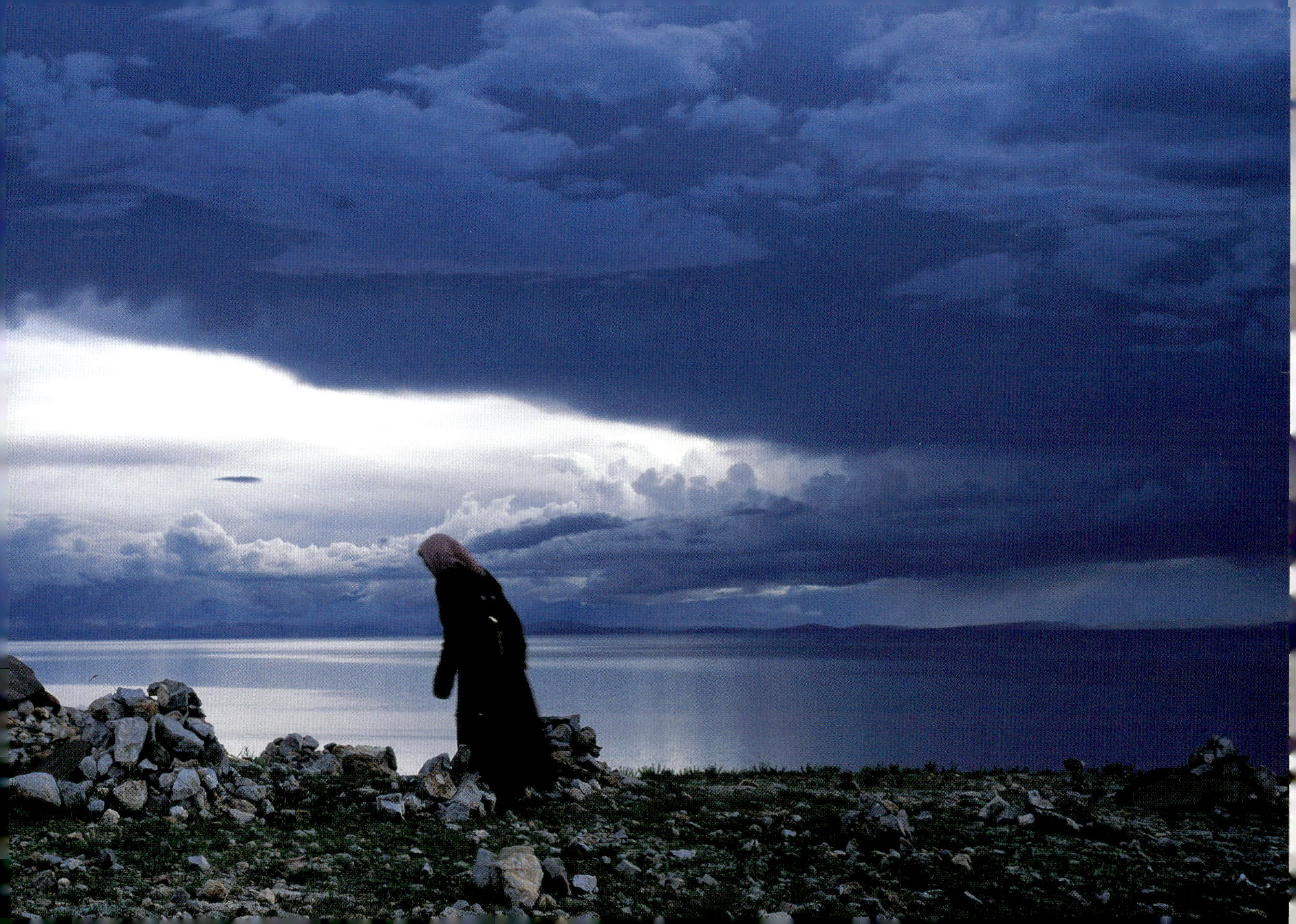

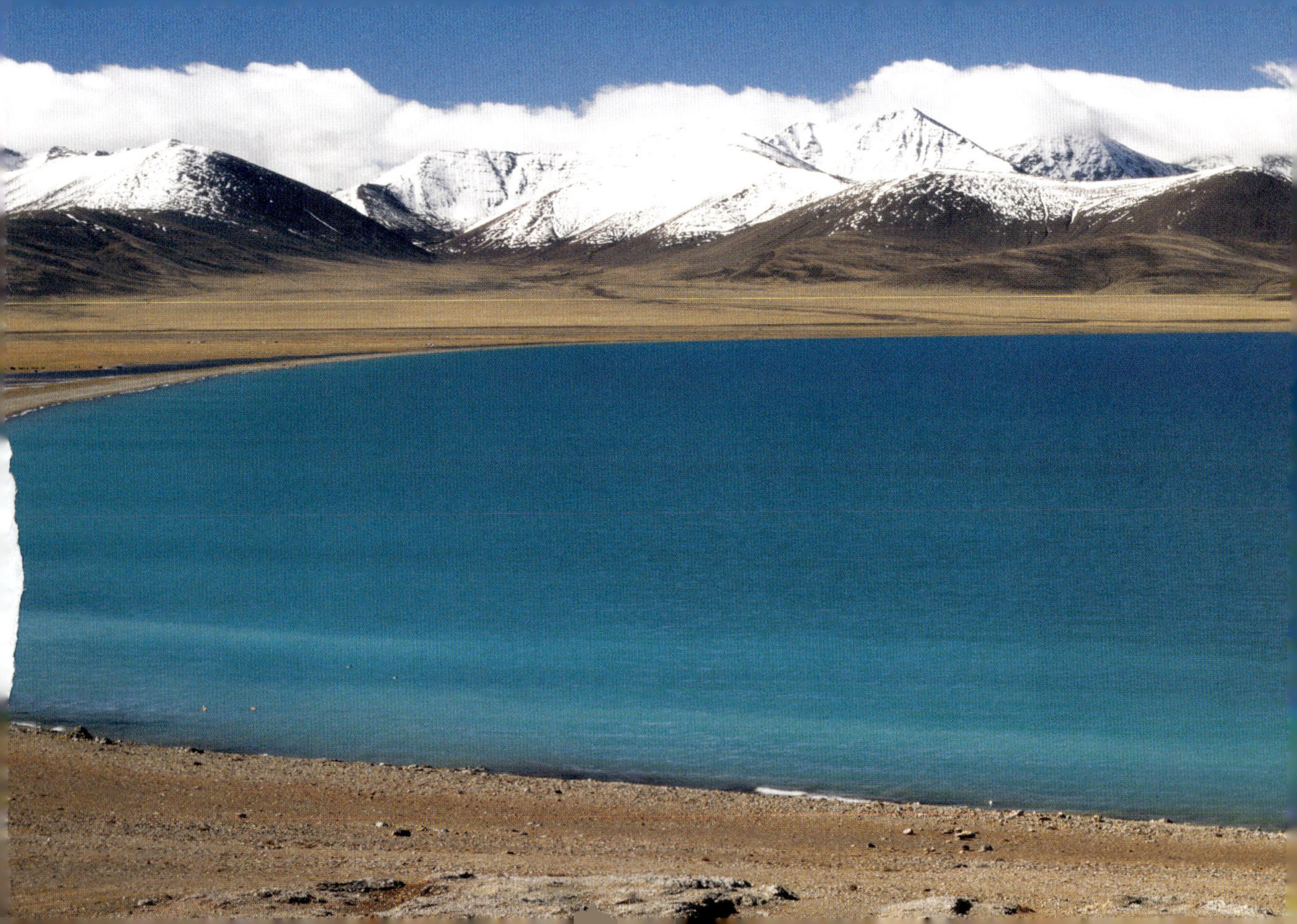

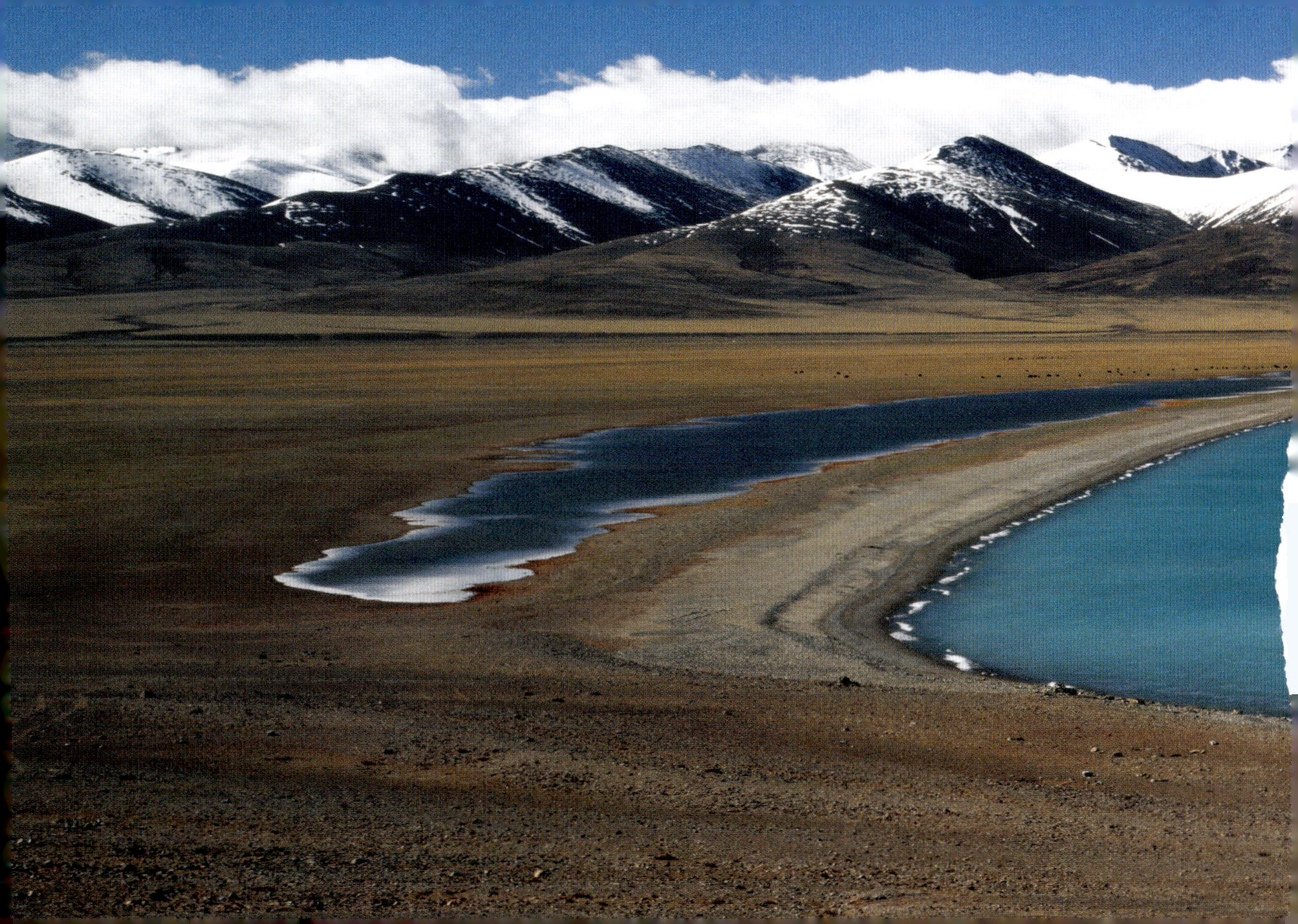

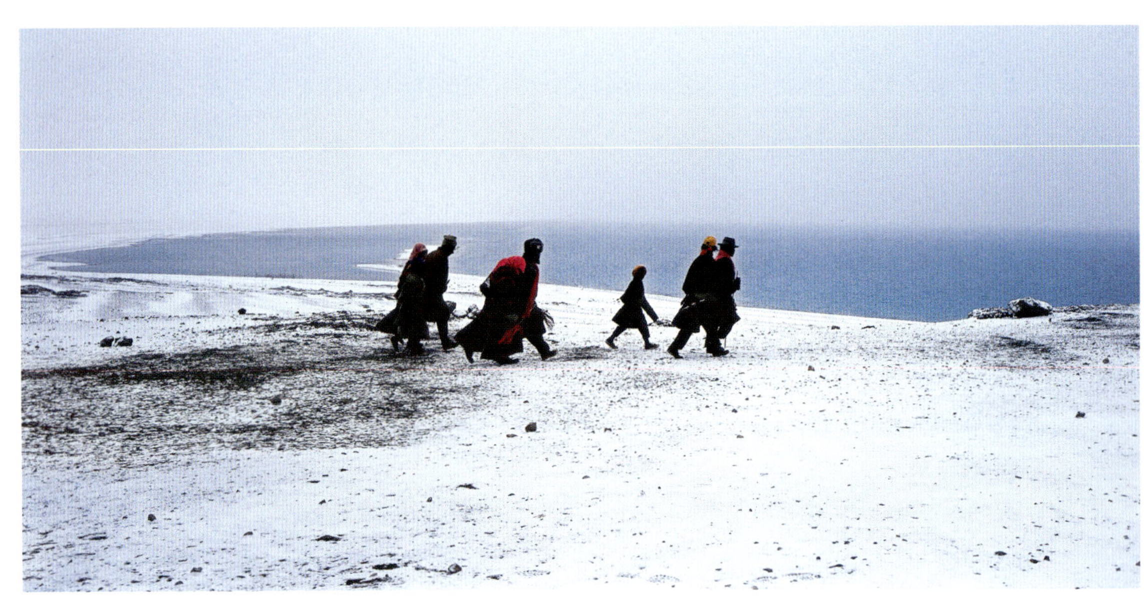

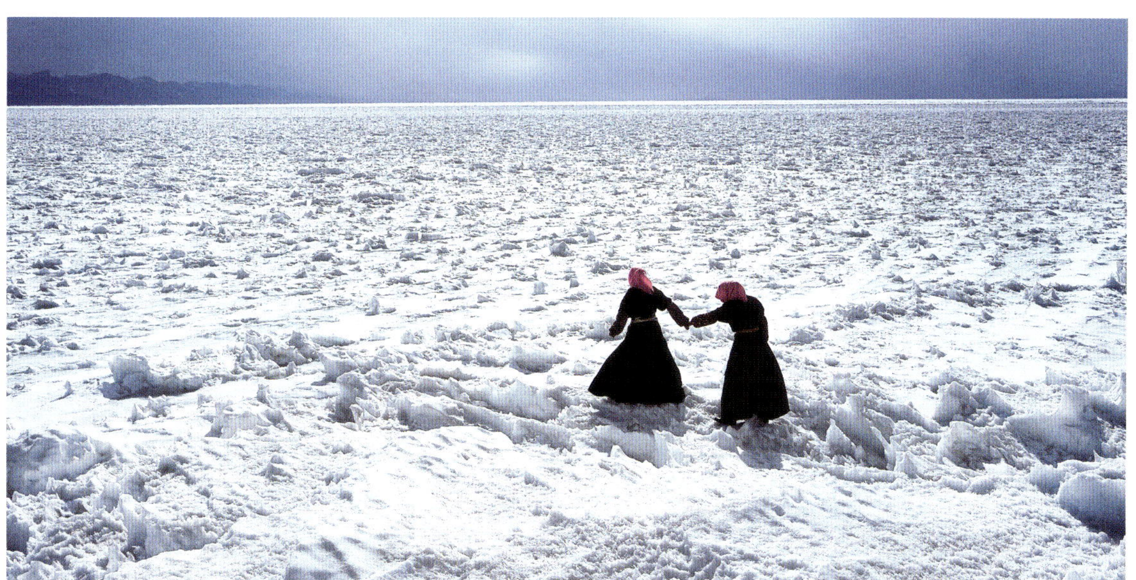

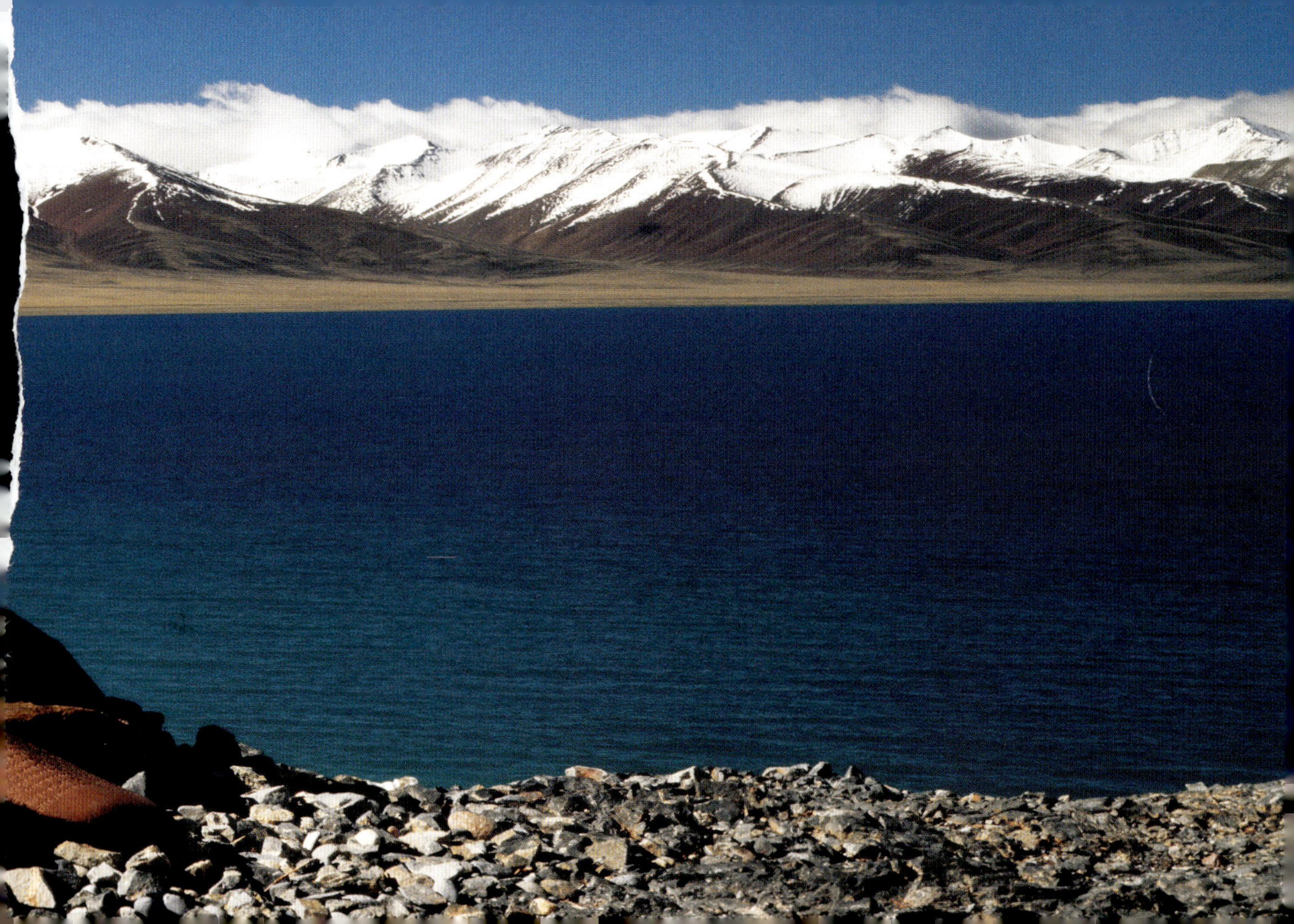

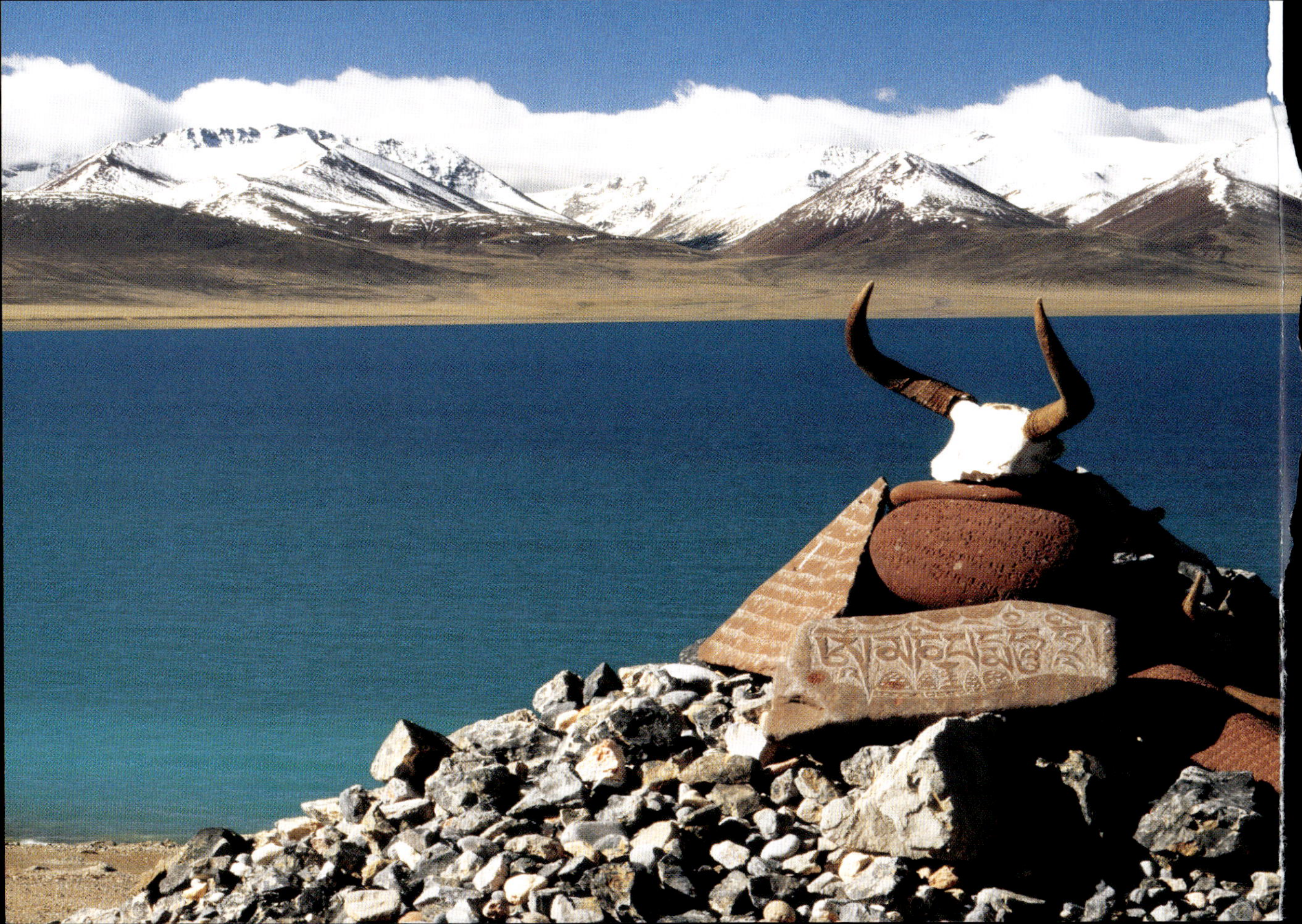

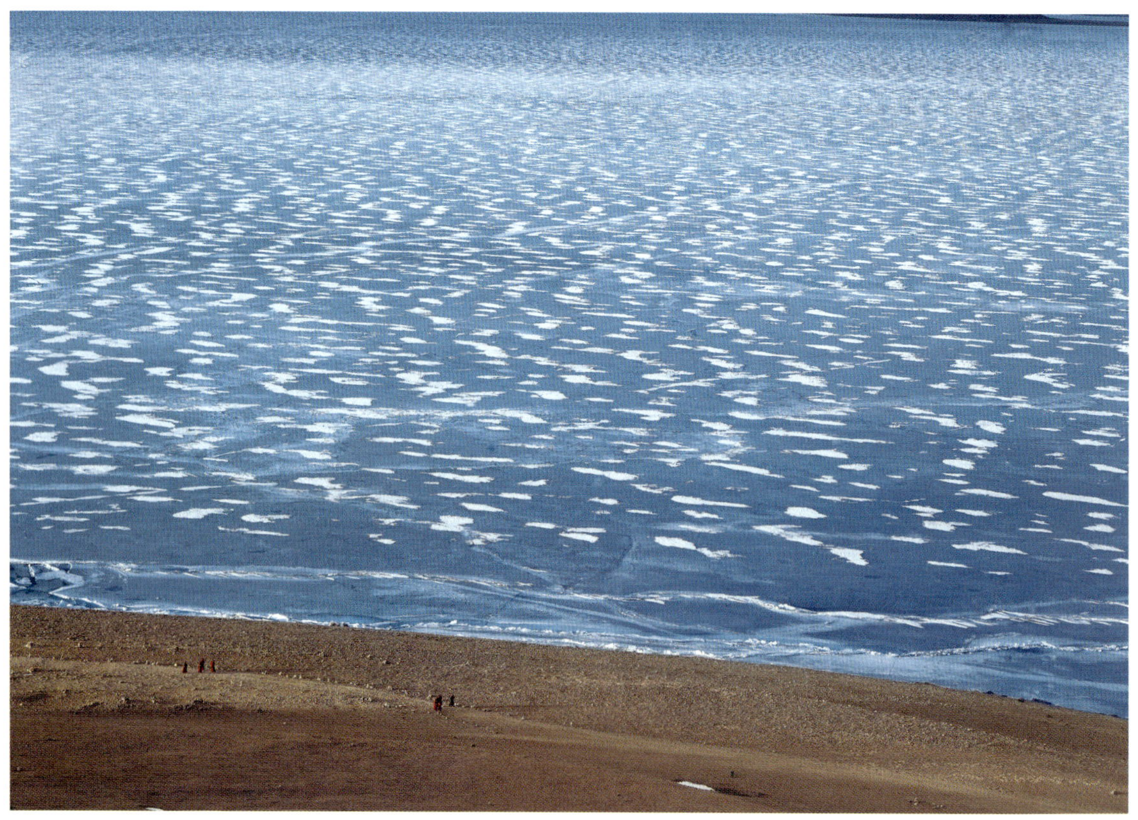

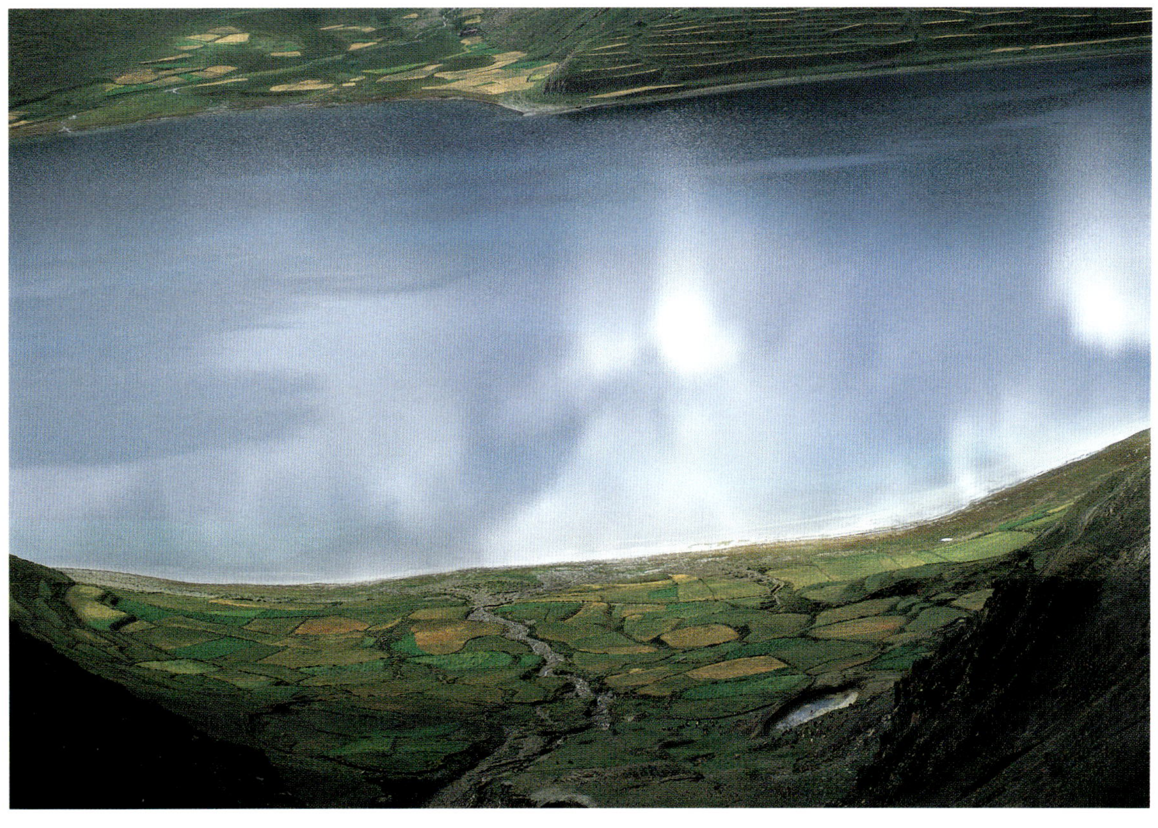

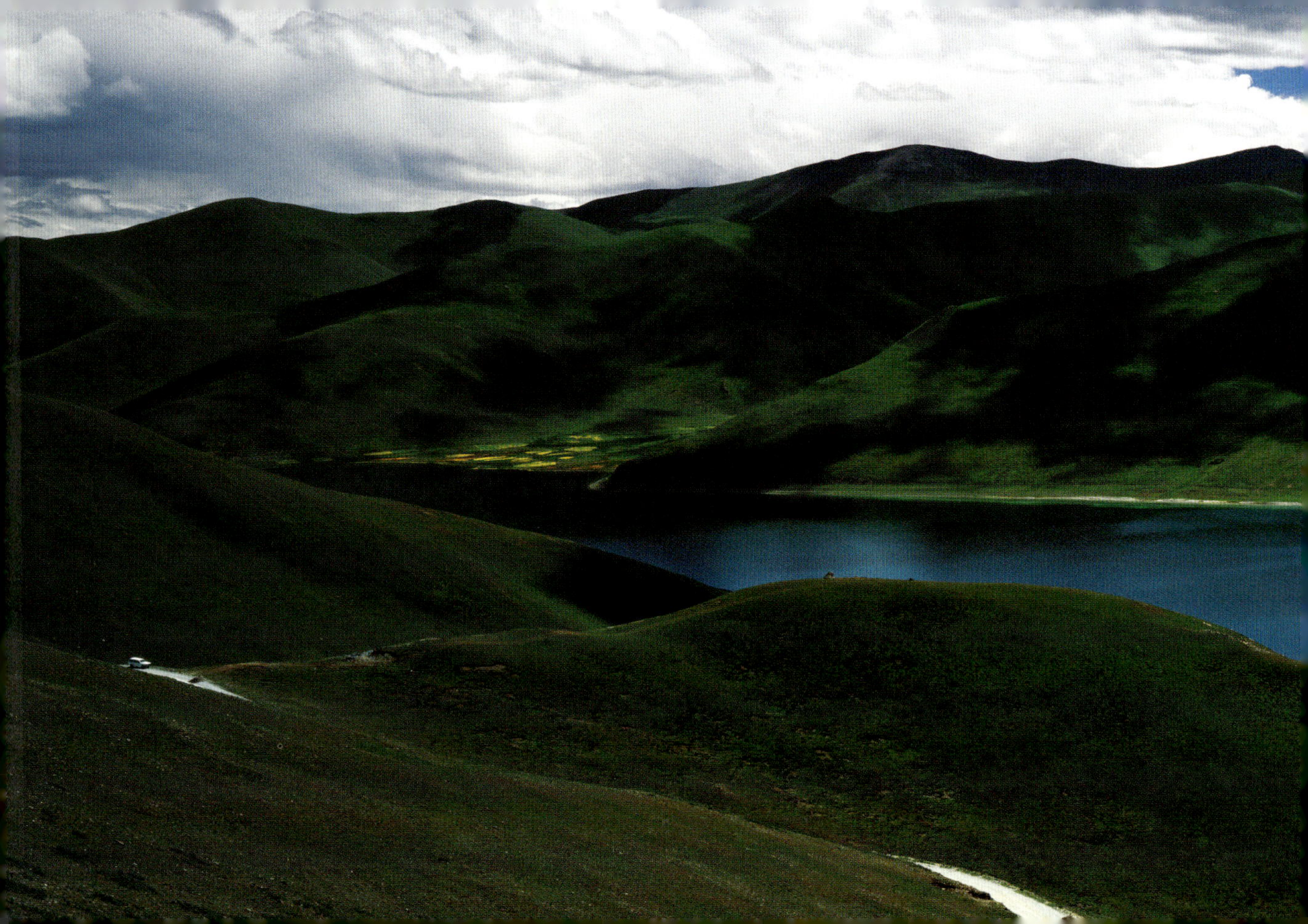

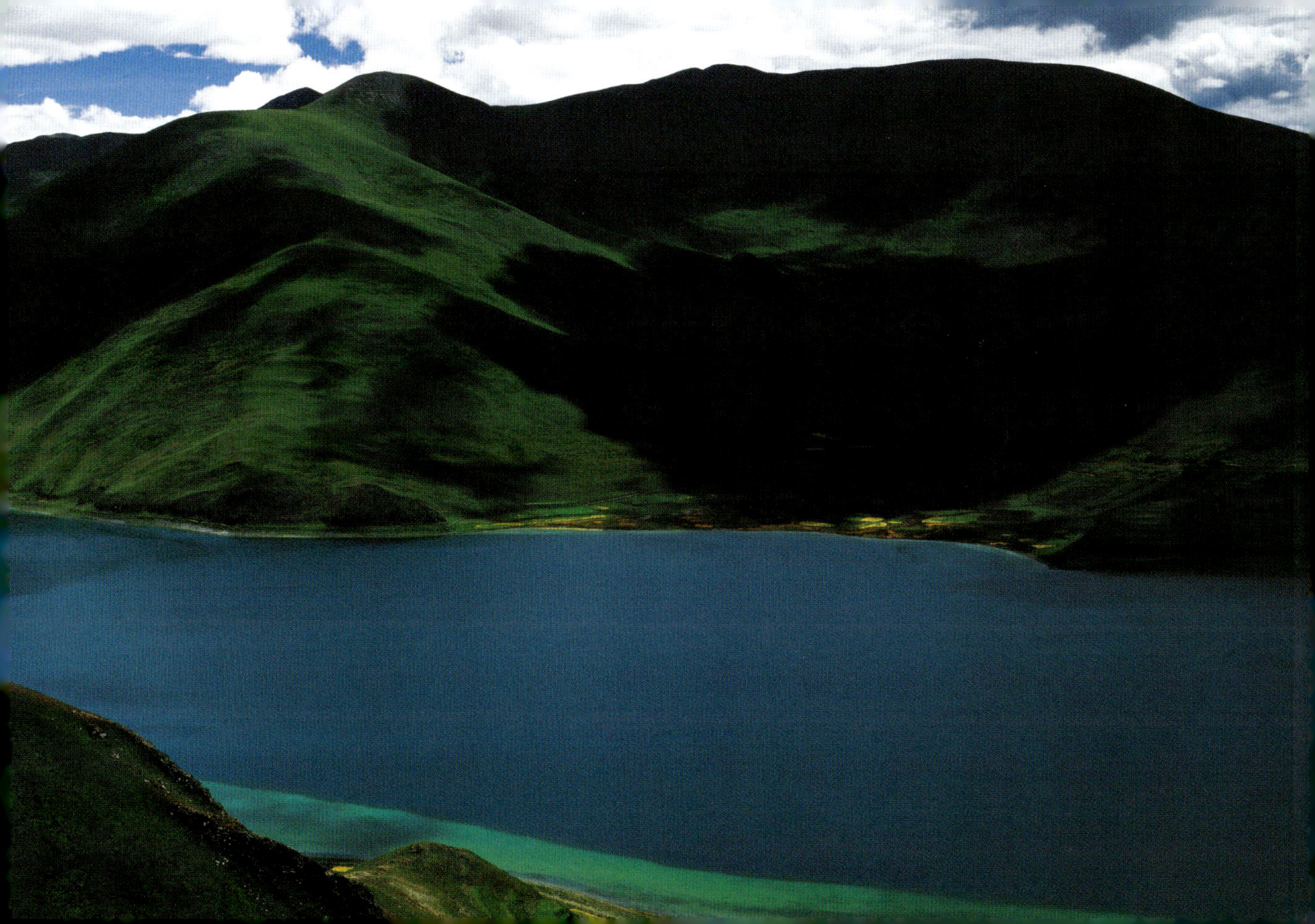

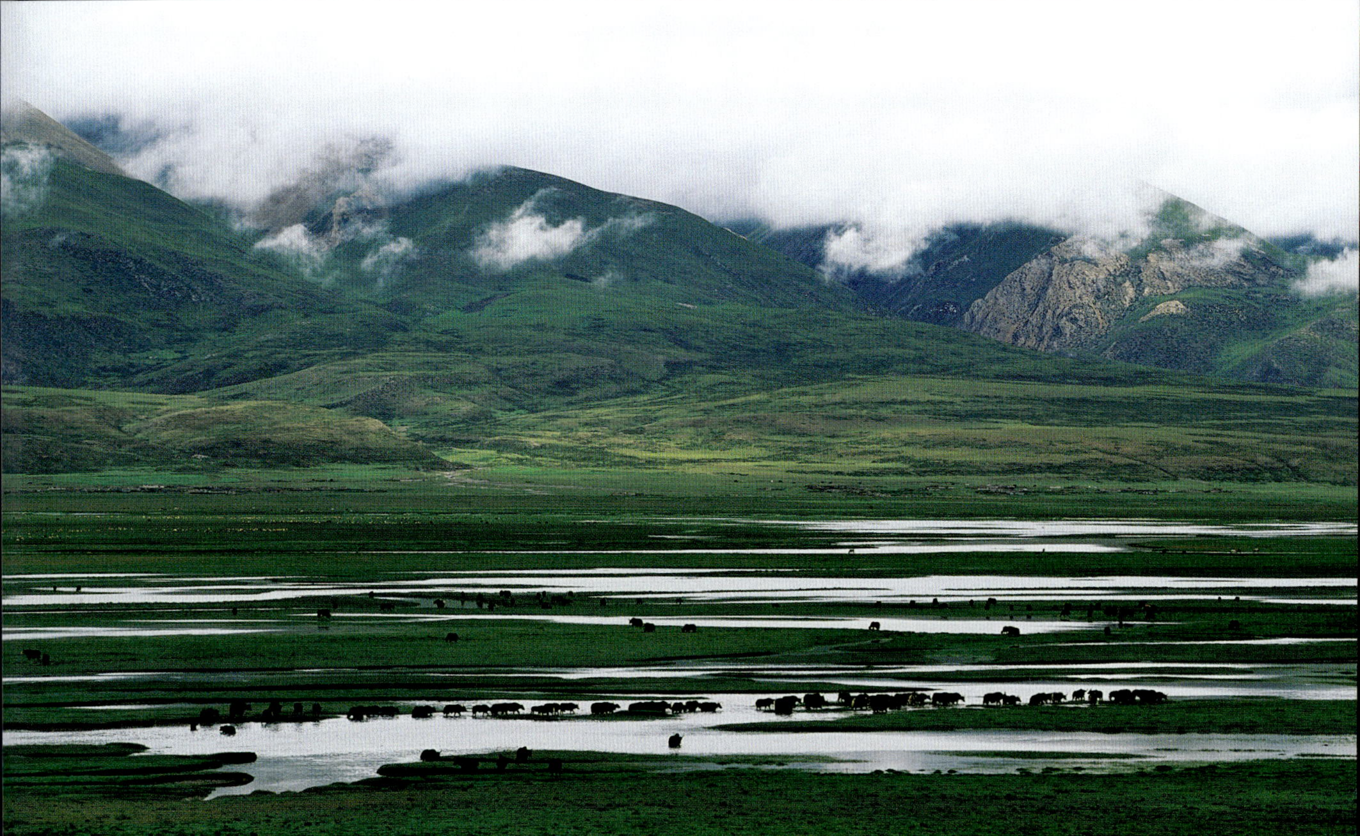

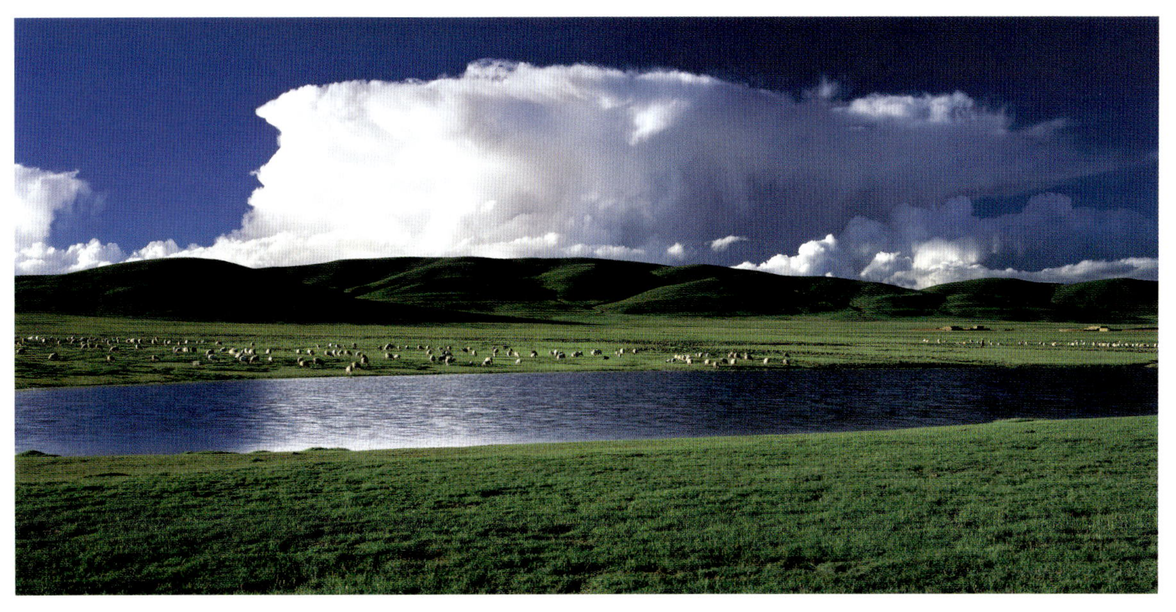

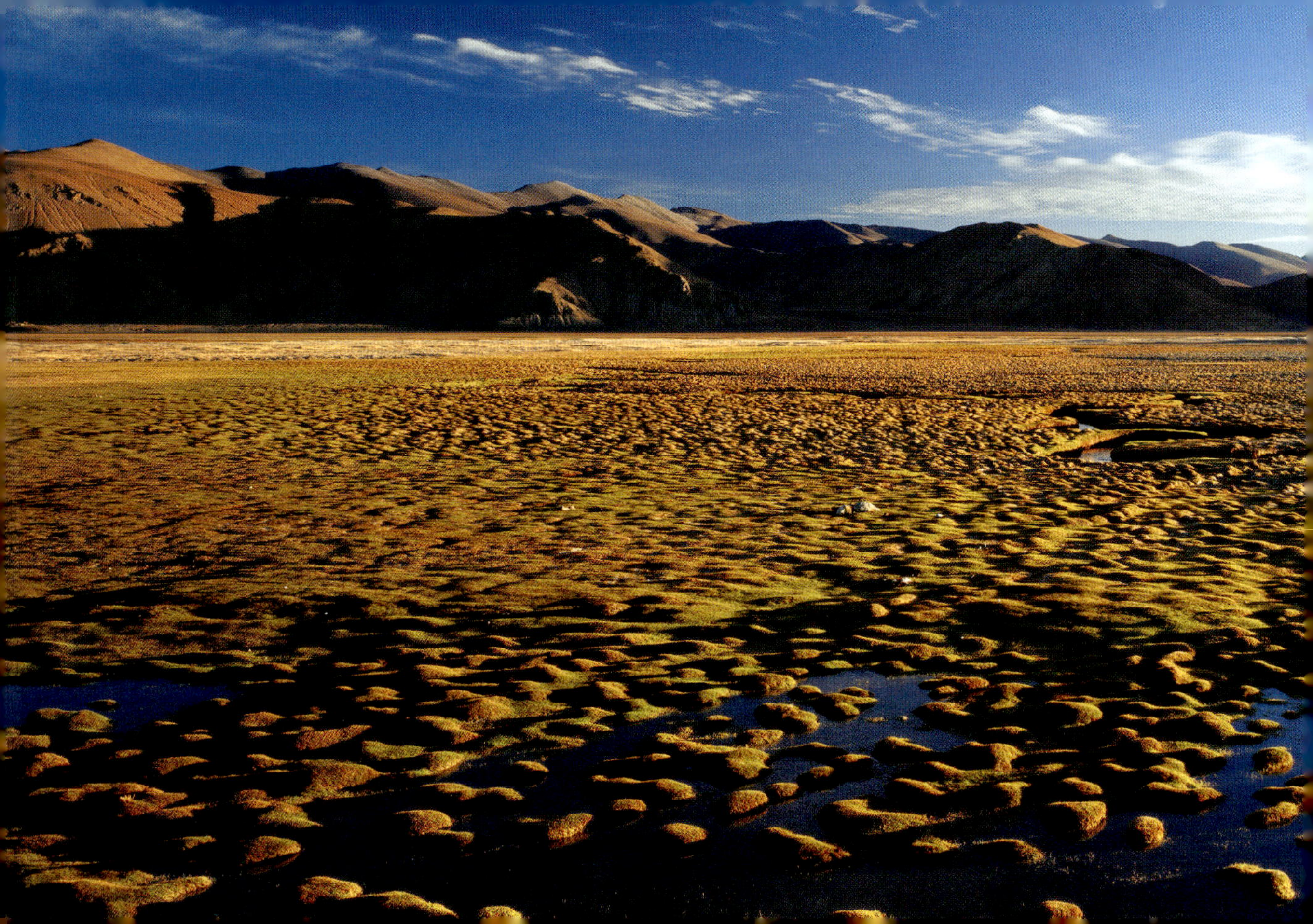

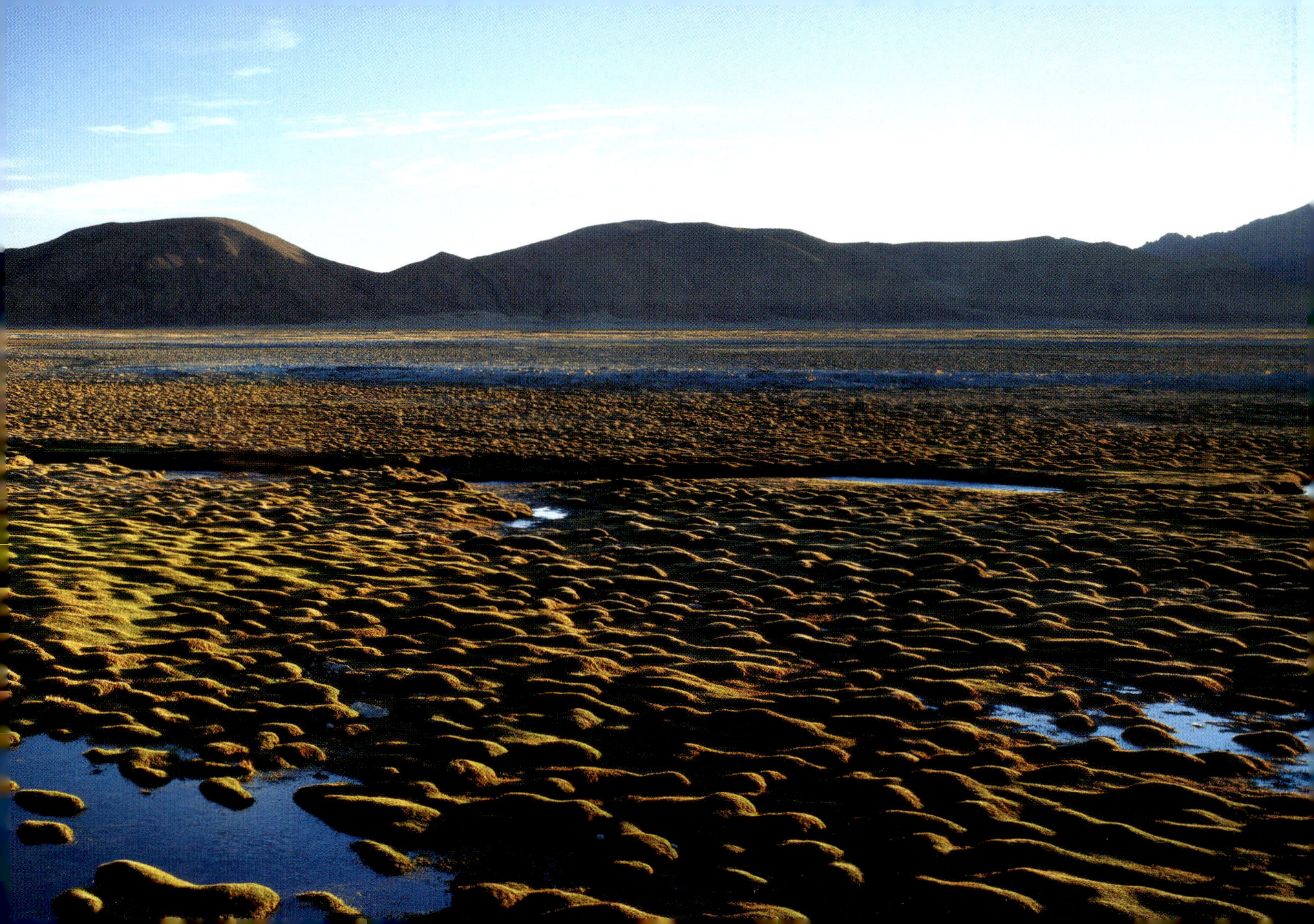

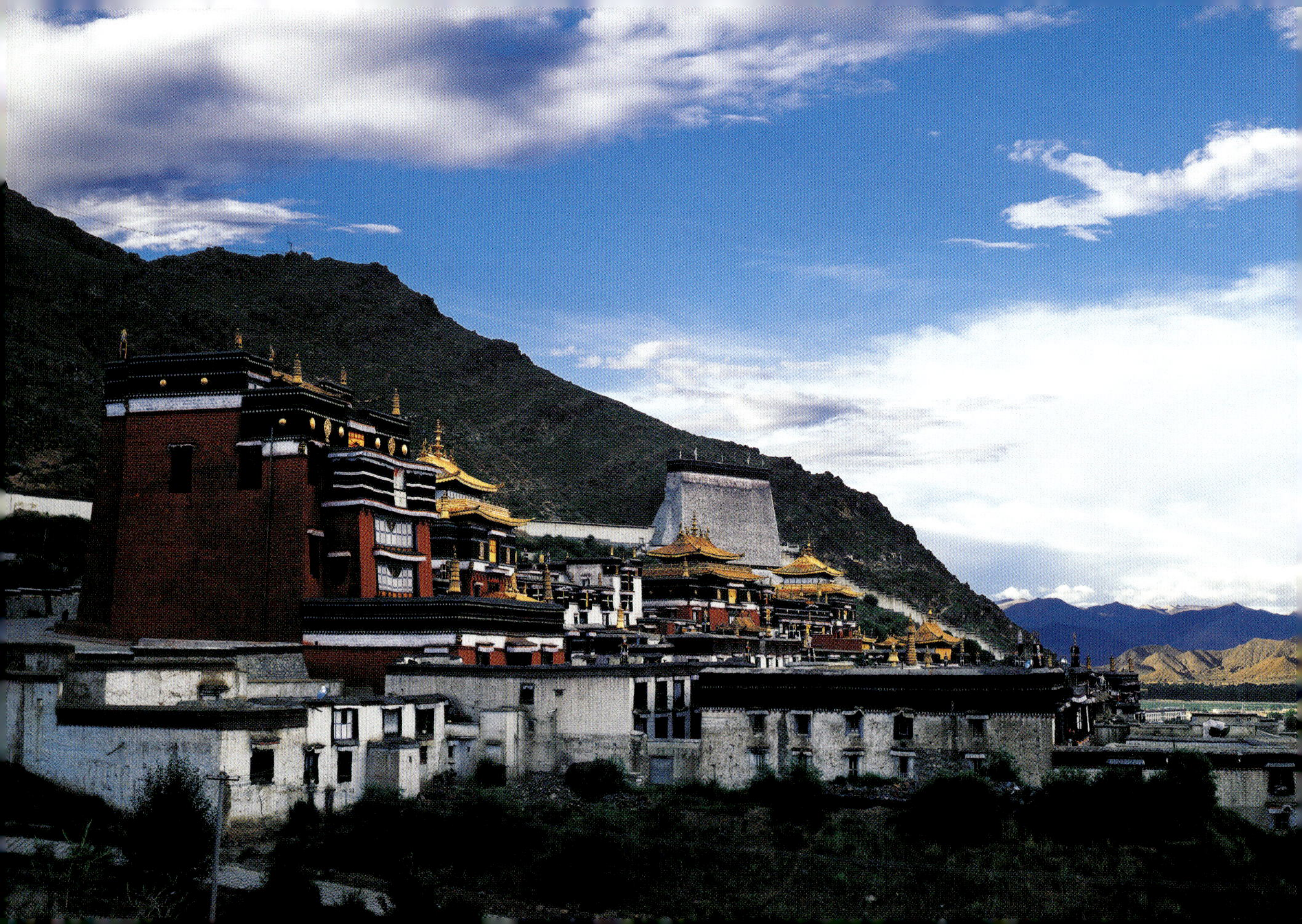

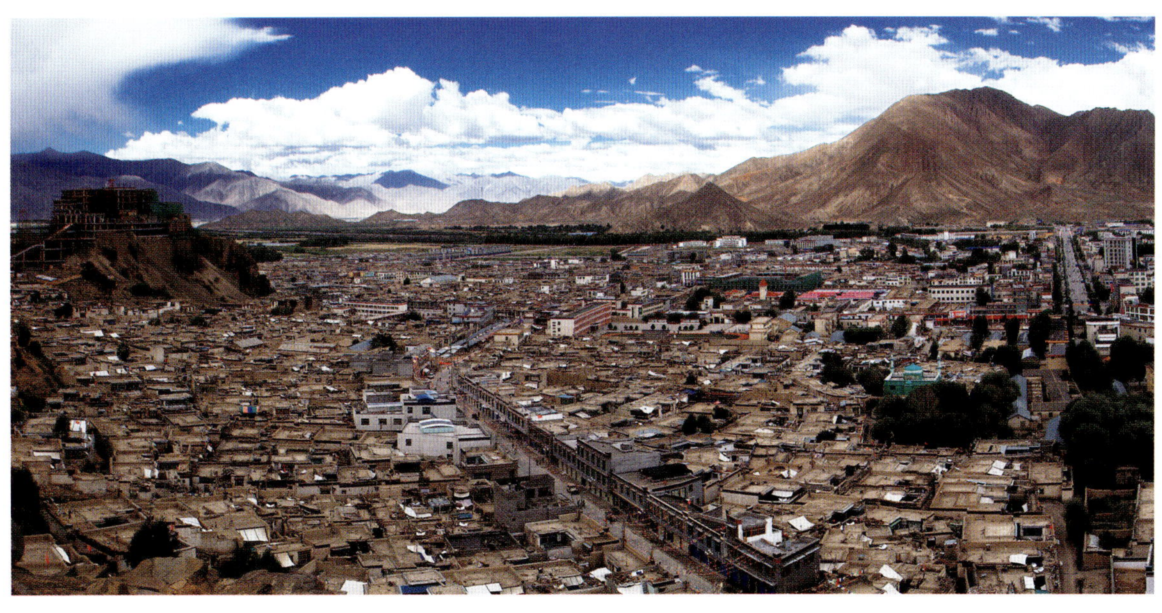

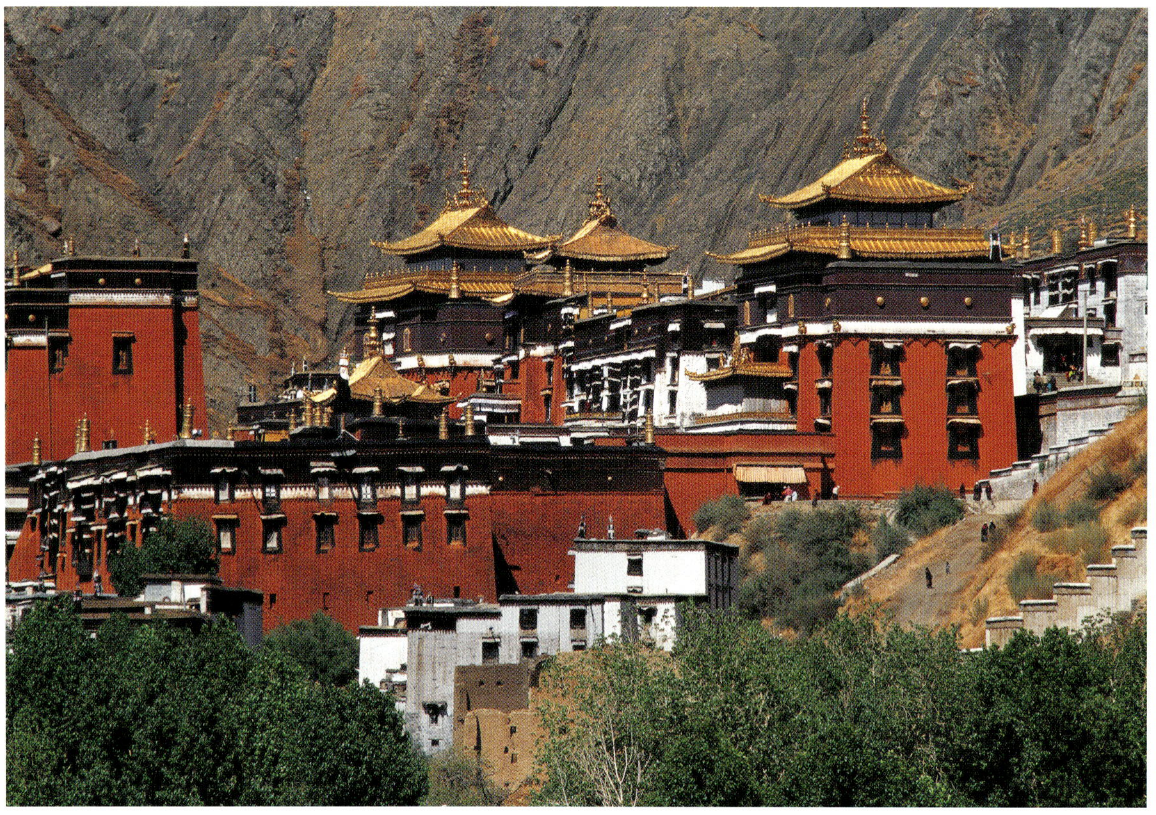

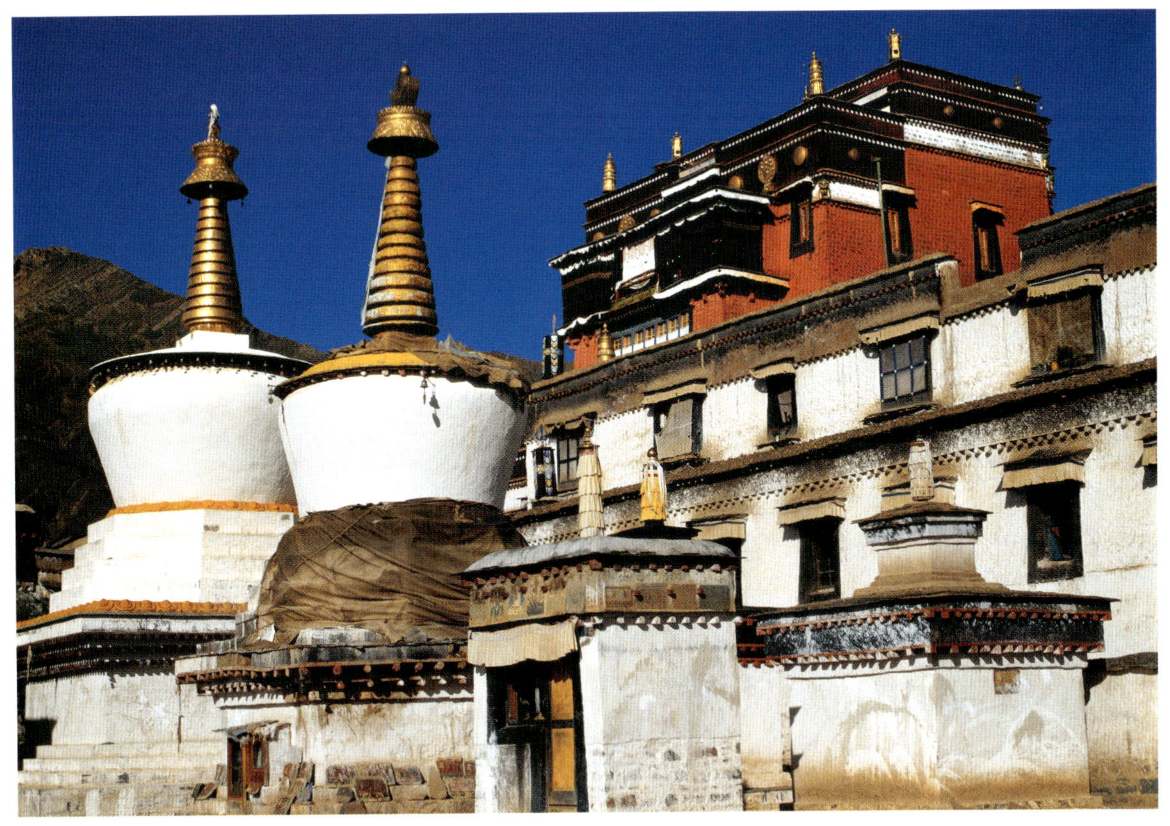

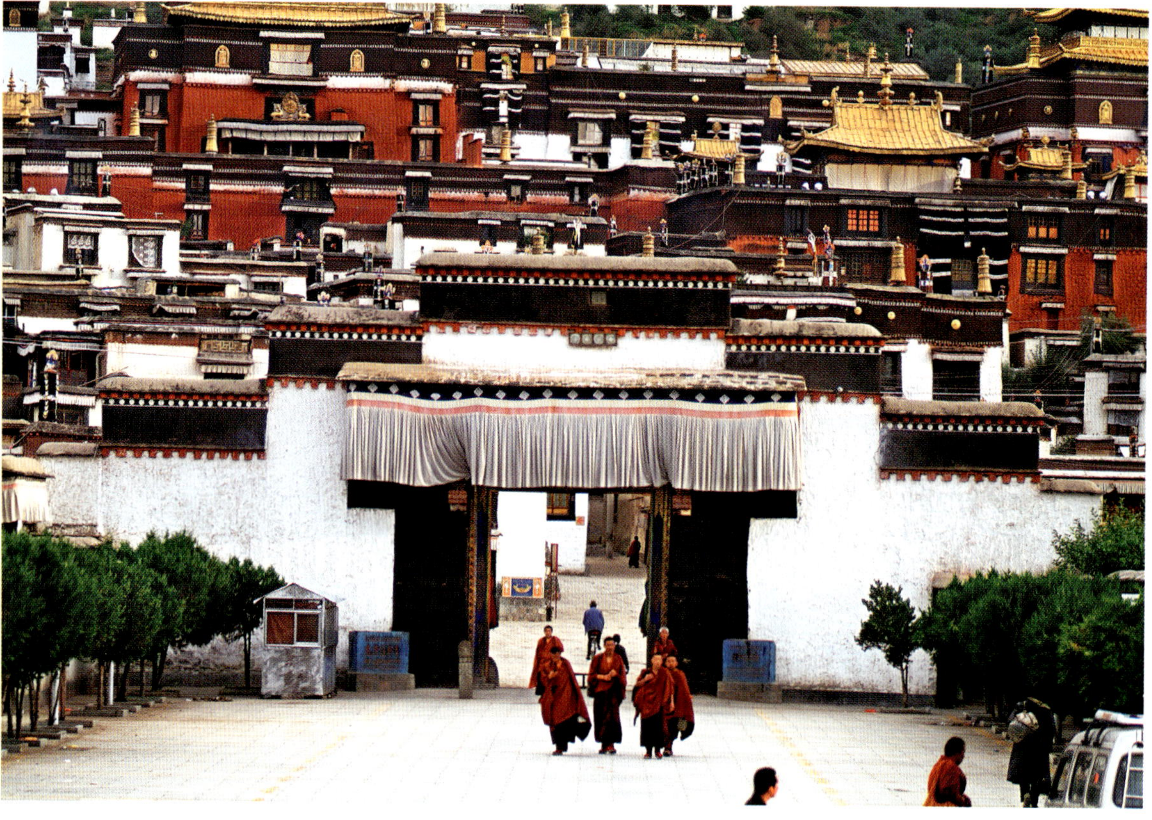

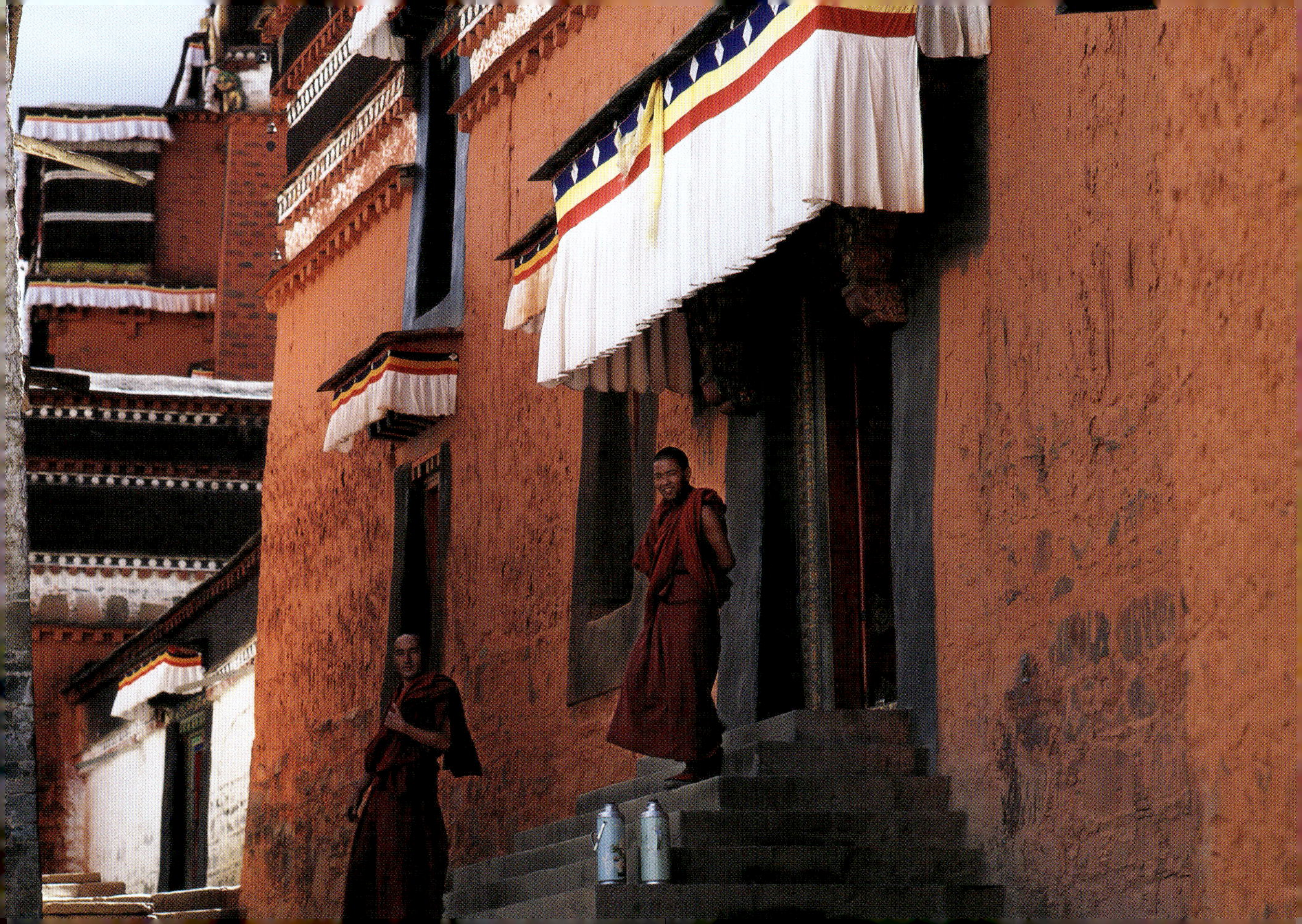

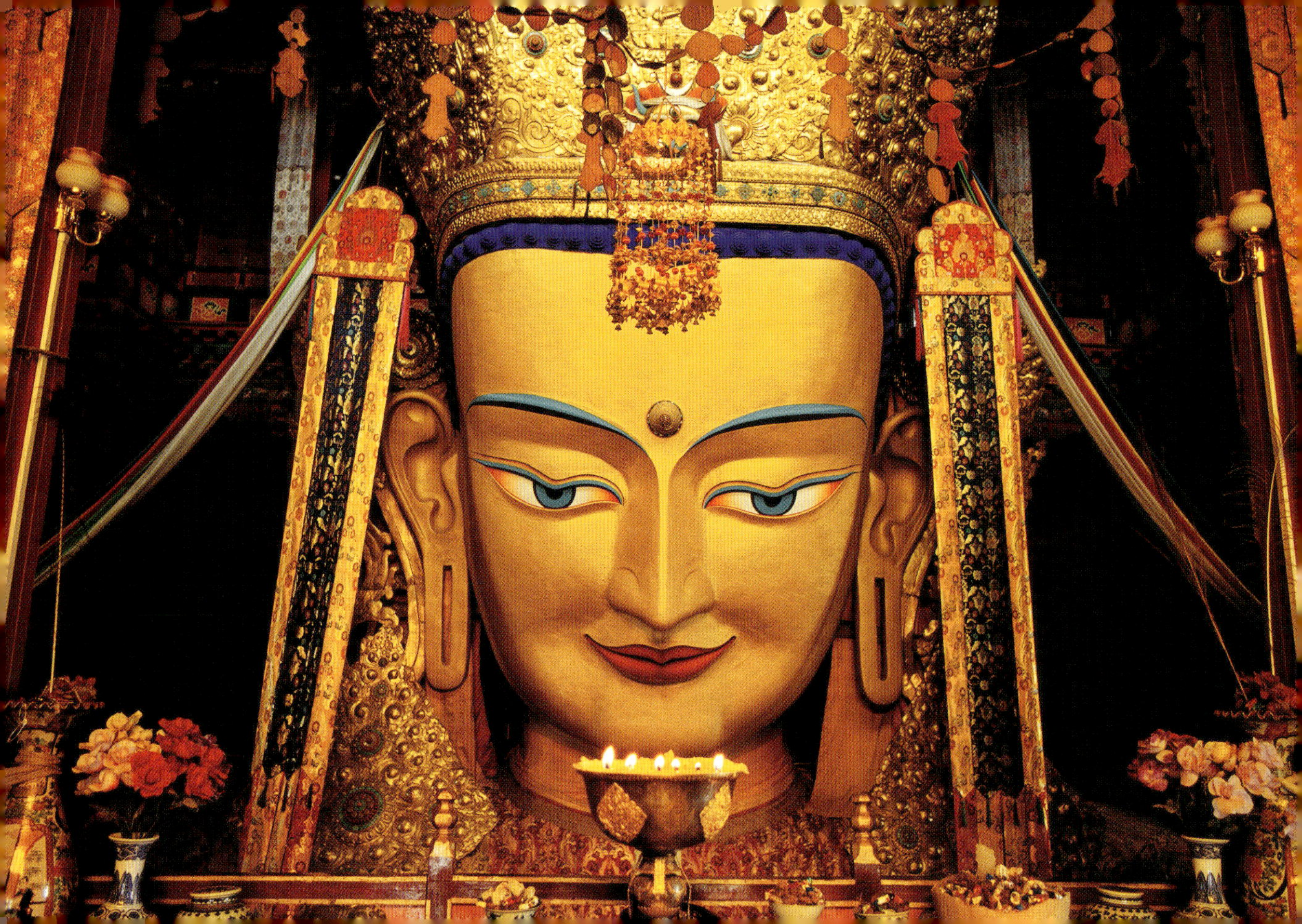

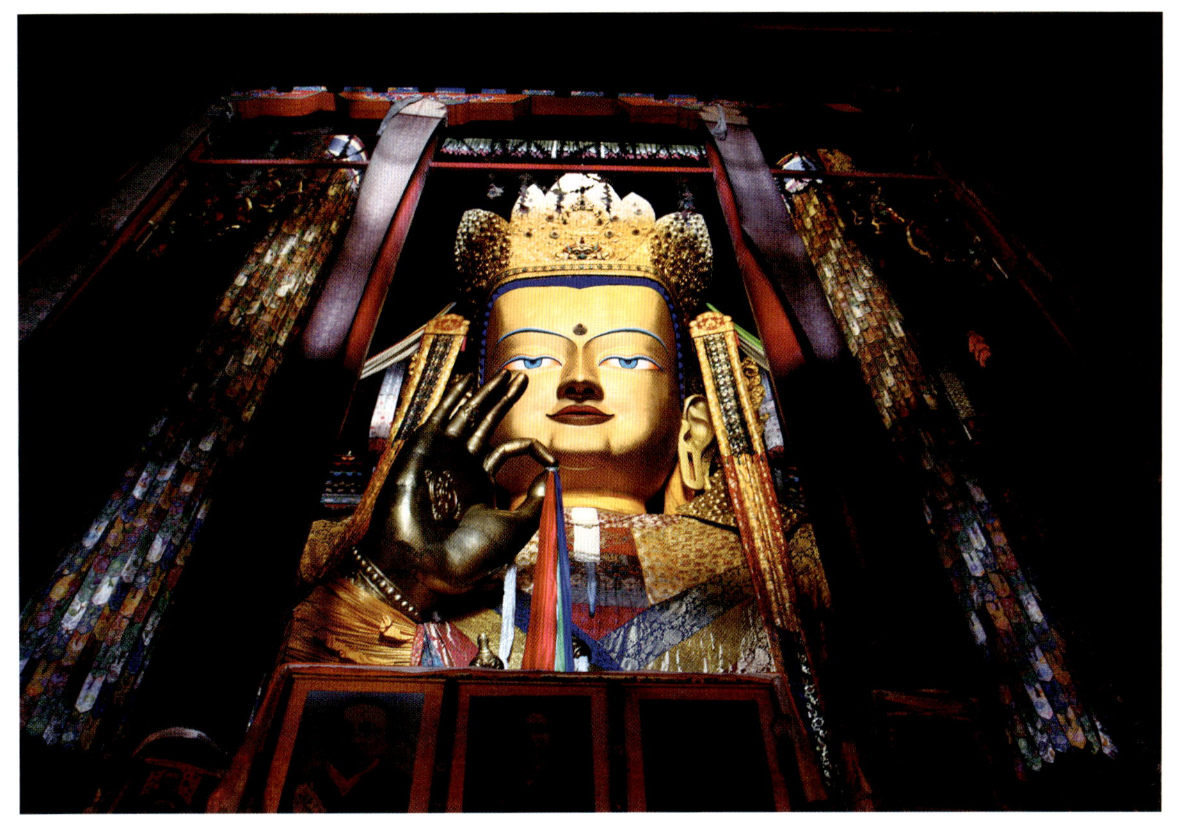

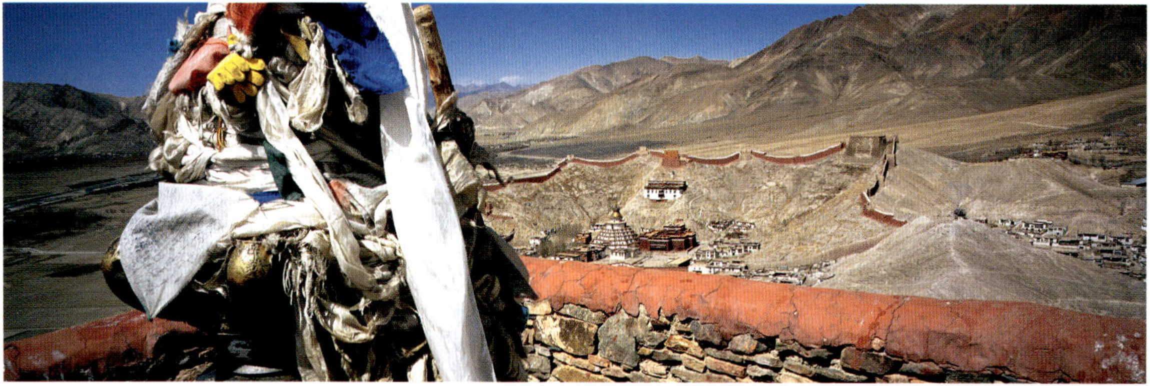

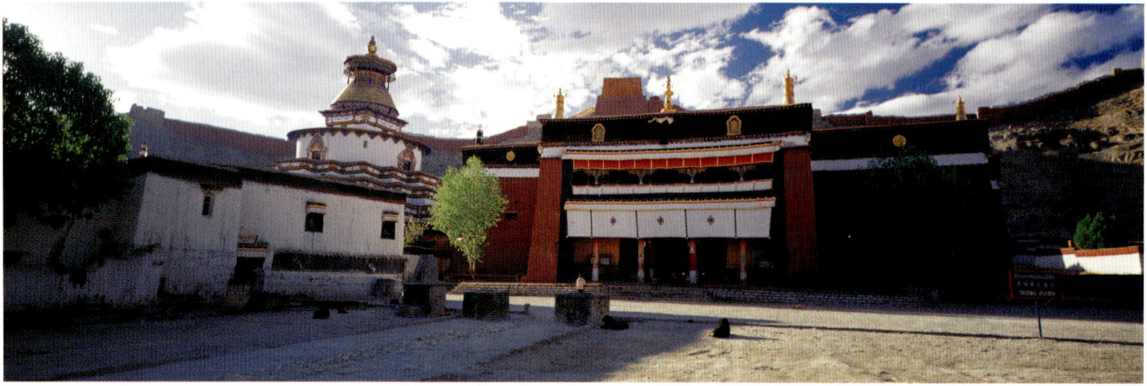

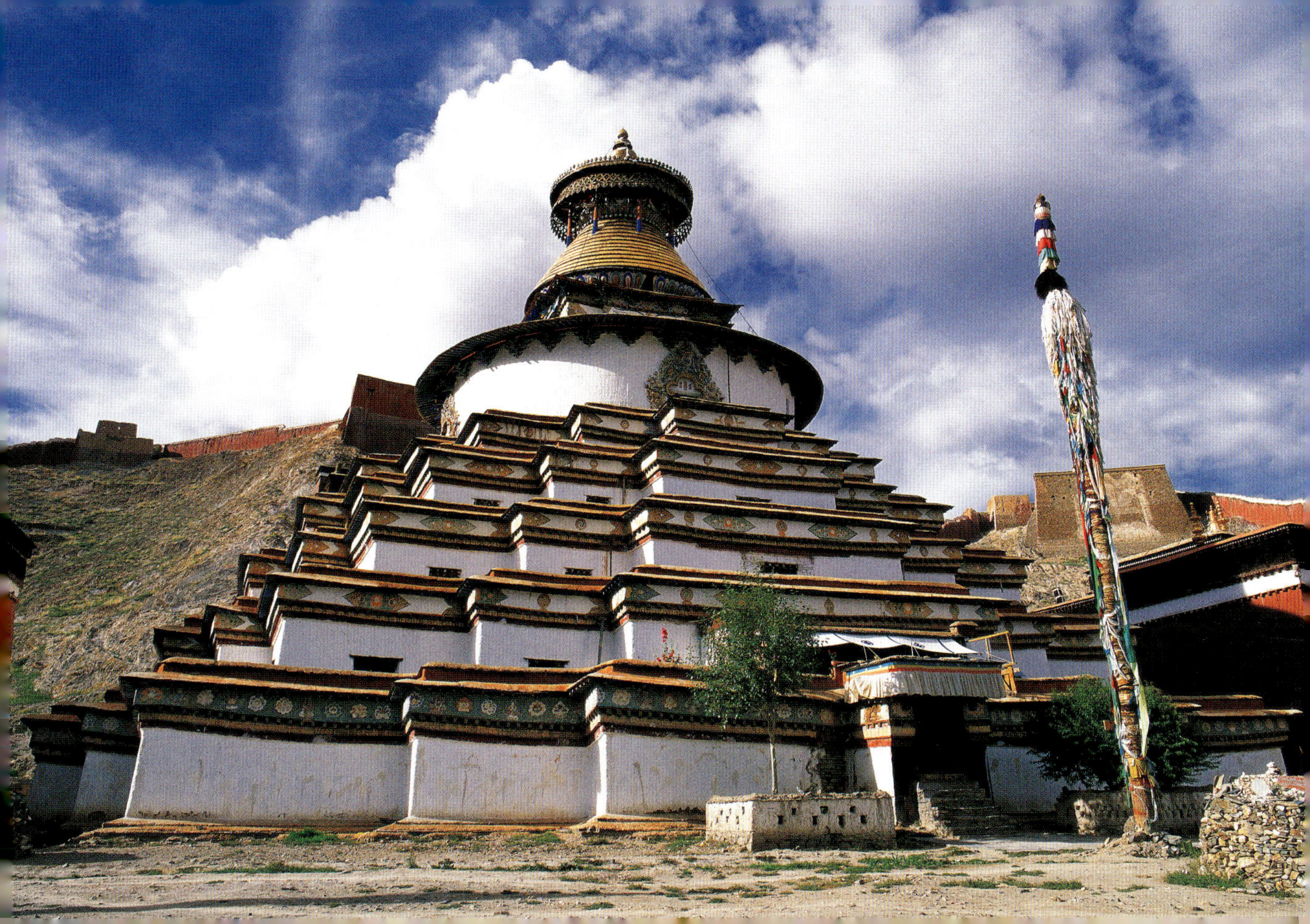

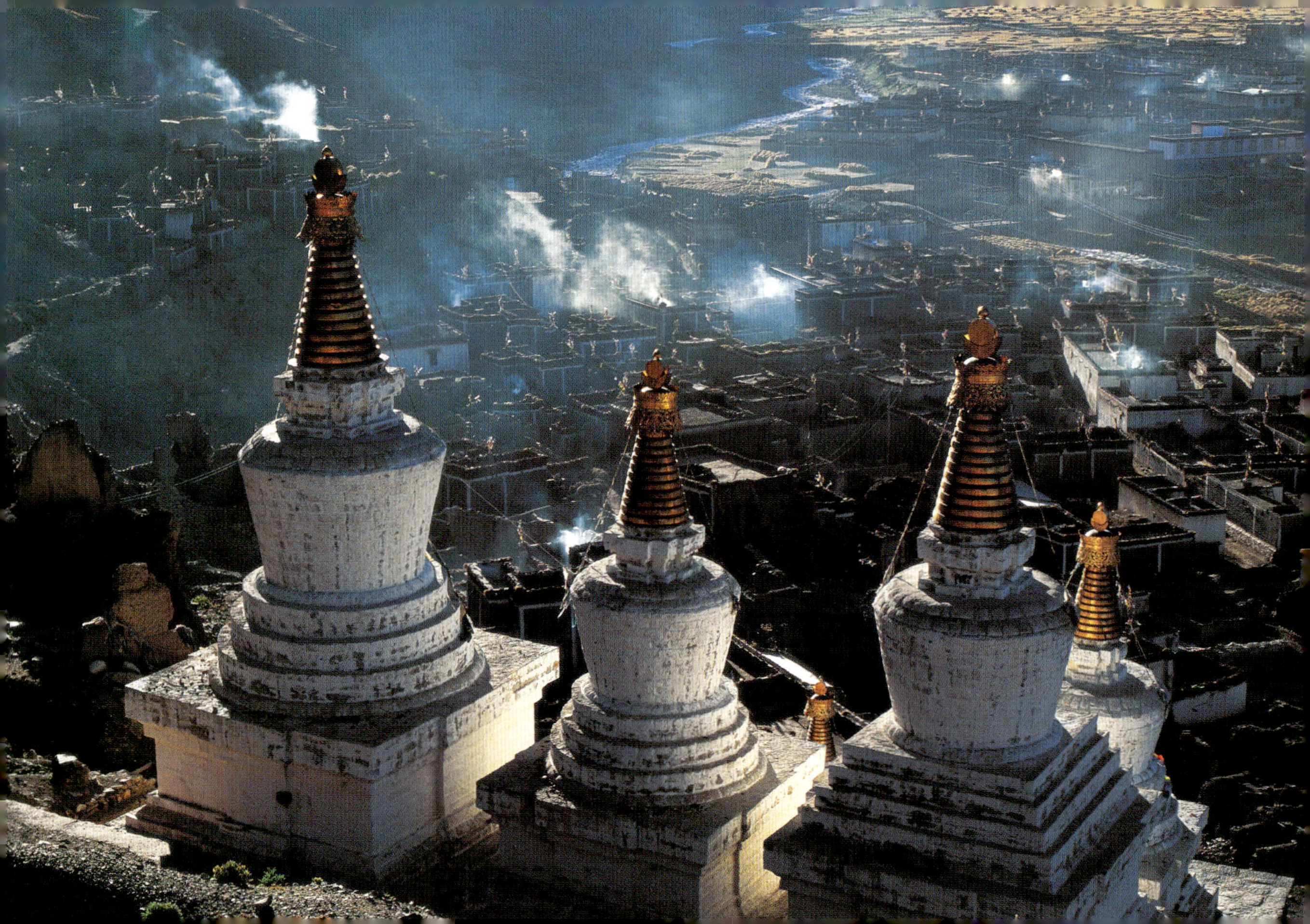

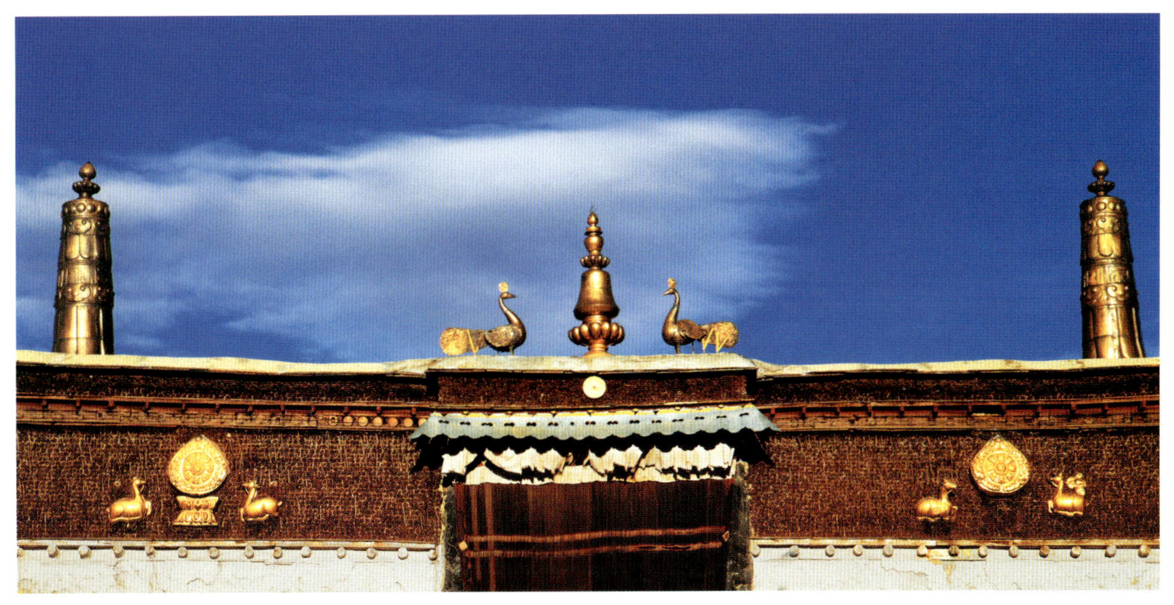

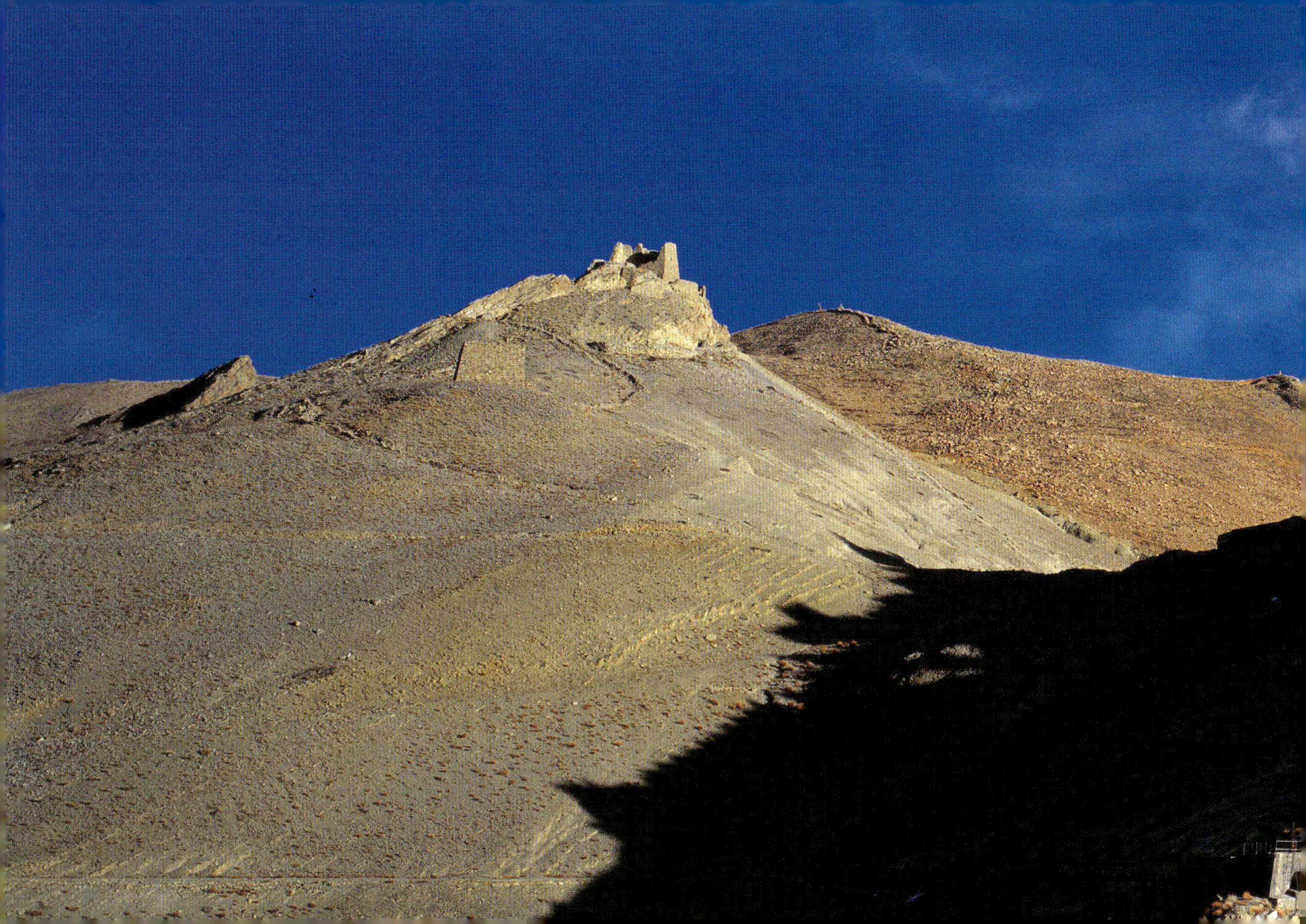

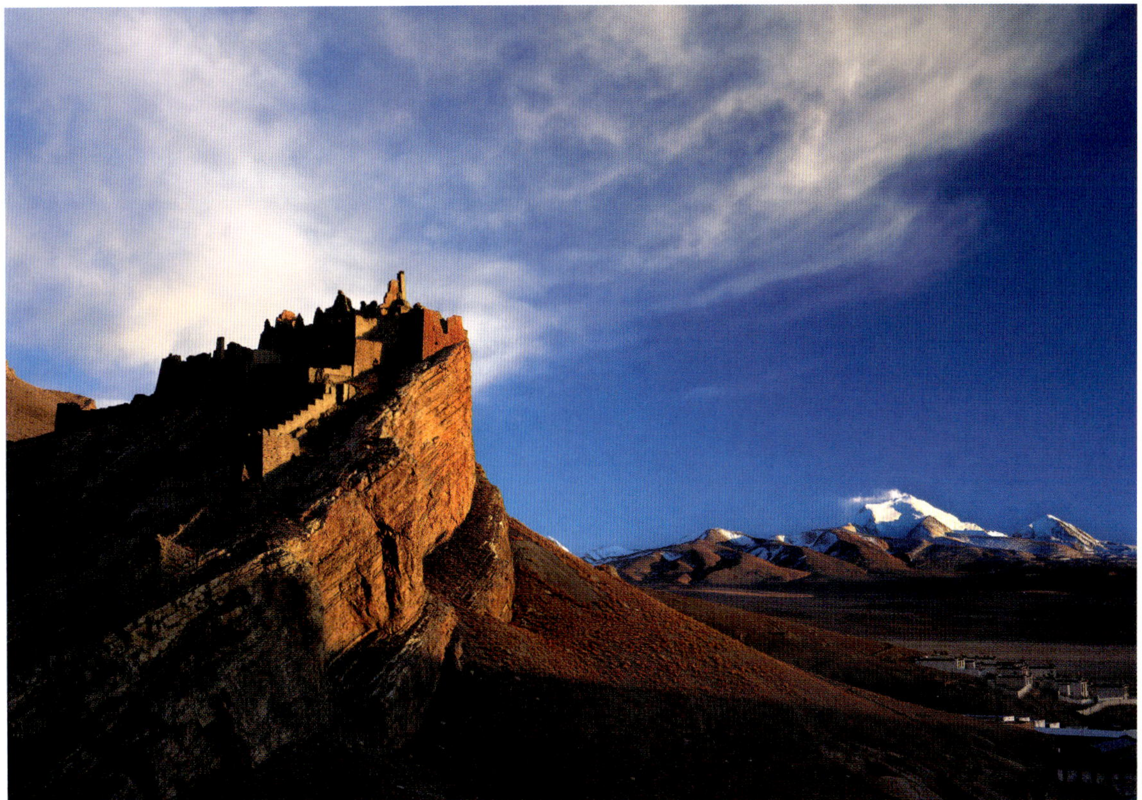

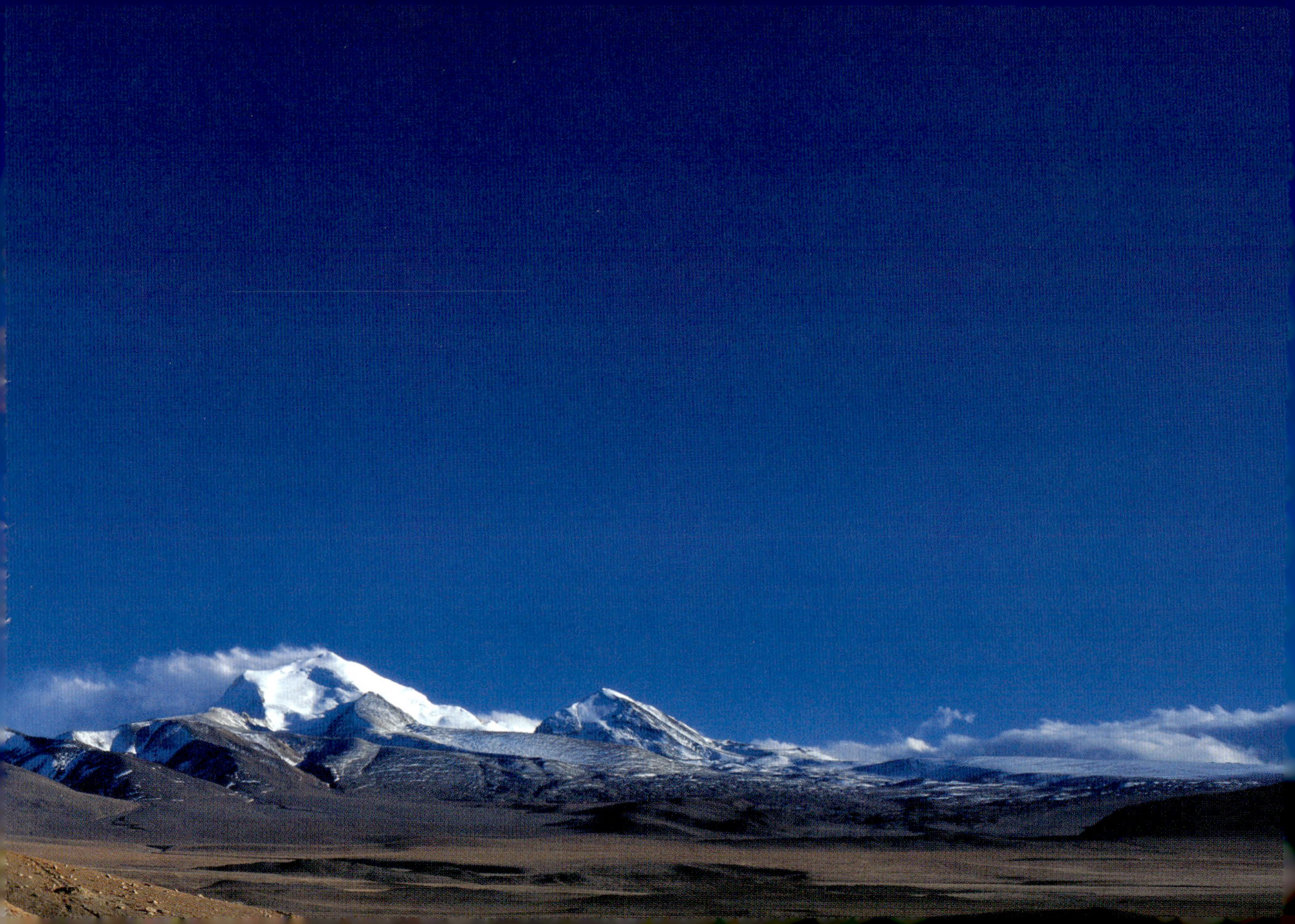

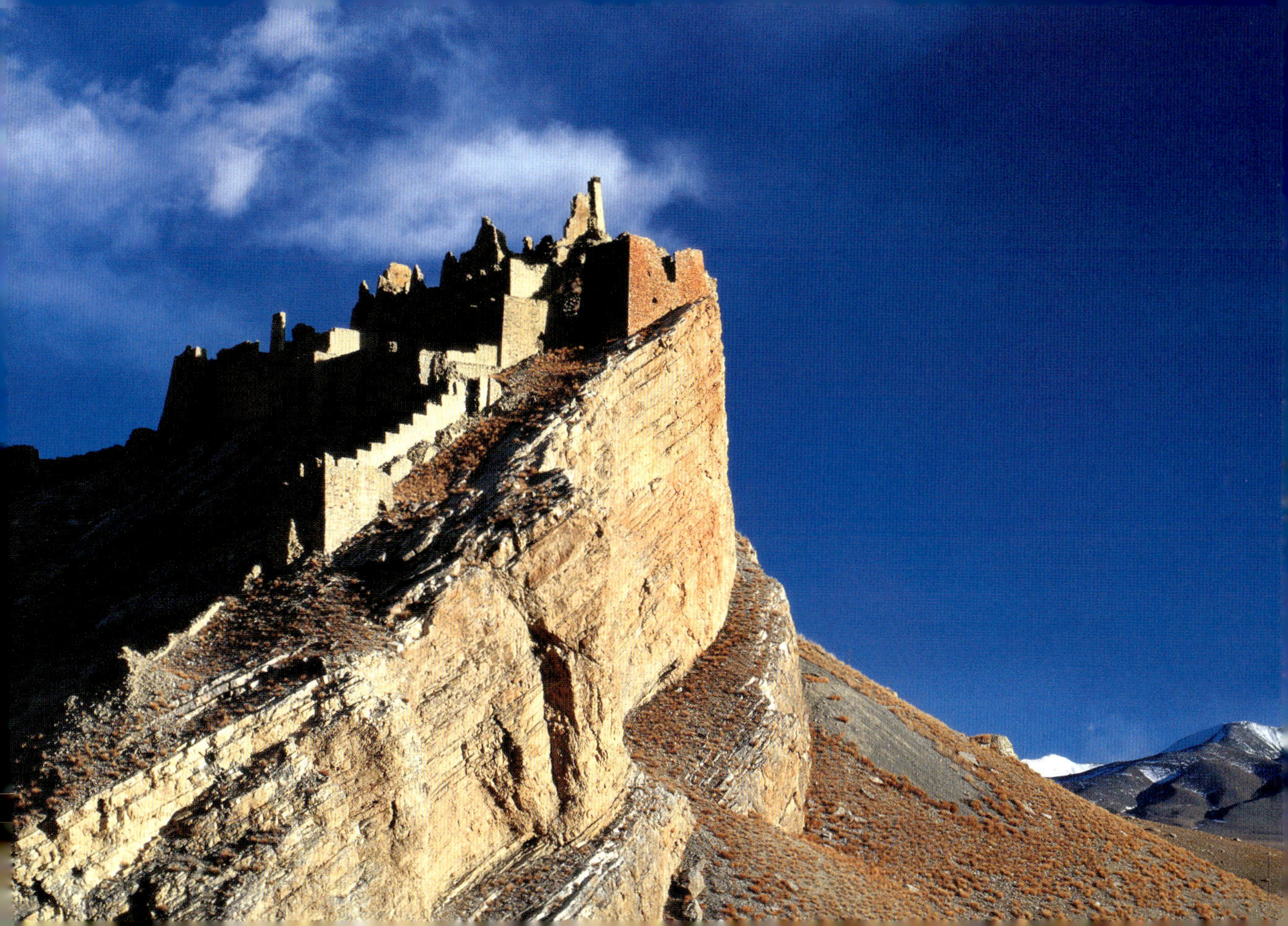

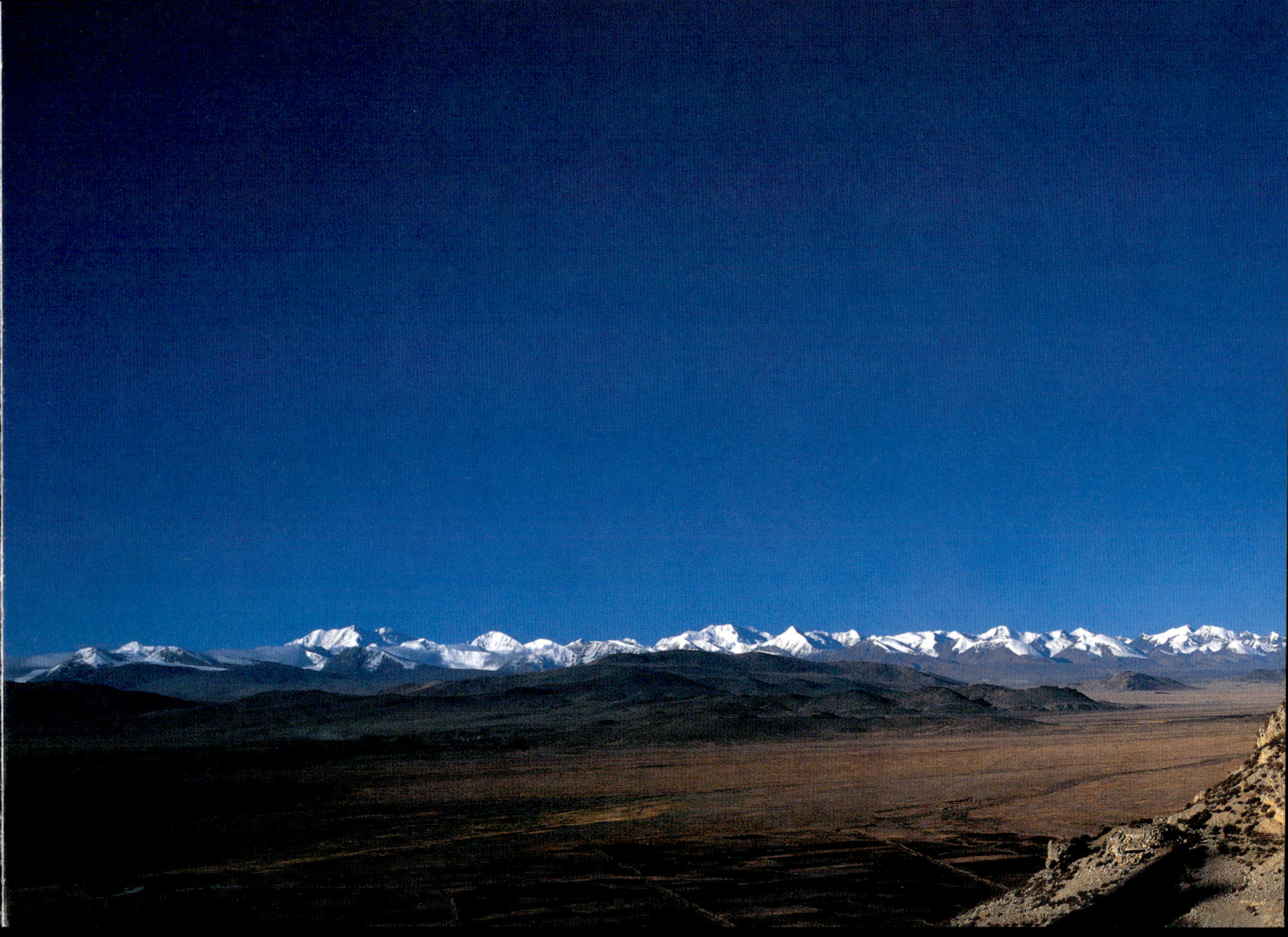

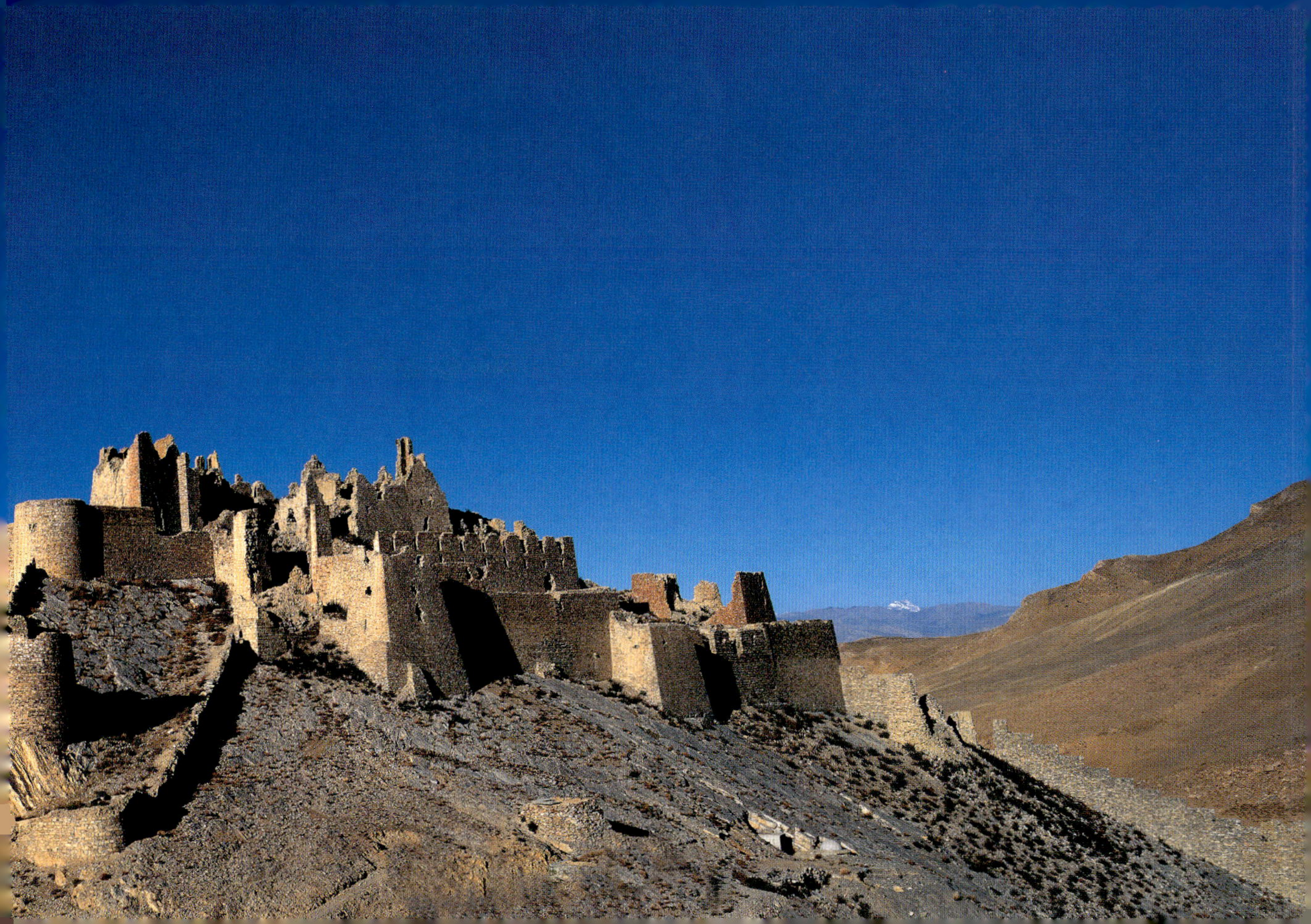

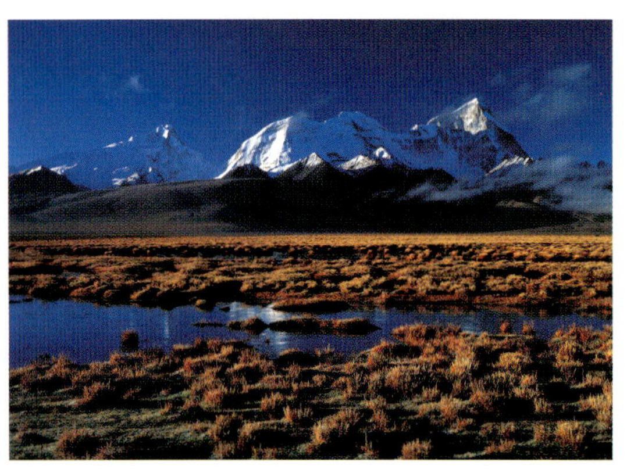

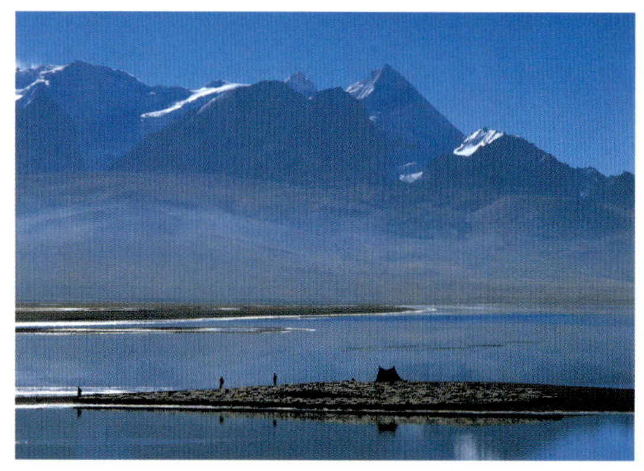

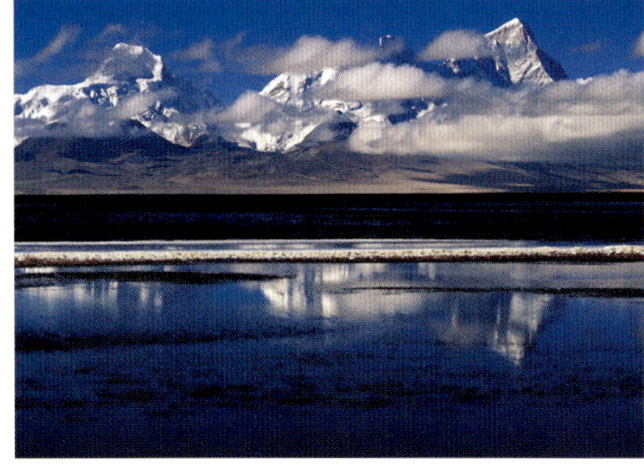

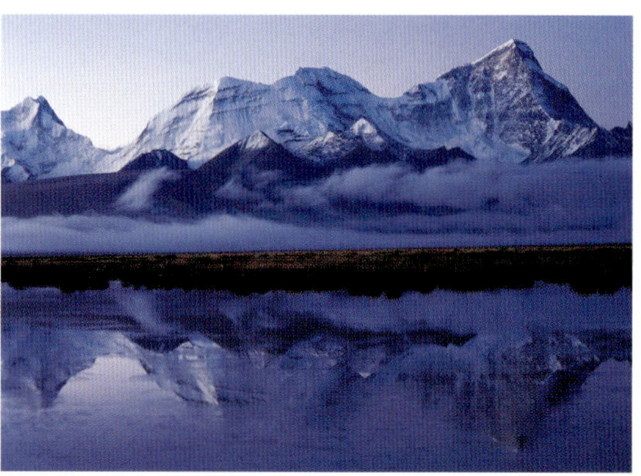

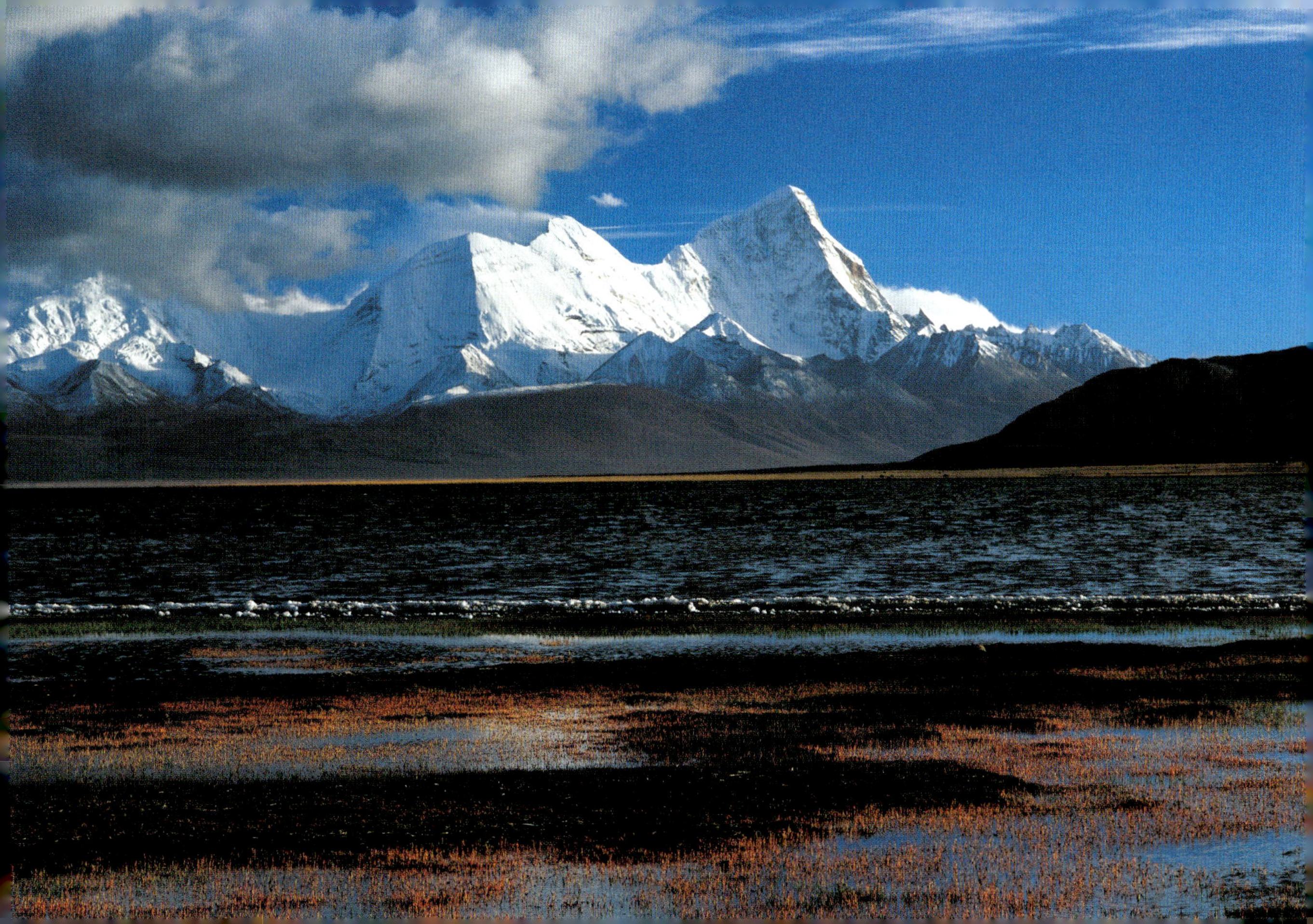

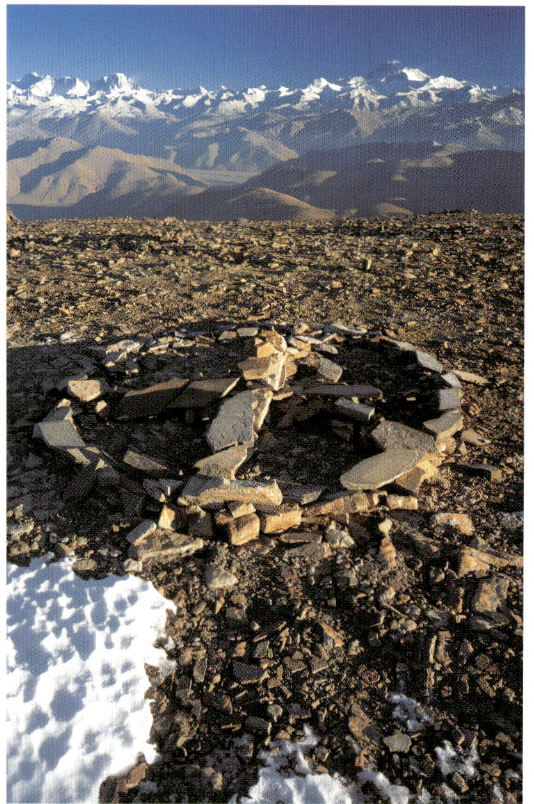

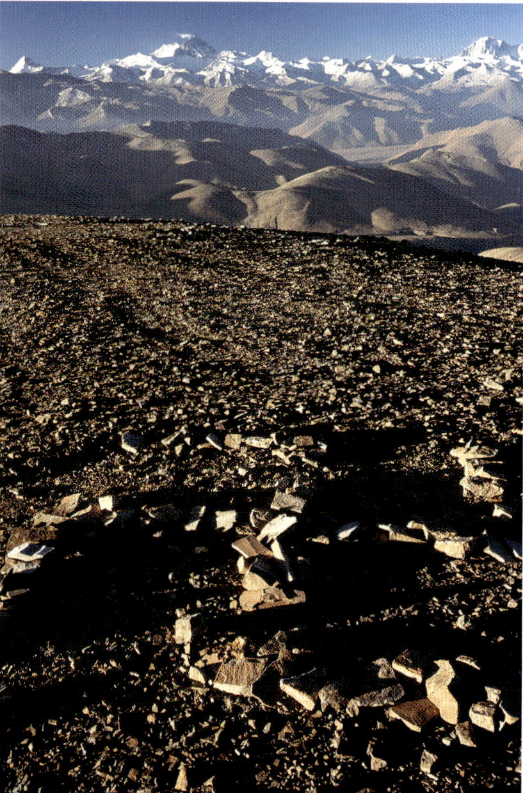

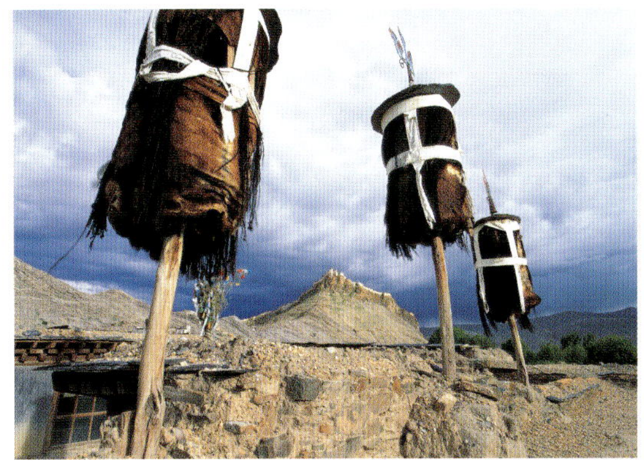

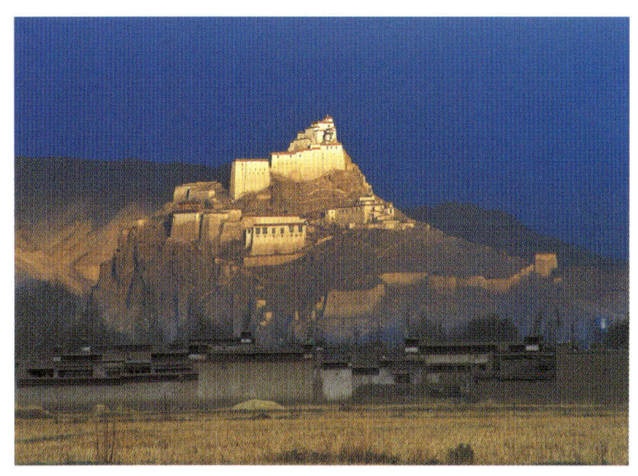

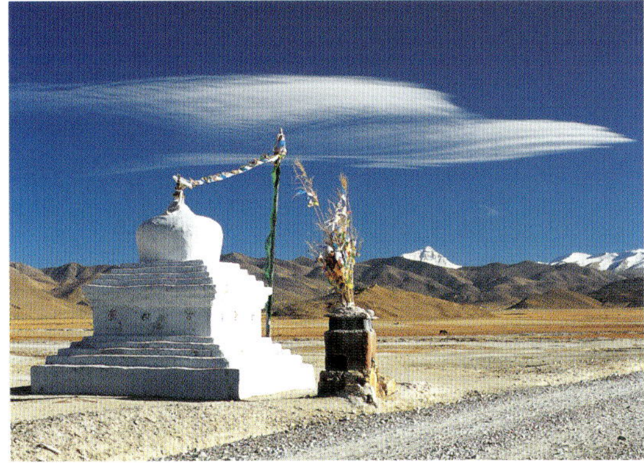

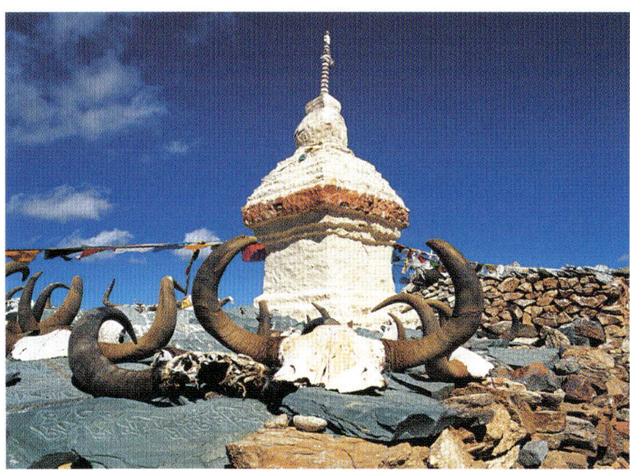

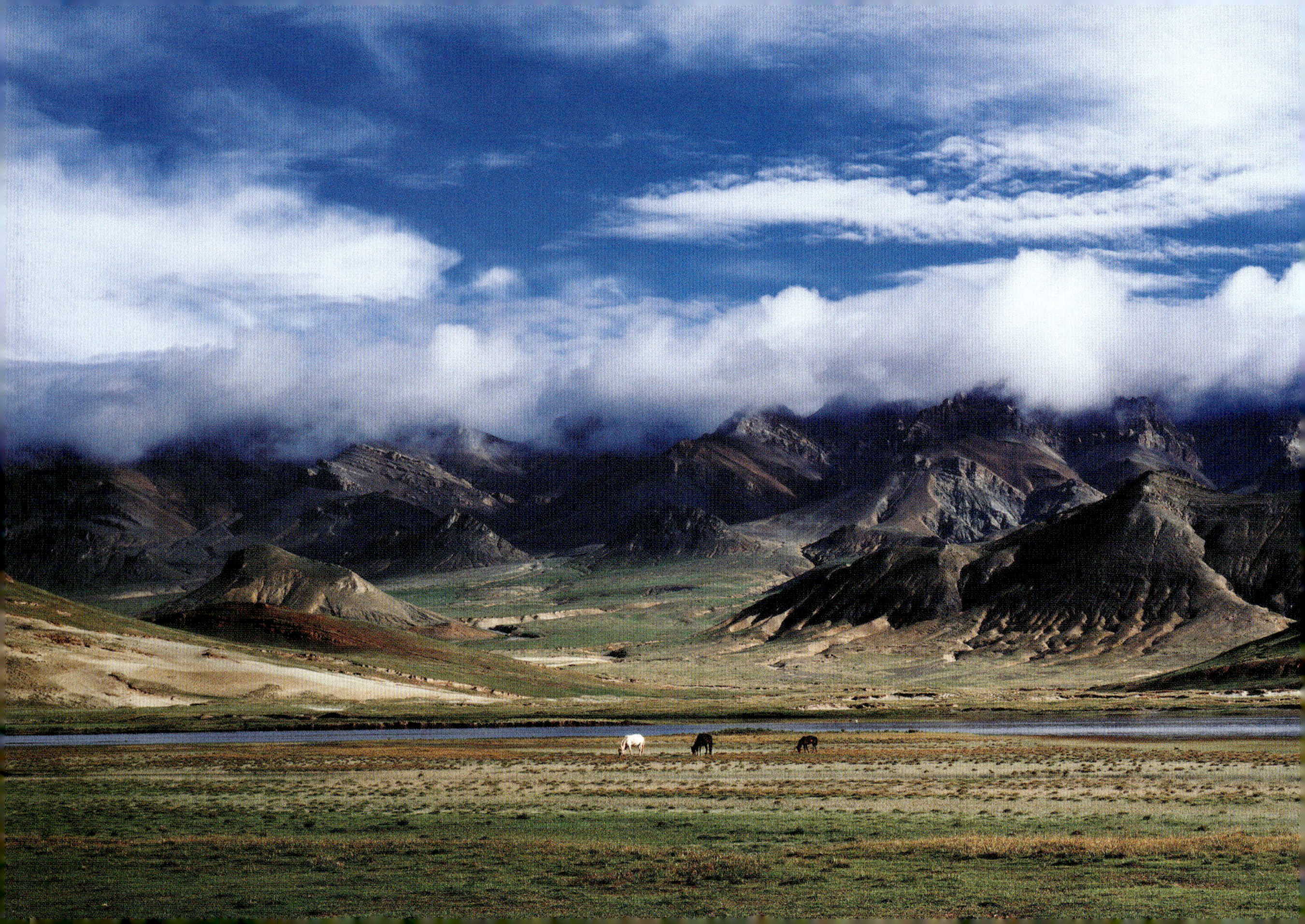

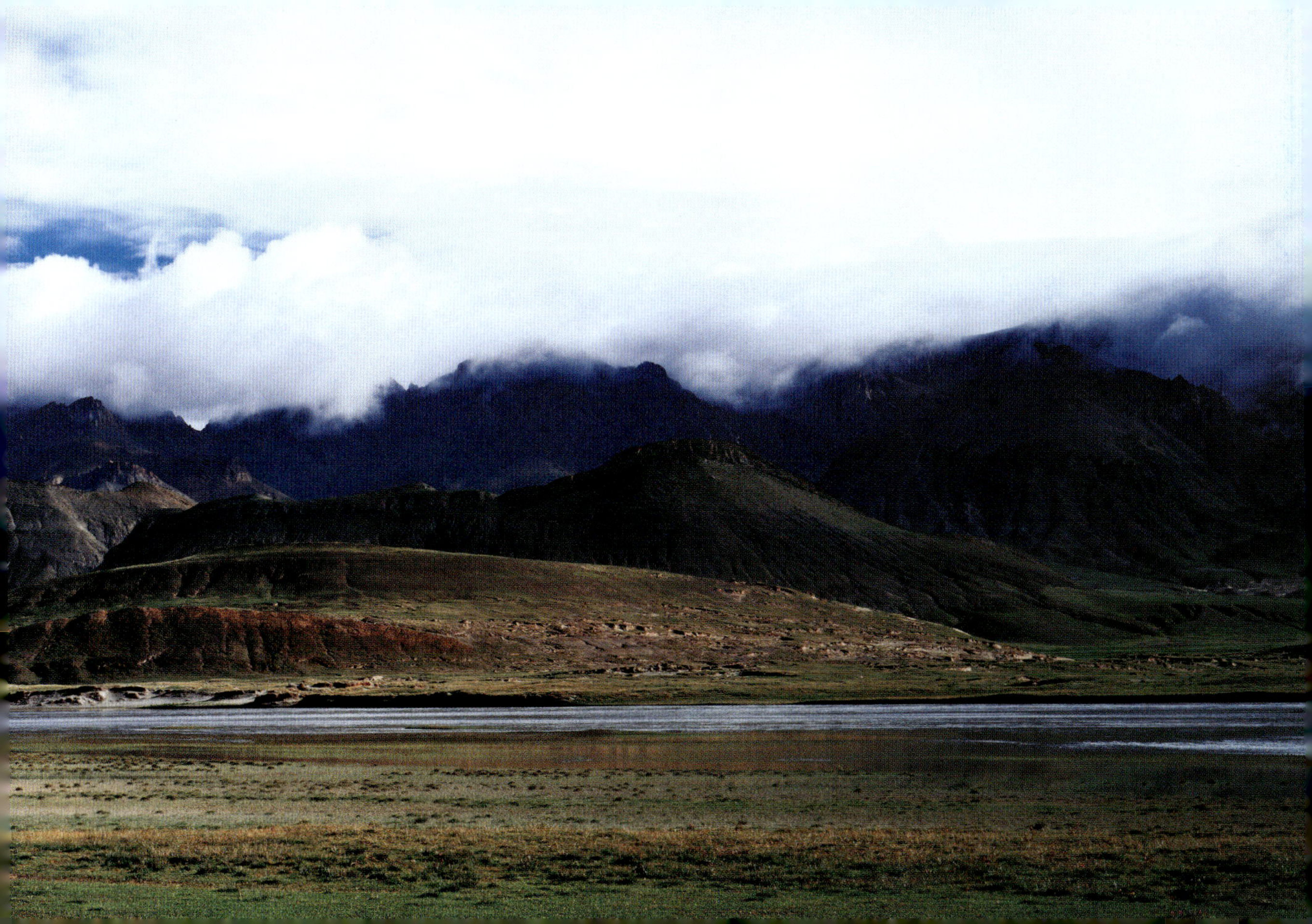

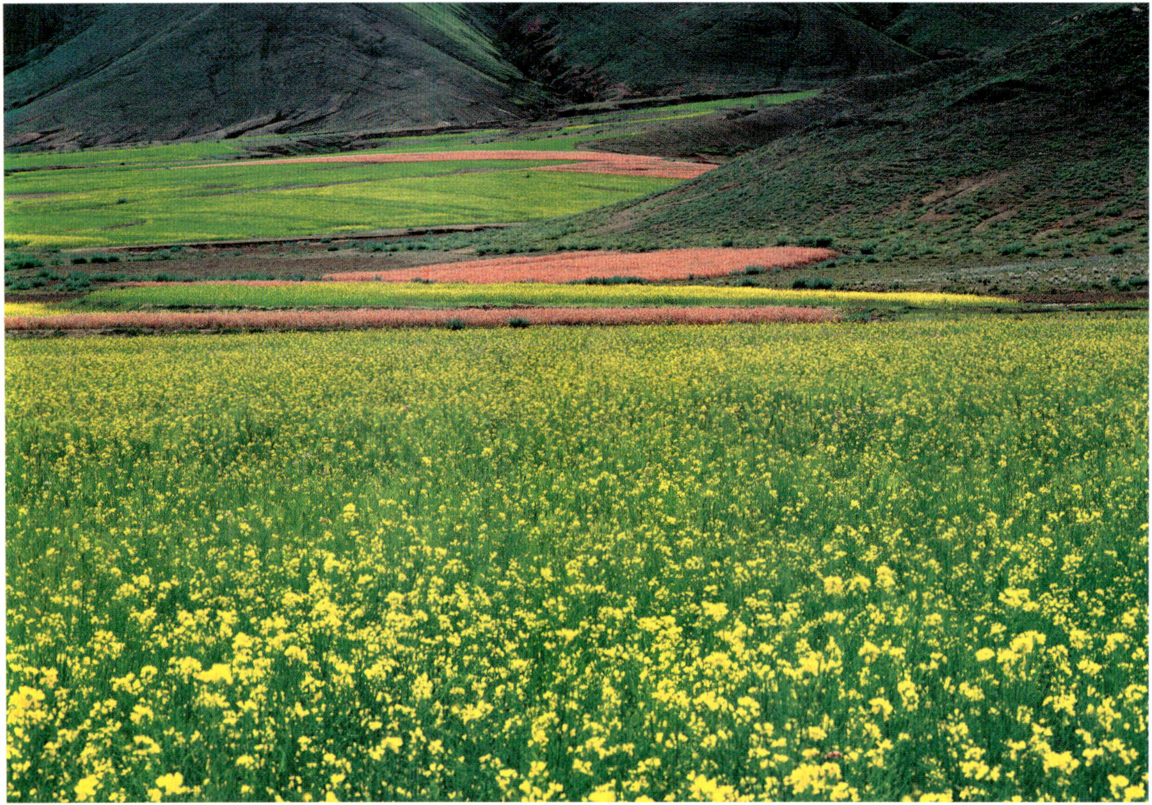

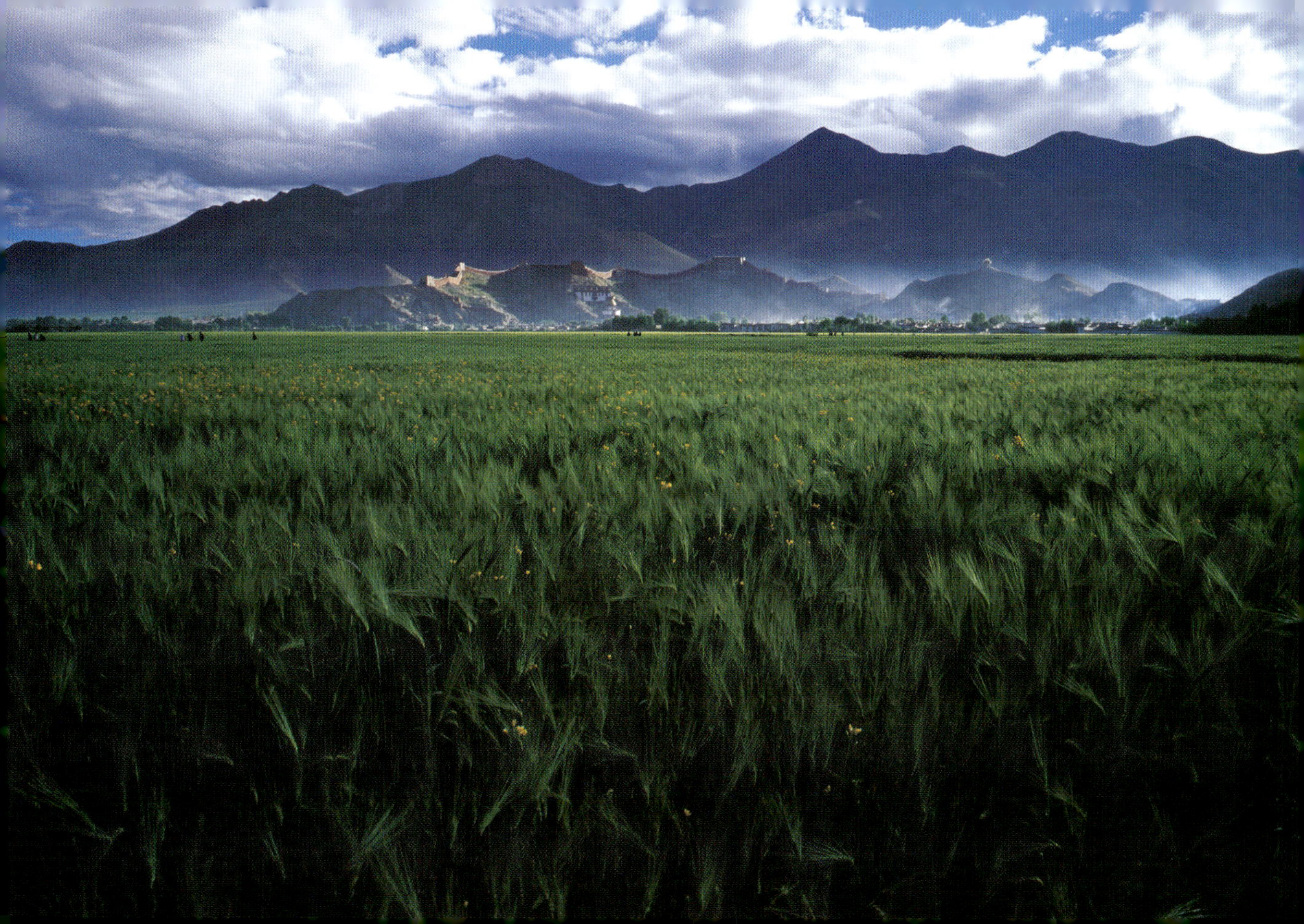

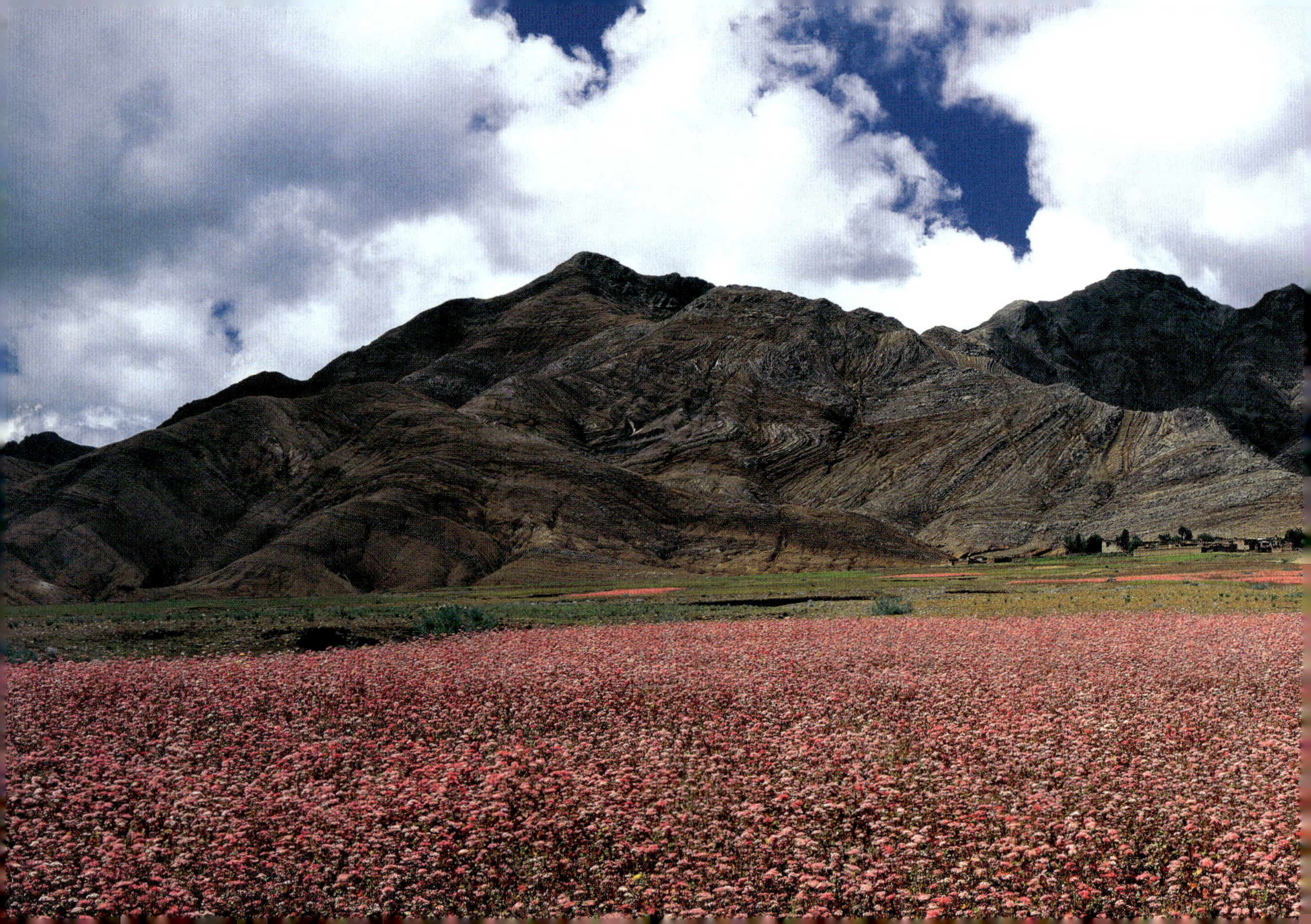

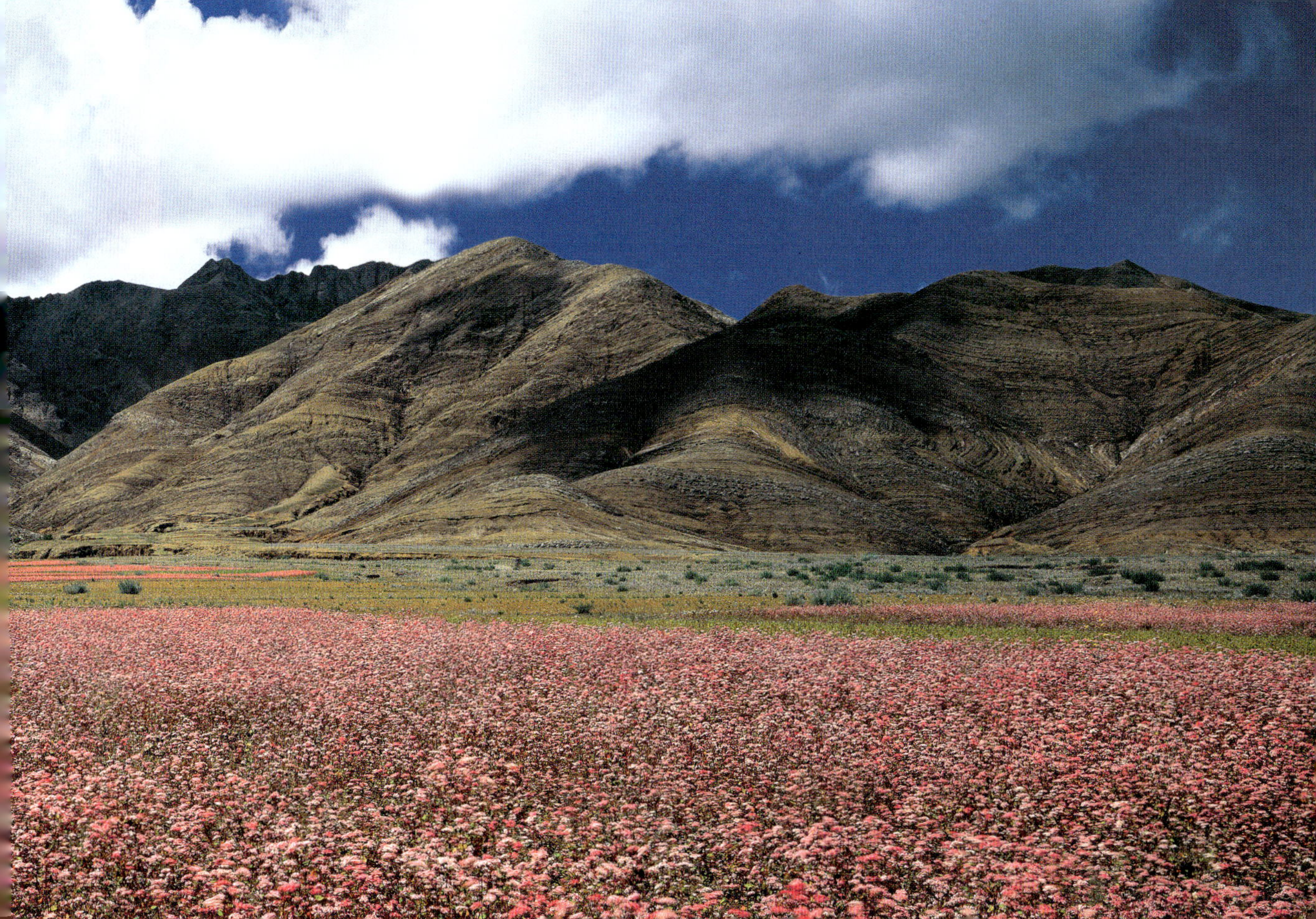

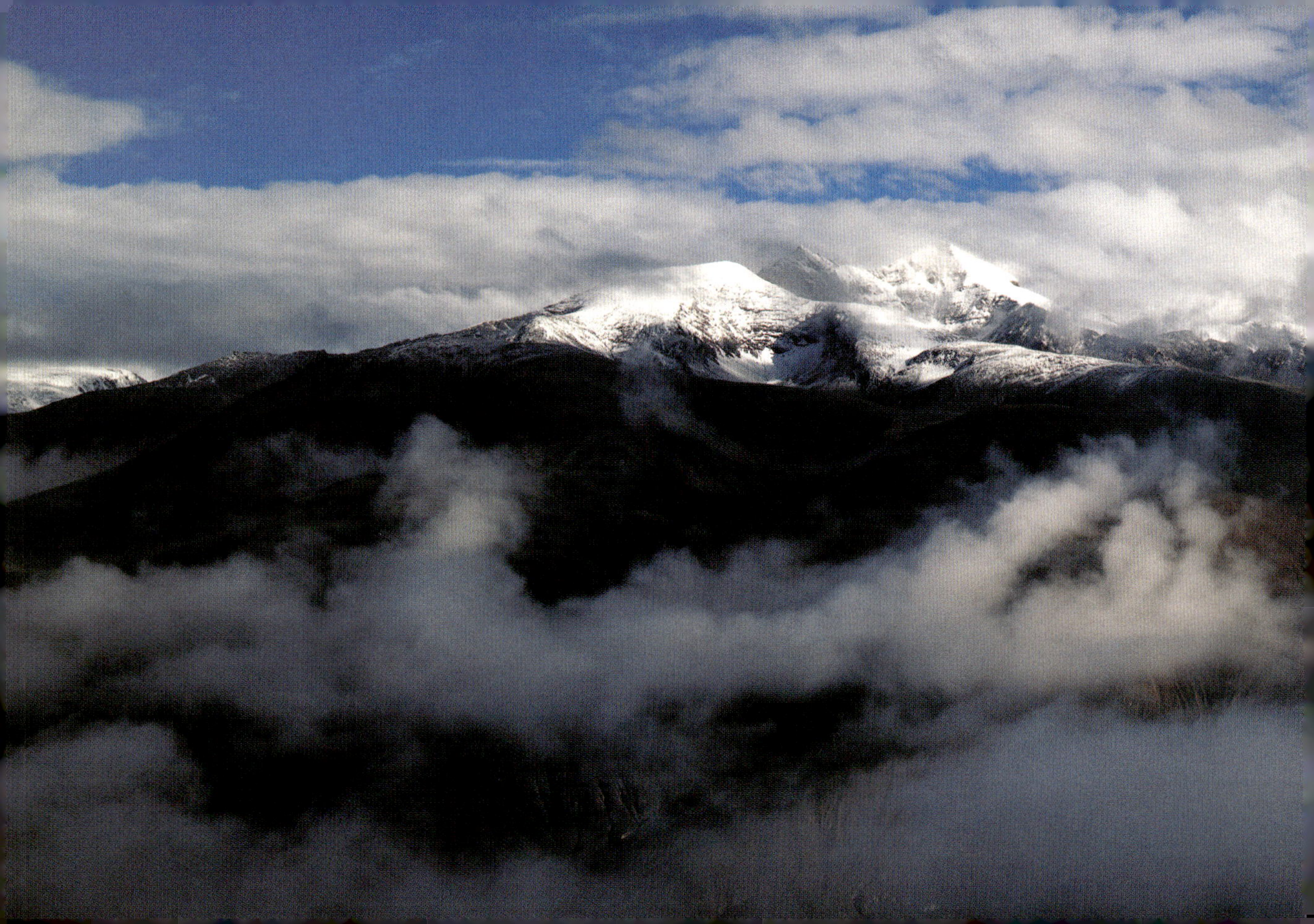

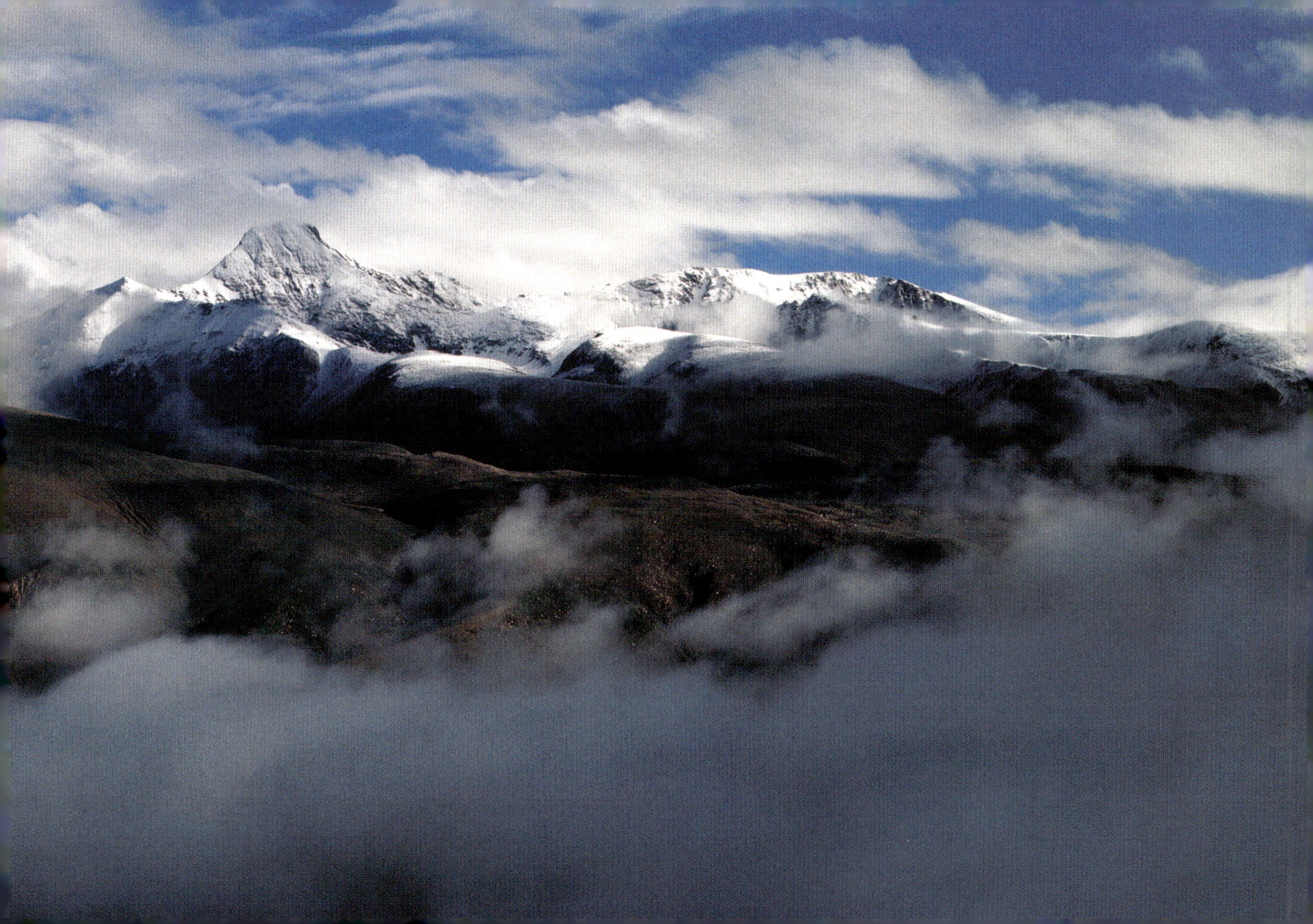

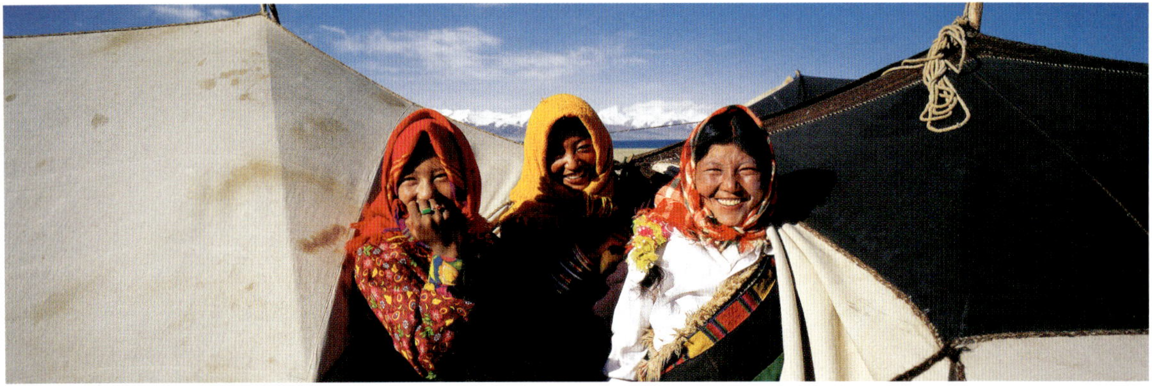

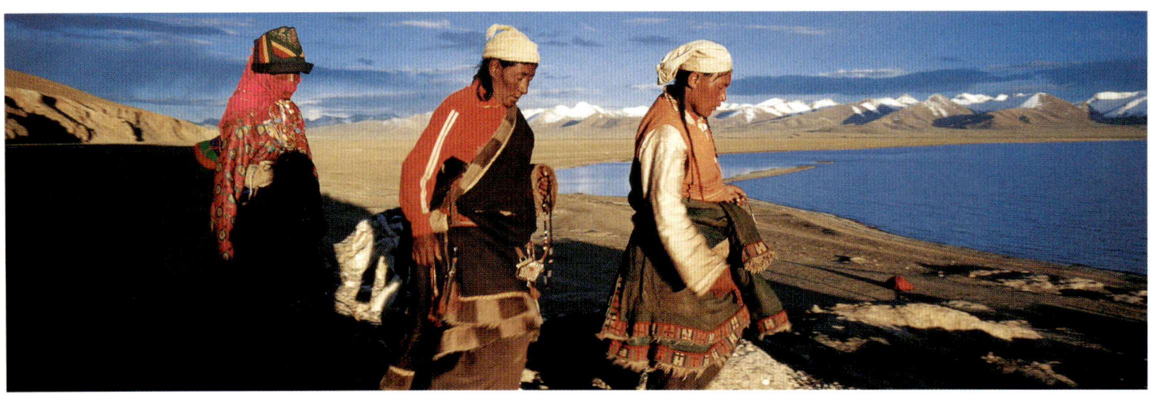

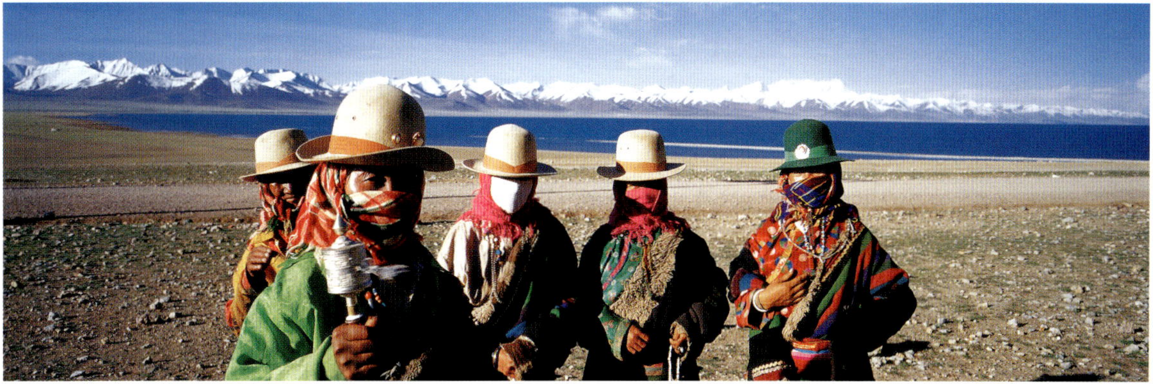

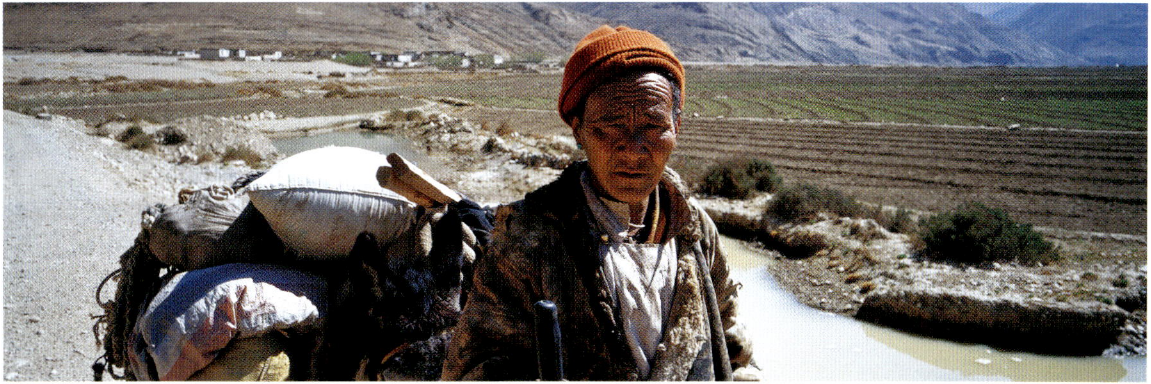

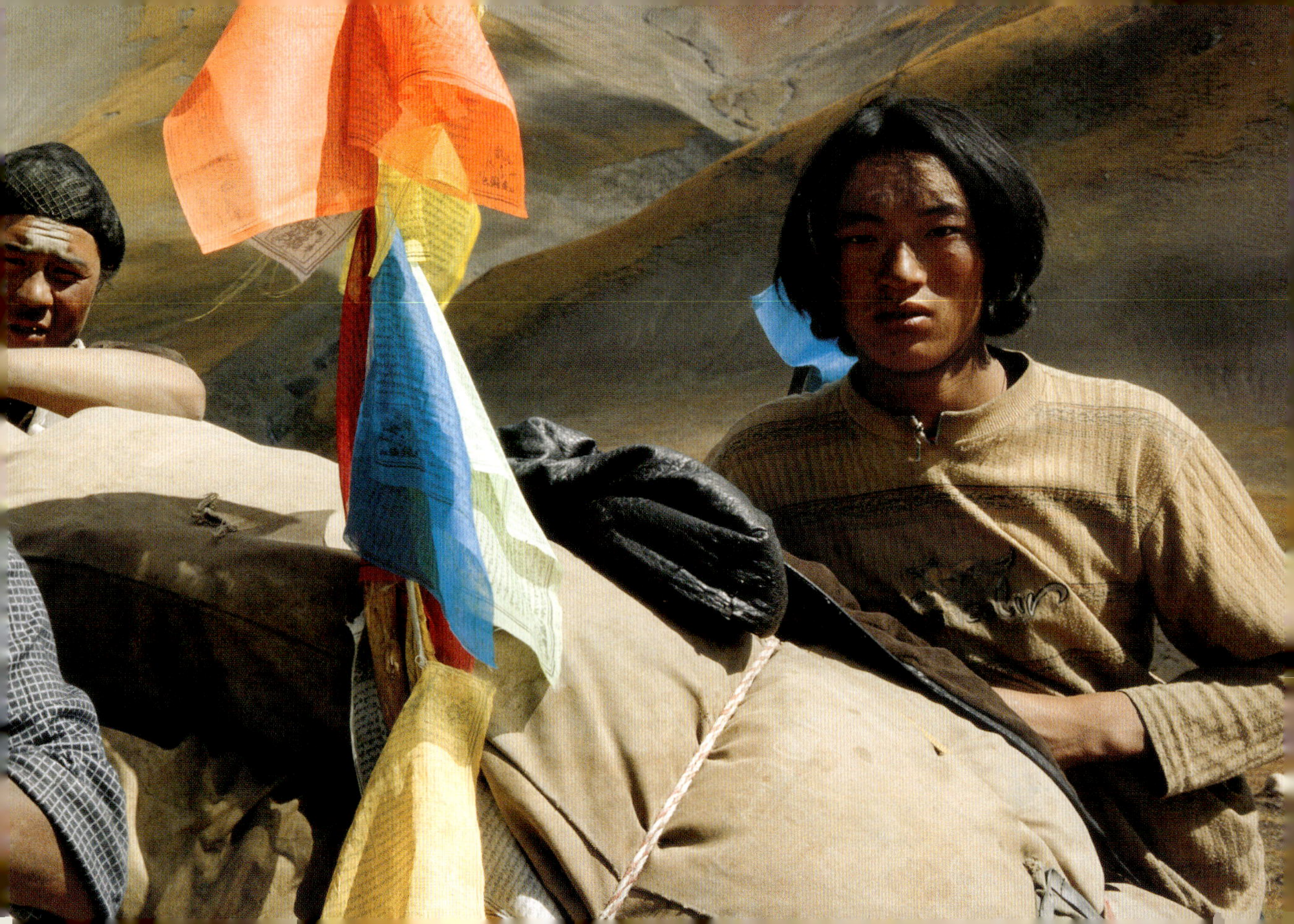

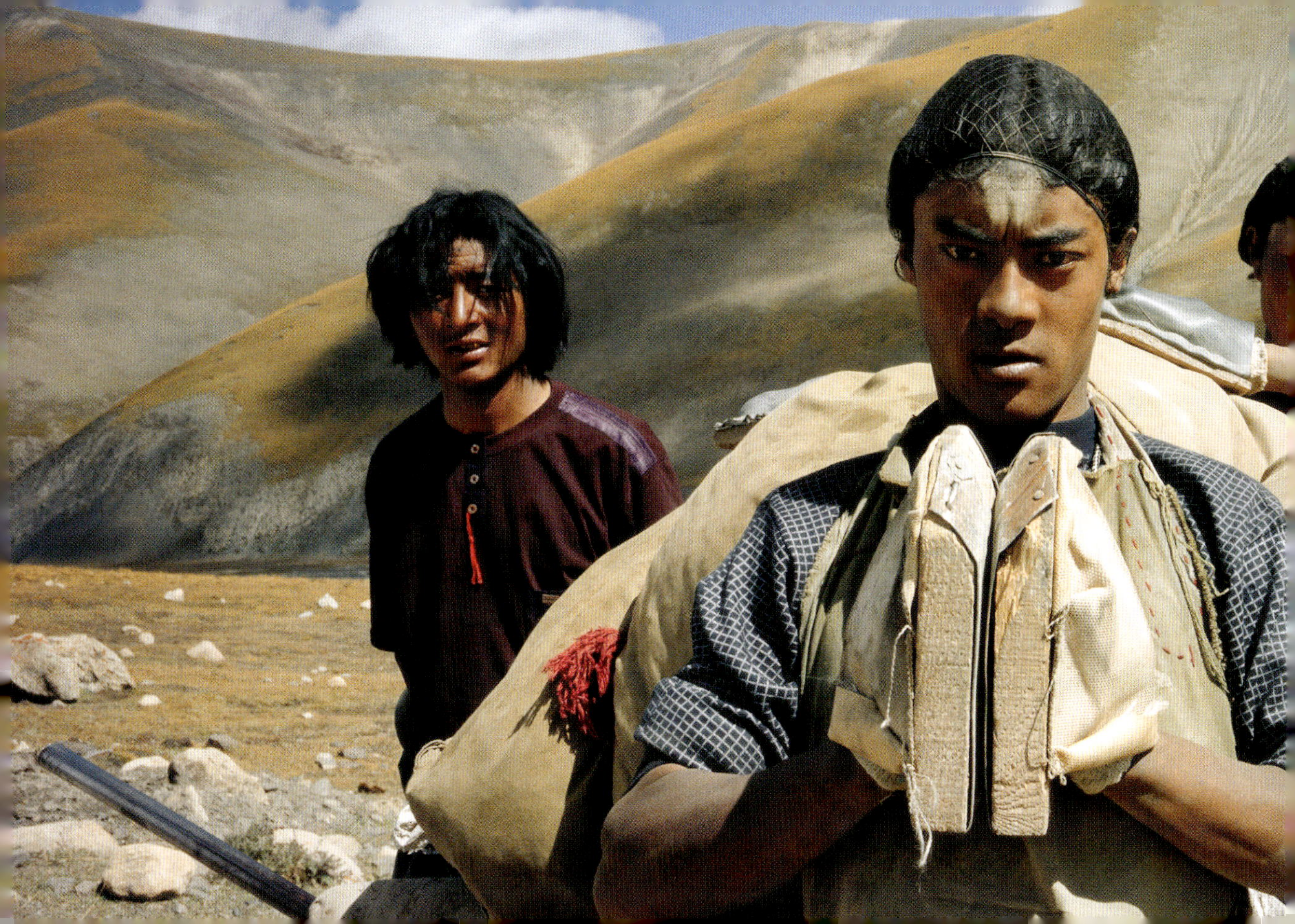

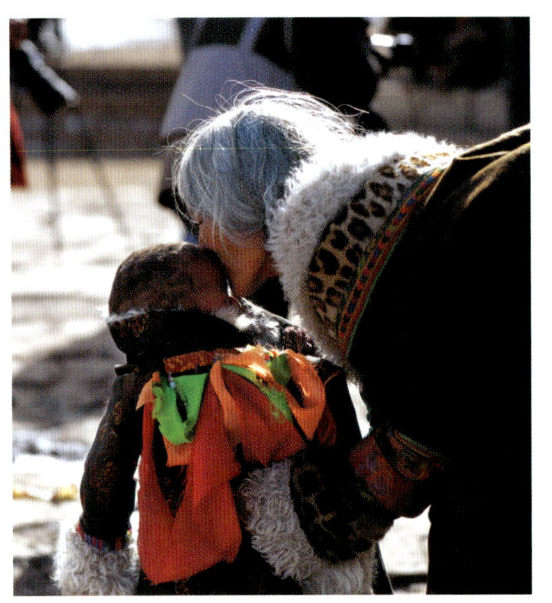

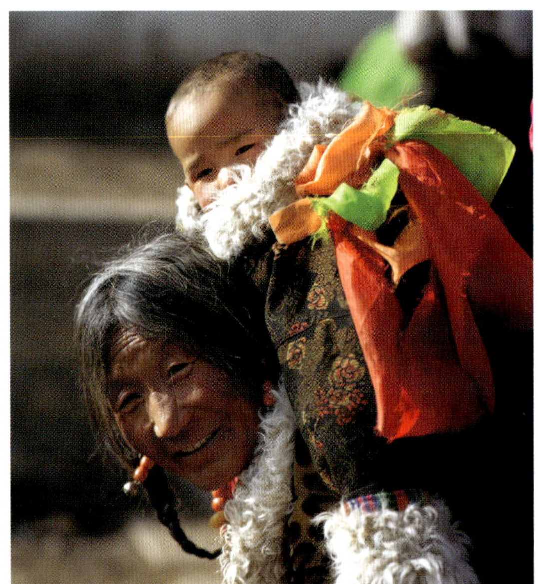

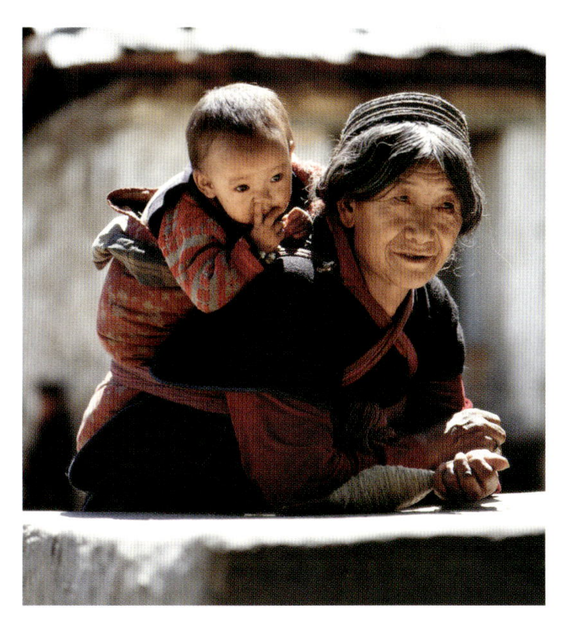

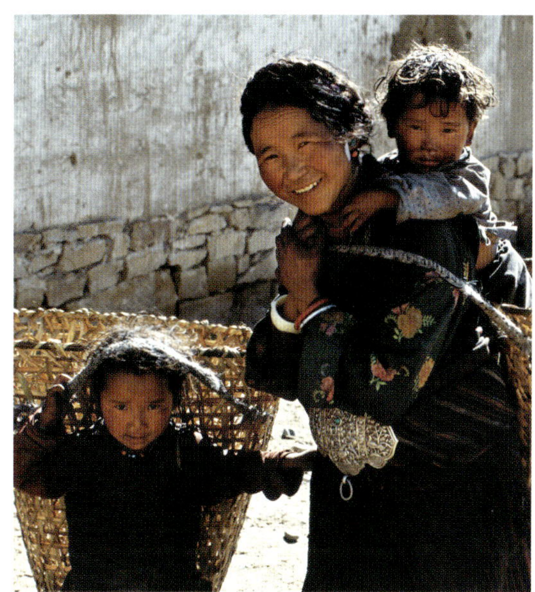

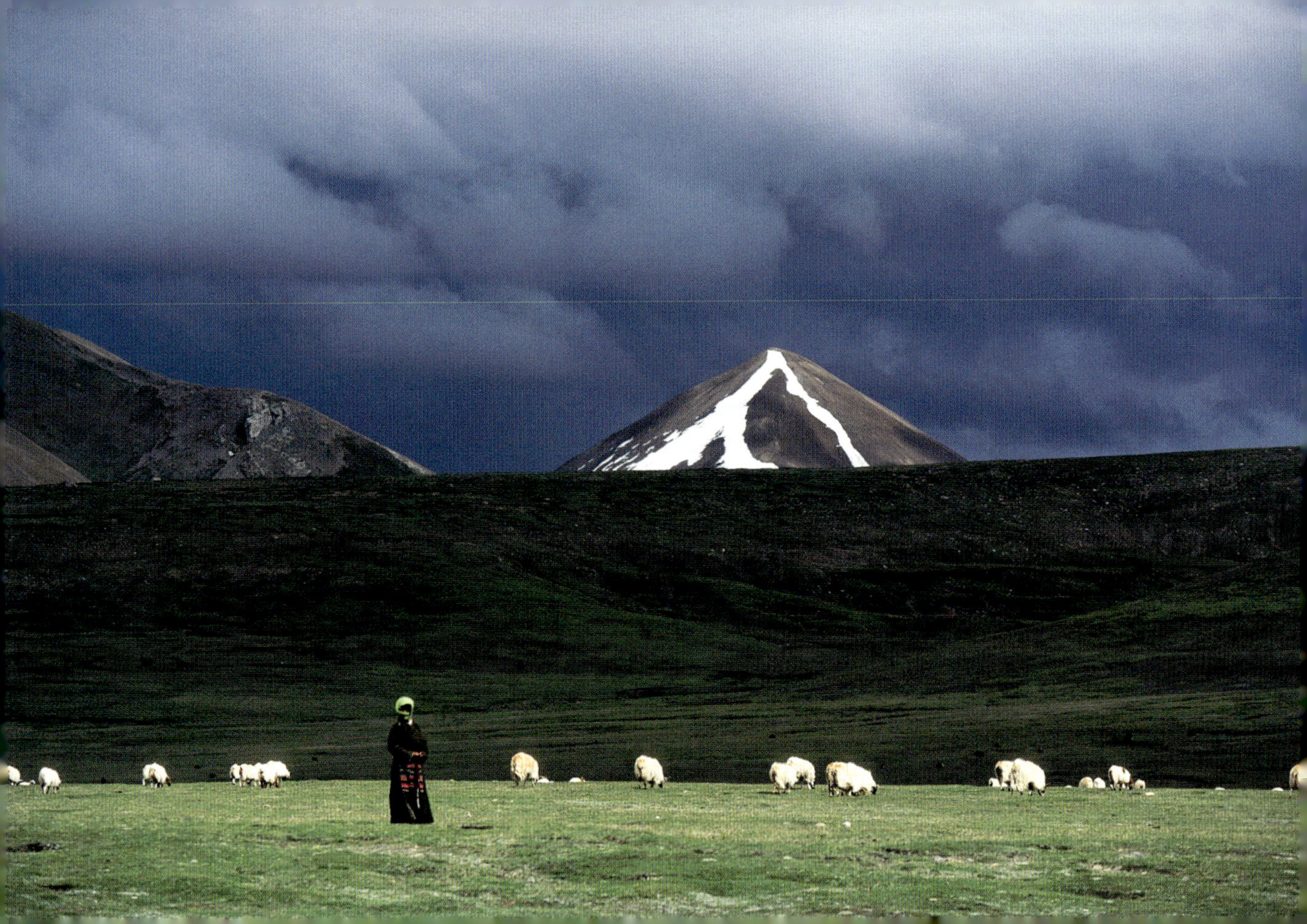

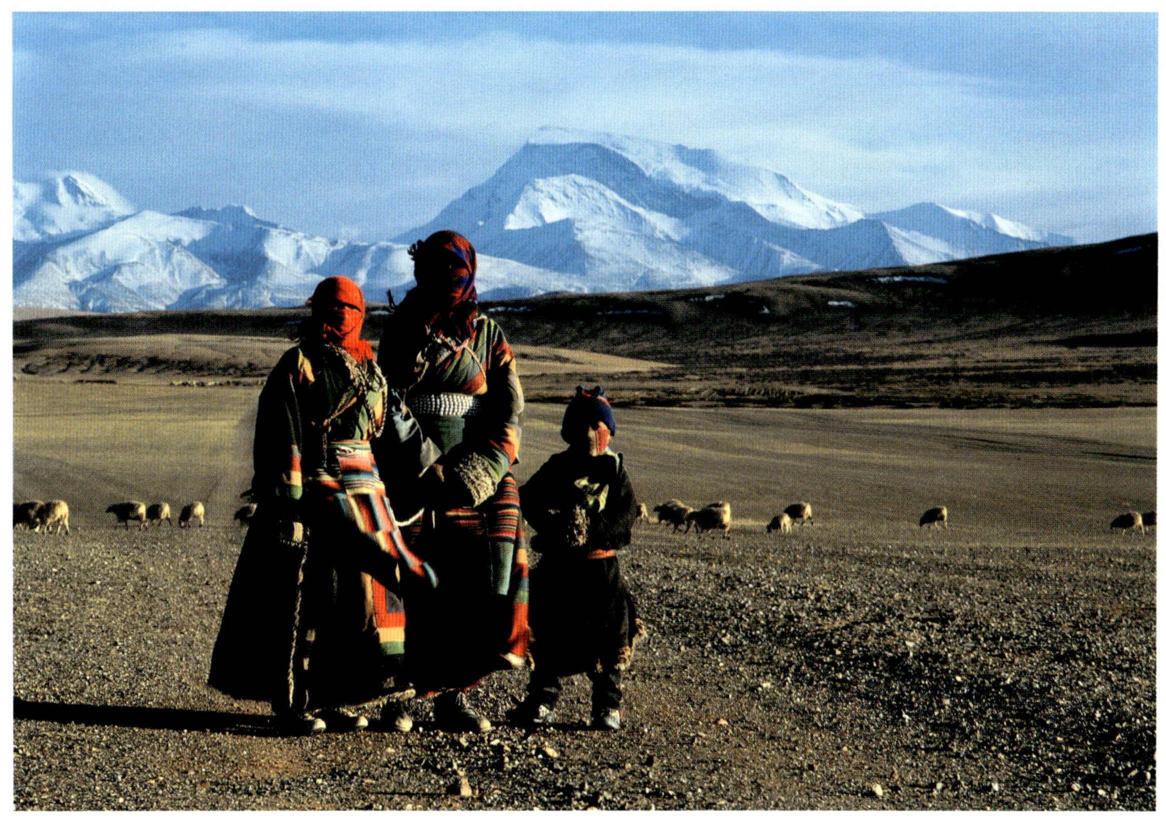

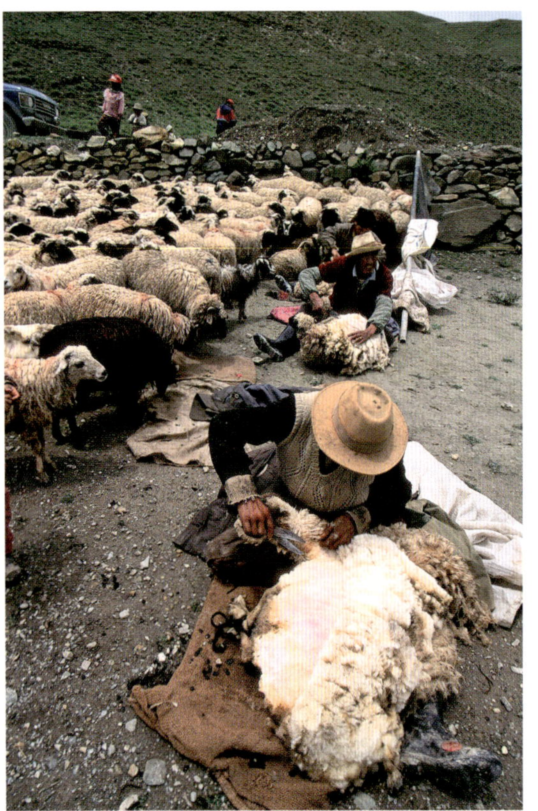

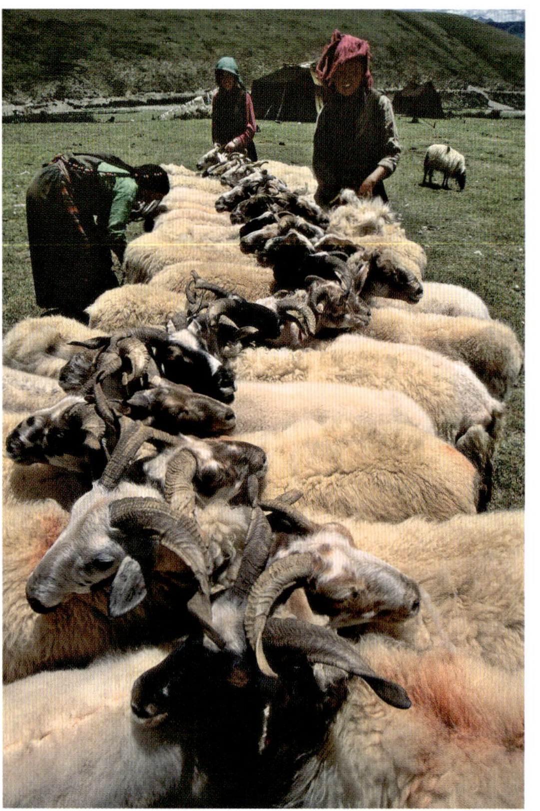

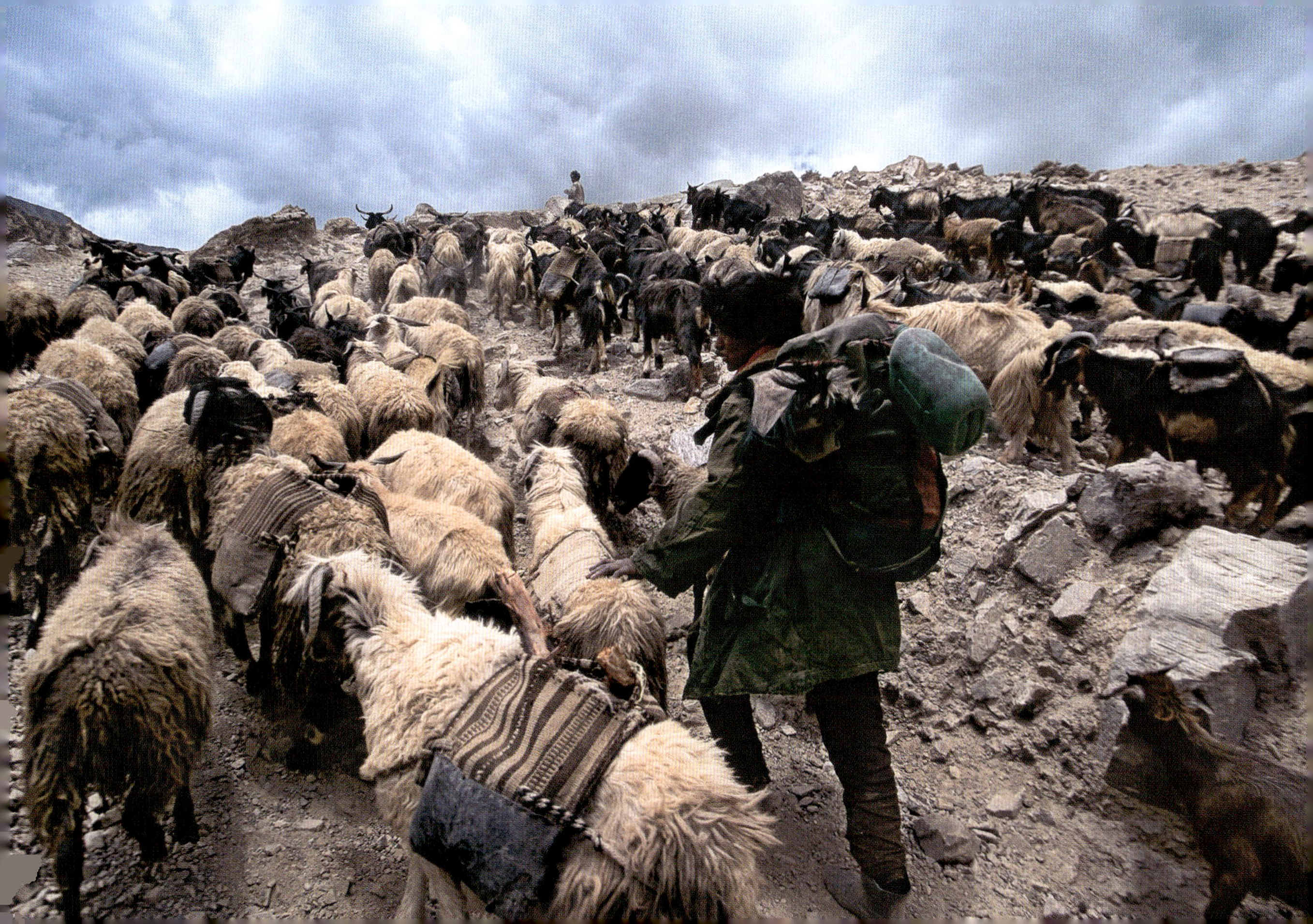

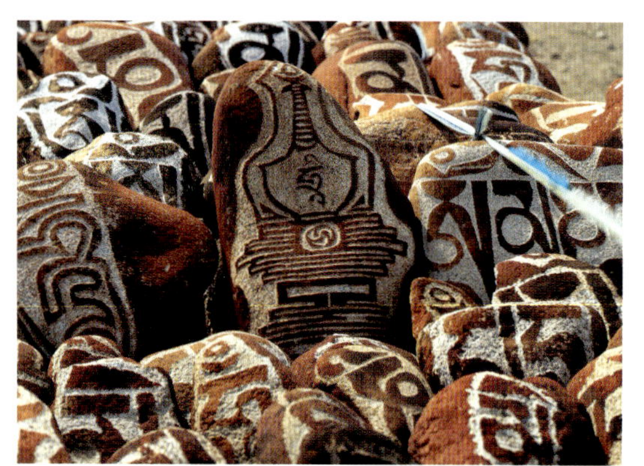

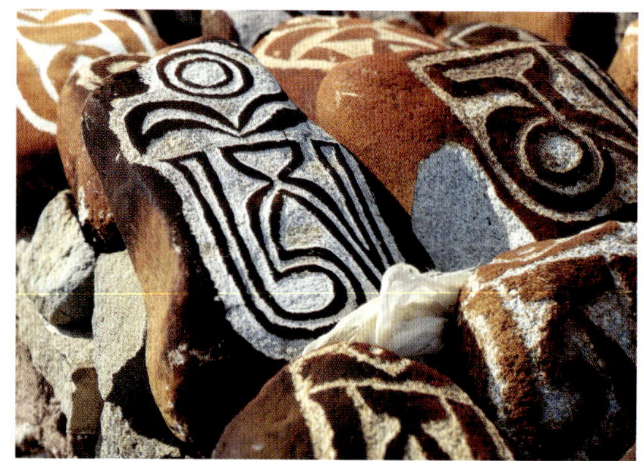

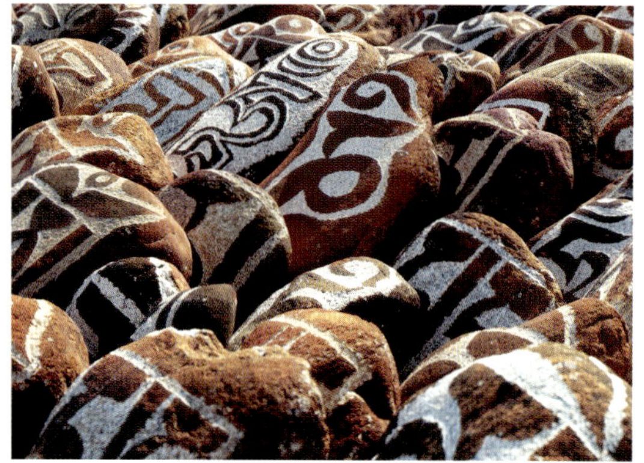

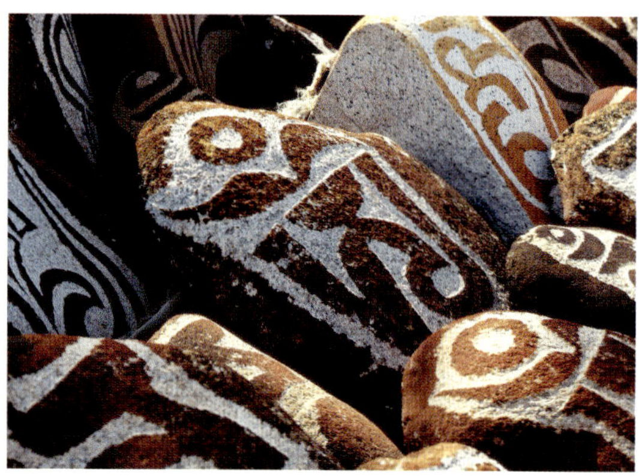

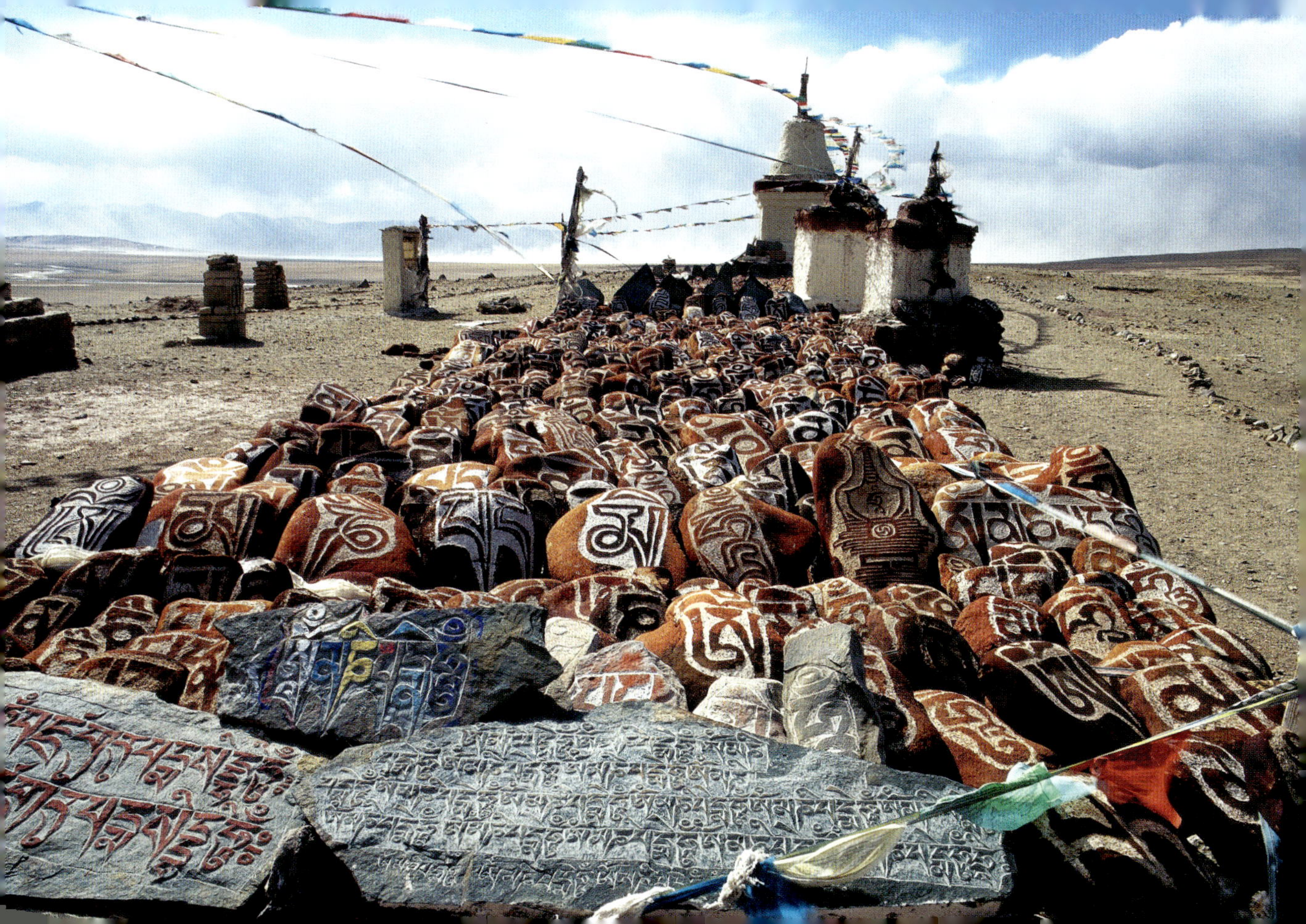

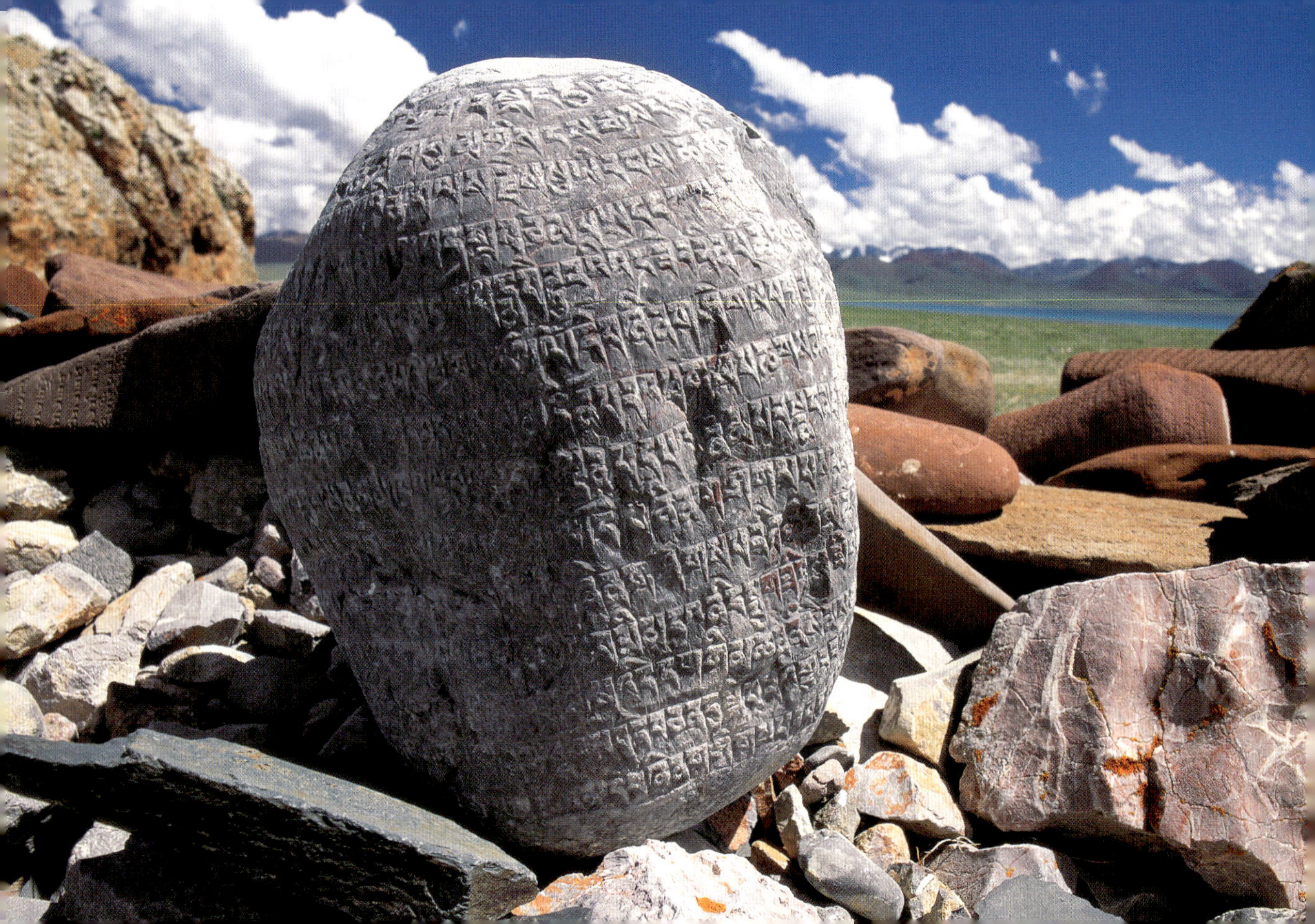

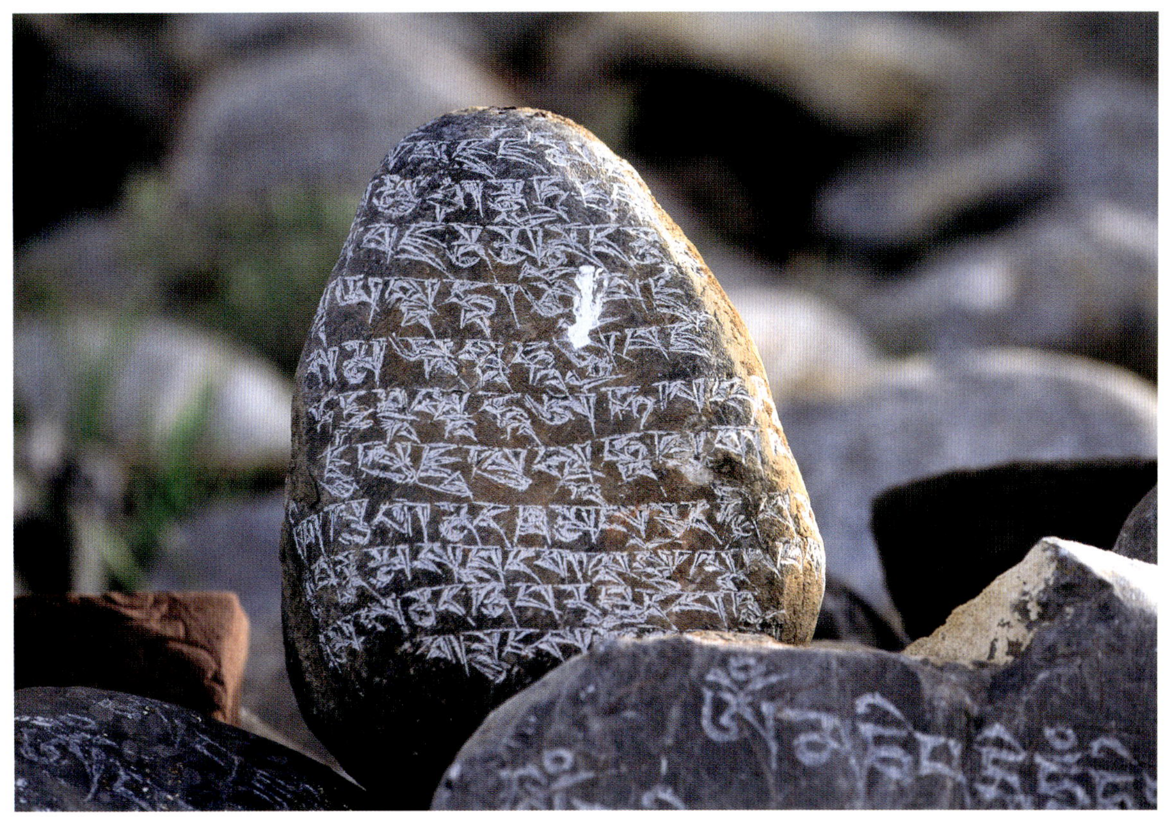

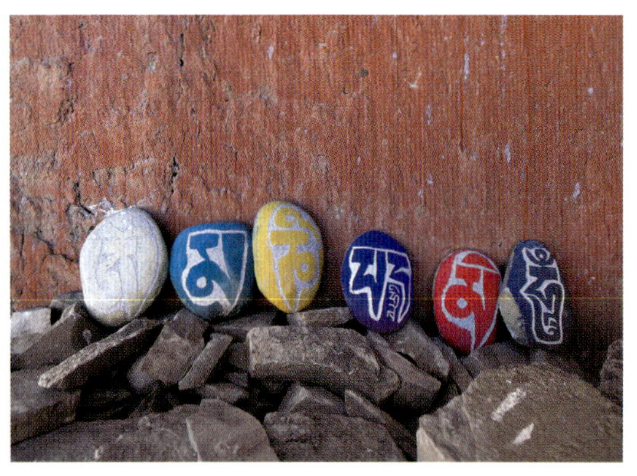

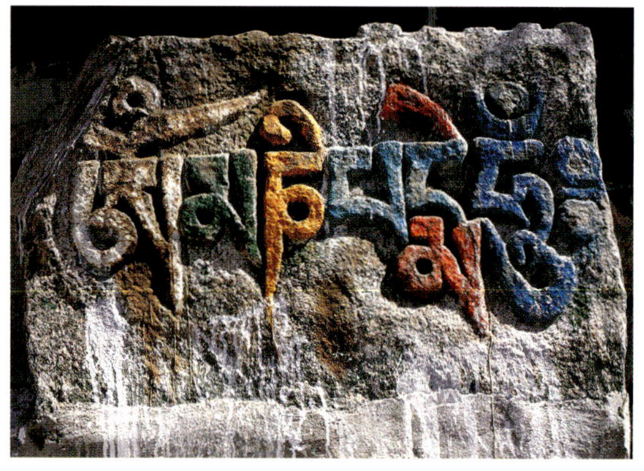

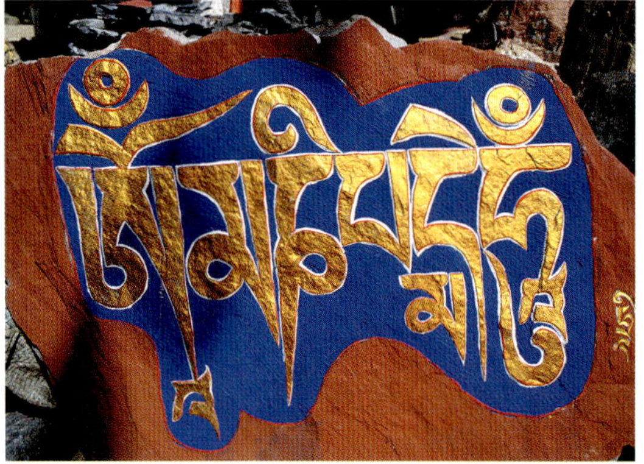

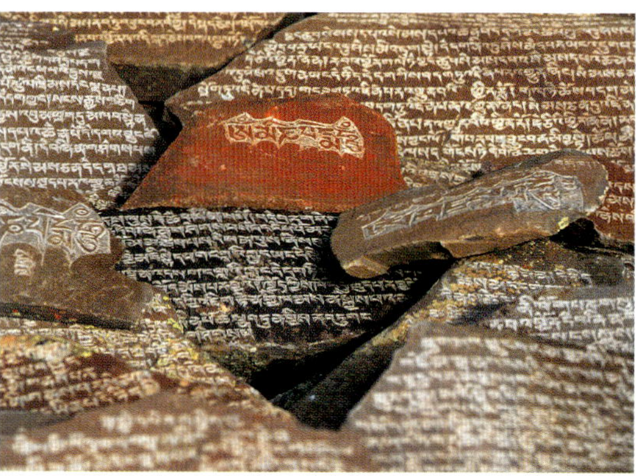

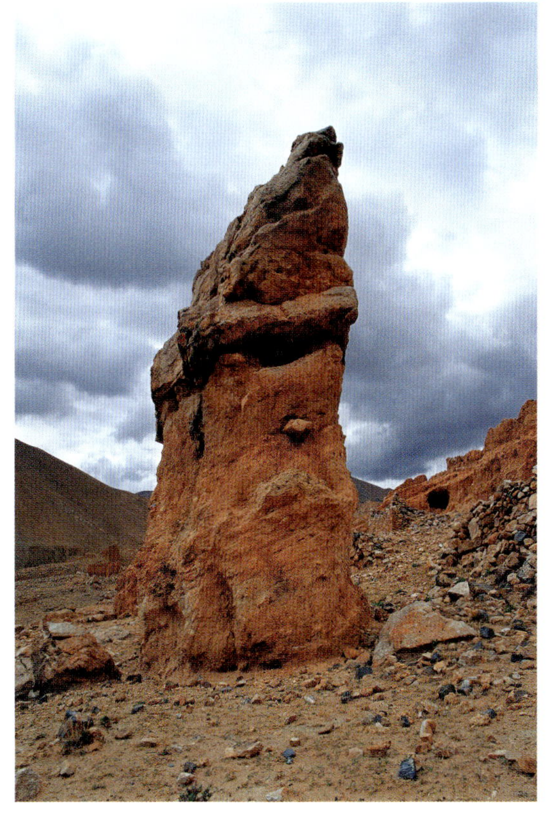

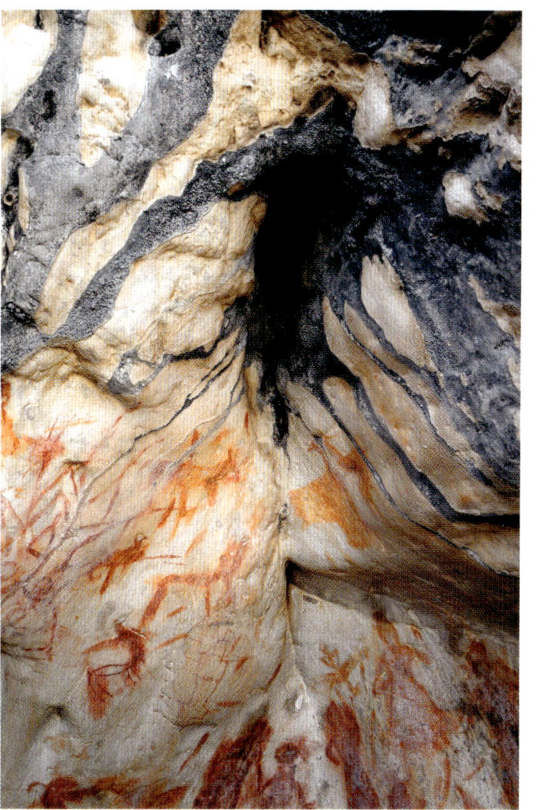

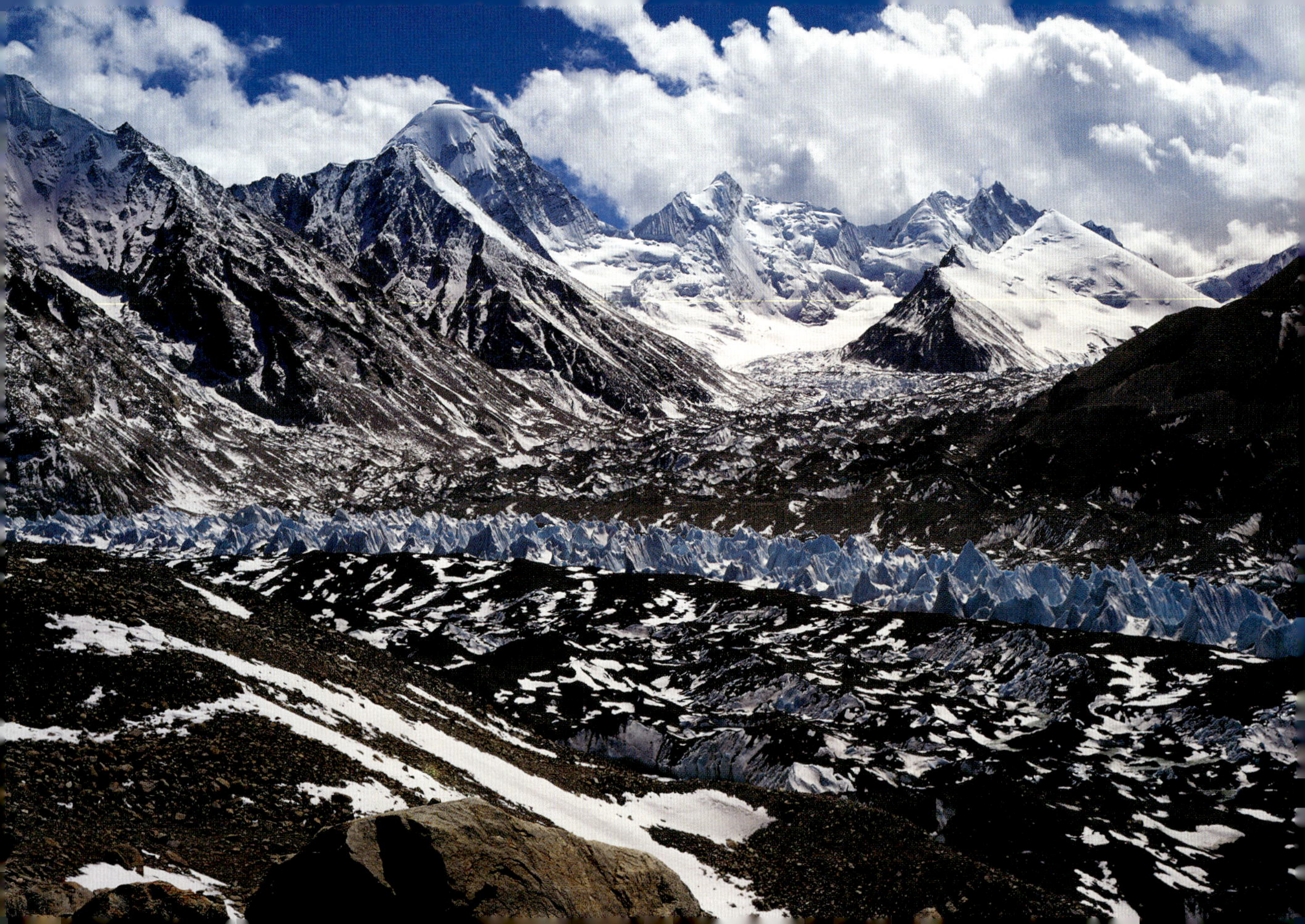

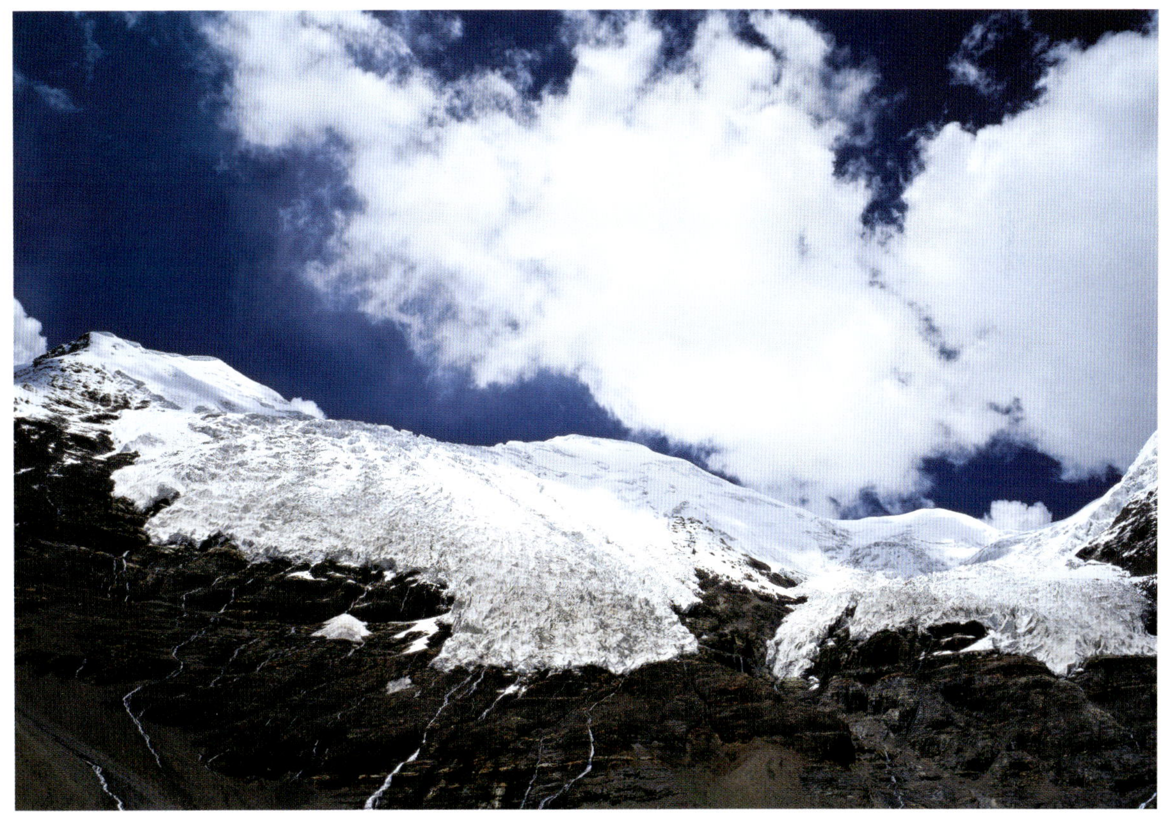

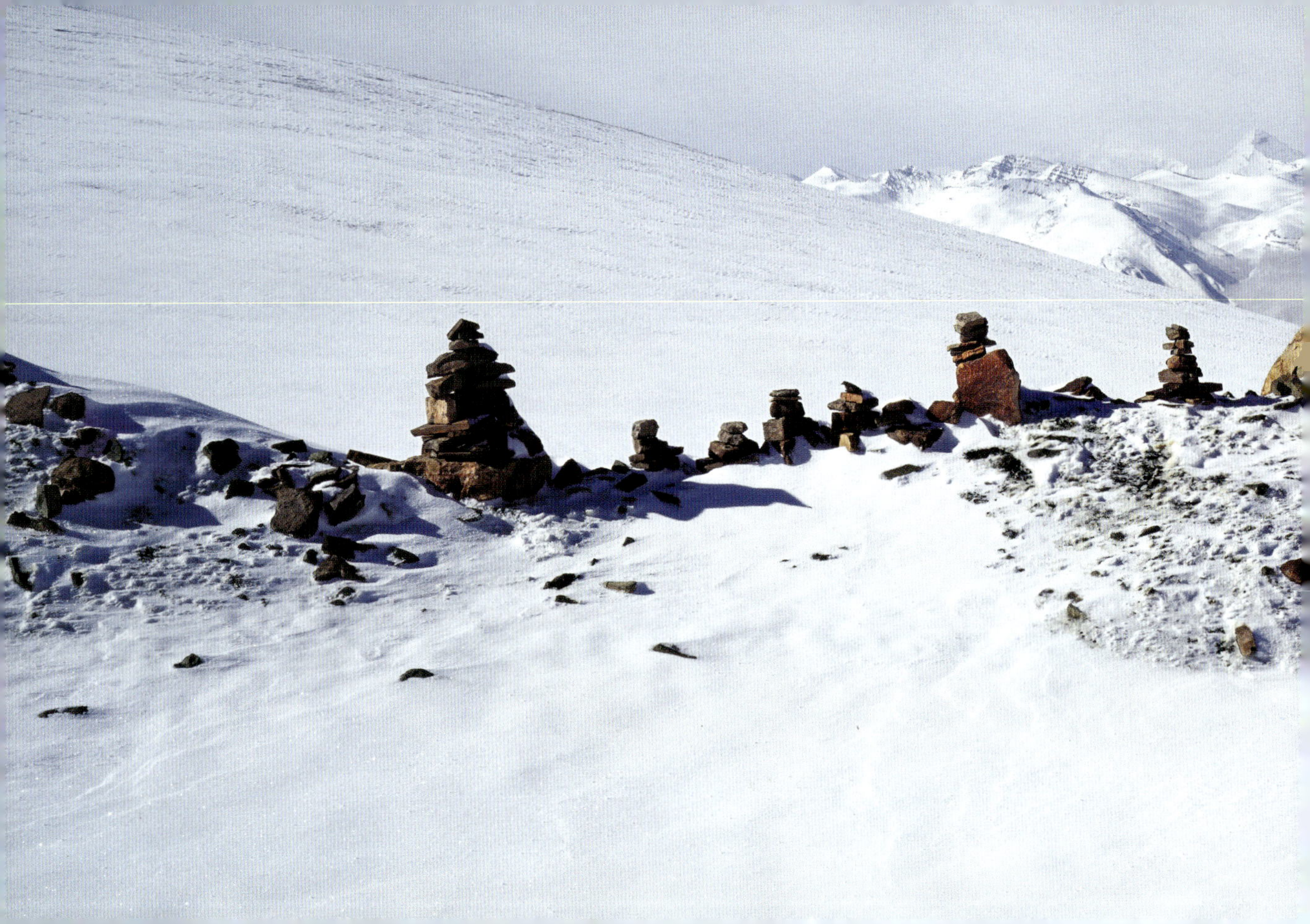

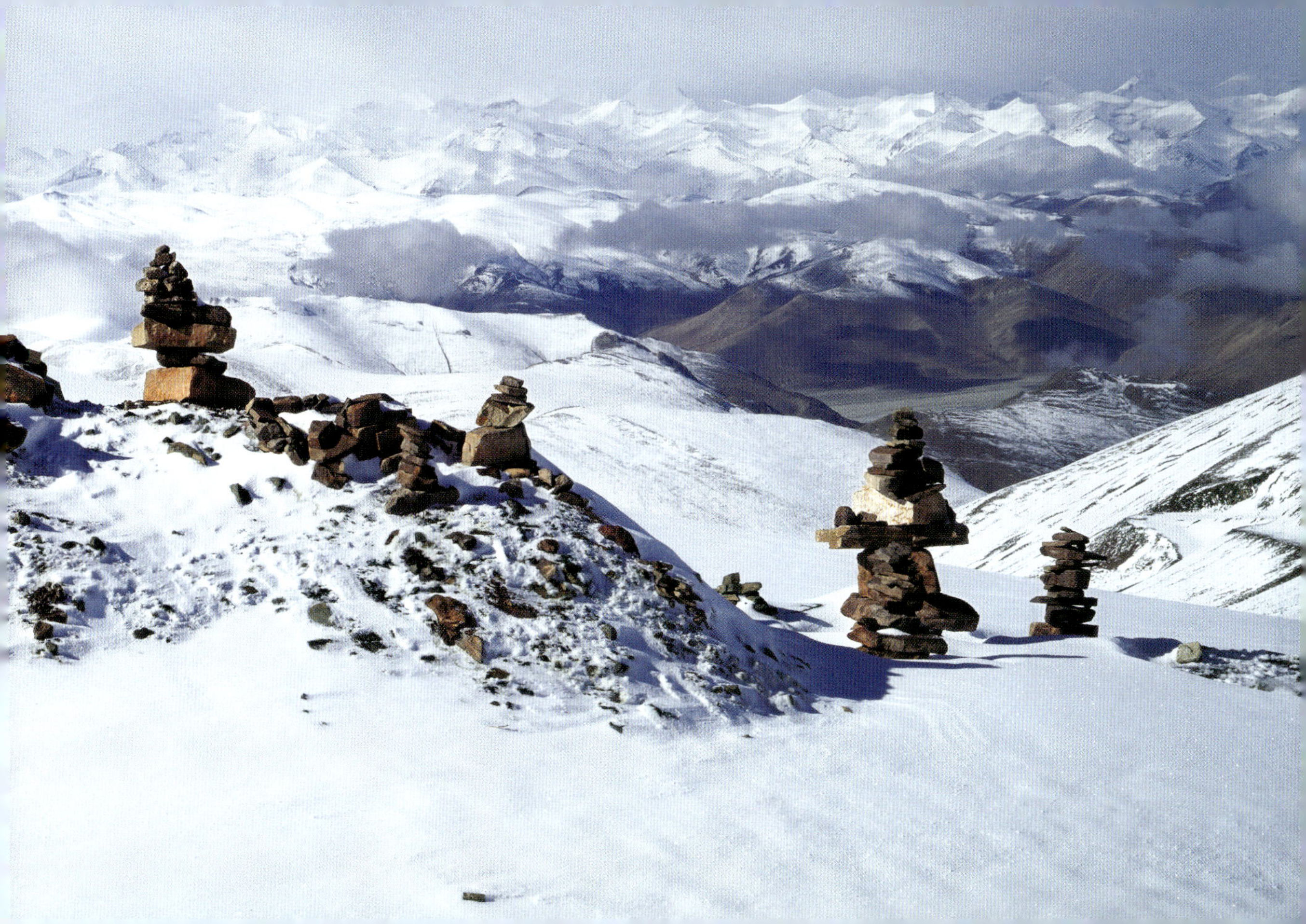

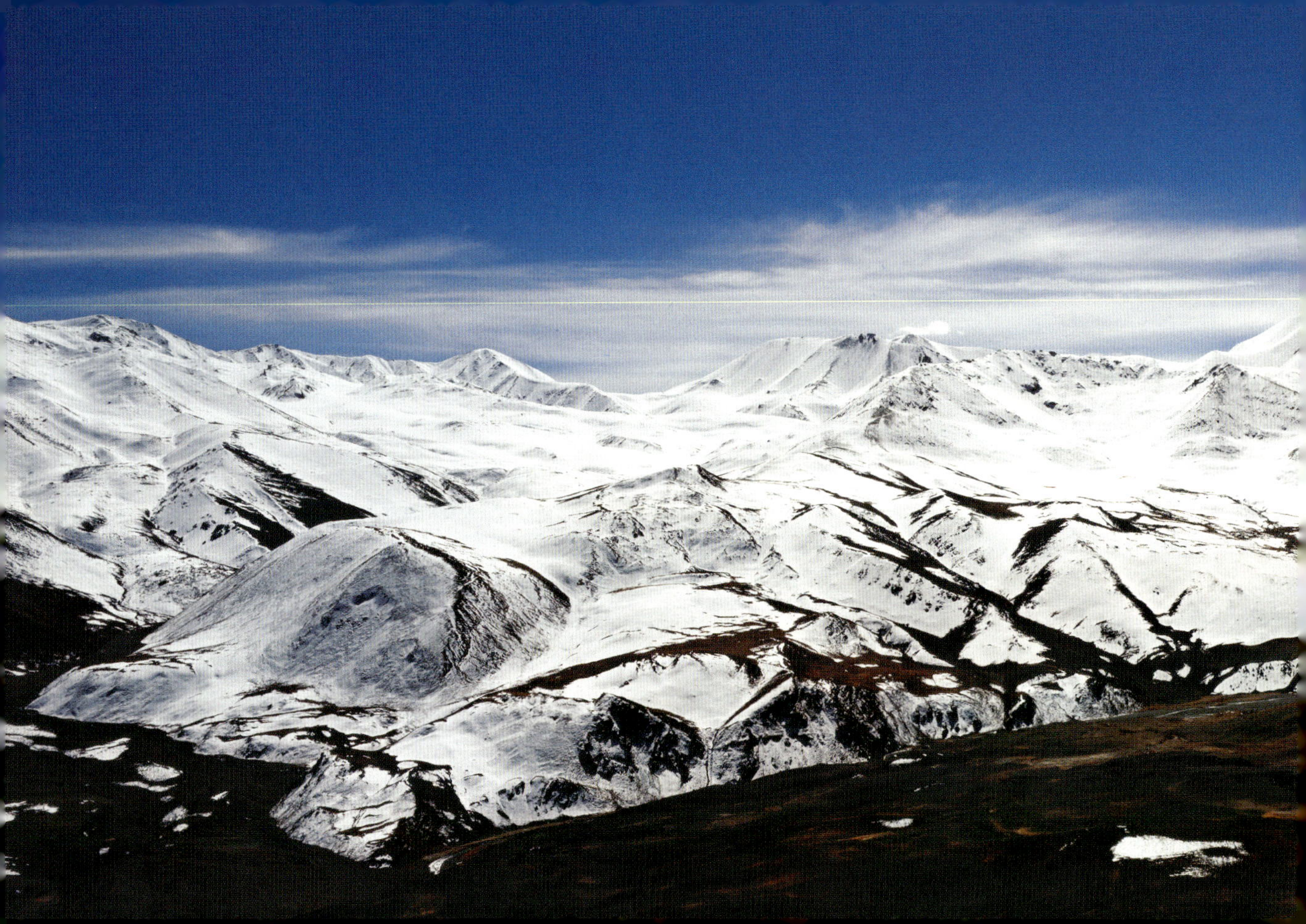

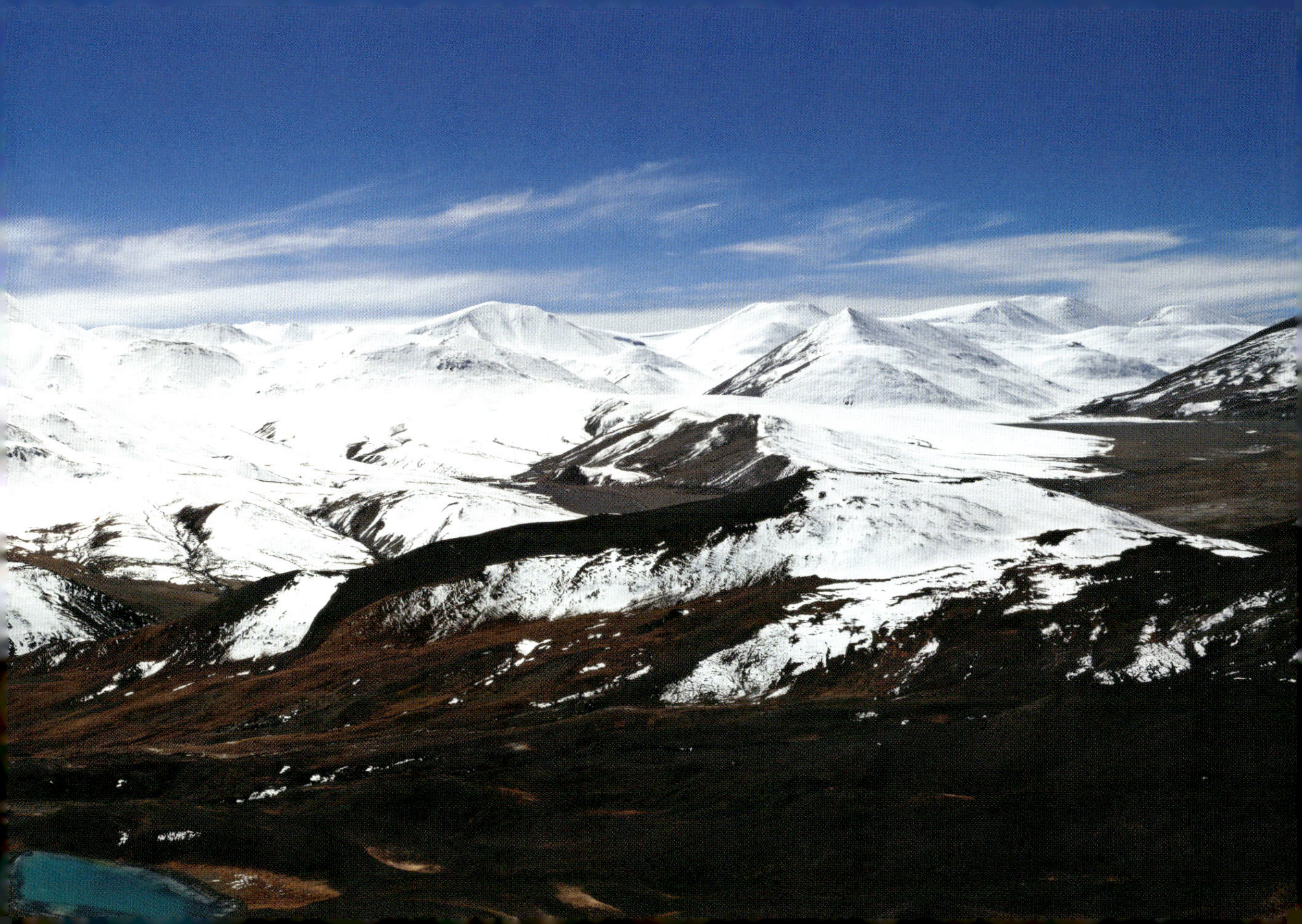

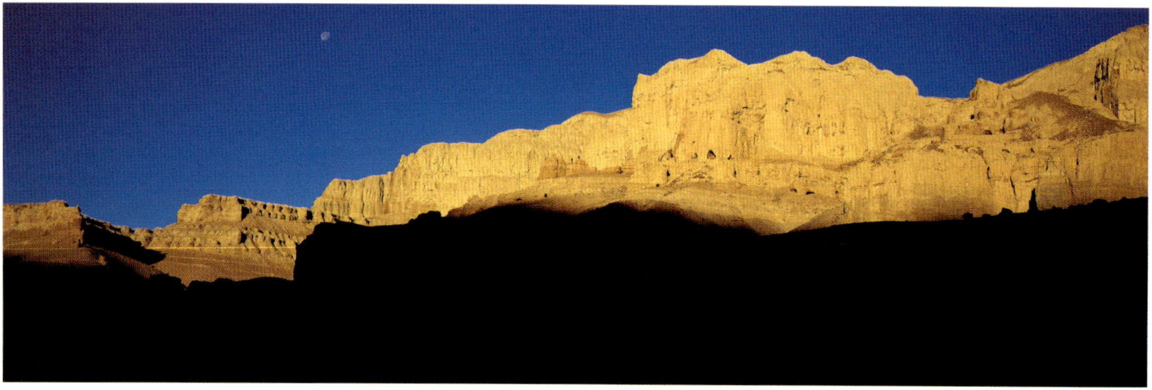

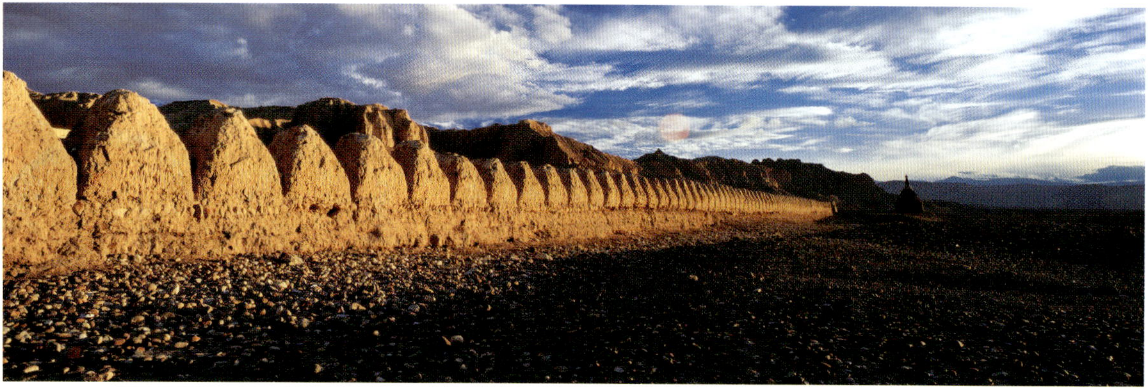

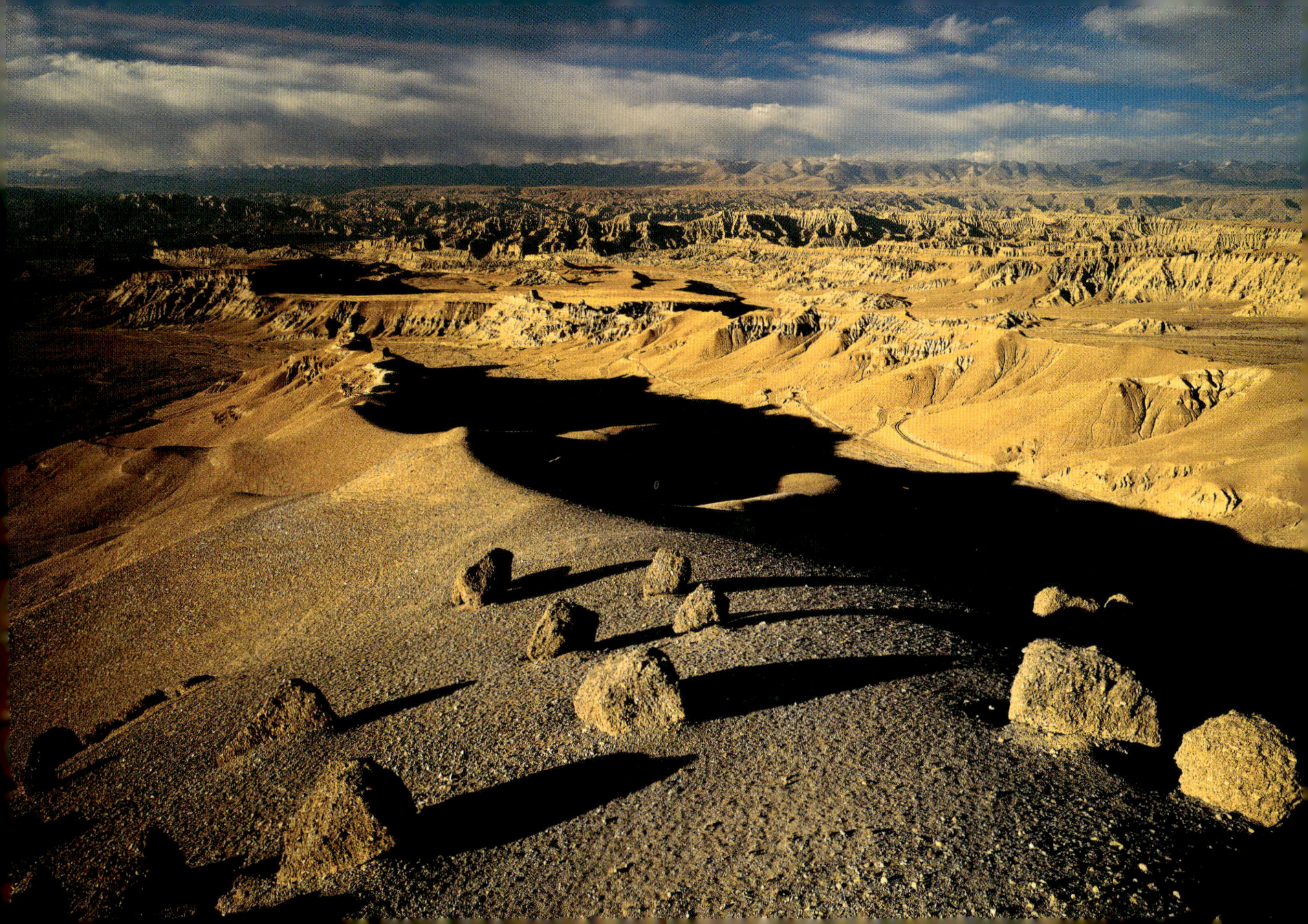

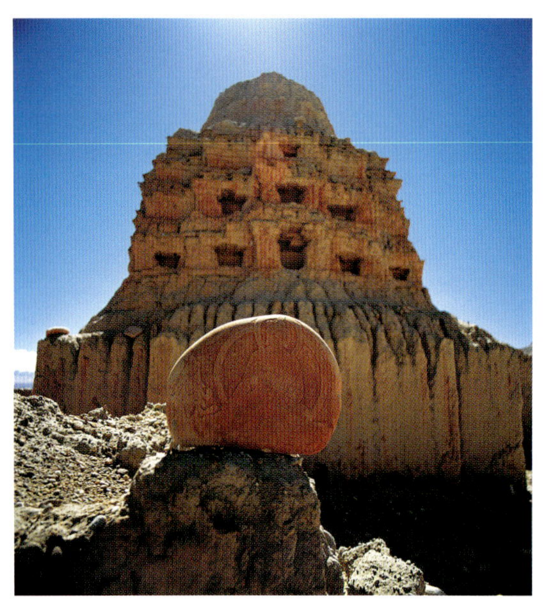

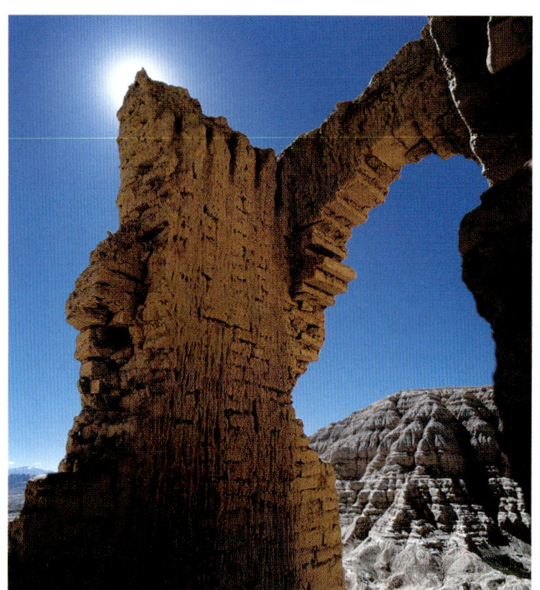

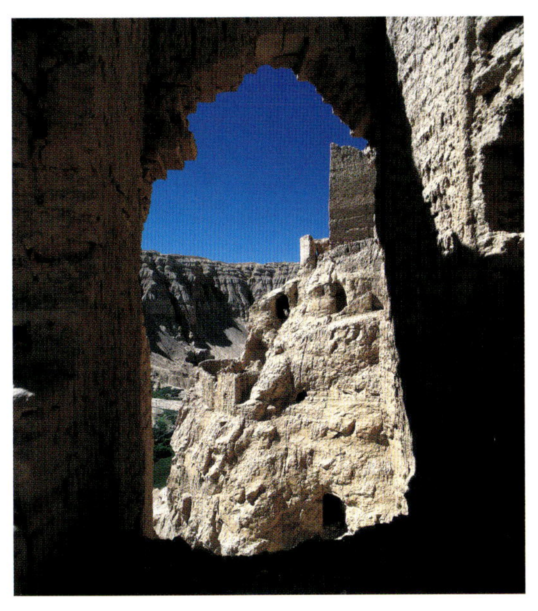

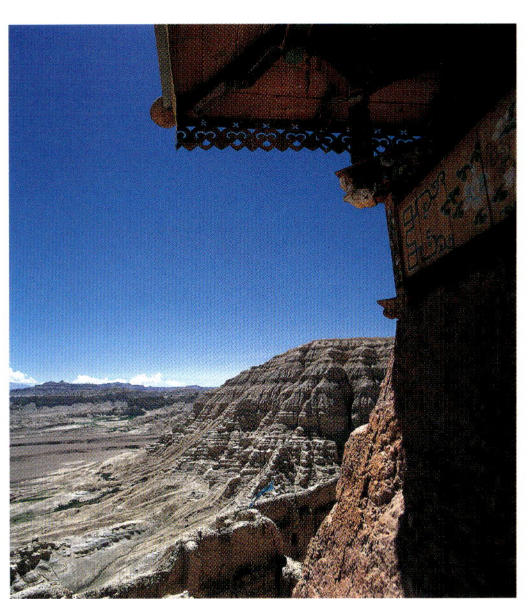

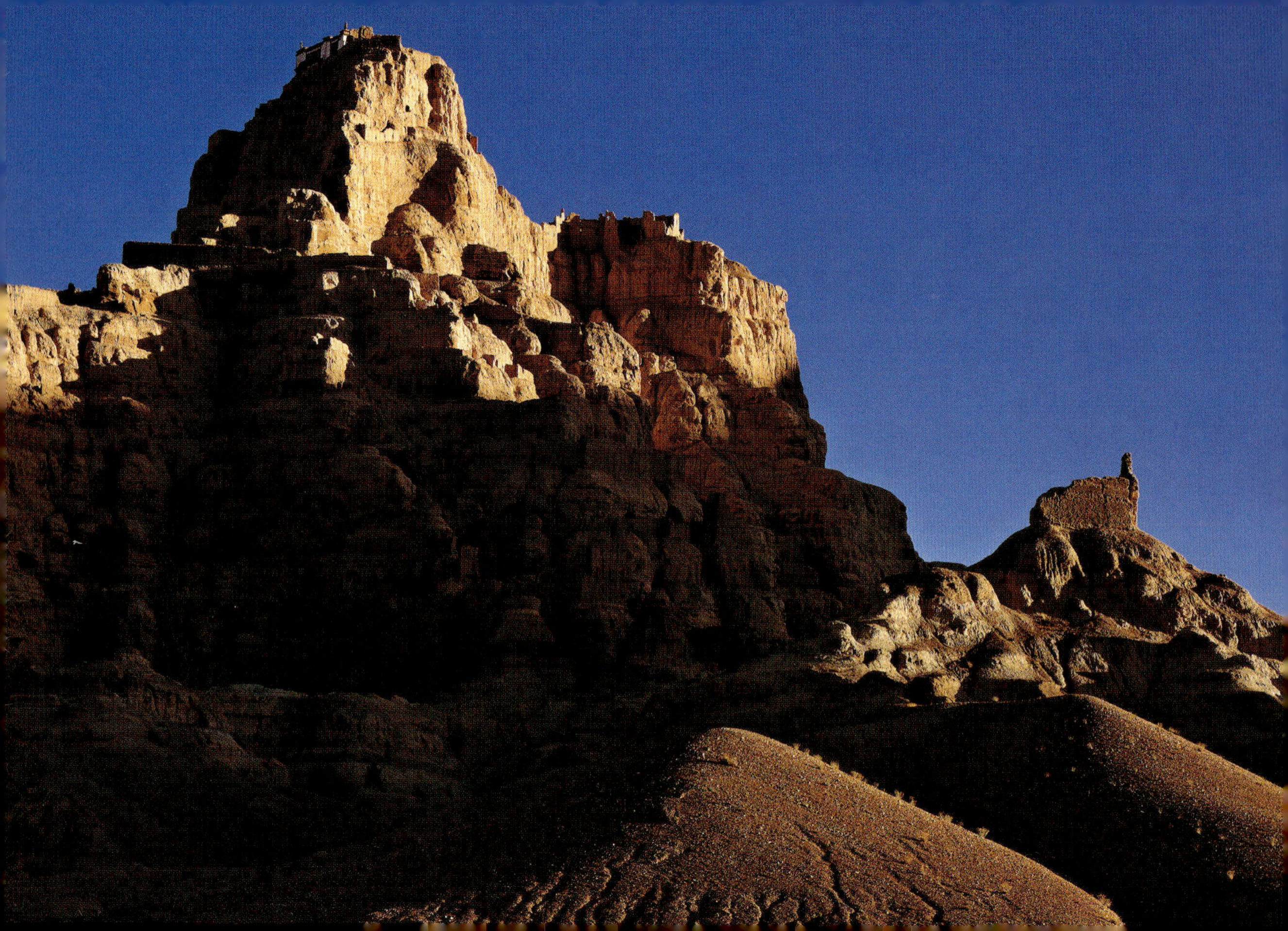

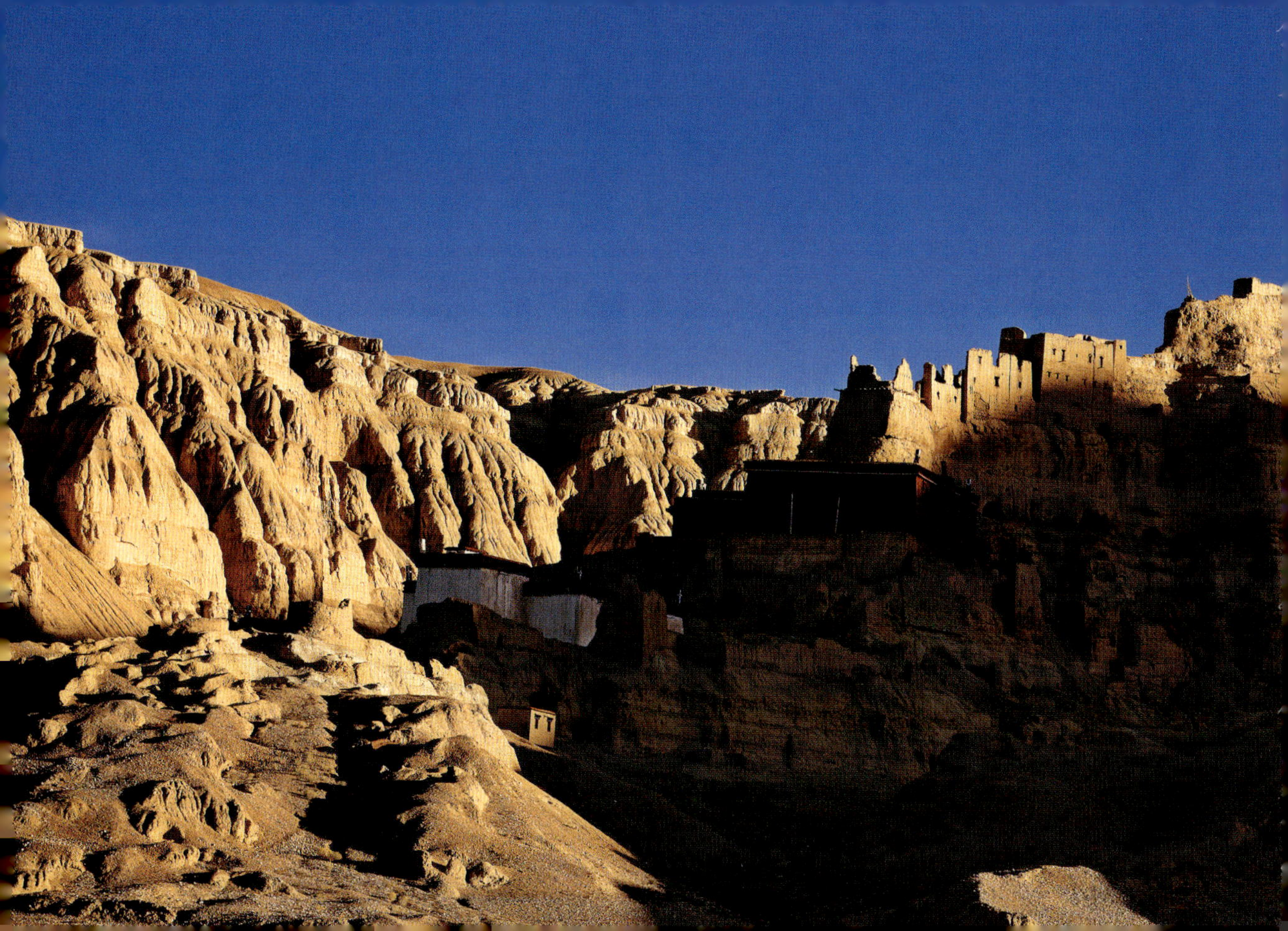

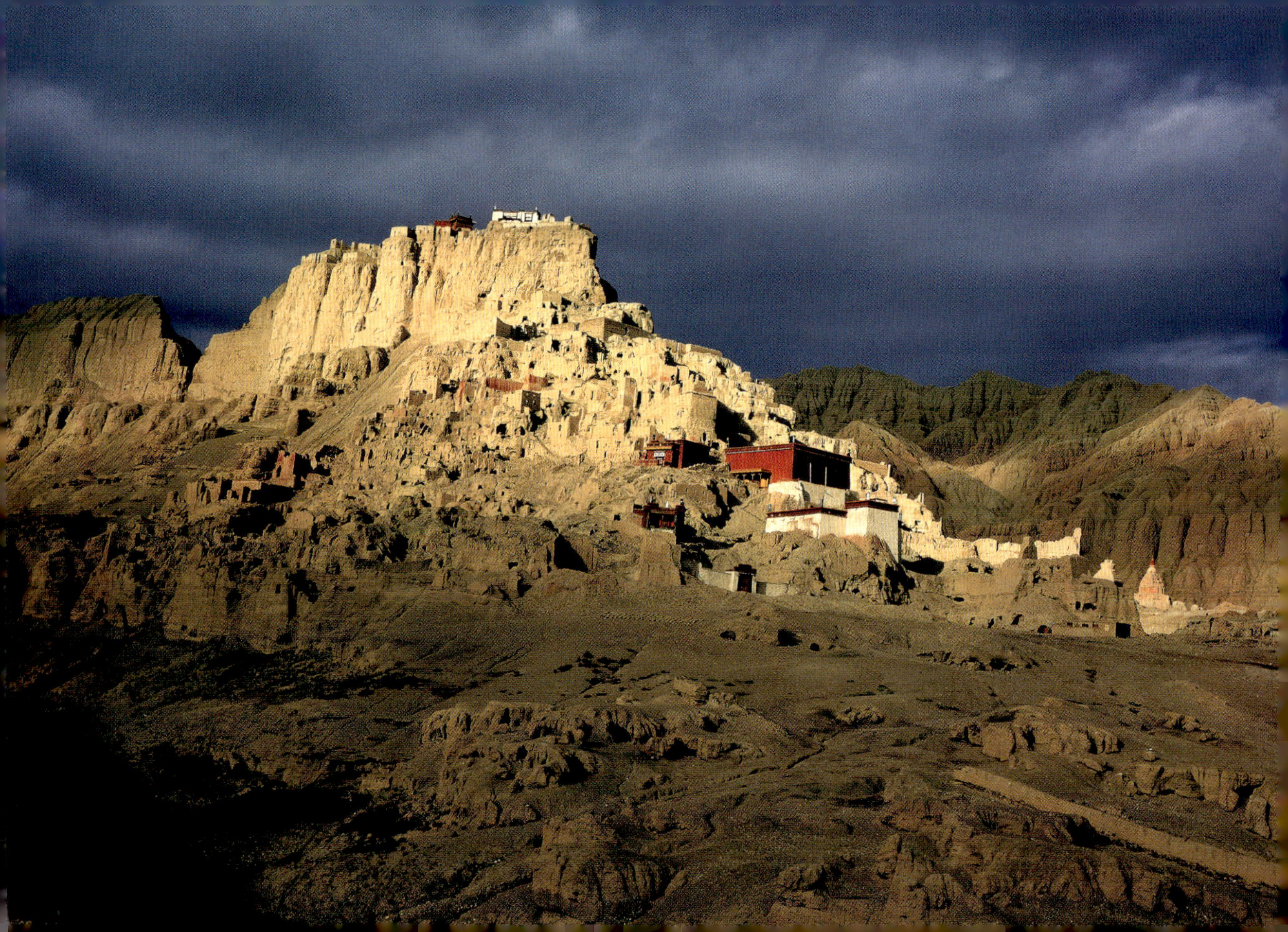

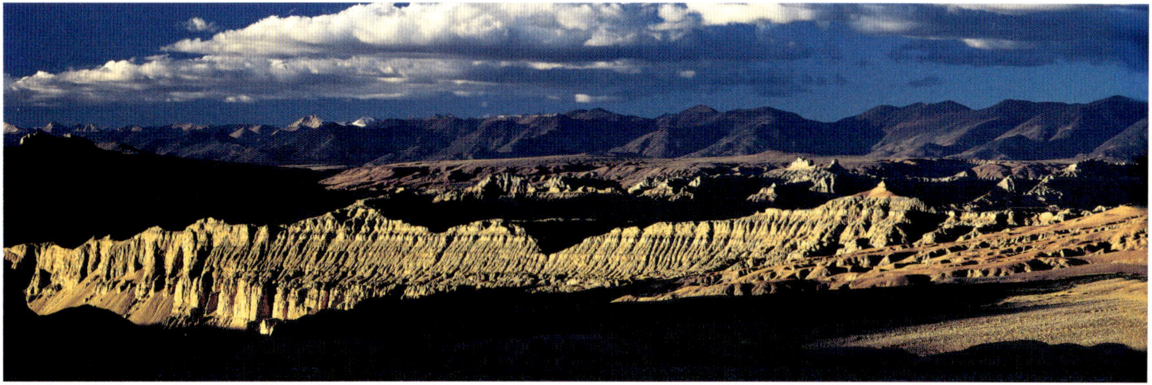

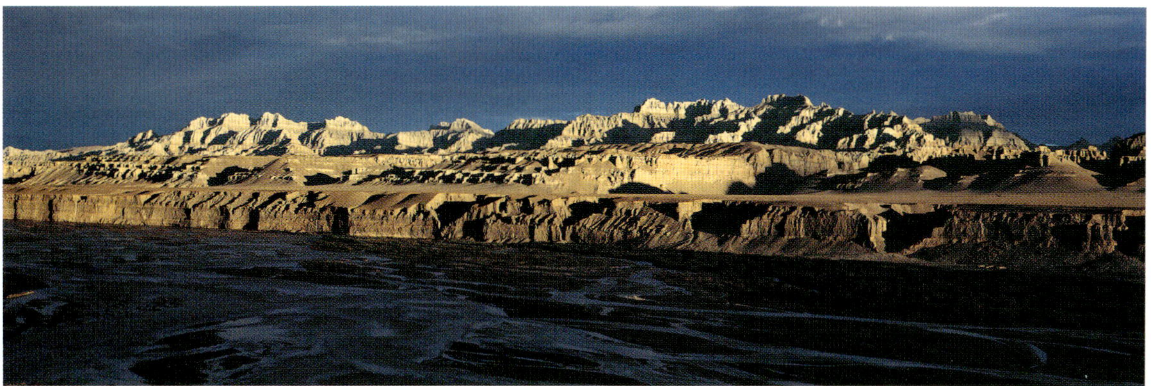

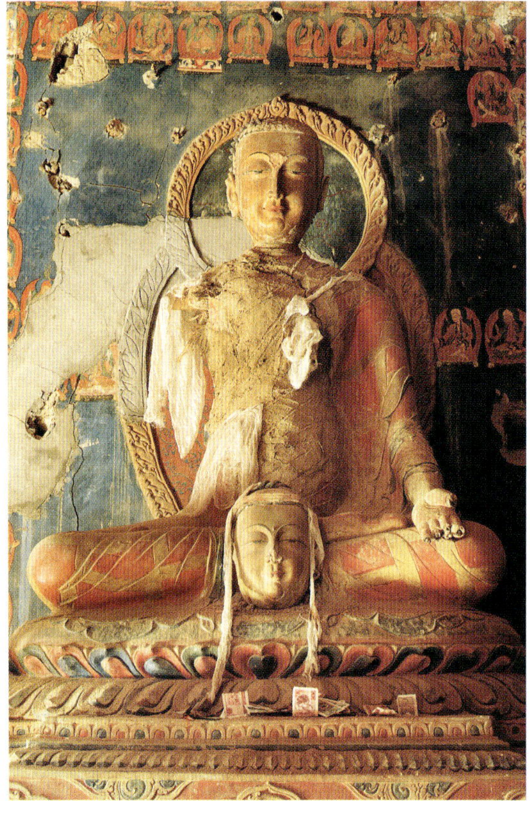

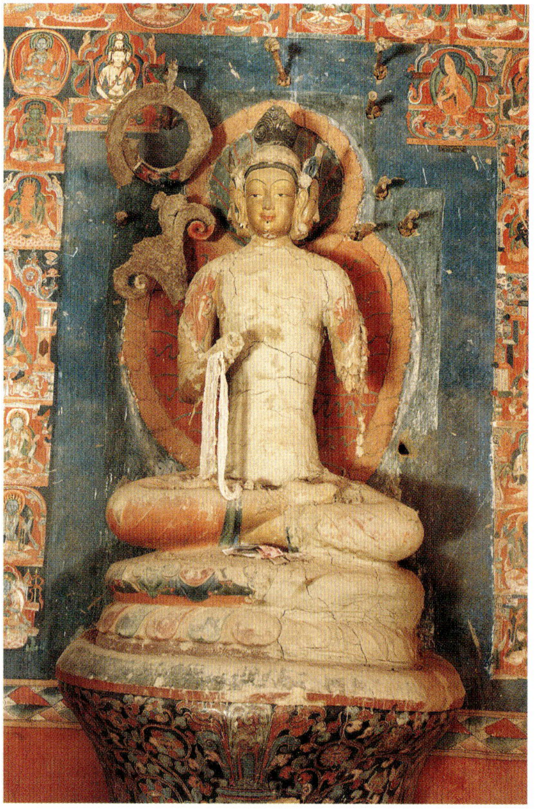

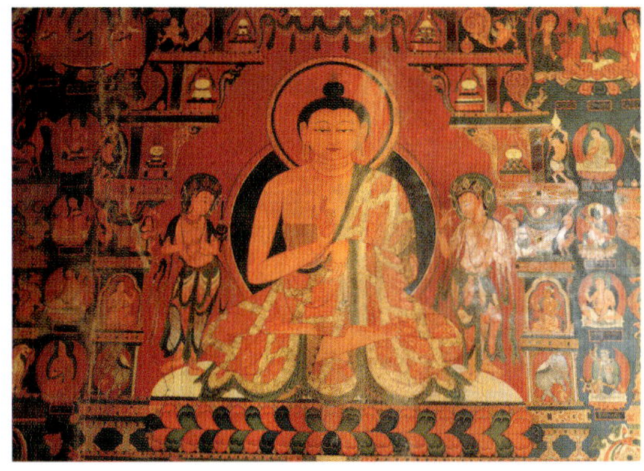
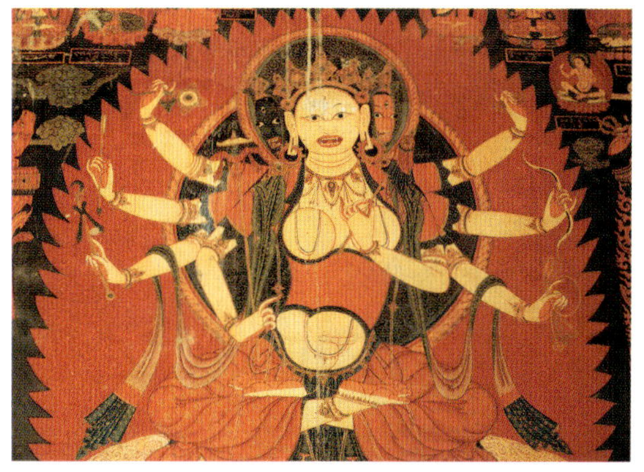

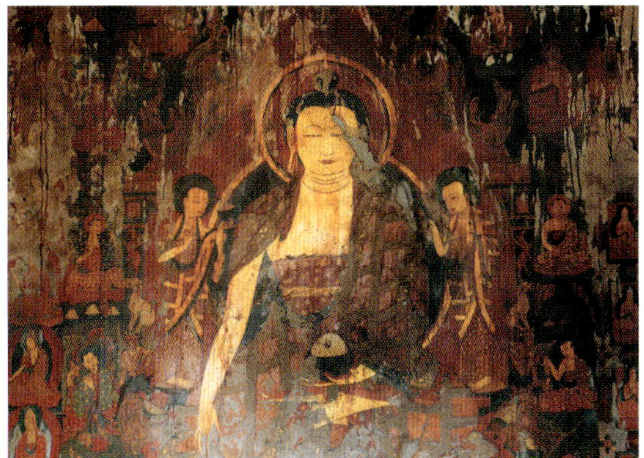
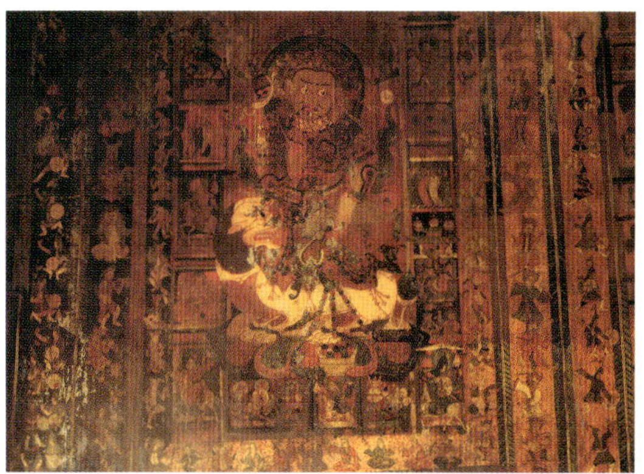

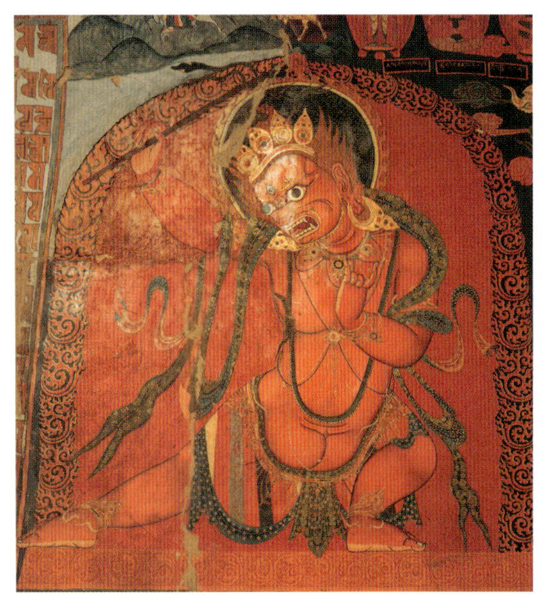

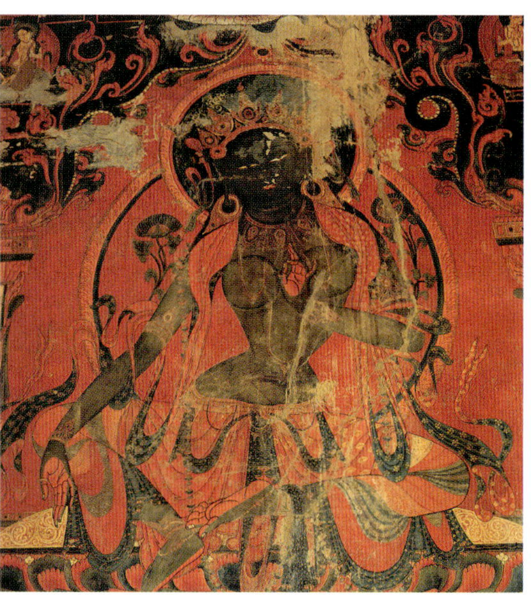

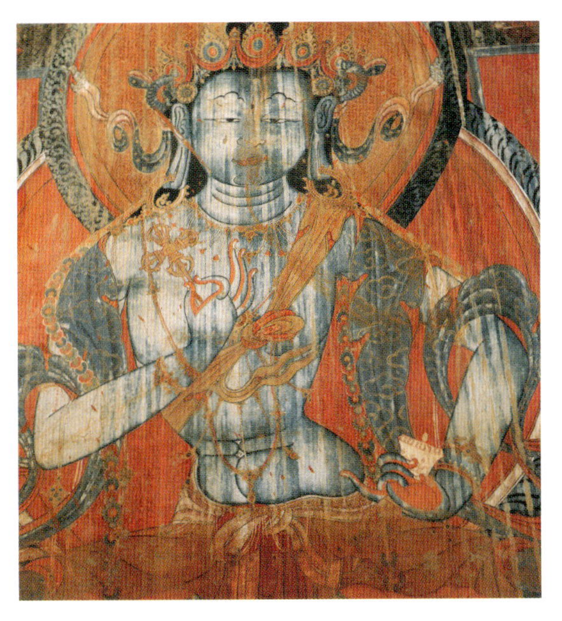

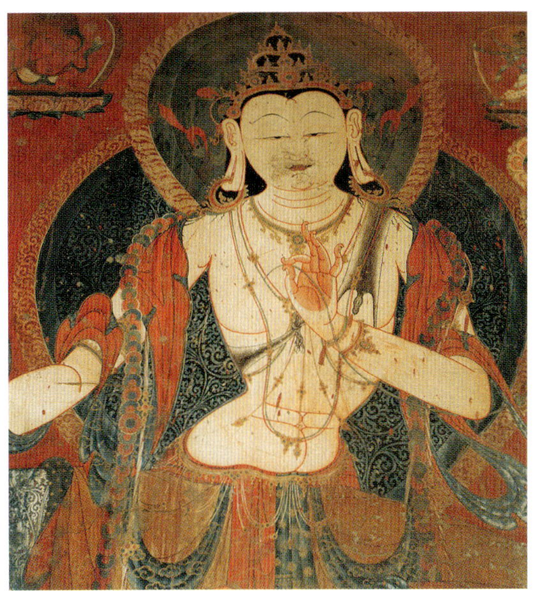

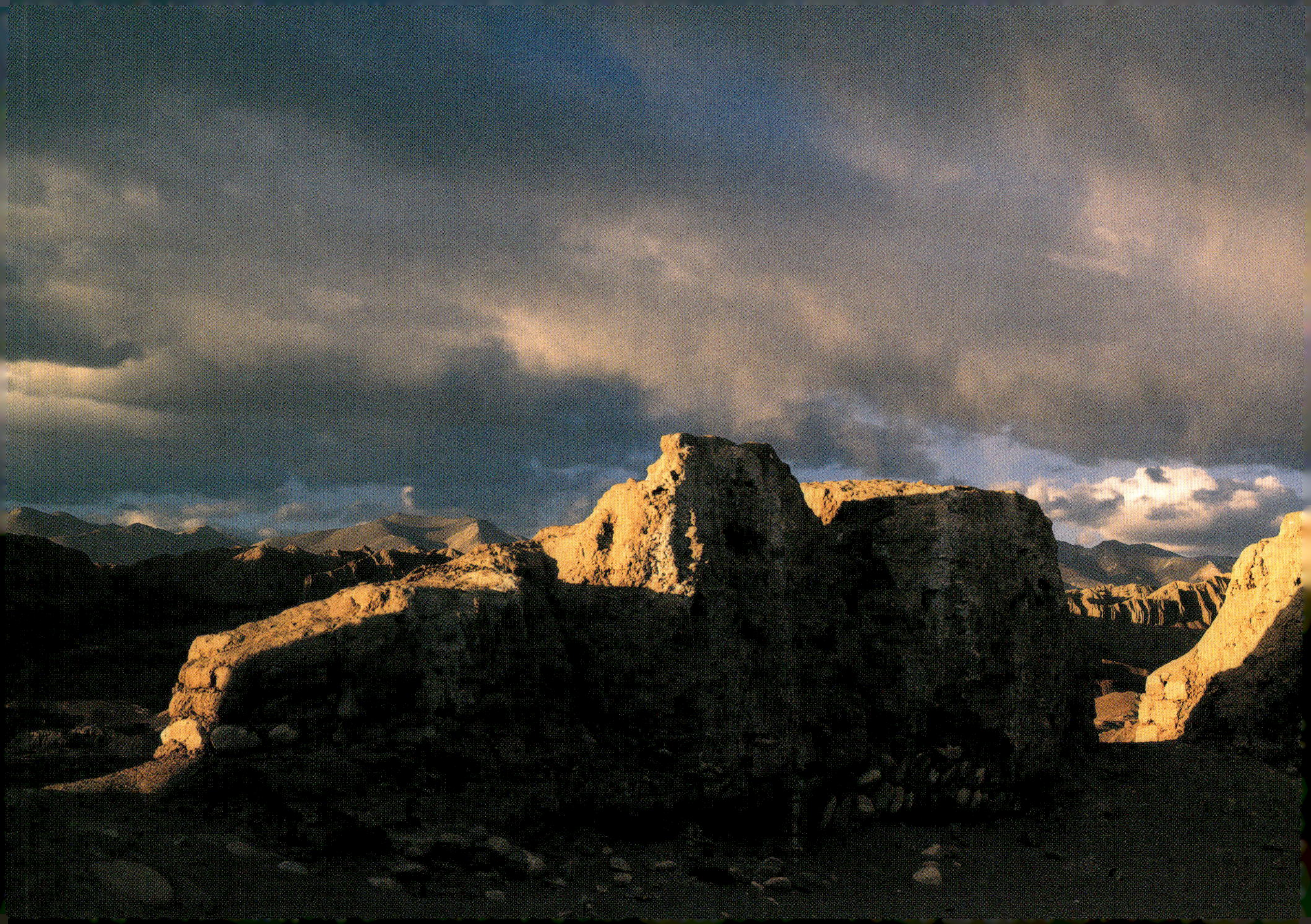

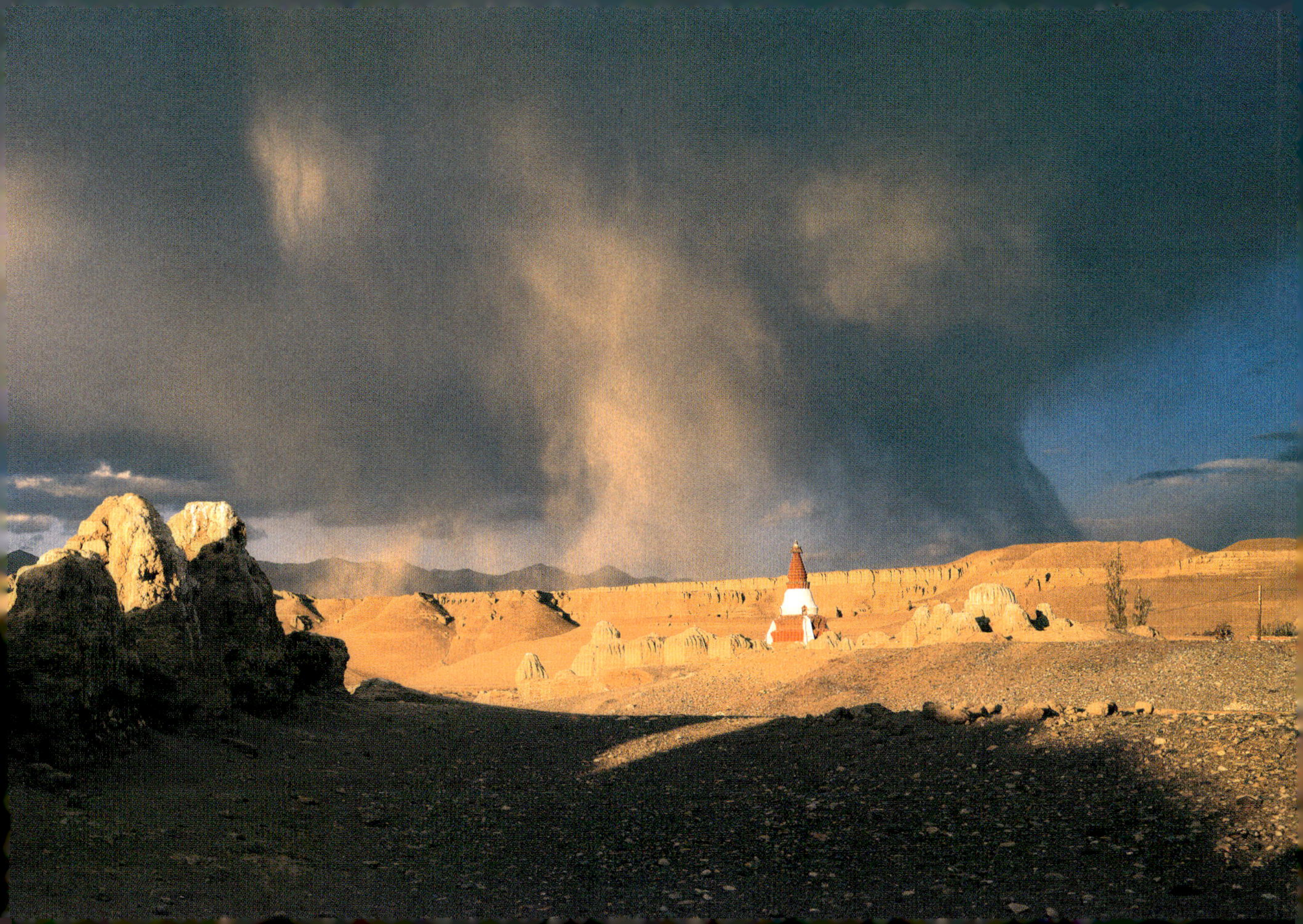

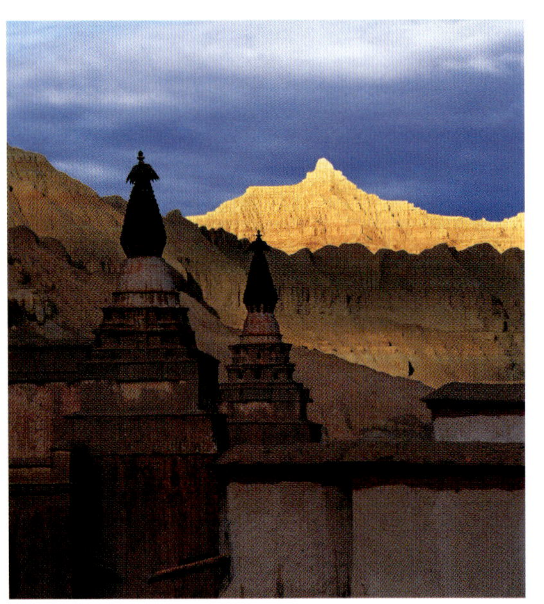

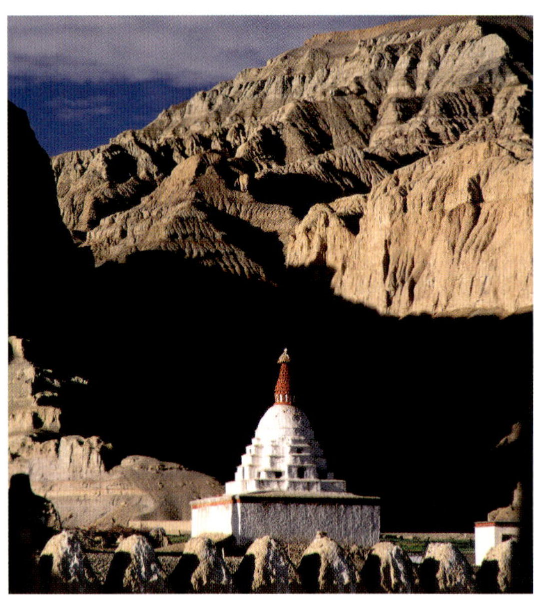

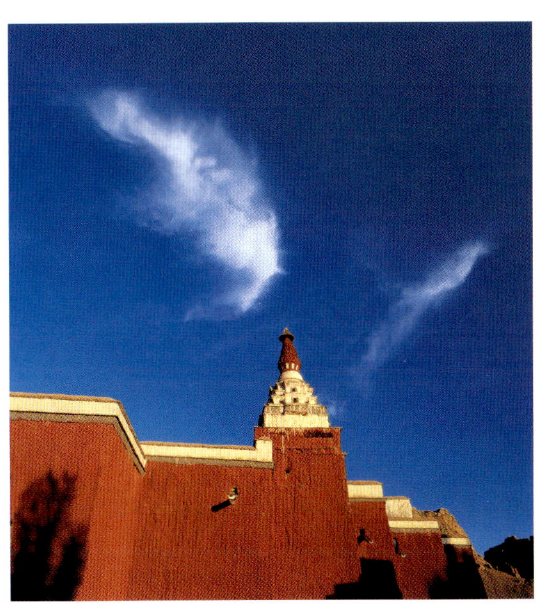

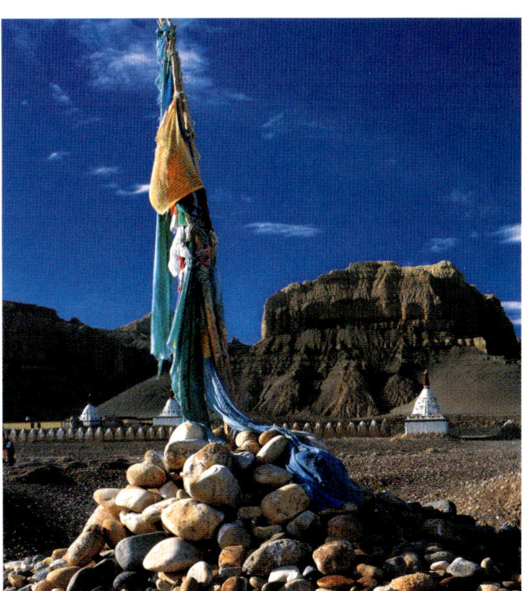

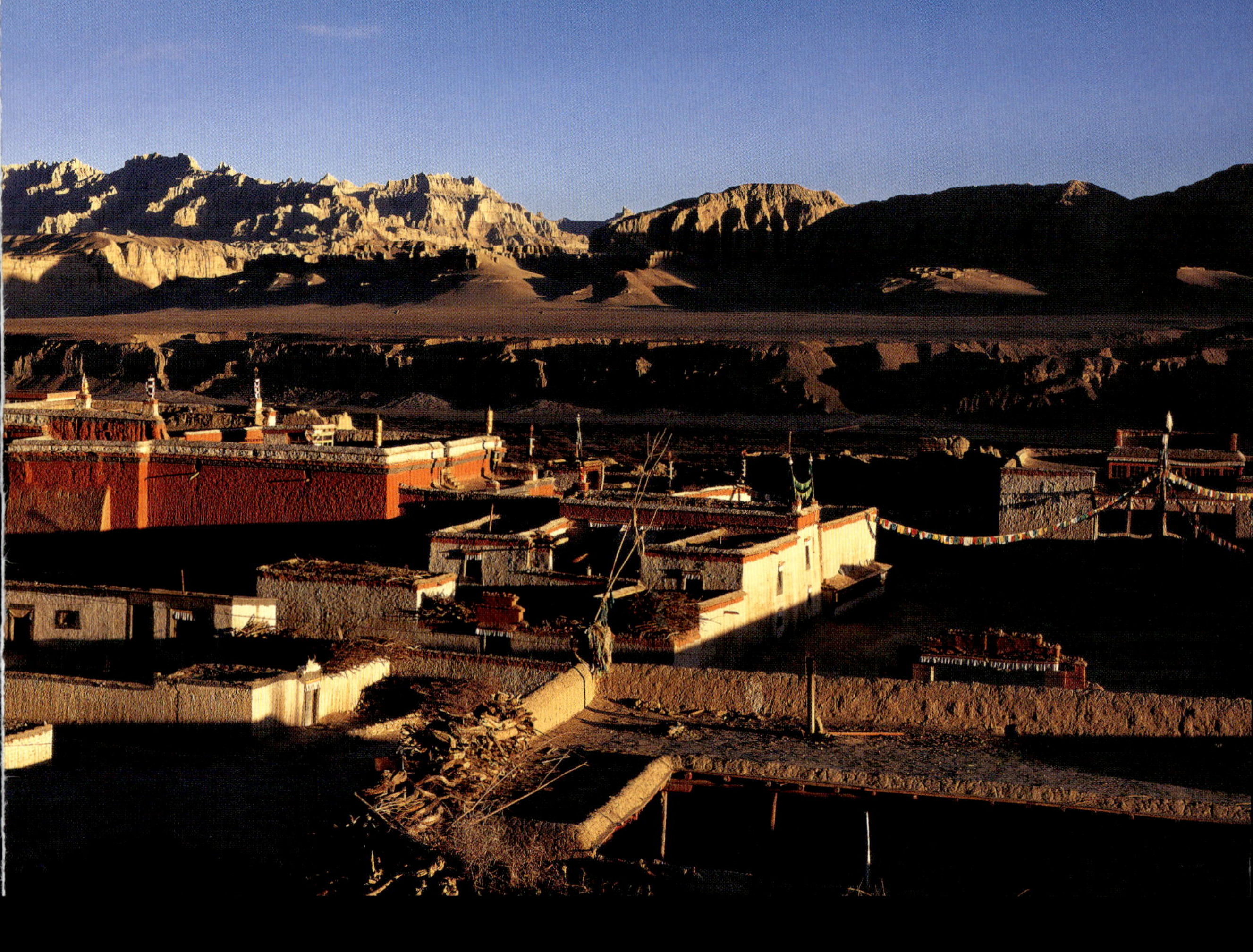

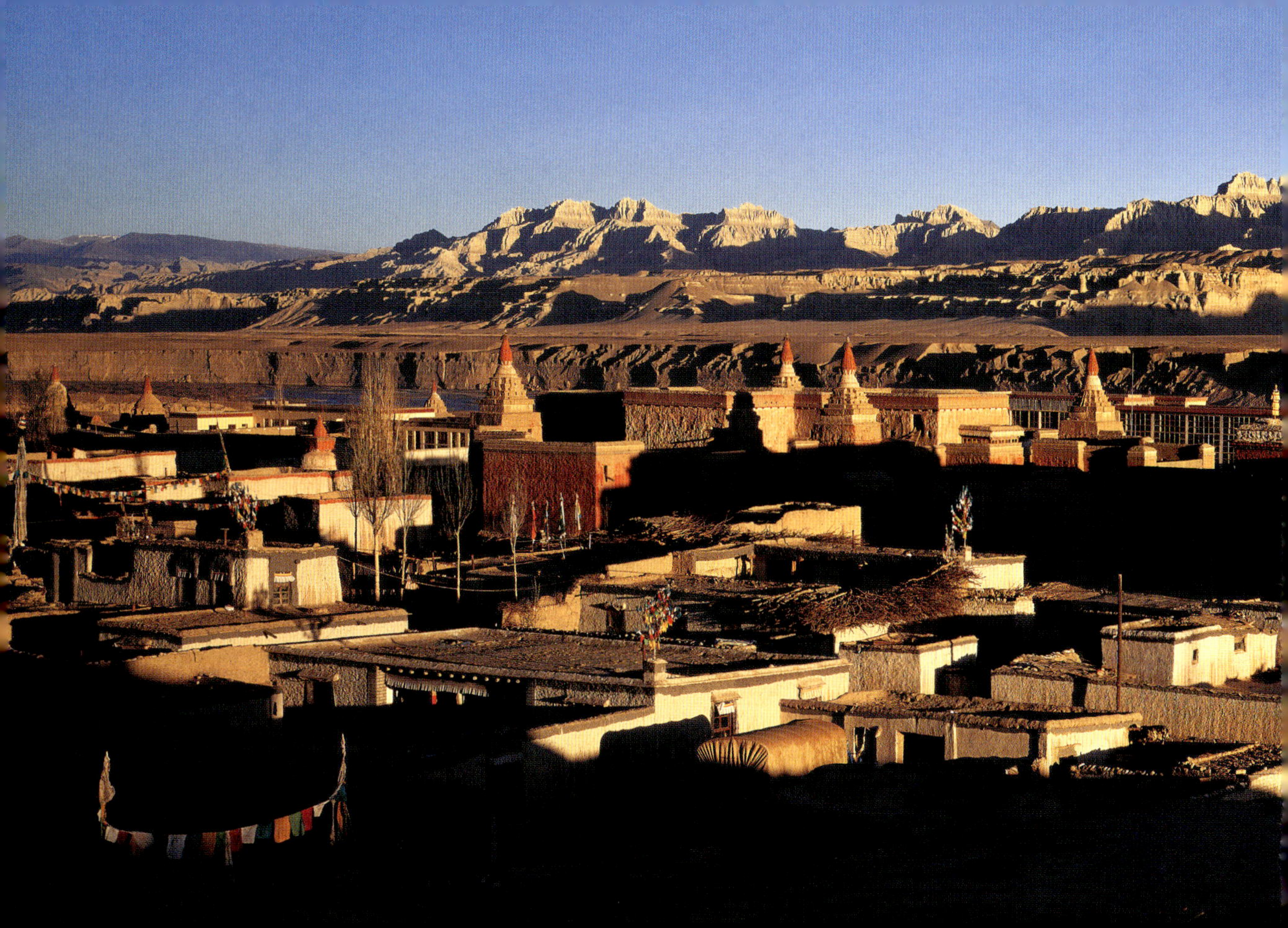

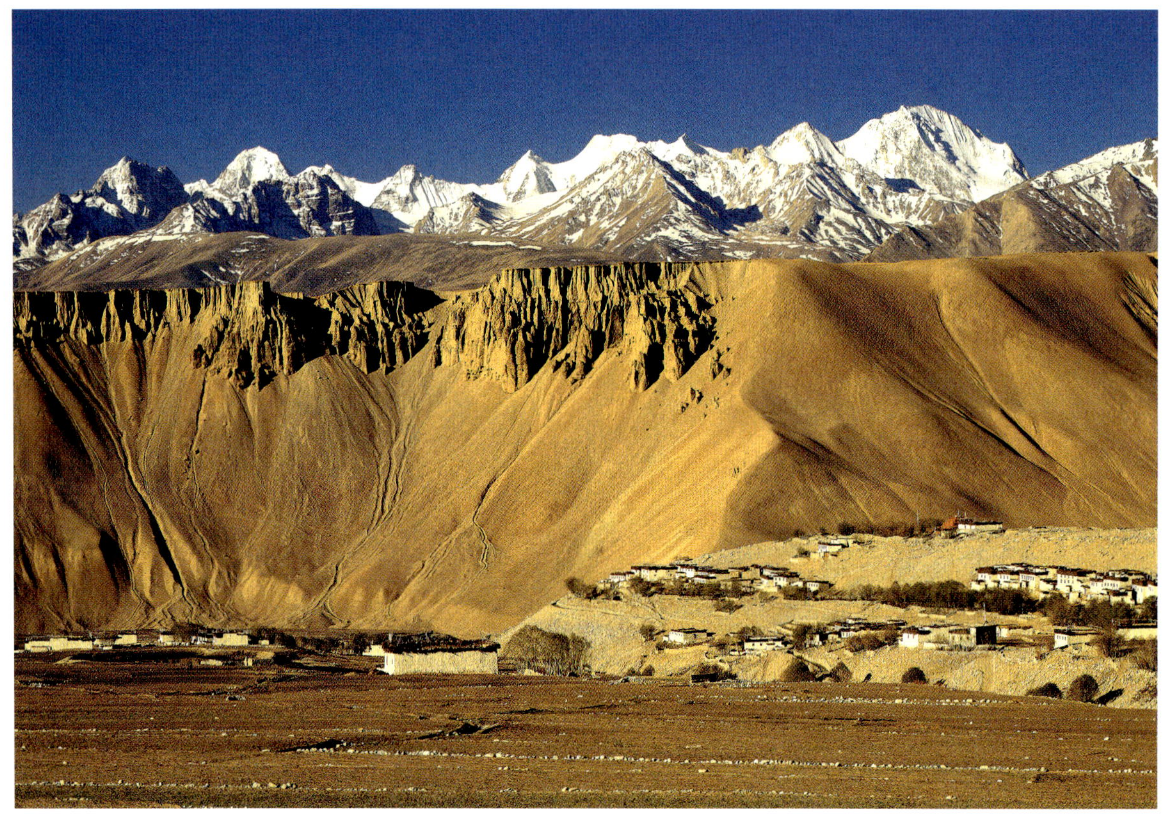

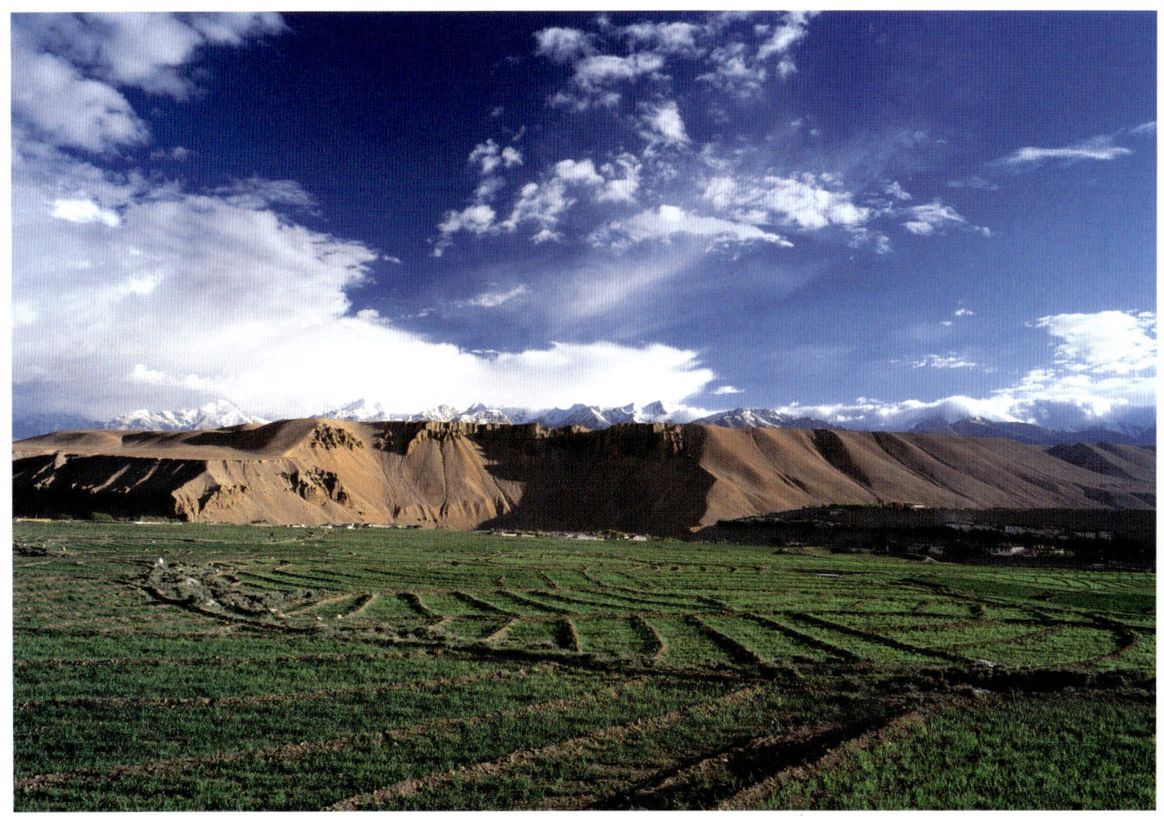

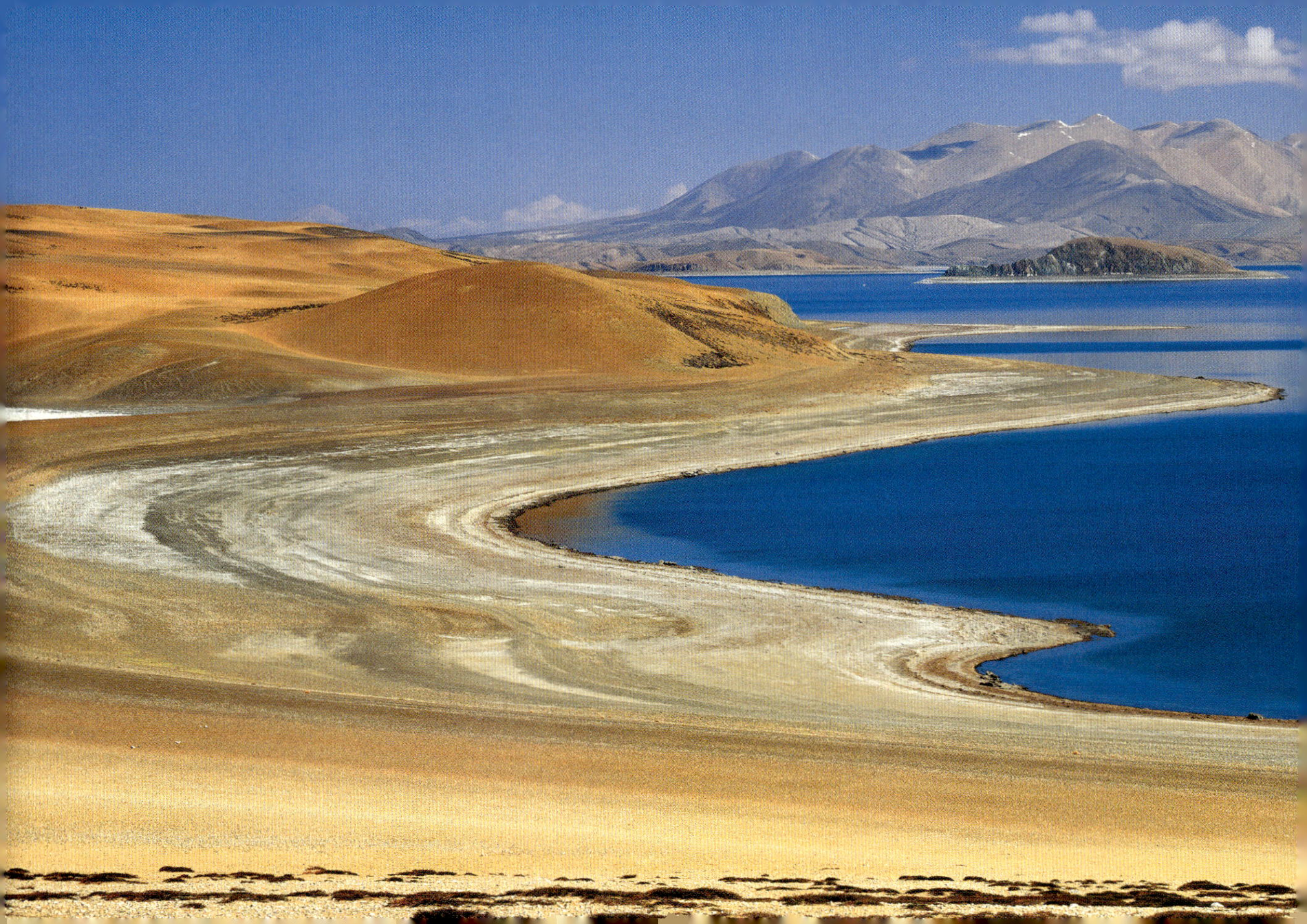

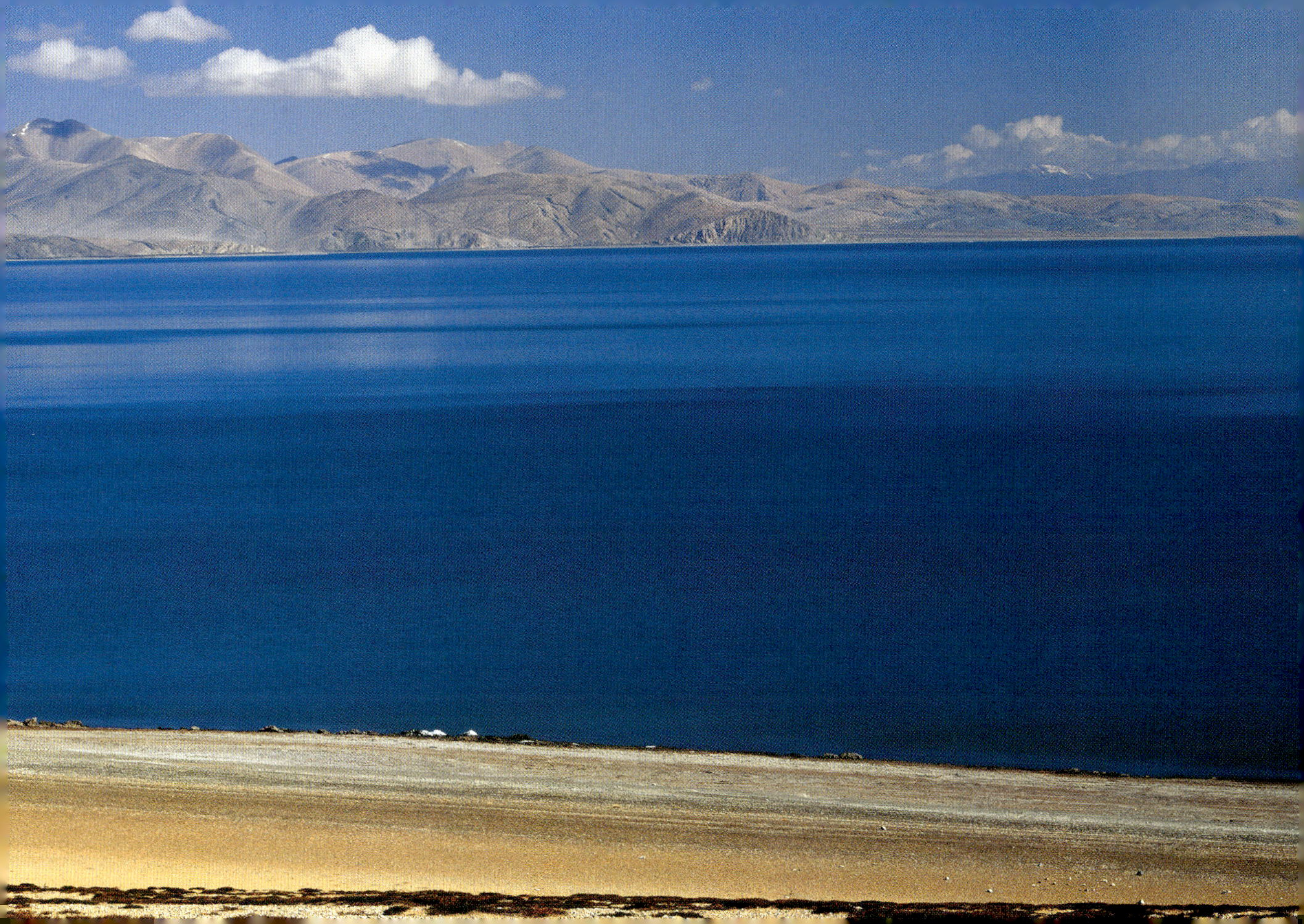

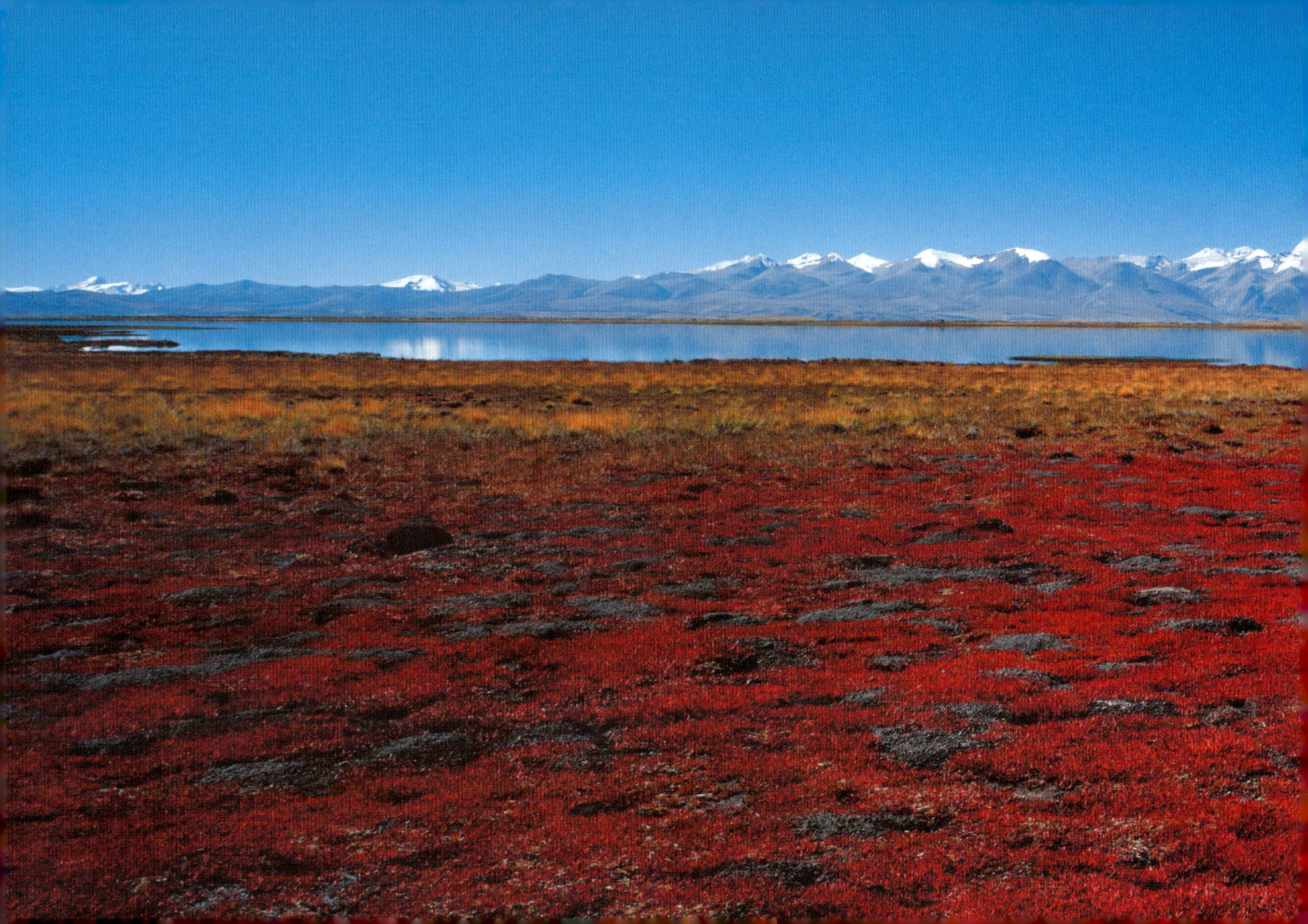

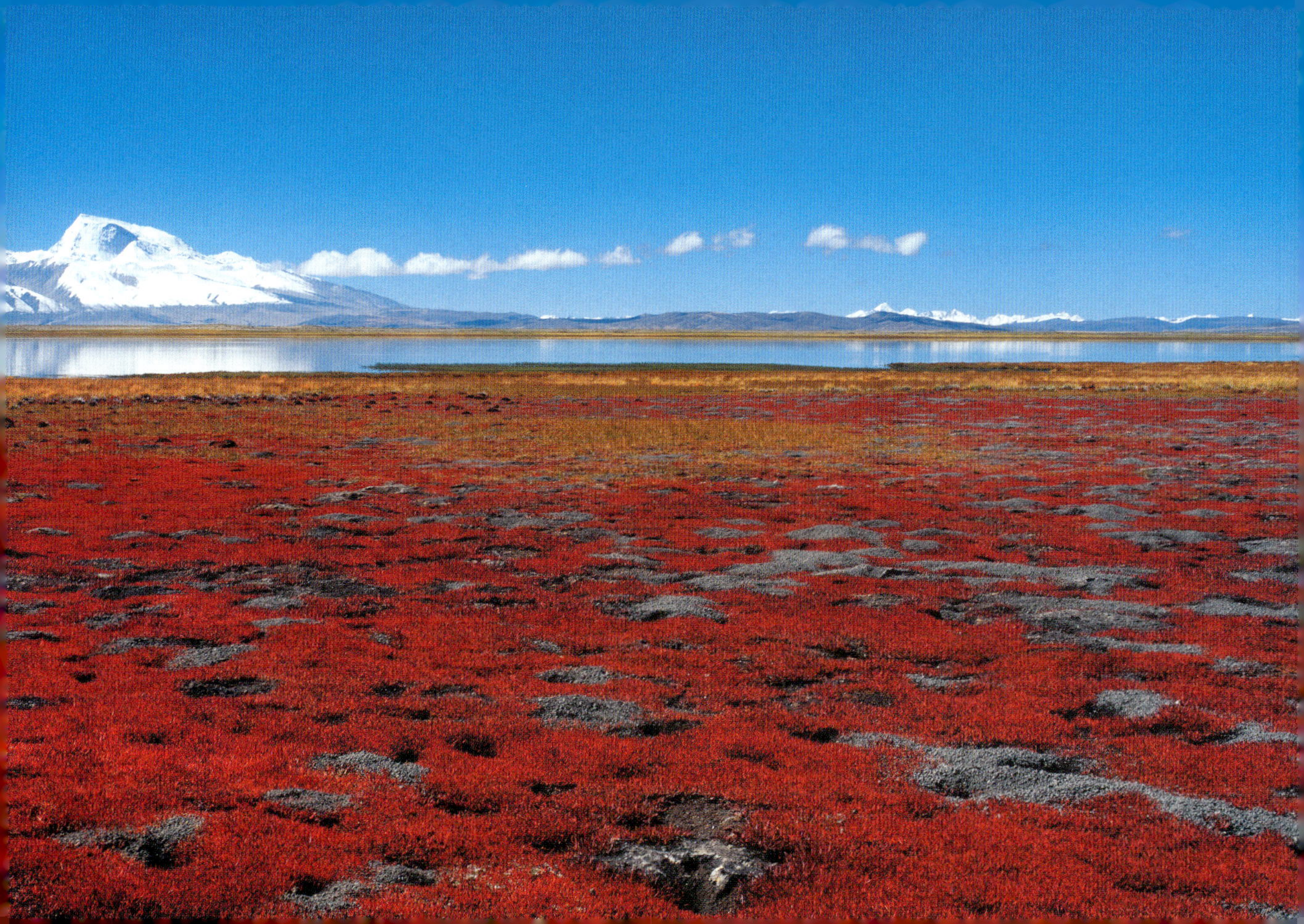

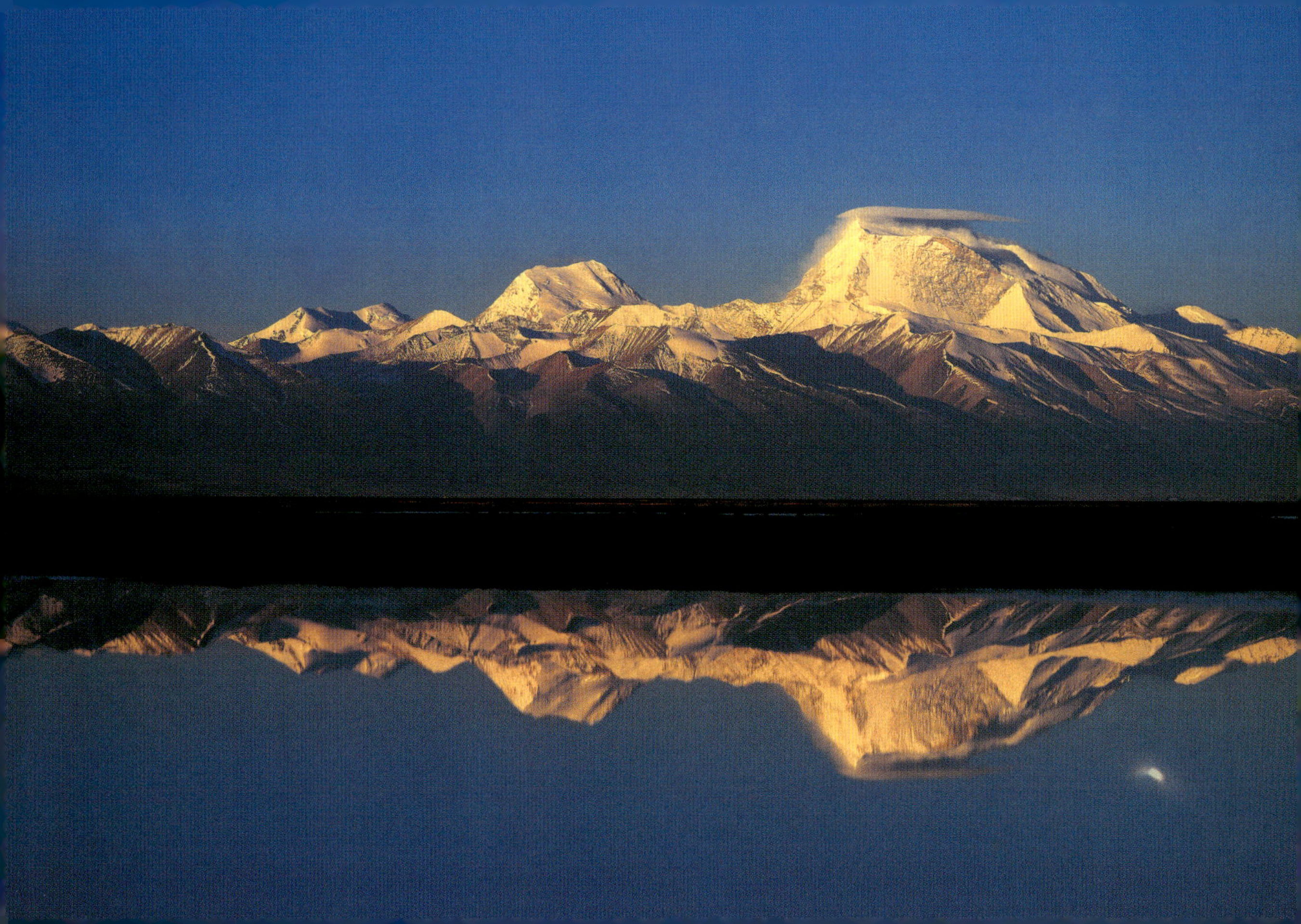

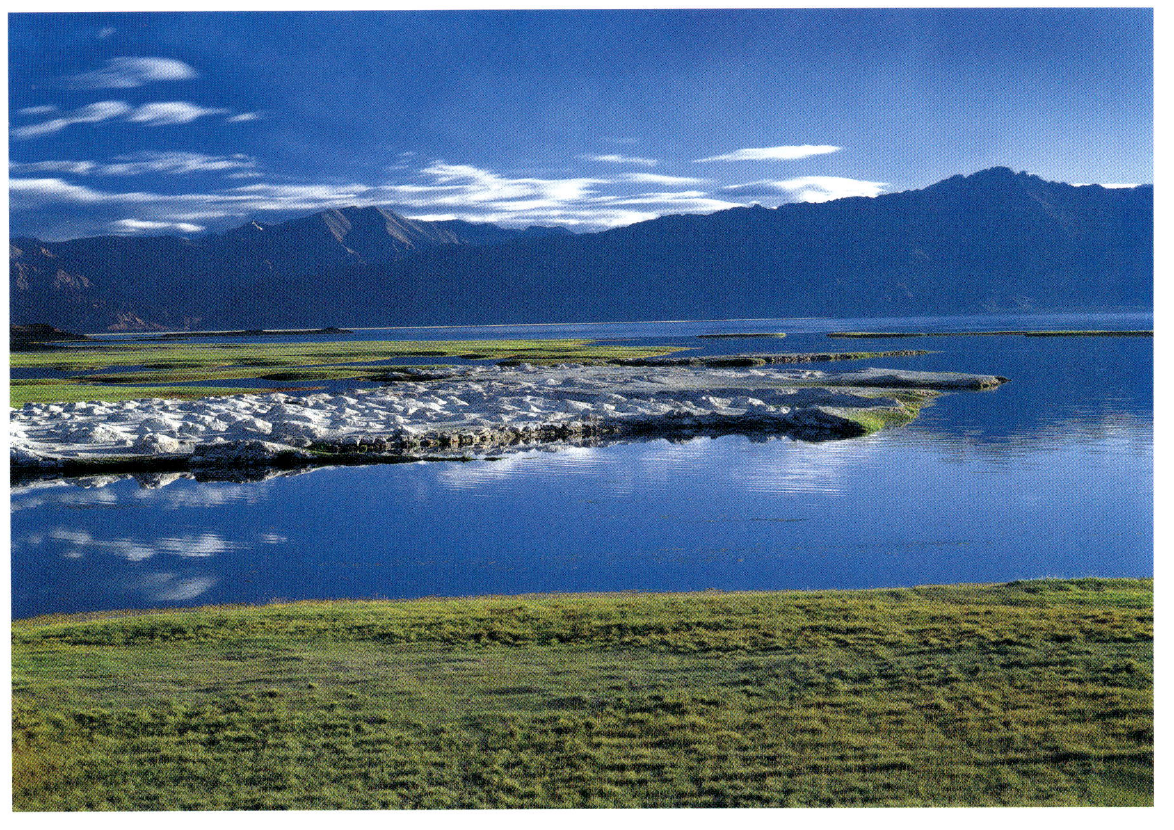

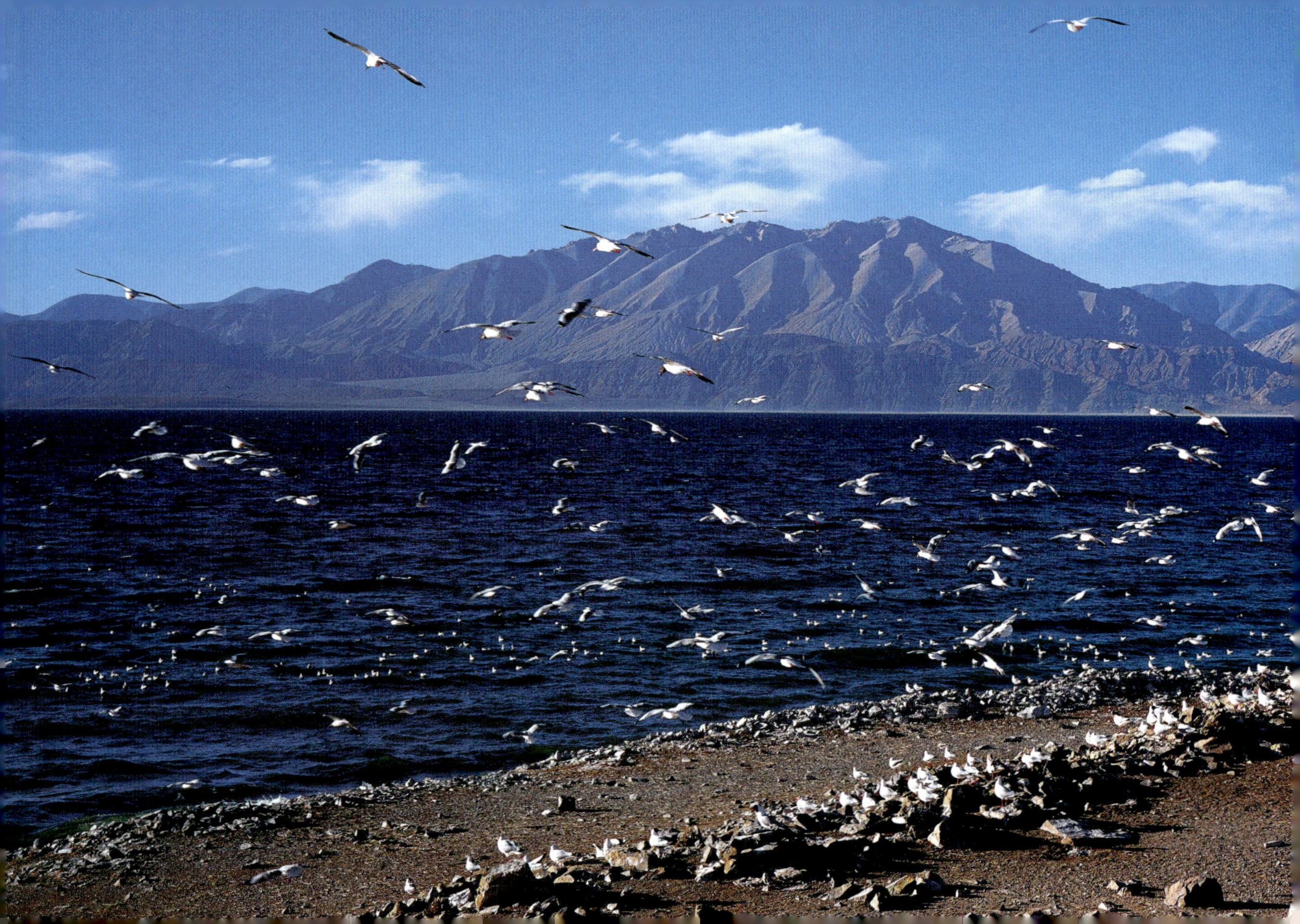

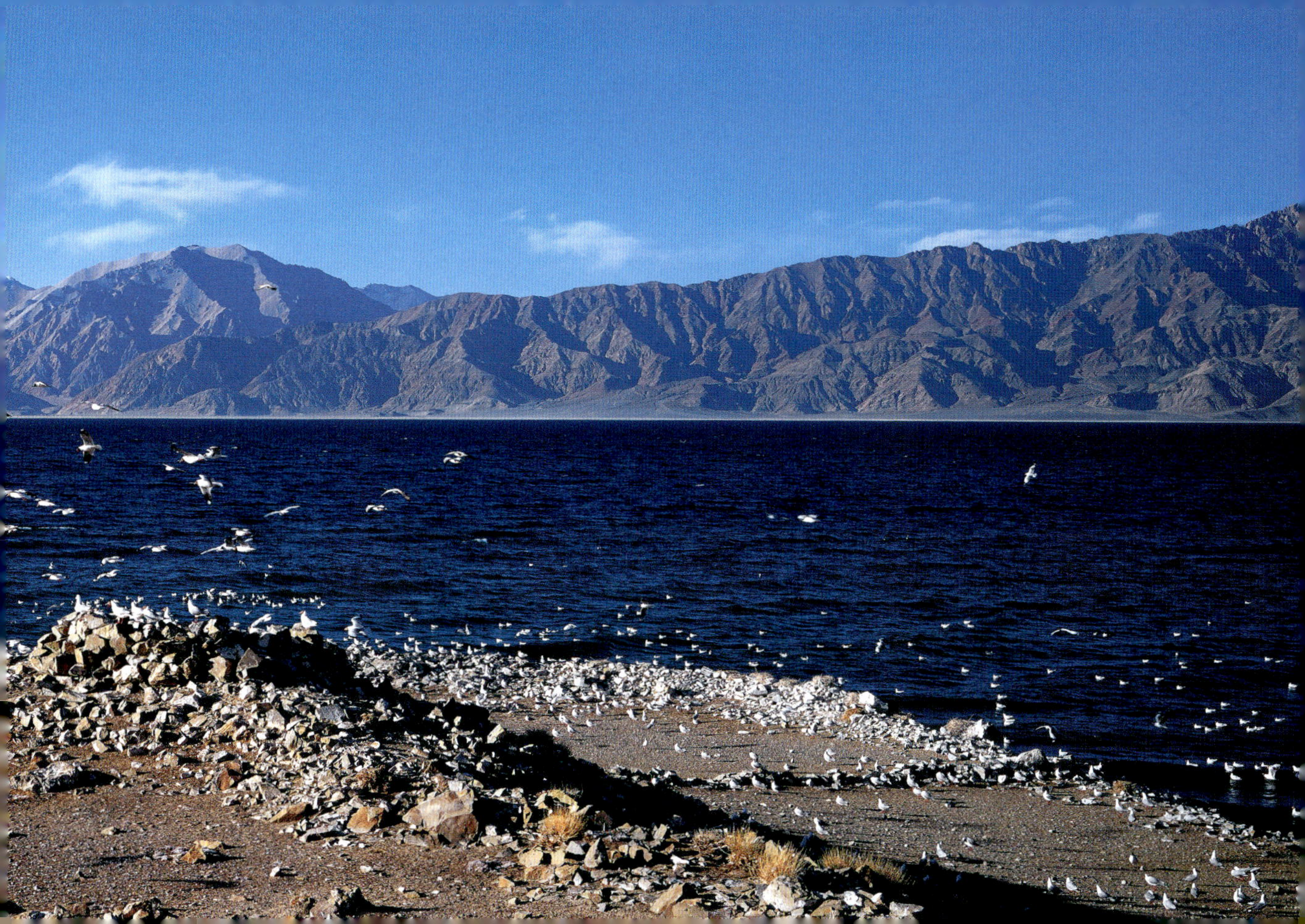

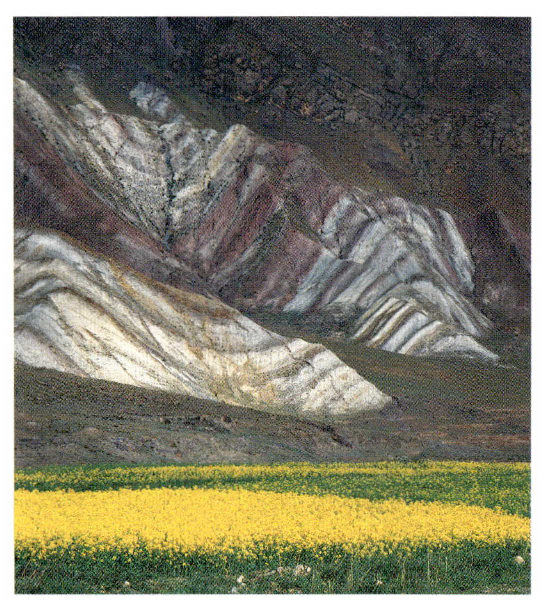

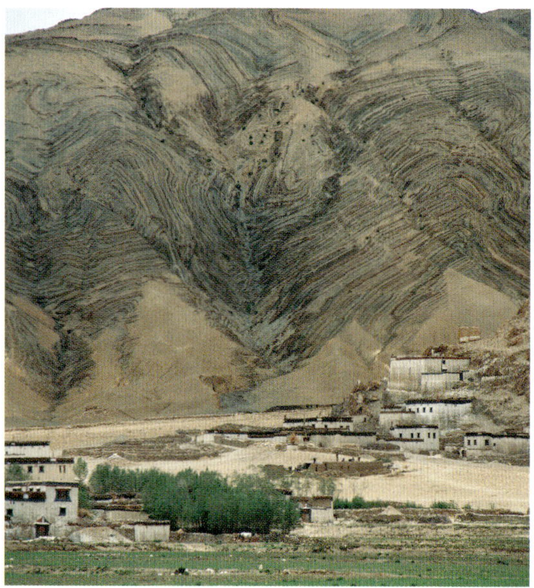

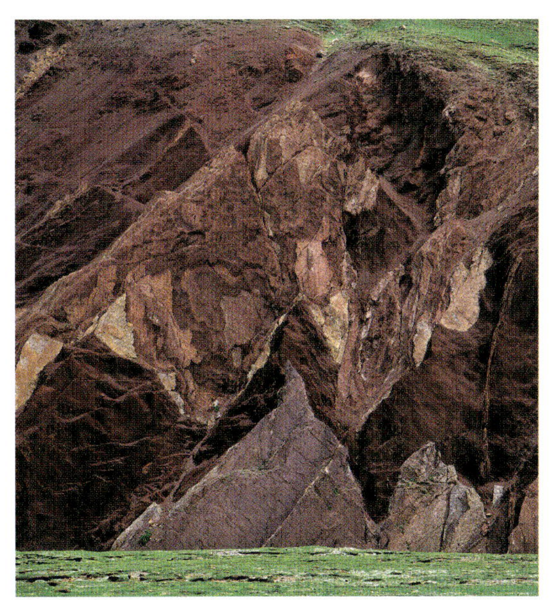

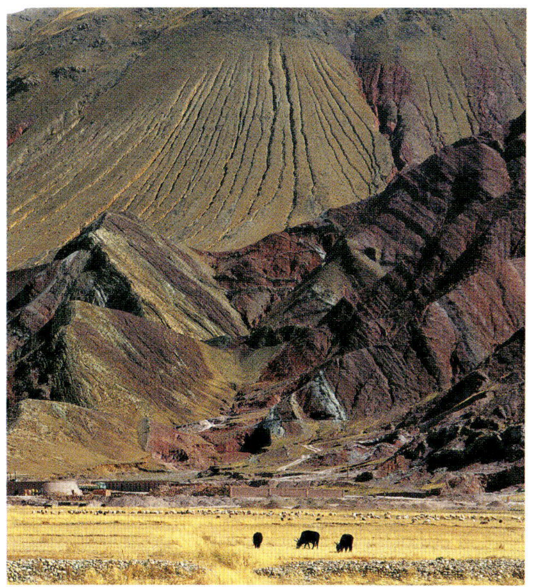

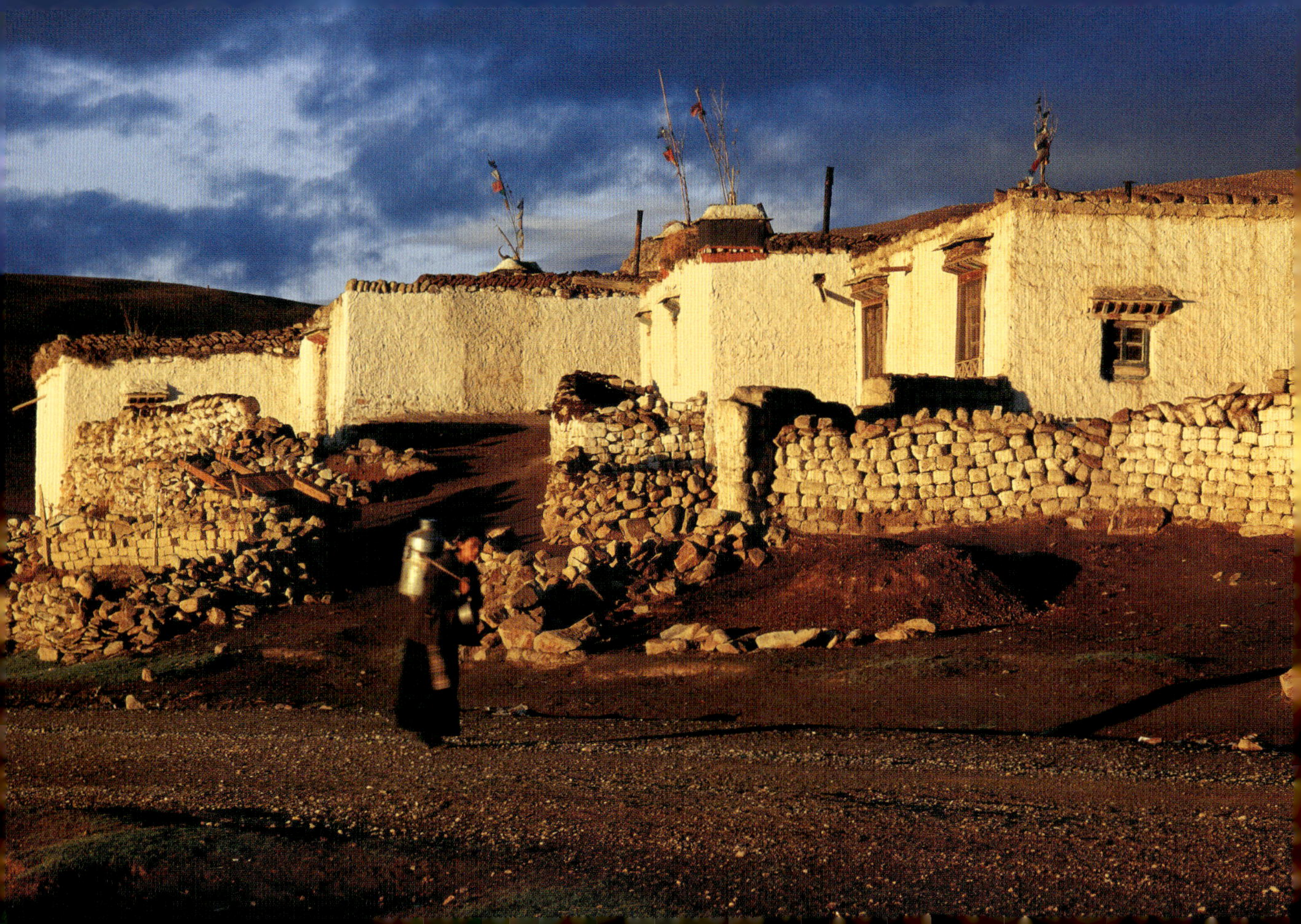

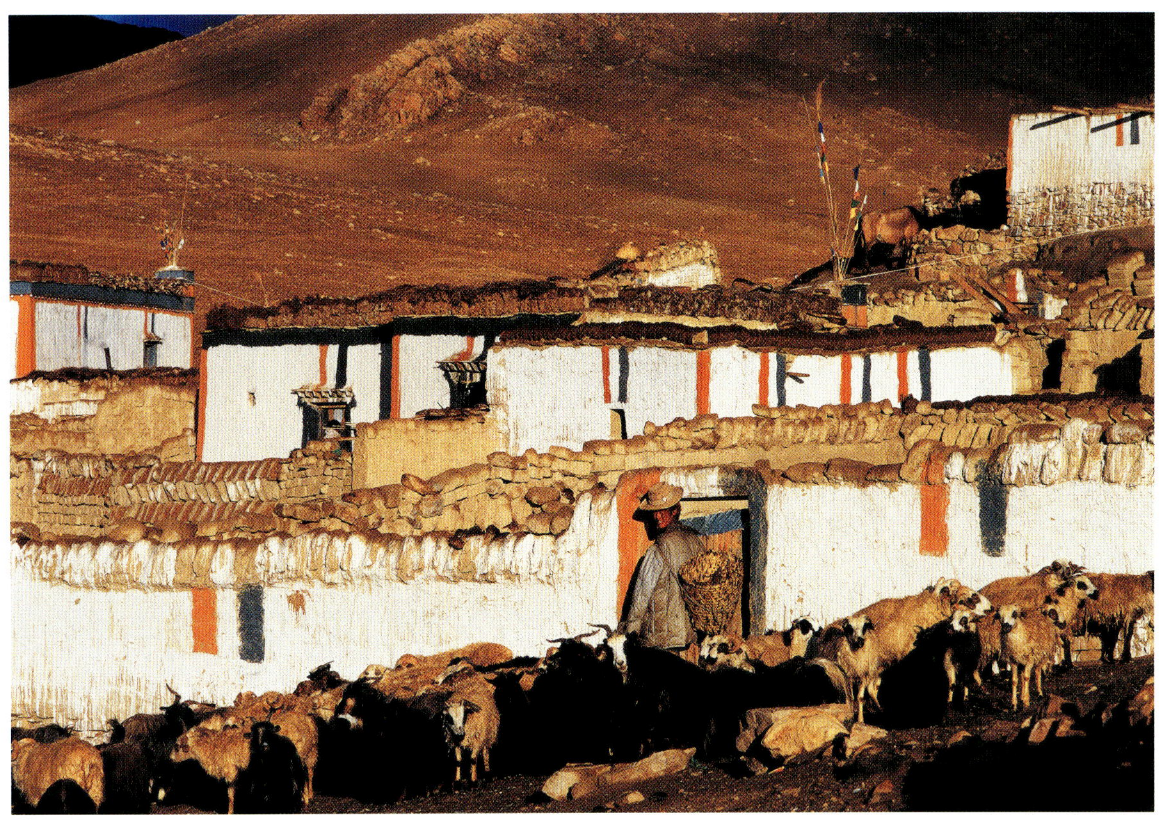

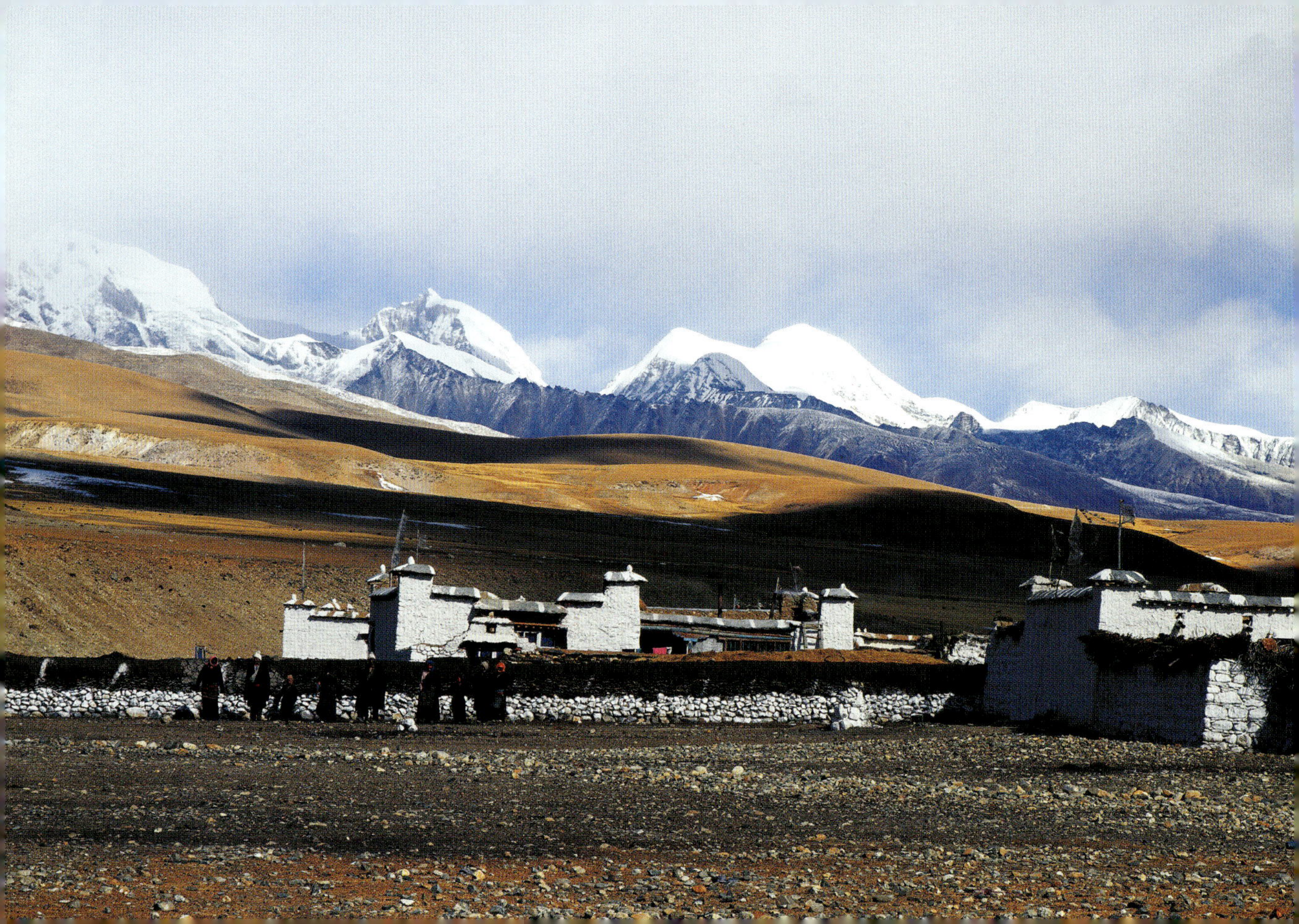

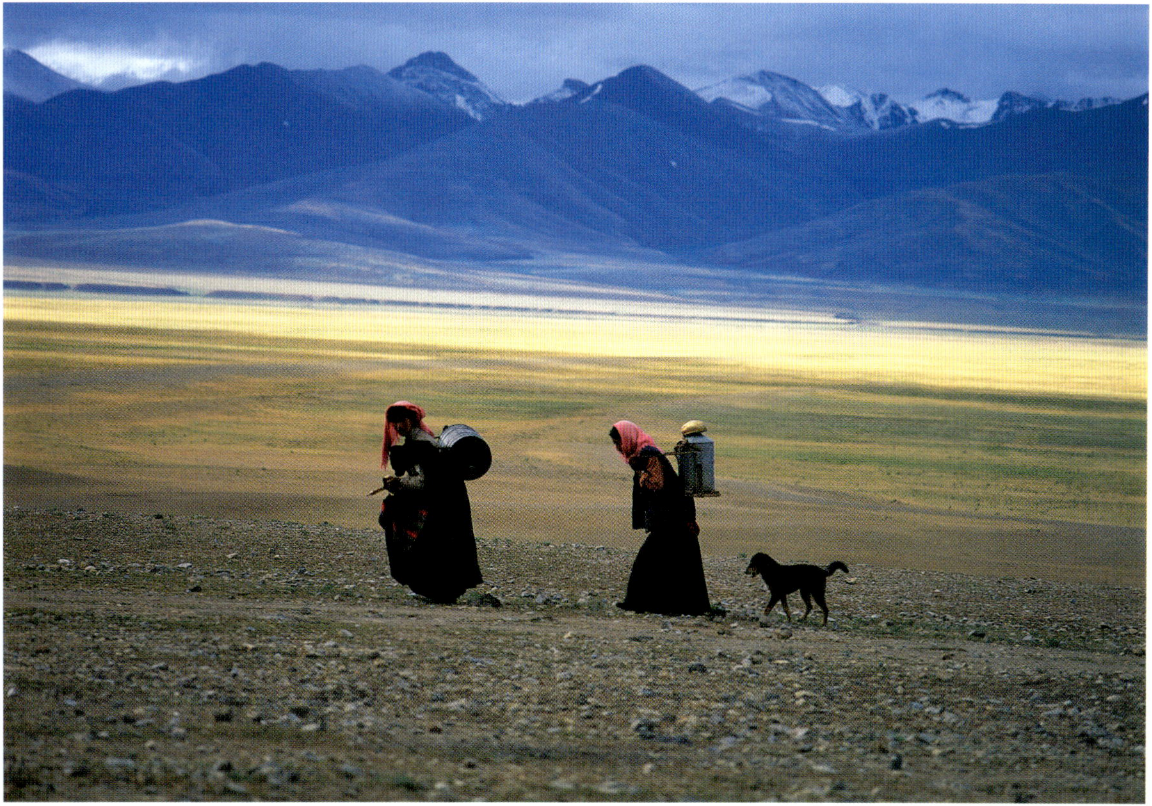

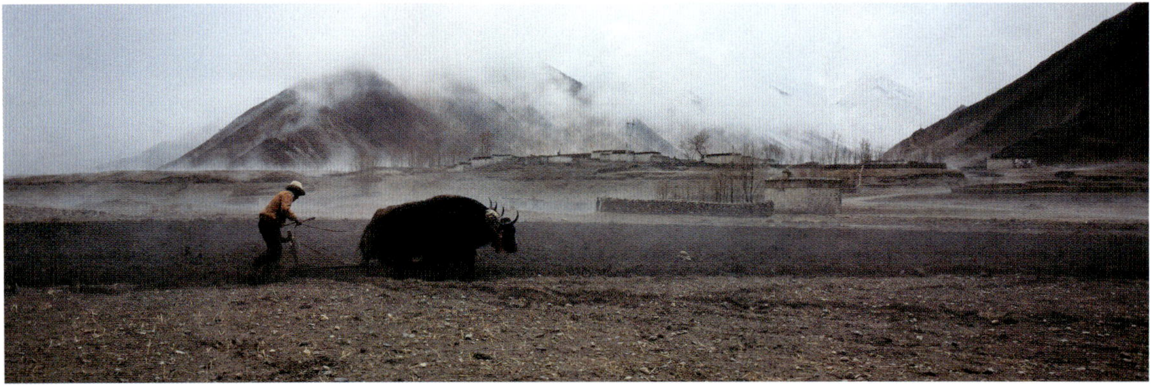

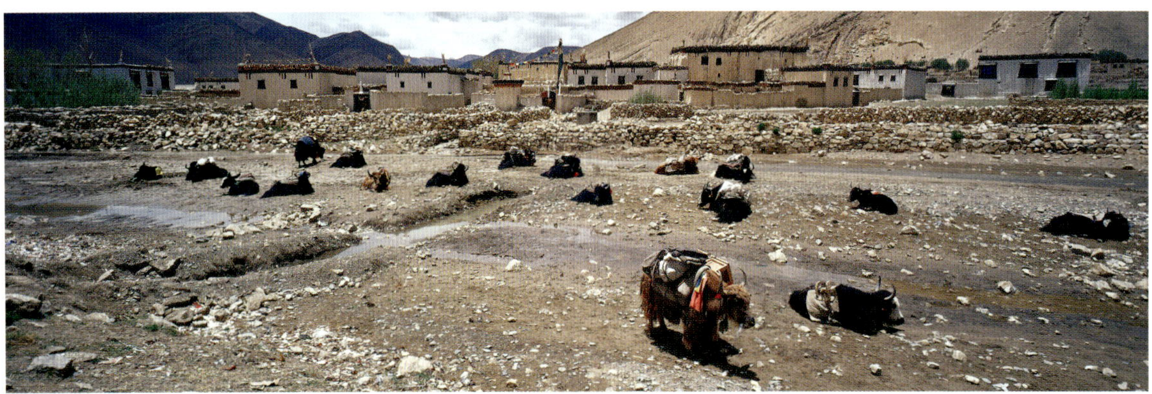

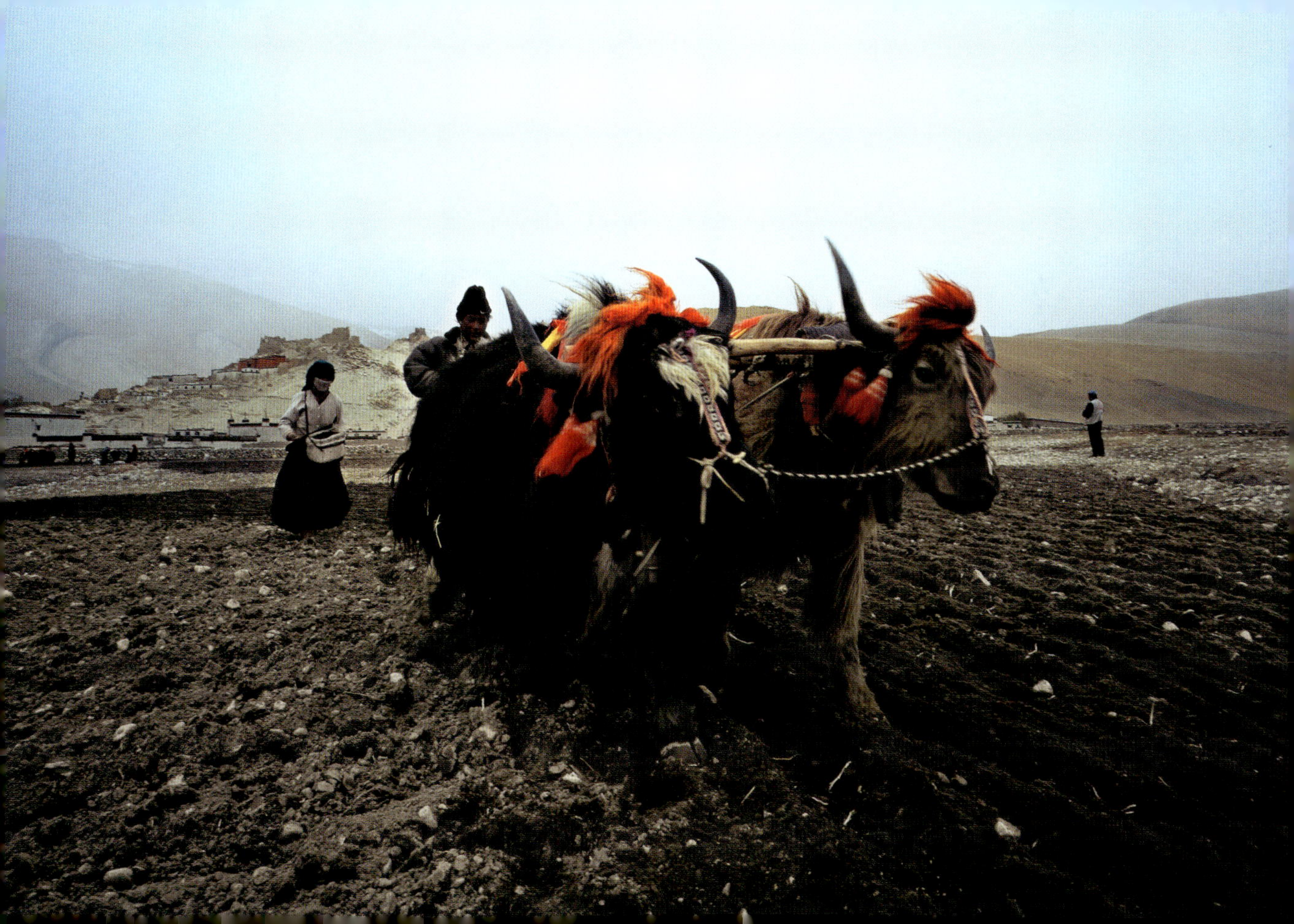

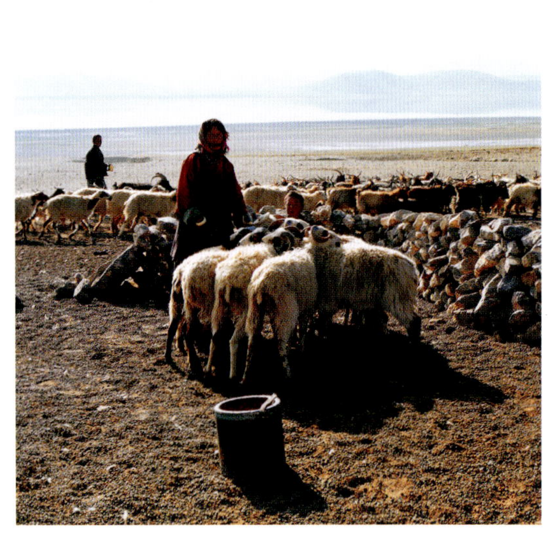

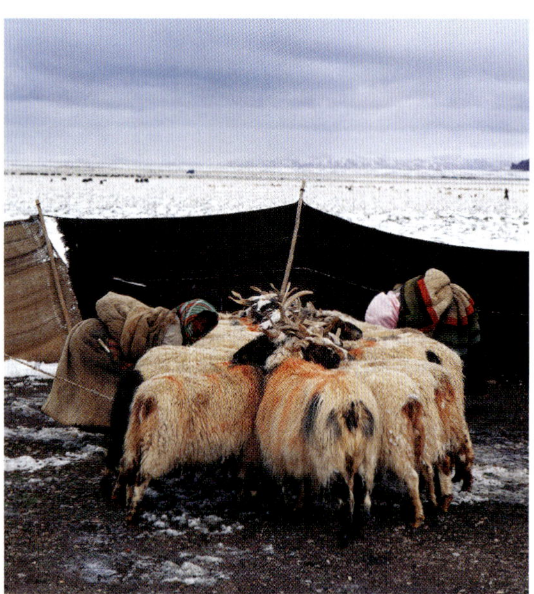

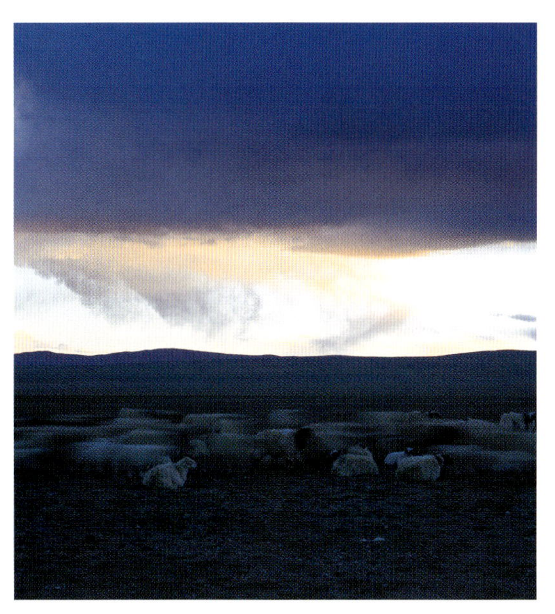

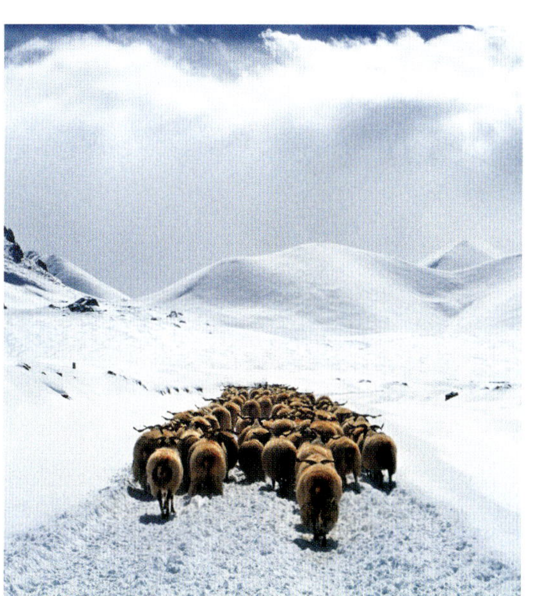

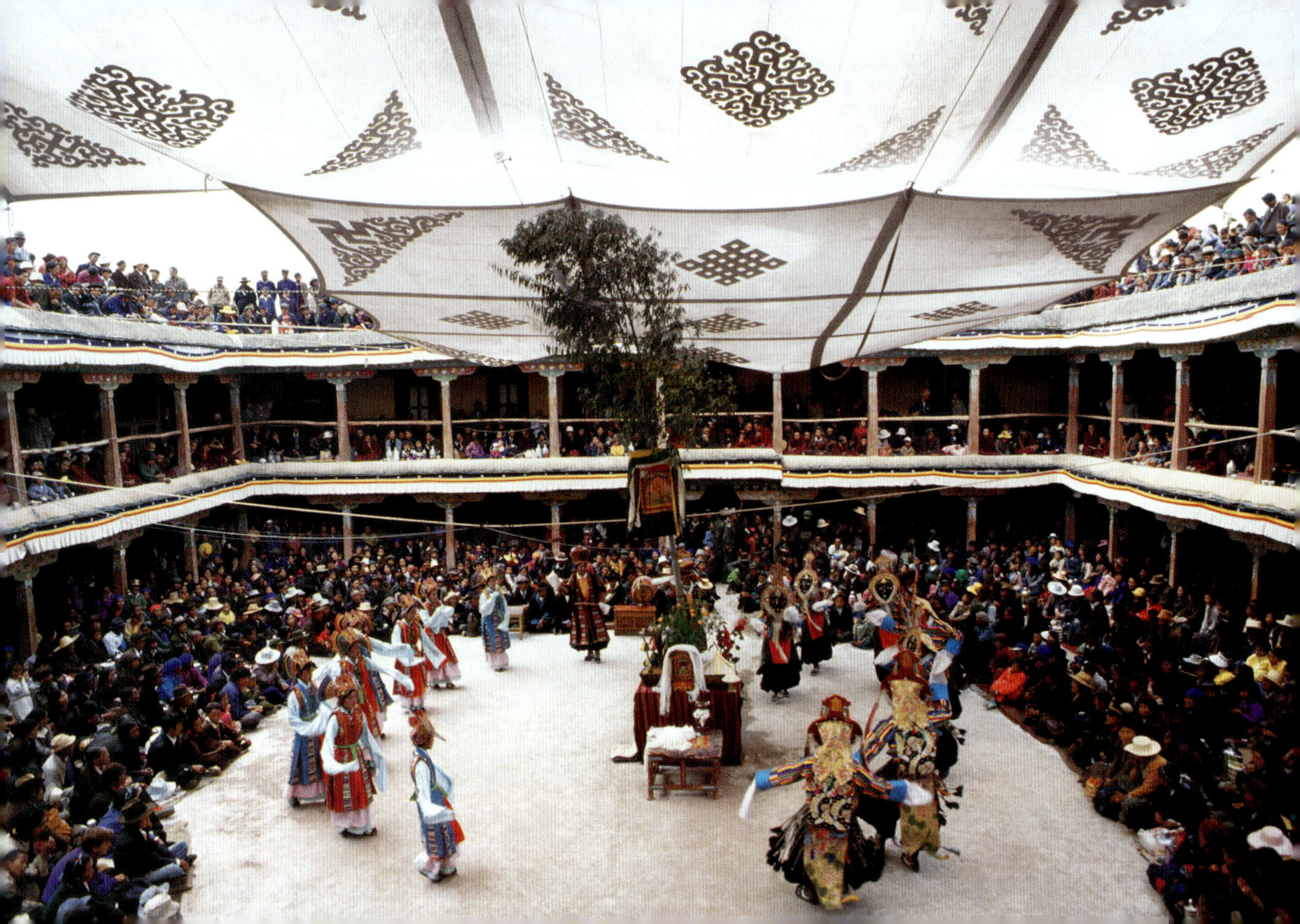

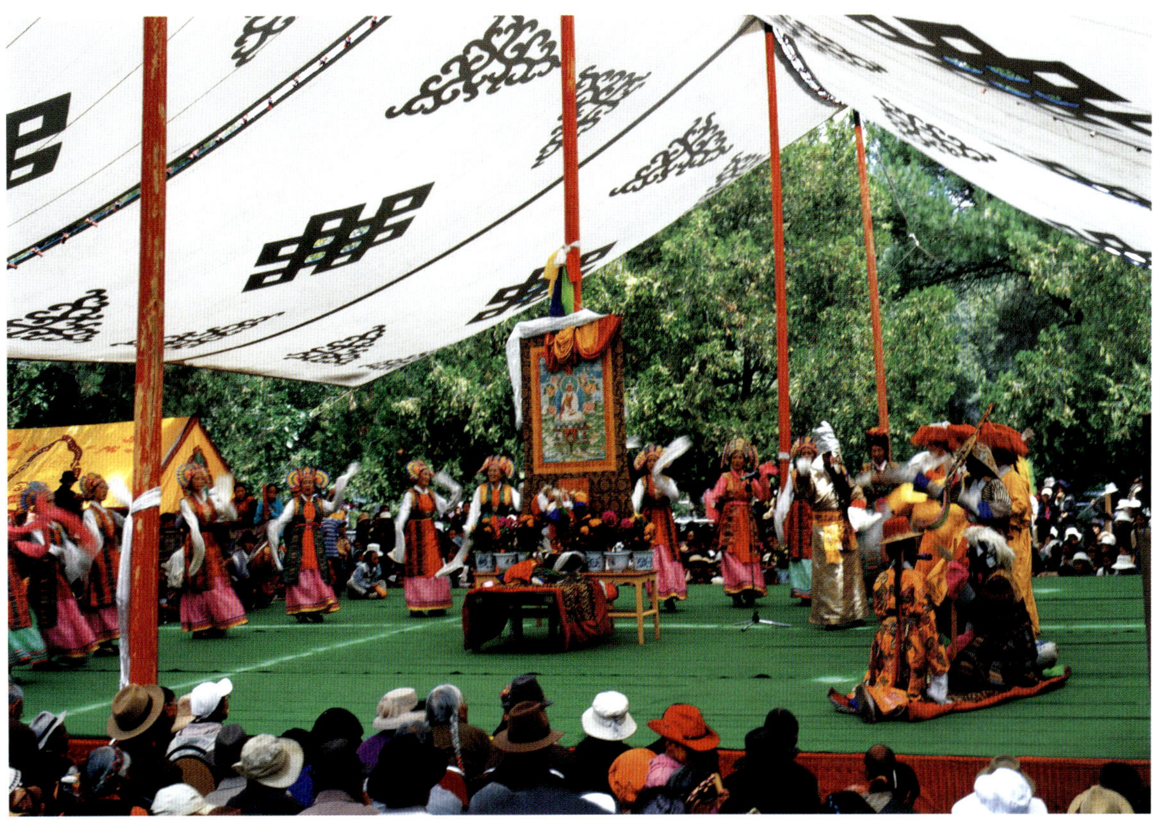

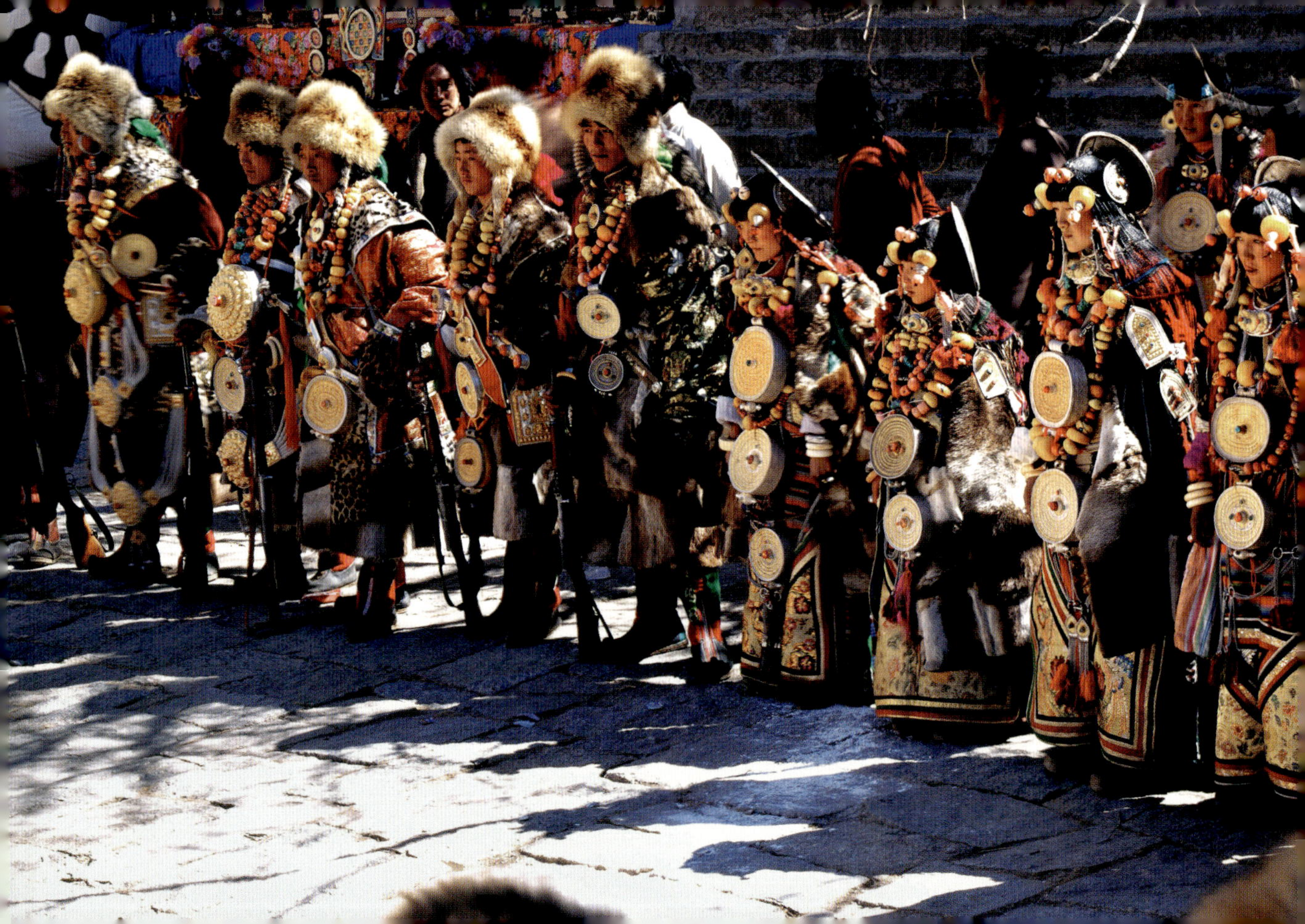

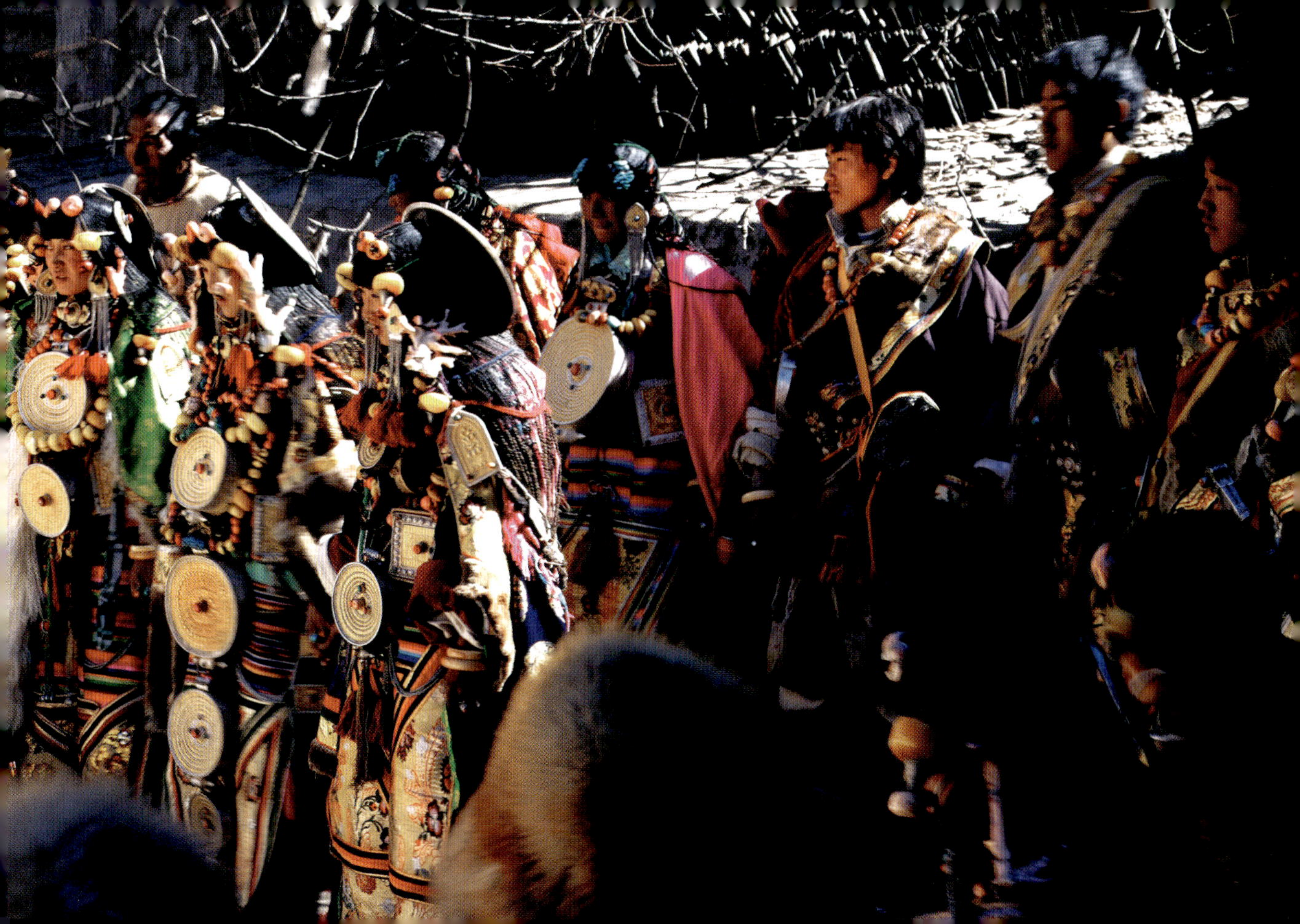

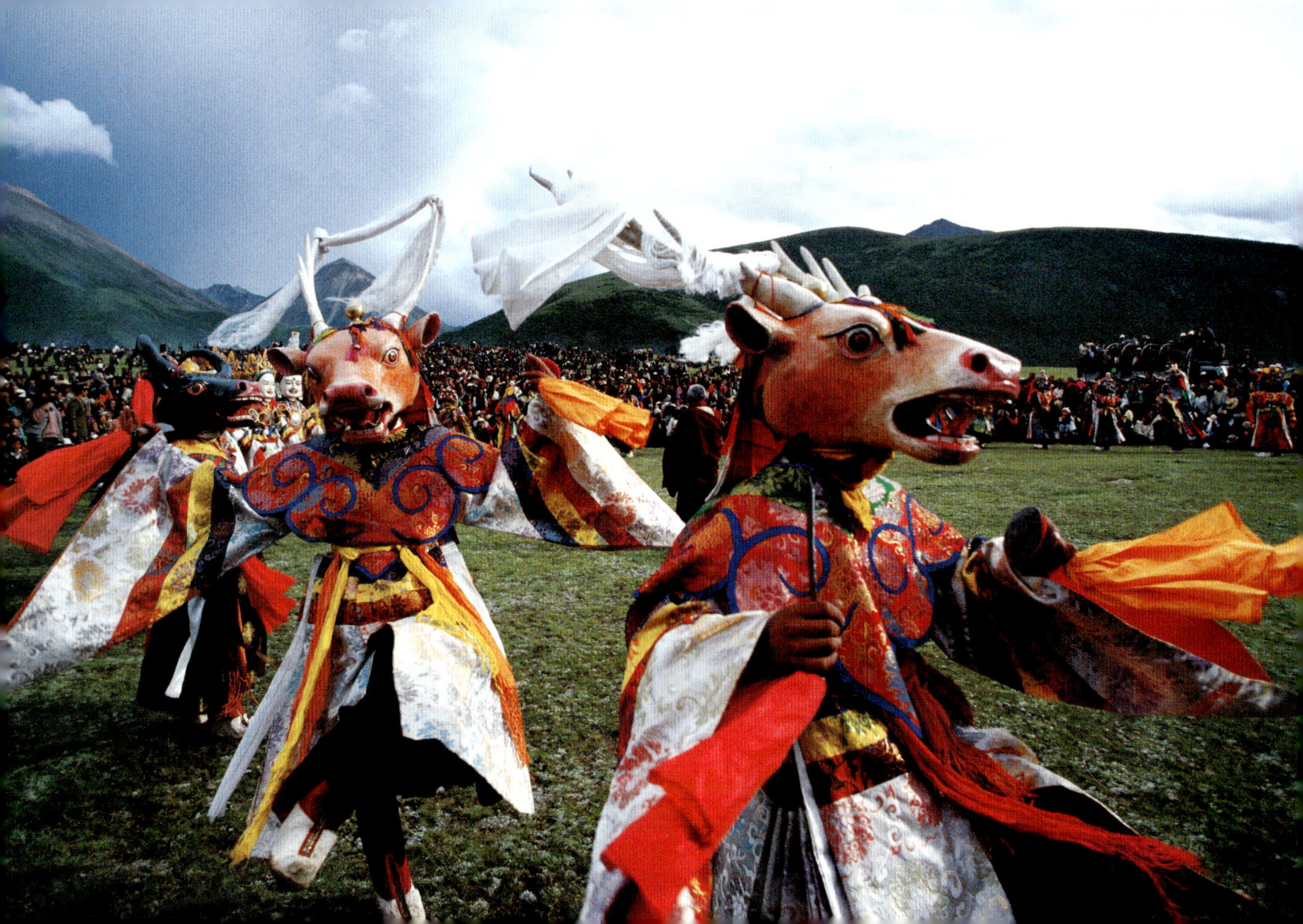

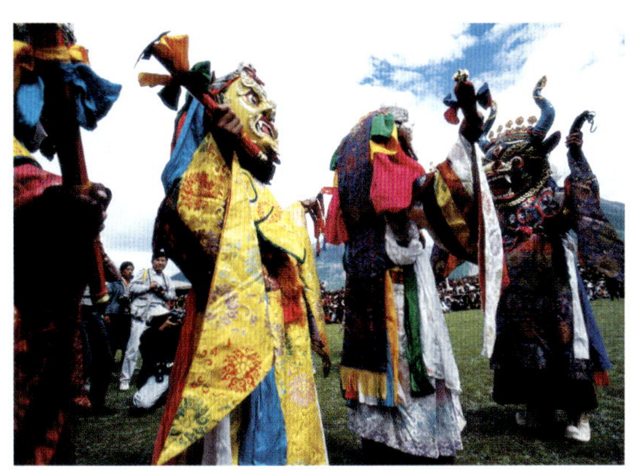

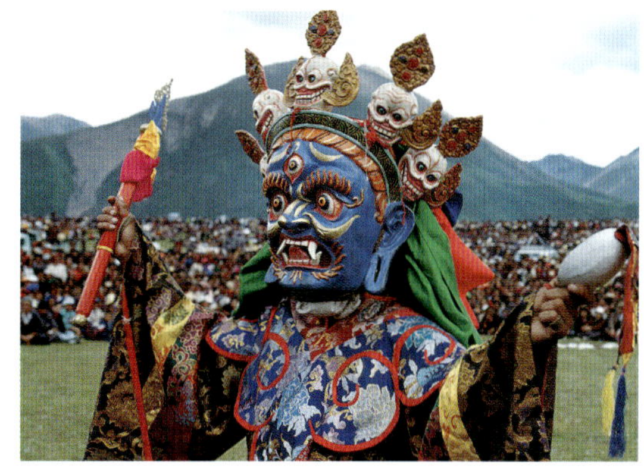

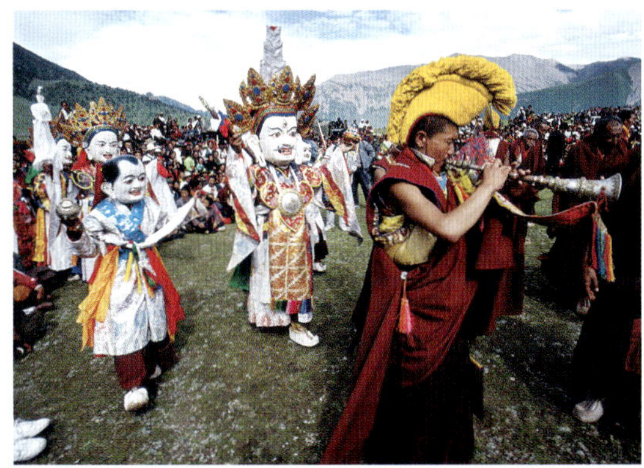

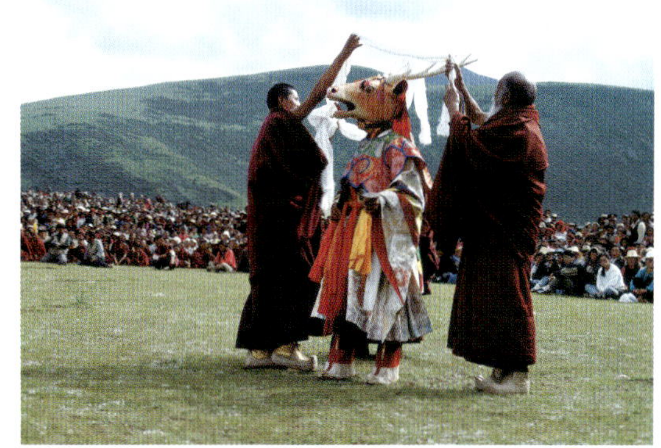

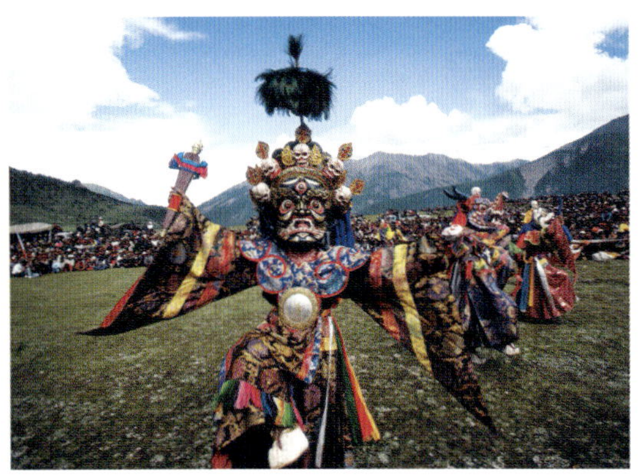

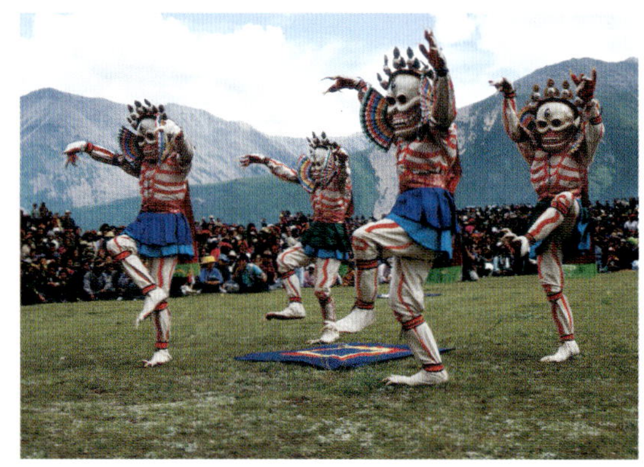

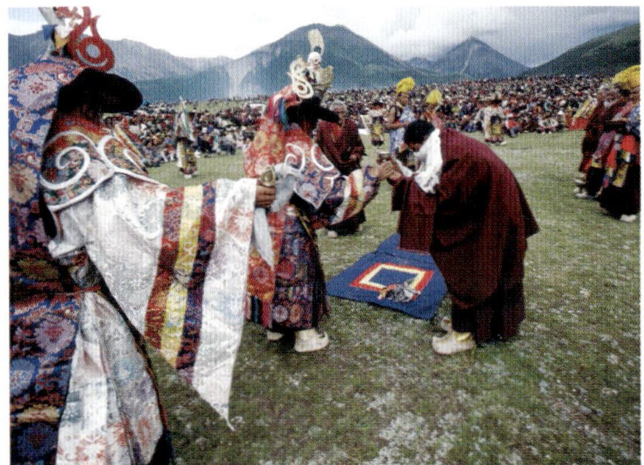

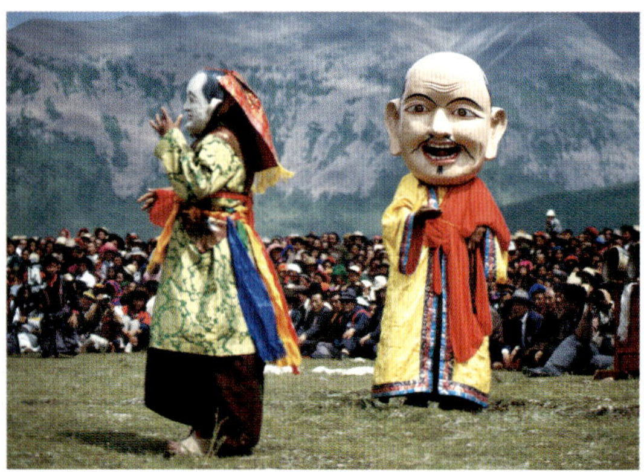

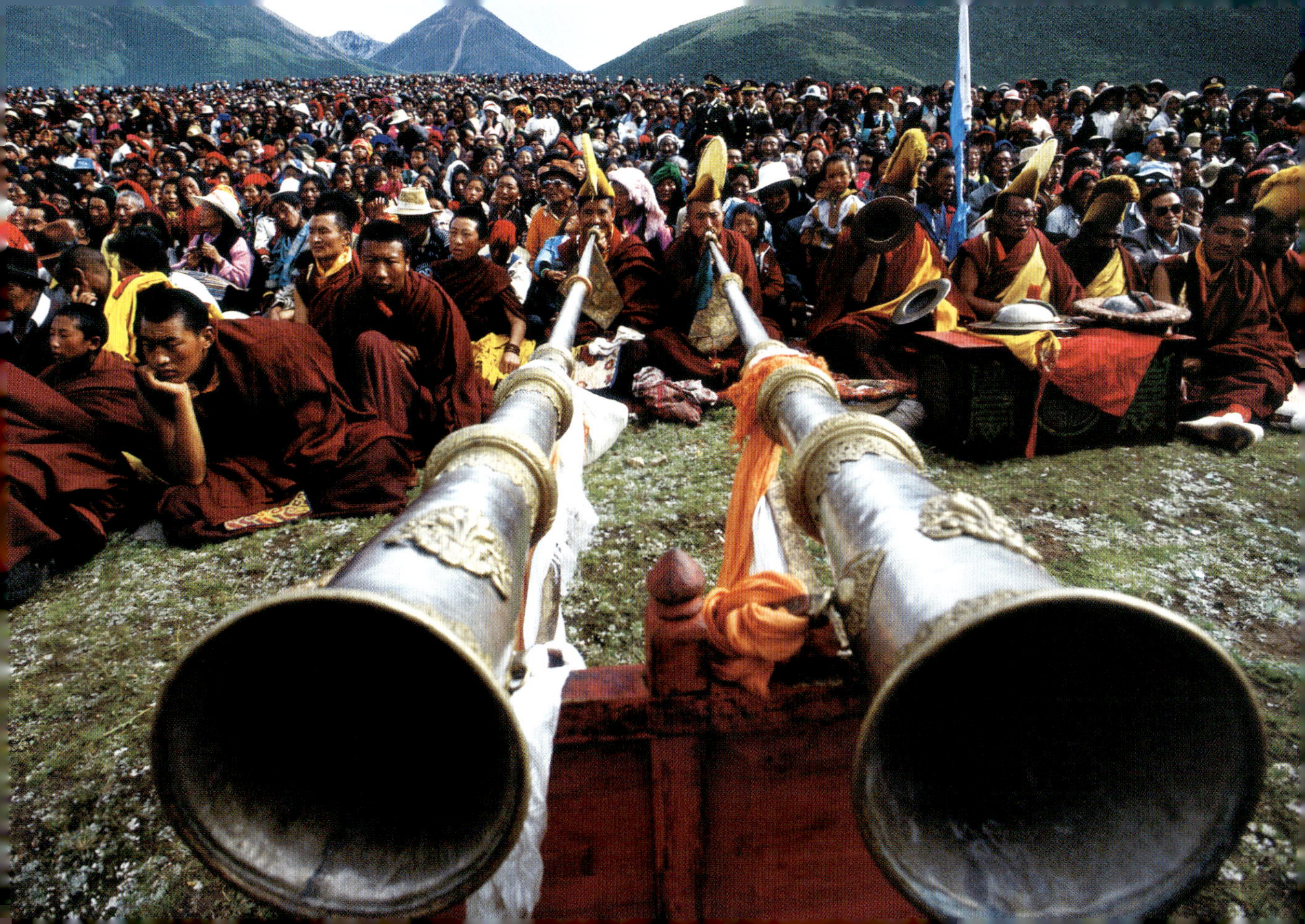

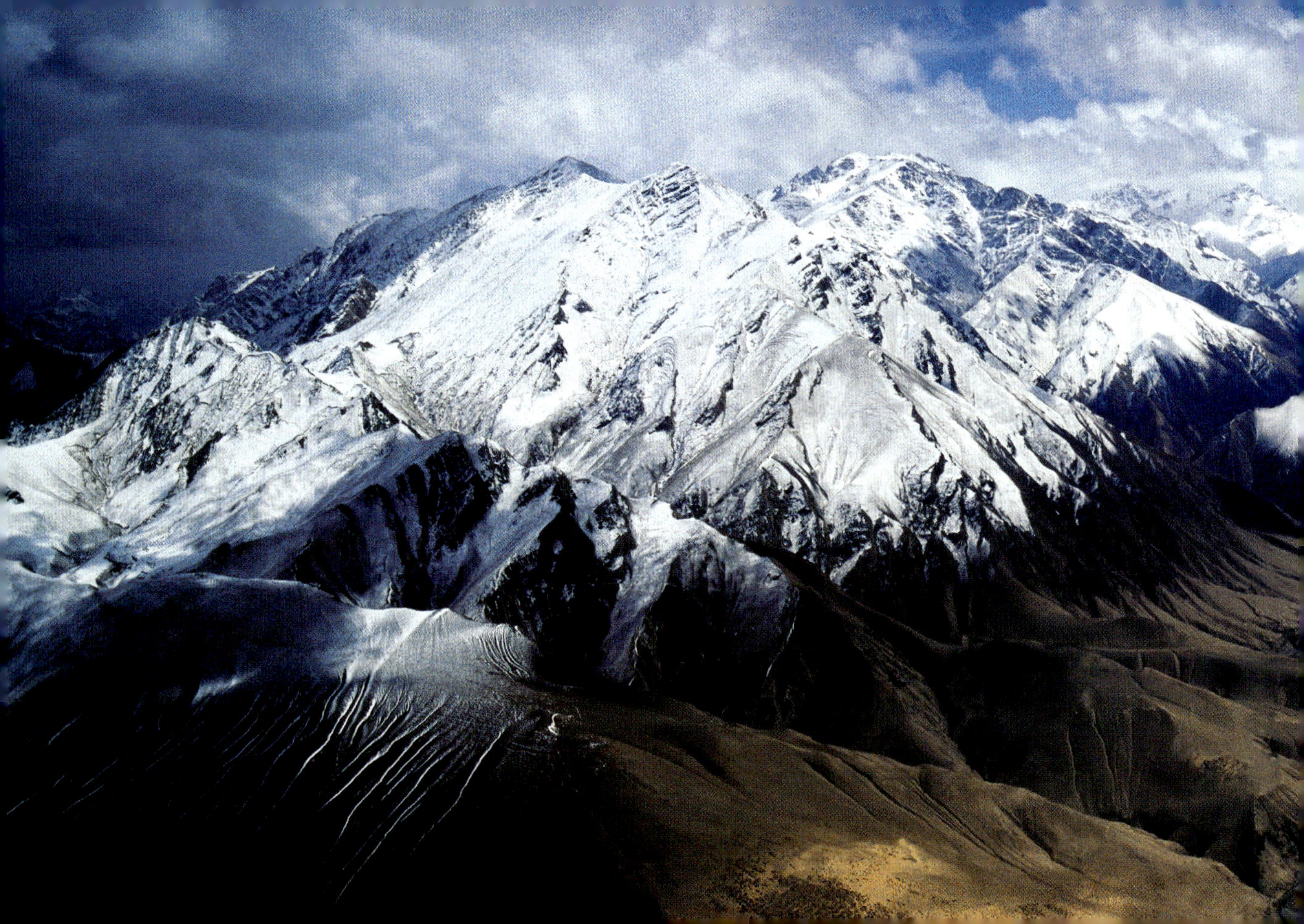

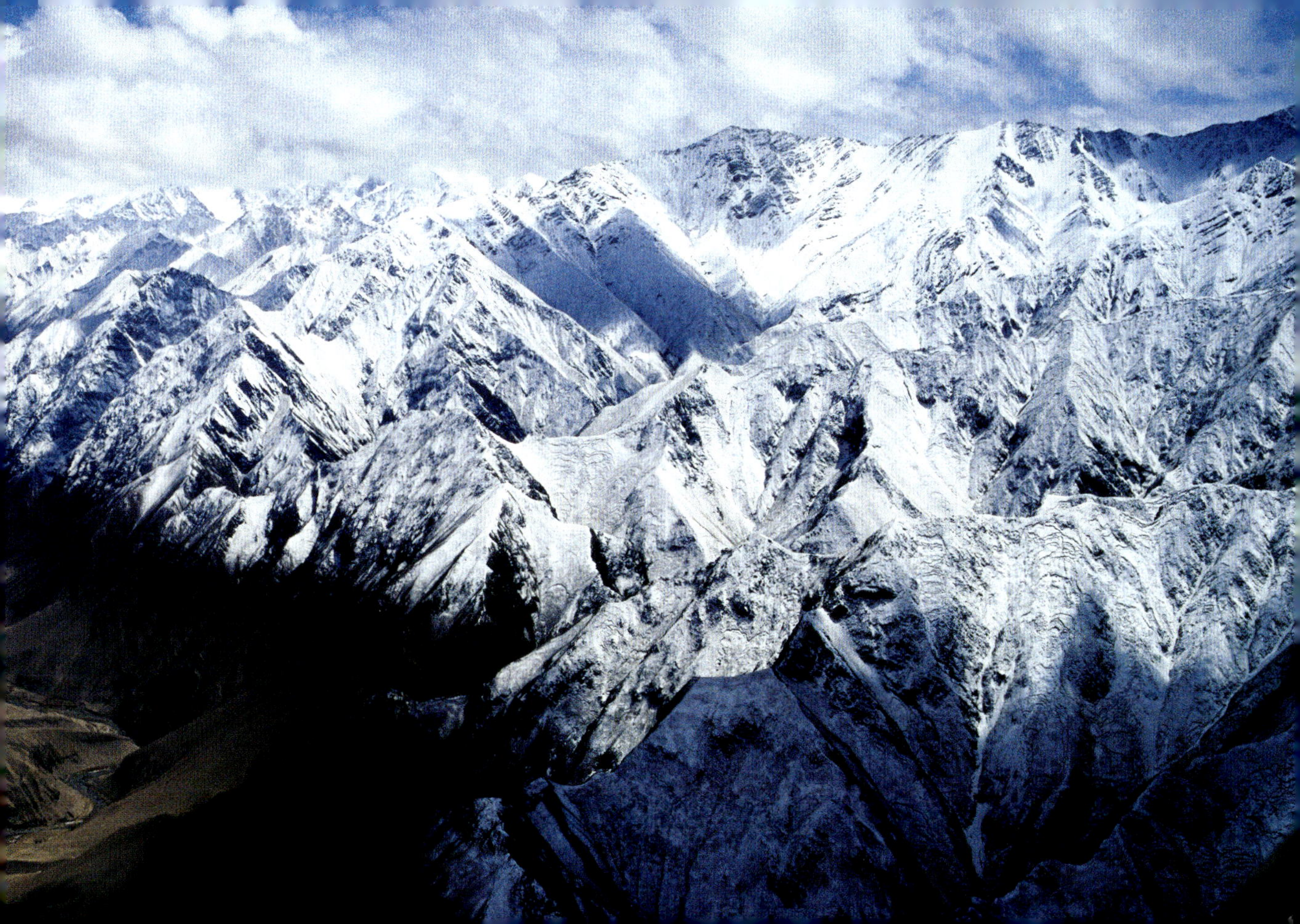

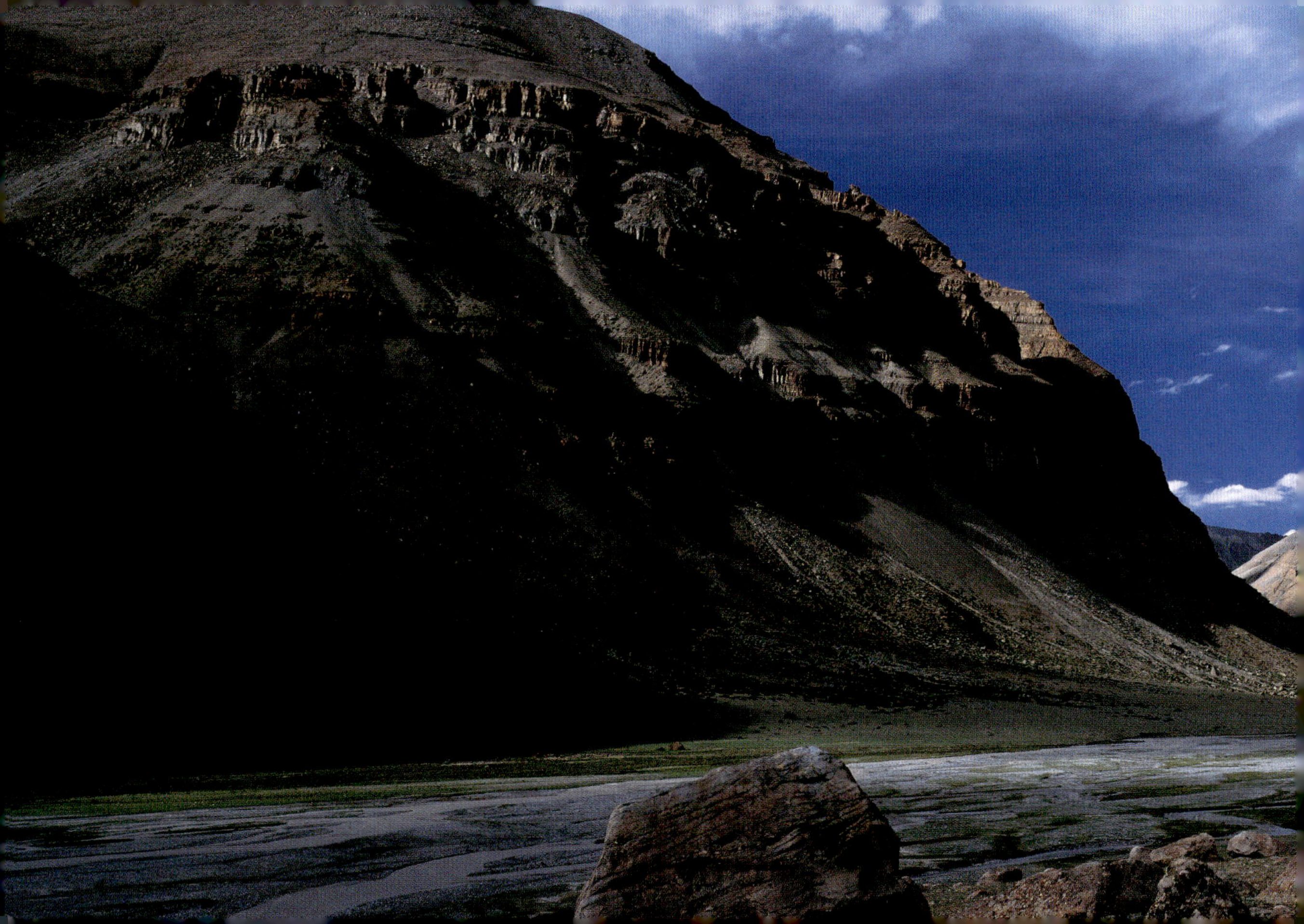

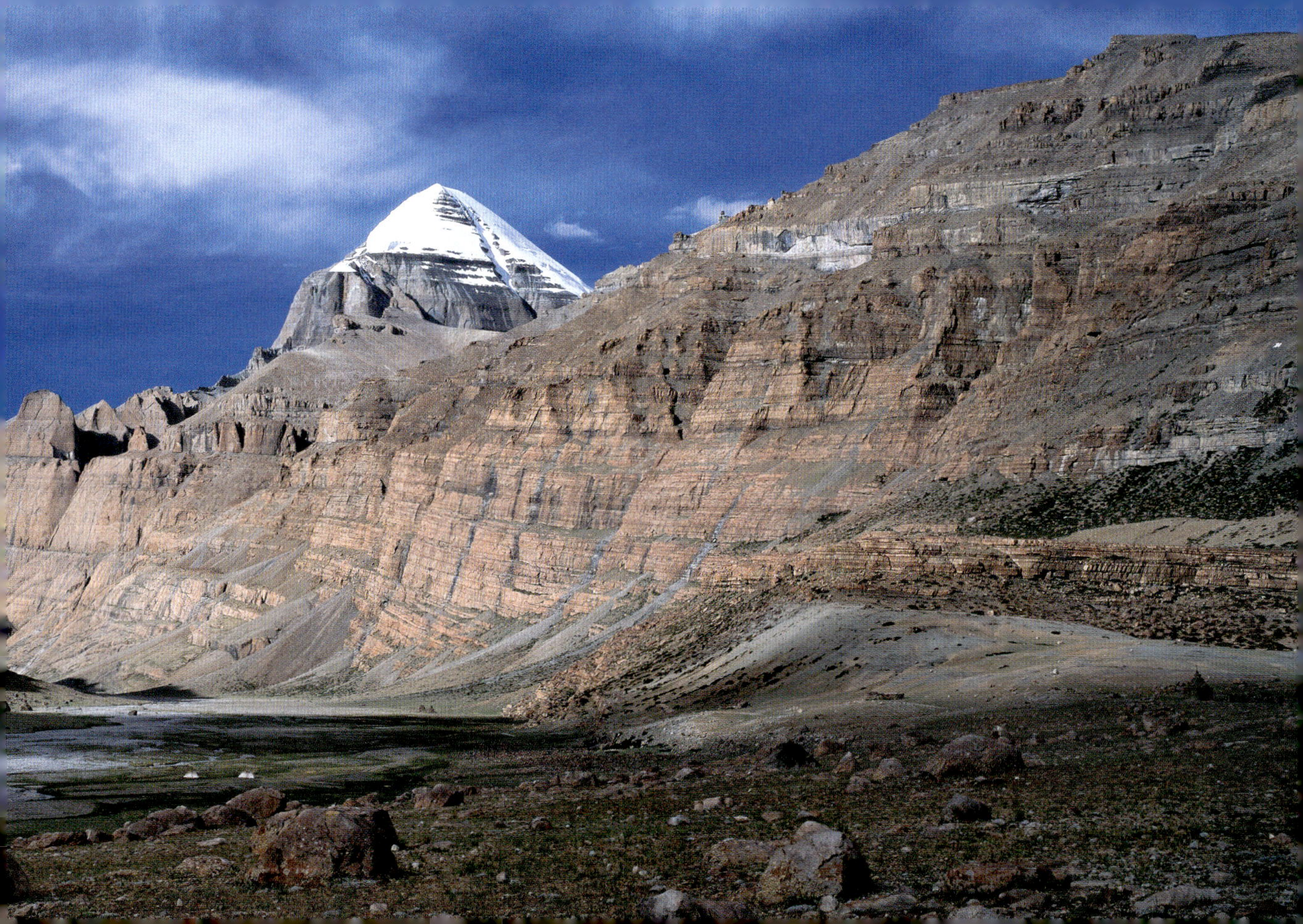

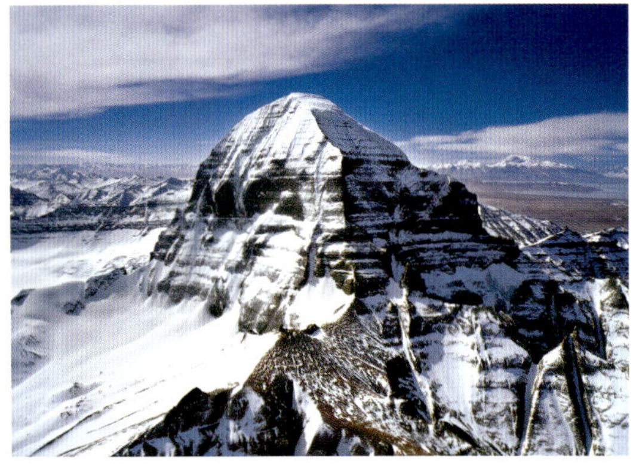

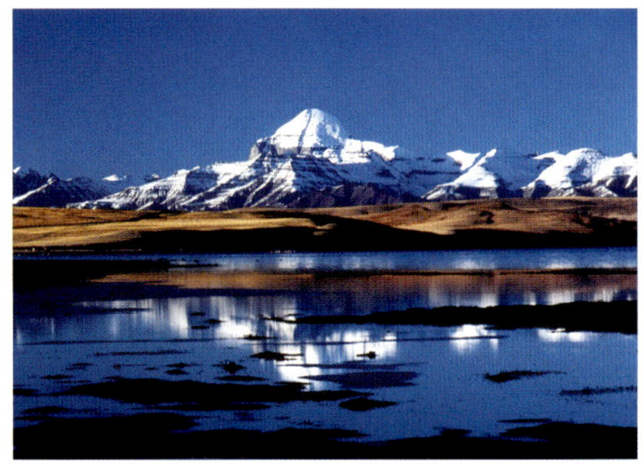

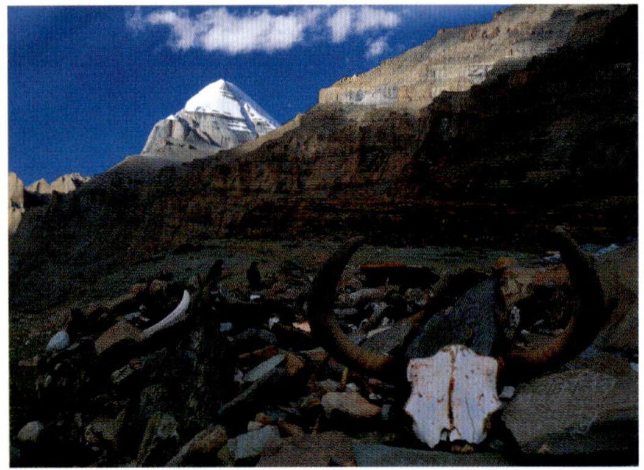

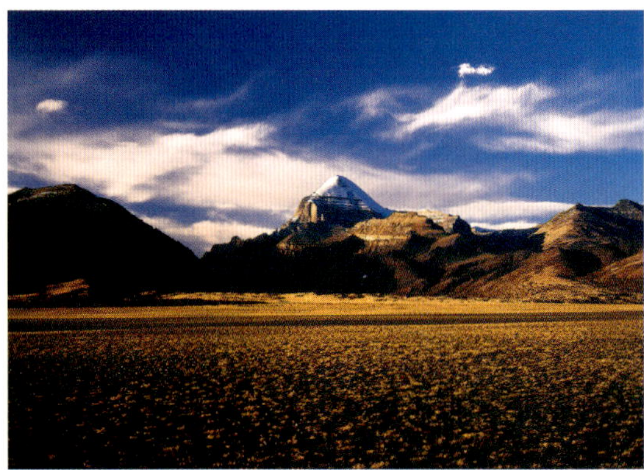

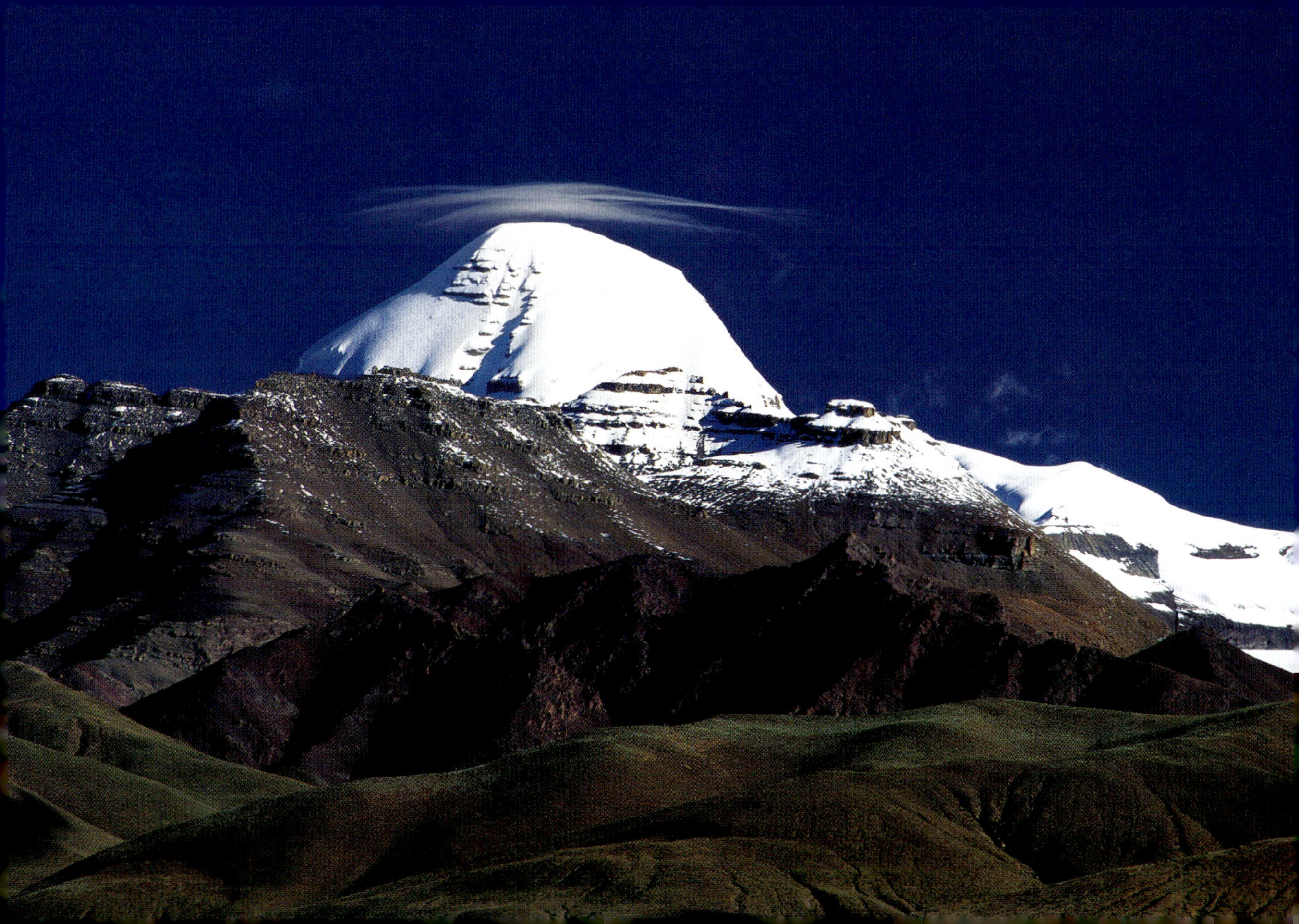

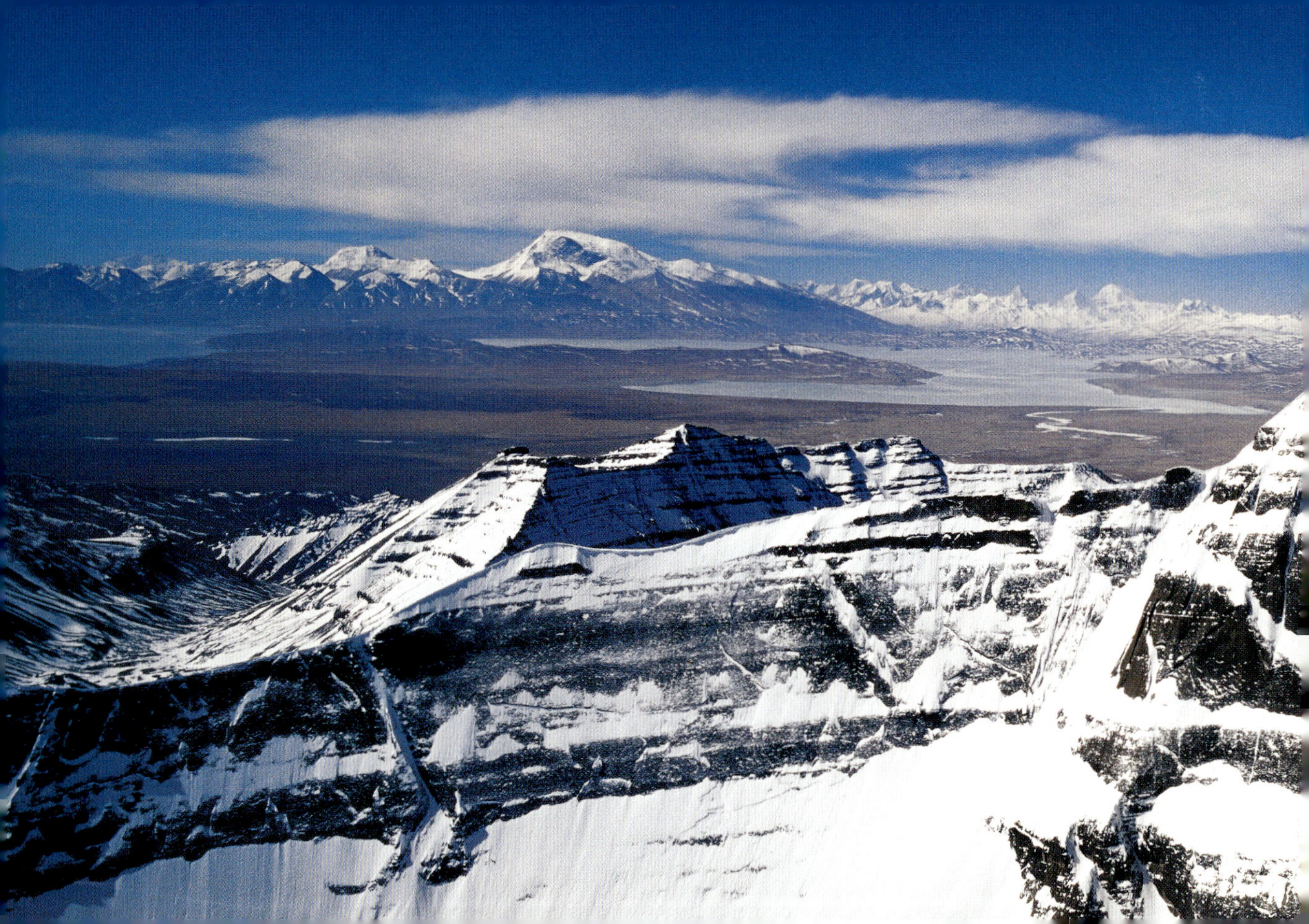

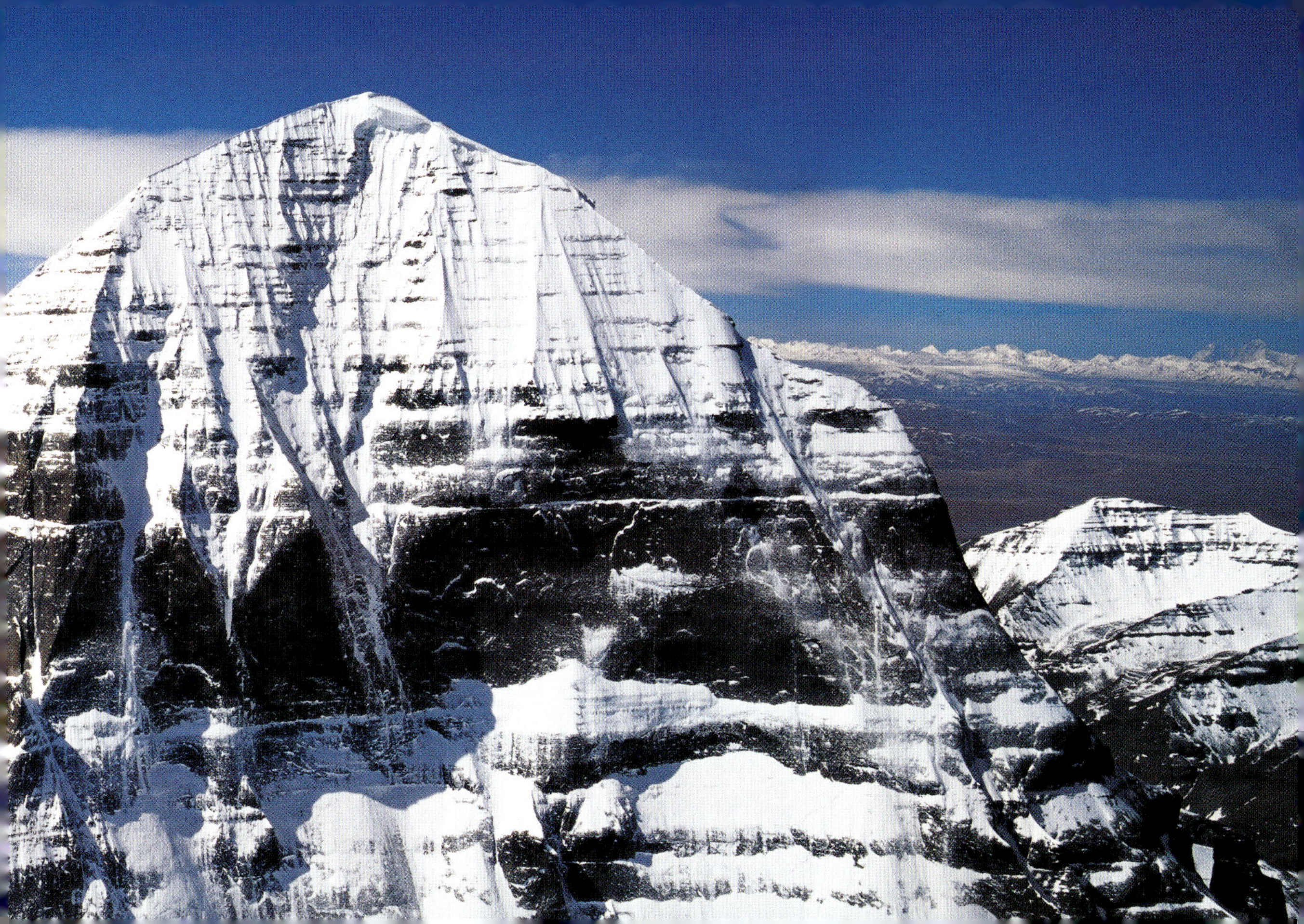

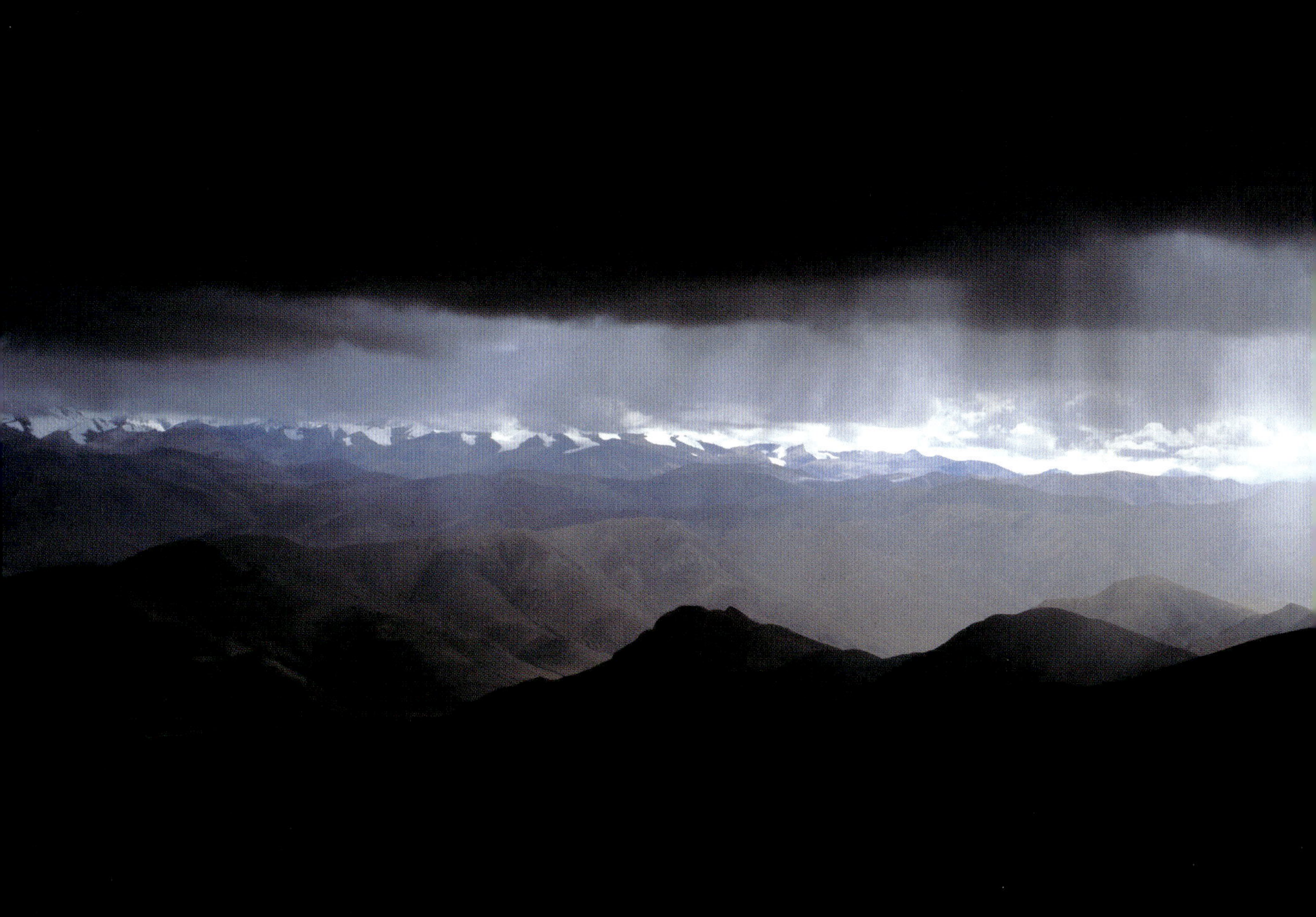

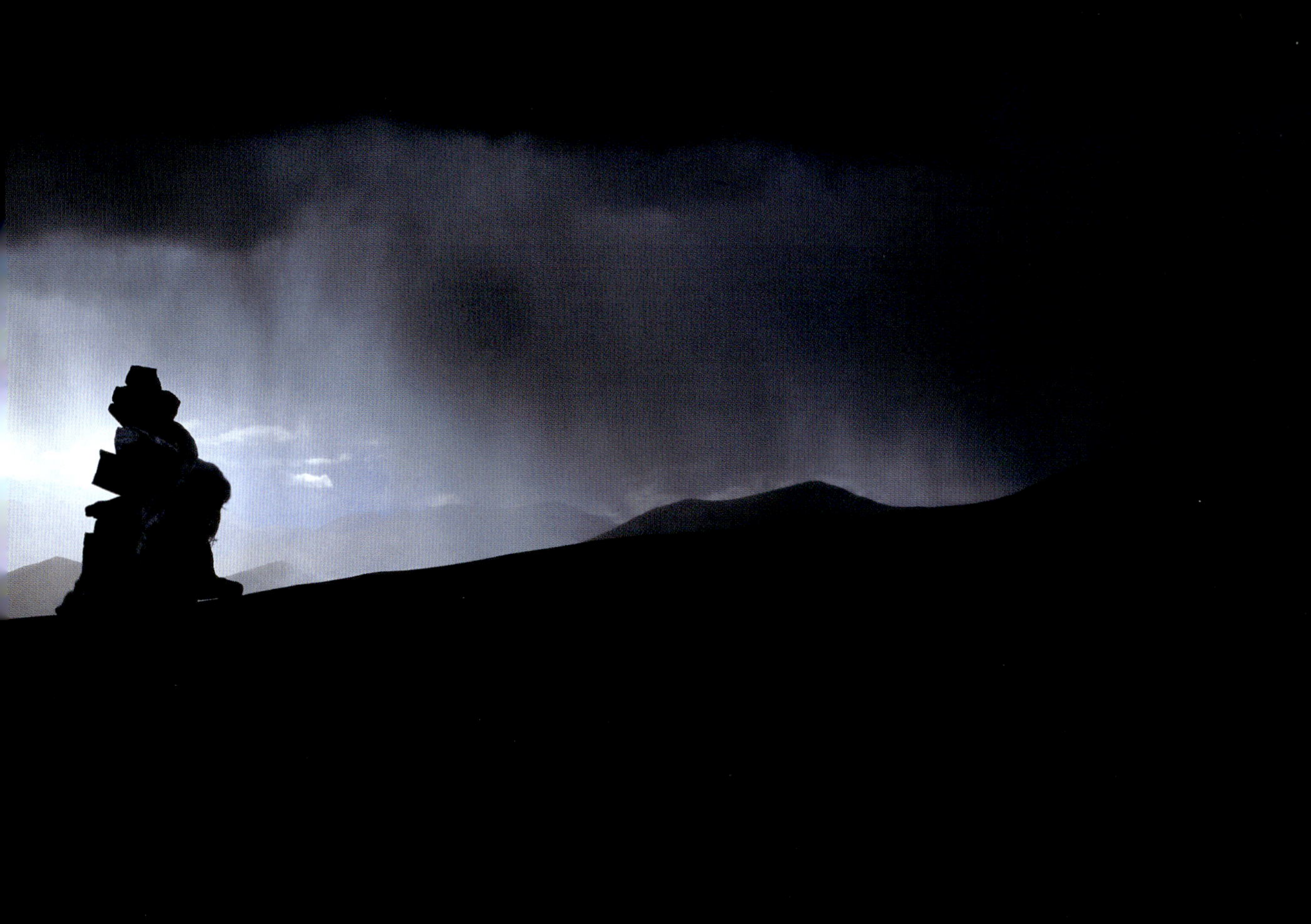

INDEX

1 Golden Dharma wheel on the roof of Jokhang Monastery
Gang Che

2-3 Mount Everest, the planet's highest peak, at an altitude of 8,844m(29,016ft), sits majestically on the roof of the world, forming different natural views at different elevations *Chengyi Sun*

6-7 Snow-covered Himalayas are one of the most splendid mountain ranges in the world *Guohua Zhong*

8-9 Mount Everest is viewed from the Rombak Monastery, from which Mount Everest is best observed *Ming Tan*

11-14 Banner-shaped clouds over Mount Everest indicate the velocity of wind *Jianjun Wang*

16-17 A bird's-eye view of the Himalaya Range; An flying eagle and Mount Everest *Xuejun Yuan* *Guohua Zhong*

18-19 Impressive Makulu peak; Various sights of Mount Everest;Kula Kangri Peak towers on the main ridge line of the middle section of the Himalaya, just like a gigantic protective screen of wall; Sights of Mount Everest; Dazzling Mount Everest with mystical colors against the setting sun *Chenyi Sun* *Jianjun Wang*

20-21 The magnificent Potala Palace, standing on the highest Plateau, is the symbol of the Qinghai-Tibetan Plateau as wells Lhasa
Chengyi Sun

22-23 The Potala Palace represents the best of Tibetan architechture; The Majestic Potala Palace *Chengyi Sun* *Gang Che*

24/27 The Potala Palace is composed of the Red Palace and White Palace. For centuries has served as the treasure house for Tibetan history, culture and arts; Downtown Lhasa seen from the Red Palace; The White Palace is where Dalai Lamas reside and handle political affairs; The Red Palace (centre) is where various religious activities are held and holy Stupas of successive Dalai Lamas are enshrined; The White Palace derives its name from the white wall which separate the two structures *Gang Che* *Panoramic Photo Gallery*

25-26 Standing against the hill, is the ancient palace complex of the Potala Palace *Ming Tan*

28-29 Bodhisattva Maitreya; Great Master Padmasambhava in the White Palace *Ming Tan*

30-31 Lobby with exquisite carvings and paintings; The interior of Potala Palace; Gorgeous embroidery decoration; Tibetan interior design focuses on symmetry, sumptuous beauty and illustrious color; Tibetan architecture pays close attention to door decoration, which perfectly matches the style of its interior; Intricate carved patterns on the doors *Ming Tan*

32-33 Buddhist Scripture debate is the preferred way for monks to learn the text of Scripture, it is also the way the senior lamas appraise their students; Scenes of passionate debate on Buddhist doctrine; Monks are full of vitality when debating Buddhist Scripture, through which they indulge in the pleasure of exploring the unknown world; Debating Buddhist Scripture and arguing interpretation are usually conducted in pairs, but participation of threes or even more is not uncommon *Chengyi Sun*

34-35 Lamas making the pilgrimage; Grand Prayer Ceremony *Panoramic Photo Gallery Gang Che*

36-37 Young monk; Young monks are playing in the snow; Young monks are having a picnic; Young monk adjusts his robe; Playful young monks , innocent as lay children *Panoramic Photo Gallery Guohua Zhou*

38-39 Praying Tibetans; Tibetans consider devout prayer to be the best way to purify the souls *Jianjun Wang Gang Che*

40-41 Devout pilgrims are prostrating fully on the ground every one step; Everlasting butter lamps; Pilgrims flock to the monastery for Buddhist services and holidays; Pious prayers *Lei Chen Jianjun Wang Chengyi Sun*

42-43 Jokhang Monastery in the early morning light *Jianjun Wang*

44/47 Tibetans call the area centered around Barkor Street Lhasa, meaning "Land of Buddha" in Tibetan; Jokhang Monastery with its red walls and golden roof; Jokhang Monastery and the Potala Palace in snow *Panoramic Photo Gallery Jianjun Wang Gang Che*

45-46 The Potala Palace is seen from dazzling golden roof of Jokhang Monastery *Ming Tan*

48-49 Jokhang Monastery; The architecture of Jokhang; Interior of Jokhang Monastery; Sharp color contrast is one of the characteristics of Tibetan architecture; Jokhang Monastery is the oldes existing wood and mud structure in Tibet *Panoramic Photo Gallery Jianjun Wang*

50-51 Dragon Decoration on the eaves of Jokhang monastery; Complicated yet exquisite Tibetan style decoration on upturned eaves; Decorations in Corners; Decorations in Corners *Ming Tan Guohua Zhong*

52-53 The Golden Life-size Statue of 12 year-old Sakyamuni, which, the legends holds, was carved according to the image of Sakyamuni himself and brought to Tibet by Princess Wen Cheng of the Tang Dynasty *Jianjun Wang*

54-55 Murals of Jokhang Monastery 1, 2, 3, 4, 5 *Gang Che*

56-57 Colorful paintings on monastery buildings 1, 2, 3 *Gang Che*

58-59 Tibetan Fairy Maiden Festival falls on October 15th of the Tibetan calendar; The tallest butter sculptures used in Grand Prayer Ceremony of Lhasa can reach over ten meters *Gang Che*

60-61 Drepung, Ganden and Sera are considered the "Great Three Monasteries" in Tibet, Drepung Monastery is considered the largest monastery in the world *Panoramic Photo Gallery*

62-63 Spectacular display of Tangka painting on annual Shoton Festival; The ceremonial display of grand Buddha painting (or Tangka); A scene of "Airing out" of Grand Buddhist painting; Monks attending a Tangka painting display festival; Annual Tangka painting display attracts large number of believers and tourists *Jianjun Wang Chengyi Sun*

64/67 Drepung Monastery is a typical Tibetan style monastery built against a hill *Gang Che*
The original name of Drepung Monastery was White Conch Drepung Monaster *Gang Che*

65-66 The Statue of Buddha Champa in the main hall *Gang Che*

68-69 Unique stone carvings at Sera Monastery; Sera Monastery is famous for its serenity and impressive surroundings *Panoramic Photo Gallery*

70-71 Famous ten- thousand-Buddha wall behind Medicine Mountain; Colorful paintings on the sides of Medicine Mountain 1, 2, 3 *Chengyi Sun Gang Che*

72-73 Drigung Monastery has one of the two most famous and auspicious sky burial sites in the world, and the largest in Tibet, Rainbow over Drigung Monastery; Drogimg Monastery sits majestically upon a steep hill; Sky burial site as seen from afar; Drigung Monastery is located on halfway up a hill *Lei Chen*

74-75 The Samyae Monastery boasts the first Tibetan Buddhist monastery possessing Buddha, the Law and monks; Perfect buildings of Samyae monastery blend architectural tradition of Tibetan, Han Chinese and Indian *Panoramic Photo Gallery Chengyi Sun*

76-77 Snow capped mountains and prayer flags; Perched on the mountain top, The towering and outstanding Yumbulagang Palace overlooks wilderness and fields *Chengyi Sun Jianjun Wang*

78-79 Peach blossom on the banks of Yarlung Zangbo River *Jianjun Wang*

80-81 The picturesque Mangkan region bordering Yunnan province; A village surrounded by terraced fields; A village by the Lancang River *Chengyi Sun Jianjun Wang*

82-83 The enchanting peach blossom valley in Nyingchi; Spring arrives Nyingchi in full splendor *Xuejun Yuan Hongwei Wang*

84/87 Qamdo region is well known for its changeable weather and large variety of plants; The Salt Well , a village in Mangkam, Qamdo, is located on the ancient Tea Horse trail; Riwoqe Monastery is a famous Gelupkpa temple; Lovely scenery in Jiaza, Jiaza refers to the Salt from Han Chinese. The legend holds that princess Wen Cheng of the Tang Dynasty came here to gave salt in charity, from which it derives its name; The town of Zham is famous for its graceful scenery *Chengyi Sun Jianjun Wang*

85-86 Lulung shows typical high altitude grassland scenes *Chengyi Sun*

88-89 A peaceful village by the snow covered lake Ra' og Co *Jianjun Wang*

90-91 Autumn descends on smooth and colorful Lake Ra´ og Co; Scenery of Yigong in Nyingchi *Yongqian Zeng Bangcai Wang*

92-93 A magical sea of clouds over Lulung *Jianjun Wang*

94-95 The Namjaghbarwa peak is famous for its complicated and precipitous mountain structure; The Namjaghbarwa Peak, covered in snow year-round and with its constant veil of clouds is mysterious and alluring *Bangcai Wang Gang Che*

96-97 The world of ice and snow *Chengyi Sun*

98-99 Lake Nam Co' s golden banks against distant snowy mountain under evening sun ; Scenery of lake Nam Co; Dark blue lake water lapping against ice and snow covered rocks; Lake Nam Co in winter; Holy and pure, no visit to Tibet is complete without a visit to lake Nam Co . *Xuejun Yuan Jianjun Wang Chengyi Sun*

100-101 Gigantic rocks with prayer flags by the lake *Jianjun Wang*

102-103 Colorful prayer flags, Tibetans firmly believe Buddhist Scripture is chanted once with each flutter of prayer flags, continuously conveying the best wishes of people to Buddha and their seeking for blessings; Prayer flags appears as a protective canopy; White prayer flags representing the while clouds *Panoramic Photo Gallery Jianjun Wang*

104-105 The Moni stone piles of lake Nam Co, consists primarily of six-character Buddhist Scripture carved on rocks, They are alleged to possess mysterious power *Jianjun Wang*

106/111 Walking round the lake is a solemn and sacred religious ritual, prevalent in Tibet; Devout believers circling the lake *Jianjun Wang*

107-110 Lake Nam Co means "Lake of Heaven" in Tibetans, one of the three sacred lakes in Tibet *Chengyi Sun*

112-113 Vast lake Nam Co and the lamas walking around it; Lake Yamzho Yumco is one of three sacred lakes in Tibet *Jianjun Wang Xuejun Yuan*

114-115 Lake Yamzho Yumco, the largest inland lake on the Northern slope of the Himalayas, is famous for its picturesque scenery *Chengyi Sun*

116-117 Pastoral life on grassland in Tibet; Water, grassy pastures and white clouds *Jianjun Wang Xuejun Yuan*

118-119 The lush grasslands within Mount Everest Natural Reserves *Jianjun Wang*

120-121 Tashilhunpo monastery is a colossal compound with a history of nearly 600 years and serves as the seat of Panchen Lamas; Tashilhunpo monastery is to the west of the city- Xigaze *Gang Che Lei Chen*

122-123 Tashilhunpo monastery is built again Tara's Mountain; The Stupa-tomb at Tashilhunpo monastery *Chengyi Sun Weixiong Liu*

124-125 The entrance to the Tashilhunpo manastery; Lamas at Tashilhunpo Monastery *Panoramic Photo Gallery Jianjun Wang*

126-127 Golden Statue of Buddha Champa is the biggest sitting bronze Buddha in the world; Majestic statue of Buddha Champa stands 23 meters high *Gang Che Jianjun Wang*

128-129 Solemn and sacred Baiju monastery; Magnificent Baiju monastery in Gyangze is a colossal complex *Panoramic Photo Gallery Jianjun Wang*

130-131 Saga Temple overlooking the entire town; Delicate architectural detail of Saga Temple *Guohua Zhong Gang Che*

132/135 Gamba Castle; Gamba Castle under evening sun glow *Jianjun Wang*

136-137 Gamba Castle, standing on the mountain range for over 600 years, remains magnificent *Chengyi Sun*

138-139 Beautiful Lake Gala; Mysterious Lake Gala; Mirror like Lake Gala; Lake Gala in wintertime; Gala lake with snowy mountains and white clouds in the background *Chengyi Sun Guohua Zhong*

140-141 Auspicious totem made of stone piles; Swastika made of stones is a Buddhist symbol of harmony and enlightenment; The fortress of Gyangze as viewed from Baiju monastery; Majestic ancient fortress of Gyangze; Buddhist Pagoda by the road; Buddhist pagoda and Mani stone piles *Jianjun Wang Jianjun Wang Guohua Zhong Weixiong Liu*

142-143 Scenery of Dingye *Chengyi Sun*

144-145 A field of yellow cole flower; Fields of billowing barley in Xigaze. Barley has been cultivated in Tibet for over 3,500 years *Chengyi Sun*

146-147 Buckwheat flowers in Xigaze *Chengyi Sun*

148-149 Spectacular yet mysterious scenery in Ge'gyai, through which the Himalayas cut from east to west *Chengyi Sun*

150 /153 Smiling Tibetans walk around the lake in prayer, believing a full circuit will bring them blessings from god; Pious ritual of walking in circle around the lake; Tibetans spinning Prayer wheels; Old man on the road *Jianjun Wang*

151- 152 Young people make the long journey to the Holy City on a pilgrimage, prostrating fully on the ground every six paces *Gang Che*

154-155 Happy , yet quiet, old Tibetan and his child 2; Old Tibetan and their children; Tibetan women and children *Guohua Zhong Chengyi Sun*

156-157 Tibetan herdsmen are managing a flock of sheep; A nomad family on the Plateau *Jianjun Wang*

158-159 Herders shearing their sheep 1; Herders shearing their sheep 2; Herdsman and his flock *Jianjun Wang*

160-161 Part of colorful Mani stone piles 1; Part of colorful Mani stone piles 2; Part of colorful Mani stone piles 3; Part of colorful Mani stone piles 4; Mani stone piles can be found throughout Tibet *Jianjun Wang*

162-163 Huge Mani stone by the lake; Mani stones inscribed with Buddhist Scripture *Jianjun Wang*

164-165 Mani stones in various shapes and colors, are inscribed with six-character Scripture 1; Mani stones in various shapes and colors, are inscribed with six-character Scripture 2; Mani stones in various shapes and colors, are inscribed with six-character Scripture 3; Mani stones in various shapes and colors, are inscribed with six-character Scripture 4; Phallicism created by Mother Nature-male; Phallicism created by Mother Nature-female *Jianjun Wang Gang Che Chengyi Sun*

166-167 Rombak Glacier on Mount Everest; Karela Clacier in Gyangze *Gang Che Jianjun Wang*

168-169 Mani Stone piles on the Himalayas *Chengyi Sun*

170-171 The Himalayan means the land of ice and snow in Tibetan *Chengyi Sun*

172-173 The ruins of the Guge Kingdom to the west of Zanda county date back to Xiangxiong Kingdom in the 9th century; Chortens at Tholinf monastery; Vast and desolate Zanda clay forest *Chengyi Sun Jianjun Wang*

174/177 The ruins of the once splendid Guge Kingdom; Abandoned capital on the plateau; According to legends the ruins of the Guge Kingdom mysteriously disappeared in one night; The ruins of the Guge Kingdom *Guohua Zhong*

175-176 The ruins of the Guge Kingdom remain standing on a high ridge *Chengyi Sun*

178-179 The ruins of the Guge Kingdom; Unique topography of Zanda clay Forest; Landscape in Zanda *Xuejun Yuan Chengyi Sun*

180-181 The gold and silver images of Buddha at the ruins of the Guge Kingdom. 1; The gold and silver images of Buddha at the ruins of the Guge Kingdom. 2; Exquisite Buddhist mural unearthed from the Guge Kingdom 1; Exquisite Buddhist mural unearthed from the Guge Kingdom 2; Breathtaking murals from the Guge Kingdom; The awesome murals from the Guge Kingdom *Chengyi Sun*

182-183 The murals at Tholing Monastery dates back to eleventh century; Buddhist murals at Tholing Monastery; Vivid Buddhist mural at Tholing Monastery 1; Vivid Buddhist mural at Tholing Monastery 2 *Chengyi Sun*

184-185 Clay forest at Tholing Monastery *Chengyi Sun*

186/189 The architecture of Tholing Monastery is the characteristic of Indian, Nepalese and Ladakh; Chortens and clay forest at Tholing Monastery match each other well; Majestic Tholing Monastery under the blue sky; Mani Stone piles at Tholing Monastery
Jianjun Wang

187-188 The ruins of Tholing Monastery, which was built in the beginning of the 11th century *Chengyi Sun*

190-191 The golden peaks of Burang in autumn; Landscape in Burang county, Ngari region, Burang is surrounded by Snowy mountains and serves as the south-western gate of the Qinghai-Tibetan Plateau *Chengyi Sun* *Jianjun Wang*

192-193 Lake Lhaang Co lies to the west of Lake Mapam Yumco, Tibetans describe its beauty as equaling that of beautiful crescent moon
Chengyi Sun

194-195 Beautiful and glamourous lake Mapam Yumco in autumn
Guohua Zhong

196-197 Lake Mapam Yumco is called Number one sacred lakes; Lake Pangong Co *Chengyi Sun*

198-199 Lake Pangong Co, meaning Long-necked swan in Tibetan, is a world famous lake situated in a valley amid high mountains on the border between China and Indian-controlled Kashmir
Chengyi Sun

200-201 Evidence of the Himalayas rising from the ancient Tethys sea-fold mountain; The folds of the Himalayas; Distinctive to pography of Nyainqentanglha mountain; Incredible folds of the Himalayas
Jianjun Wang *Gang Che*

202-203 Typical Tibetan house 1; Typical Tibetan house 2
Chengyi Sun *Gang Che*

204-205 The snowy mountains provide a beautiful background for those who live below them; Tibetan women carrying water
Gang Che *Jianjun Wang*

206-207 Yaks, mammals living on the highest elevation grasslands, are perfect as animals for transportation; Yaks are bovine species special to Tibetan Plateau; Yaks are the most important animals to the Tibetan people *Jianjun Wang*

208-209 Herdsmen on high altitude grasslands and their flocks 1; Herdsmen on high altitude grasslands and their flocks 2; Cold–resistant flocks on Tibetan Plateau; Flocks on winter grasslands in Northe Tibet *Gang Che* *Chengyi Sun*

210-211 Unique traditional Tibetan opera. Tibetan opera has a long history and very popular among Tibetans; Grand Tibetan opera performance *Gang Che* *Chengyi Sun*

212-213 Tibetans celebrate a festival in their splendid attire
Panoramic Photo Gallery

214-215 Changmo Dance is an ancient and unique art form in Tibetan culture. Changmo dancers with various colorful masks; The role of dancers can be identified by the masks they wear; Simple yet enchanting Changmo dance ceremony; Changmo dancers are from lamas at Radreng monastery *Guohua Zhong*

216-217 Changmo dance is one of the important rituals on the Paltung Tanbo Festival at Radreng Monastery, the festival combines religious activity with that of commercial and entertainment; Mysterious Changmo dance ritual; Changmo dance ritual aims at driving away the devils and promoting Buddhism; Changmo dance ritual expresses the best wishes of Titetans; Grand Paltung Tanbo Festival *Guohua Zhong*

218-219 Magnificent Gangdise Mountain *Ligui Wang*

220-221 Kangrinboqe, a universally recognized sacred mountain, is revered as the center of the world by believers in Hinduism and Tibetan Buddhism *Jianjun Wang*

222-223 Kangrinboqe Mountain at an altitude of 6,656 meters above sea level; Sacred Mountain; Kangriboqe peak covered with snow year-around as seen from a distance; Mysterious Kangriboqe Mountain; Amazing Kangriboqe Mountain veiled in clouds *Ligui Wang Gang Che Jianjun Wang Chengyi Sun Xuejun Yuan*

224- 225 Kangriboqe is the center of the universe in the minds of believers *Ligui Wang*

226- 227 Silent Mani Stone piles watching the Holy Himalayas *Jianjun Wang*

Editorial and Publishing Committee of *Tibet:*

Chairman: Jingyan Zhang

Vice Chairman: Wenli Xu

Committee Members: Guang Guo, Jianjun Wang, Chengyi Sun, Gang Che, Mei Yu, Xiaoqiang Yi

Chief Editor: Guang Guo

Photographers: Gang Che, Ligui Wang, Hongwei Wang, Jianjun Wang, Bangcai Wang, Weixiong Liu,Chengyi Sun, Lei Chen, Guohua Zhong, Xuejun Yuan,Yongqian Zeng, Ming Tan, Panoramic Photo Gallery

Editor: Dafu Jiang, Yu Mang, Geneviève Rudolf

Assistant Editor: Hui Zhang, Yao Wang, Yue Ran, Yuan Ren, Yuhai Zhang, Xu Song

English Translator: Hongjun Ma, Xiaoqiang Yi

Tibet

First published in the United Kingdom in November 2009 by

CYPI PRESS

Chief Editor: Guang Guo

Add: 79 College Road, Harrow Middlesex, Greater London, HA1 1BD, United Kingdom

E-mail: sales@cypi.net editor@cypi.net

Website: www.cypi.co.uk

ISBN: 978-0-9556057-6-5

Printed in China